THE ATLAS OF
Endangered
Species

THE ATLAS OF
Endangered
Species

Editor: John A. Burton

Pictures supplied by Bruce Coleman Ltd

MACMILLAN LIBRARY REFERENCE USA
NEW YORK

Contents

A QUARTO BOOK

Copyright © 1991 and 1999 (revised edition)
Quarto Inc.

Macmillan Library Reference USA
1633 Broadway,
New York, New York 10019

Library of Congress Cataloging-in-Publication
Data
The atlas of endangered species/editor John
A. Burton. -- 2nd ed.
    p. cm.
    Includes bibliographical references (p.)
and index.
    Summary: Describes the various animals and
plants throughout the world whose survival is
being threatened and the steps being taken to
save them from extinction.
    ISBN 0-02-865034-4 (alk. paper)
    1. Endangered species -- Juvenile literature.
2. Endangered plants-- Juvenile literature.
3. Nature conservation--Juvenile literature.
[1. Endangered species. 2. Rare plants.
3. Nature conservation. 4. Environmental
protection.]   I. Burton, John A.
QH75.A85   1988
333.95'22--dc21   98-44328
                           CIP
                           AC

This book was designed and produced by
Quarto Publishing plc
The Old Brewery, 6 Blundell Street
London N7 9BH

Senior Editor Sally MacEachern
Editor Judy Maxwell
Index Dawn Butcher
Designers Hazel Edington, Julie Francis
Maps Janos Marffy, Malcolm Swanston
Illustrations Ann Savage, Wayne Ford, Paul
Richardson, Rob Shone
Picture Manager Gill Metcalf
Art Director Moira Clinch

Typeset by Central Southern Typesetters,
Eastbourne
Manufactured in Hong Kong by Regent
Publishing Services Ltd
Printed by Leefung Asco Printers Limited,
China

10 9 8 7 6 5 4 3

Printed in China

Foreword

The worldwide endangerment of plants and animals is a phenomenon of the twentieth century. It is a product of the continuing use of more and more natural resources for a constantly growing human population. With more people and their needs for food, fuel, and shelter, there is less room for wild life. As a result, most wildlife species are endangered primarily because of loss of habitat. However, this is not the sole cause of endangerment.

Decimation of the world's fish resources has occurred because of rising demand for fish products and an improved technology, which allows us not only to harvest a sustainable number annually, but to make an almost clean sweep of many high-demand species such as swordfish, tuna, cod, and haddock. Industrial pollution eliminates habitat, poisoning waterways and aquatic life world wide. Dams cut off migration and access to breeding or feeding areas. Alien species introduced to new habitats without controls choke out or eliminate native species by taking over their habitat, by competing with them for nest holes, by eating them, or by bringing new diseases to which the native species are susceptible.

It is for these reasons that island forms have been particularly hard hit, as rats, cats, snakes, pigs, and other introduced species establish themselves. Flightless birds, small reptiles, and amphibians are often eliminated. Trade in animal products, such as rhinoceros horn or crocodile skins, and in live animals, such as parrots, is often responsible for reducing species numbers. However, almost all endangerments are the result, directly or indirectly, of growing human populations. Until we control human population growth, the endangerment so characteristic of the twentieth century will accelerate into the twenty-first. By 2020, twenty per cent or more of the plants and animals on earth will be threatened - the most massive short-term extinction since the elimination of the dinosaurs.

One key to understanding and reversing the loss of species is knowledge. Perhaps no group of species on earth is better known than the world's birds. Out of the approximately 9,700 species of bird, 1,100 are endangered or

Left Peregrine Falcon
(Falco peregrinus).

Right Black Rhinoceros
(Diceros bicornis).

Right *Tiger*
(Panthera tigris).

threatened. Numerous other species have been greatly depleted, although they still exist in large numbers. The thorough documentation of the status of birds has led, in an increasing number of cases, to concentrated governmental and private action. In New Zealand, where most native bird species are endangered, whole islands, which are free of rats and predators, have been set aside to act as genetic reservoirs for the future. The Seychelles Warbler, for instance, had been reduced to a few tens of birds on one island, but now has a population of over a thousand on several islands. The Peregrine Falcon, once extirpated in the United States, flies free once again and its population is expanding - the result of a public and private conservation initiative.

Although birds are the best-documented class of species from a scientific standpoint, the continued decline of large mammals is probably more obvious to the general public. Twenty years ago large number of rhinoceros still inhabited East Africa's national parks, and a fair number were found outside the parks. Now, rhinoceros are restricted to remnant or reintroduced populations, and are objects of intense interest and stewardship by park managers. In India, tigers have been reduced from over 100,000 at the turn of the century to a few thousand today. In the far north, the once-secure Polar Bear is now found to have elevated amounts of PCB in its body fat, poisons that are being passed to coming generations of bears as they nurse in their birth caves. If we can manage to save sufficient high-quality habitat for the world's large mammals, many other terrestrial species will be saved with them.

To keep what we have, and to bring back species long eliminated, will required commitment and funds far beyond that which has been expended to date. Fortunately, we have new tools in the conservation battle coming on line every day. The Internet is an instant source of information on environmental matters, and a way of sharing strategies for saving what is left of nature among environmentalists and the general public. Information and databases shared by governments and private organizations are allowing us to approach problems in a unified and cooperative way. Lear's Macaw, reduced to a few hundred individuals and restricted to dry forests of Brazil, will be augmented by birds confiscated from unscrupulous pet dealers and collectors from many countries who have been part of a a smuggling network. Internation cooperation and law enforcement are increasing because of shared information. Television, reaching more and more people world-wide every year, conveys vivid images of the natural world, often provoking an intense desire to protect it. The present generation will be more interested in wildlife and, if they are to reverse present decline, must know more about it. In 1983, the conservation movement received an enormous boost from the Convention on Trade and Endangered Species of Wild Fauna and Flora (CITES), the first global convention on wildlife. The renewed commitment of governments to the recent Biodiversity Convention and the Global Environmental Fund, and the growth of non-profit conservation organizations world-wide will also help. There is a great deal to be done, but already there are bright spots as individual species are recovering, being protected, or being reintroduced.

In the end, wild endangered species are no more endangered than we are ourselves – by our own population growth, pollution, and the hostilities and conflict brought on by resource competition. Endangered wildlife and our own survival are intertwined – a fact we are still learning.

In this Atlas, John Burton has provided valuable information and a tool to aid in our commitment to endangered species protection. It is information we all need to absorb and to share with others.

Dr. Gerard Bertrand
Massachusetts Audubon Society

| **Below** *Polar Bear* (Ursus maritimus).

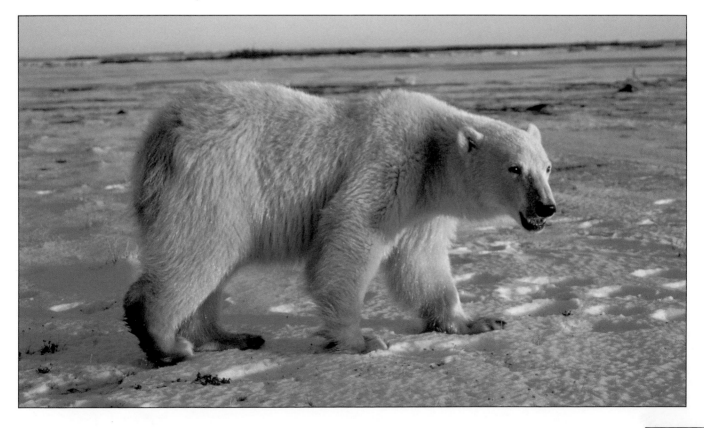

Introduction

This book gives an overview of some of the problems facing wildlife as we begin the twenty-first century. The plants and animals within each and every different region of the world share certain characteristic, and these have led biologists to divide the world into biogeographical regions. While the fate of life in all regions is interlinked, this book focuses on each region in turn so that its wildlife can be examined in greater detail.

Among the species of most concern throughout the world are those confined or endemic to single islands or groups of islands. Because of their isolation and often small numbers they are particularly vulnerable to any environmental changes. In addition to the oceanic islands there are habitat "islands" on the continents, such as small mountain ranges surrounded by plains, isolated lakes, and cave systems. Also, people are increasingly creating "islands," for

Above *Fiddler Crab* (Uca).

Above right *Ice shelf, Admiral Byrd Bay, Antarctica.*

many parks and reserves are totally surrounded by agricultural lands. Indeed, in most of the developed world agricultural lands are now some of the least species-rich habitats in the world. Research has demonstrated that there are critical sizes for islands, including reserves, below which the numbers of species that can be supported drop dramatically.

The threats currently facing the wildlife of islands and other areas include natural catastrophes, and even gradual change. The natural catastrophes that produce the most dramatic effects are those most similar to large-scale industrial pollution: volcanic eruptions. That of Mount St. Helens, USA, in May 1980 produced a plume of airborne ash and pumice that stretched almost a mile into the sky and affected the global climate for over a year. The only species likely to be made extinct by volcanic eruptions, or other natural disasters including hurricanes, tsunami (tidal waves), and floods, are those confined to islands.

Such natural catastrophes can now be manipulated by people. At a conference held in Stockholm in 1984, papers were given which showed how much environmental damage could be done by using small-scale nuclear explosions to trigger volcanic eruptions. As long ago as 1978 a Convention on Environmental Modification (Enmod 1977) came into force, and it applies to the UK, USA, Russia, and over 40 other countries. This seeks to protect the world from

Left Cattleya skinneri, *the national flower of Costa Rica.*

environmental warfare and other disruptive activities. Unfortunately it is difficult to enforce, and so may be as ineffective as the various other conventions seeking to prevent the use of chemical and bacteriological weapons in war. Thousands of acres of Vietnam are still affected by the defoliants sprayed by US forces, and it may be decades, or even centuries, before they recover. Through these and countless other activities, people have become the most significant threat to the majority of species facing extinction.

THE CAUSES OF EXTINCTION

It is becoming apparent that we are witnessing one of the greatest waves of extinction that has ever occurred. Extinction is a natural process and all species eventually become extinct. Some only exist for less than half a million years, while some exist almost unchanged for many millions of years. The Tuataras of New Zealand, for instance, are virtually indistinguishable from their Jurassic ancestors. However, catastrophic extinctions can occur. The dinosaurs of North America are believed to have been wiped out when a gigantic meteor hit the coast of Mexico. The impact was so huge that the repercussions would have been global and would have lasted for many years, if not centuries. The wave of extinctions we are experiencing now is less dramatic, but may be on the same scale. (Remember that, in geological terms, the period between the industrial revolution and two centuries from now, would be invisible in the strata of the future.) And if global warming continues at the rates currently being predicted, then extinctions will occur at an exponentially increasing rate. Even if the worst predictions of are not fulfilled, all the other causes of concern remain.

HUNTING

From earliest times, human hunters have caused the extinction of many species. For instance, before humans colonized the Americas they contained a much greater diversity of large mammals, including mammoths and camels. With the spread of Stone Age hunters, over 100 species of mammal became extinct. Until the eighteenth century it was mainly large species that were hunted to extinction, and most animals managed to survive in remote areas. Then Europeans began traveling regularly all over the globe, and guns became more accurate and easy to handle. By the end of the nineteenth century, the gun had brought one of the most numerous birds in the world, the Passenger Pigeon, to the brink of extinction, it had reduced the Californian Condor to a level where its future was probably doomed, and had aided the extermination of many species in the Pacific.

Today hunting is, in theory, regulated in most parts of the world, but it remains a major threat to the survival of birds and mammals in particular. Sport hunting, though the most questionable perhaps on moral grounds, generally has the least impact. Commercial hunting for ivory, skins, hides, and other products has rarely been effectively controlled and it continues to lead to the extinction of species.

As the twenty-first century begins, though, it is probably plant species that are under the greater threat from direct exploitation. The plant equivalent of hunting, collecting, is endangering many species including rare orchids and cacti, and even rare species of timber tree.

POLLUTION

Our food is contaminated with hundreds of pesticides and other chemicals. While we may only consume small amounts, large quantities run off into the rivers and accumulate in the soil. In addition huge amounts of pollutants, many of which will persist in the environment for decades, are being pumped directly into rivers, seas, and the atmosphere. Oil slicks are the most visible marine pollutants and cause serious mortalities among sea mammals and birds. Even more dangerous, perhaps, are the hundreds of miles of "ghost" nets – fishing nets that drift in the oceans, ensnaring and drowning fish, seabirds, seals, dolphins, and turtles.

The effects of atmospheric pollution may be far more grave. In particular, some of the gases produced by industry rise up in the atmosphere and trap the sun's heat through the so-called greenhouse effect. The USA, the countries of the former USSR, and China are the chief producers of these gases, followed by Brazil, India, and Germany. Concern that these gases will result in global warming is now widespread.

HABITAT DESTRUCTION

This is undoubtedly the most significant threat to the greatest number of species, and, is also the most difficult to prevent.

The world's consumption of wood continues to increase, as does paper production. Some 12 million hectares (30 million acres) of tropical forest were being cleared annually in the early 1990s, and at the current rate of deforestation most experts predict that virtually all remaining tropical forests will disappear within 40 years. In many parts of the world, burgeoning human populations are displacing wildlife in an effort to turn seemingly unproductive forests into farmland, and forest fires which raged in the mid-1990s in Indonesia, Mexico and Brazil destroyed millions of acres of forest. By 2010, it is estimated that there will be very little forest left in Asia, and in West and East Africa, almost none left in Central America, and in South America the only remaining large areas of forest will be in western Brazil and the Guyana highlands. The tropical forests of the Côte d'Ivoire, Nigeria, India, and Thailand are already essentially depleted.

Responsibility for these problems does not rest solely on the poorer countries with their rapidly increasing populations. Fundamental inequalities lie at the root of much of this destruction. Much of Europe and North America, for example, is wealthy and can (at least in theory) afford the luxury of conserving the remnants of their wildlife. Unfortunately, having depleted their own natural resources, they have all too often gone on to exploit the resources of the tropical countries. Moreover, in order to repay crippling international debts, many

| **Above** Ruffed Lemur (Varecia variegata).

developing countries are forced to allow wholesale exploitation by foreign companies. Japanese lumber companies, for example, are plundering the forests of southeast Asia, and while conservationists may argue that with proper management such resources could be exploited in a sustainable way, few businesses and even fewer governments will consider investment over the timescales relevant to tropical forests.

In addition, it is the industrialized countries that are using the bulk of the world's natural resources. The average inhabitant of Canada, for example, uses 148 times more energy than a person in the Democratic Republic of Congo (formerly Zaire). Also, the importing countries insist on paying as little as possible for those raw materials.

THE CASE FOR CONSERVATION

There are a number of arguments used to promote conservation. One contends that plants and animals should be conserved simply because they enhance the world and make it a more interesting place, and because they have a *right* to exist. Another is the materialistic one, that plants and animals are useful to people. However, although superficially attractive, this view is double-edged because it encourages decisions which are based on economic principles, and which may not always be of benefit to the global ecosystem.

Above *Scarlet Tanager* (Piranga olivacea).

Left *"Gerais" grasslands, central Brazil.*

A third argument is that our survival depends on a healthy global ecosystem. The consequences of the spiraling human population and resource consumption will be as grave for us as for the natural world. When populations of any species increase, the resources upon which they depend become depleted, starvation becomes widespread, and pandemics of disease wipe out weakened populations.

As human populations have increased, people have gathered in urban areas and the potential for catastrophes has escalated. In 1986 over 40,000 people died of cholera in Africa, while since 1982 cases of AIDS have soared in many parts of the world. The toll taken by natural disasters is also great. An earthquake in China in 1976 killed over 850,000 people, while millions of people have been affected by major floods during the 1980s and 1990s. A disaster is often followed by migrations of refugee populations, thus increasing pressure on other areas and their wildlife.

Whichever justification one uses for conserving wildlife and the environment, one thing is clear: the destruction cannot continue, even in the short-term of the next few decades, without the collapse of entire ecosystems and human populations.

Biogeographic regions

Biologists have divided the world into geographic regions based on the affinities of the plants and animals that live within them. Although there is some disagreement over the precise boudaries, those shown here reflect the most widely used, and make convenient divisions for describing the world's wildlife and its regional conservation problems.

- [ ] Ice

- Mountain vegetation
  Tundra

- Boreal forest
  Conifer forest

- Mixed forest
  Broadleaf forest

- Tropical rainforest
  Monsoon forest

- Dry tropical forest
  Sub-tropical forest

- Mediterranean scrub
  Prairie
  Steppe
  Savanna

- Dry tropical scrub and thorn forest
  Desert

NEARCTIC REGION

NEOTROPIC REGION

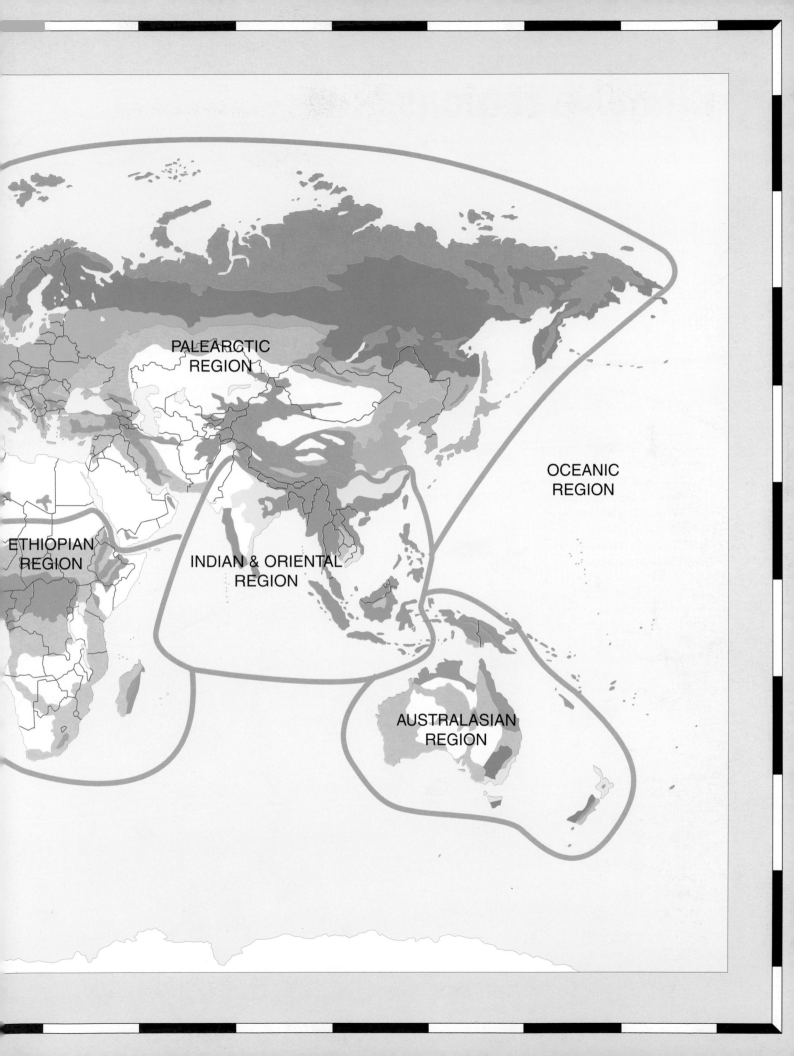

Climatic regions

Climate plays an important role in determining the distribution of plant and animal species. The arid and cooler regions have fewer species than the rich and diverse tropical moist forests. Long term changes in climate alter the distribution of wildlife. The effects of global warming may raise sea levels, causing flooding in many coastal areas. However, increased cloud cover from pollution could possibly precipitate another Ice Age. Whatever happens, one thing is certain; all the pollutants being allowed to pour into the earth's atmosphere are unlikely to have any long term benefits, and are almost certain to be doing harm.

Polar
(Ice and tundra)

Cooler humid
(Subarctic and continental

Dry
(Steppe and desert)

Warmer humid
(Marine, subtropical and Mediterranean)

Tropical humid
(Savanna and rain forest)

Natural disasters

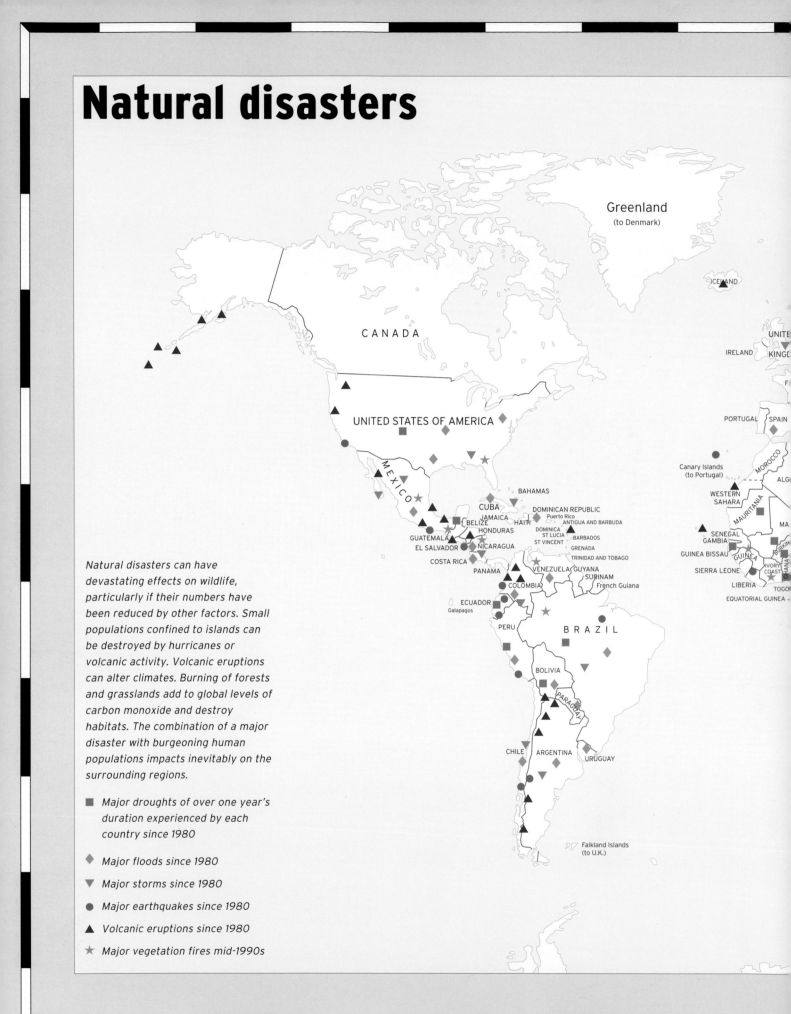

Natural disasters can have devastating effects on wildlife, particularly if their numbers have been reduced by other factors. Small populations confined to islands can be destroyed by hurricanes or volcanic activity. Volcanic eruptions can alter climates. Burning of forests and grasslands add to global levels of carbon monoxide and destroy habitats. The combination of a major disaster with burgeoning human populations impacts inevitably on the surrounding regions.

■ Major droughts of over one year's duration experienced by each country since 1980

◆ Major floods since 1980

▼ Major storms since 1980

● Major earthquakes since 1980

▲ Volcanic eruptions since 1980

★ Major vegetation fires mid-1990s

Pollution

Although pollution is rarely the actual cause of extinctions, it plays a major role in reducing populations, destroying habitats and generally upsetting the balance of ecosystems. Although, until recently, the developed world has produced most of the pollution, stricter controls have led to polluting industries being moved to parts of the world where laws are less strict. Developed countries are also attempting to reduce the amount of household waste dumped in landfills and to increase recycling.

⬜ *Areas suffering from acidic rains in early 1990s*

⬛ *Countries producing between 500,000 to 5 million tons of hazardous waste in early 1990s. Note: there is no accurate documentation for many African, South American, Asian and East European countries.*

⟋ *Polluted rivers*

▲ *Deep sea dumps*

⬜ *Areas of coastal pollution*

CANADA

UNITED STATES OF AMERICA

MEXICO

Greenland
(to Denmark)

ICELAND

IRELAND

UNITED KINGDOM

PORTUGAL SPAIN

Canary Islands
(to Portugal)

WESTERN SAHARA

MOROCCO

MAURITANIA

SENEGAL
GAMBIA

GUINEA BISSAU

SIERRA LEONE

LIBERIA

MALI

BURKINA

GUINEA

IVORY COAST

GHANA

TOGO

EQUATORIAL GUINEA

BAHAMAS

CUBA

JAMAICA

BELIZE

HONDURAS

GUATEMALA

EL SALVADOR

NICARAGUA

COSTA RICA

PANAMA

HAITI

DOMINICAN REPUBLIC

Puerto Rico

ANTIGUA AND BARBUDA

DOMINICA

ST LUCIA

ST VINCENT

BARBADOS

GRENADA

TRINIDAD AND TOBAGO

VENEZUELA GUYANA

SURINAM

French Guiana

COLOMBIA

ECUADOR

Galapagos

PERU

BRAZIL

BOLIVIA

PARAGUAY

CHILE ARGENTINA

URUGUAY

UNITED KINGDOM	NORWAY	CANADA
85, 8, 9	68, 14, 18	67, 29

Methods of disposal of household waste in the end 1990s, in per cent

Recycling waste combustion to produce energy landfill

FINLAND
66 · 30 · 4

AUSTRIA
65 · 24 · 11

USA
61 · 24 · 15

FRANCE
59 · 8 · 33

GERMANY
46 · 18 · 36

BELGIUM
43 · 3 · 54

SWEDEN
34 · 19 · 47

NETHERLANDS
30 · 28 · 42

JAPAN
21 · 5 · 74

DENMARK
20 · 25 · 55

SWITZERLAND
47 · 11 · 47

Population

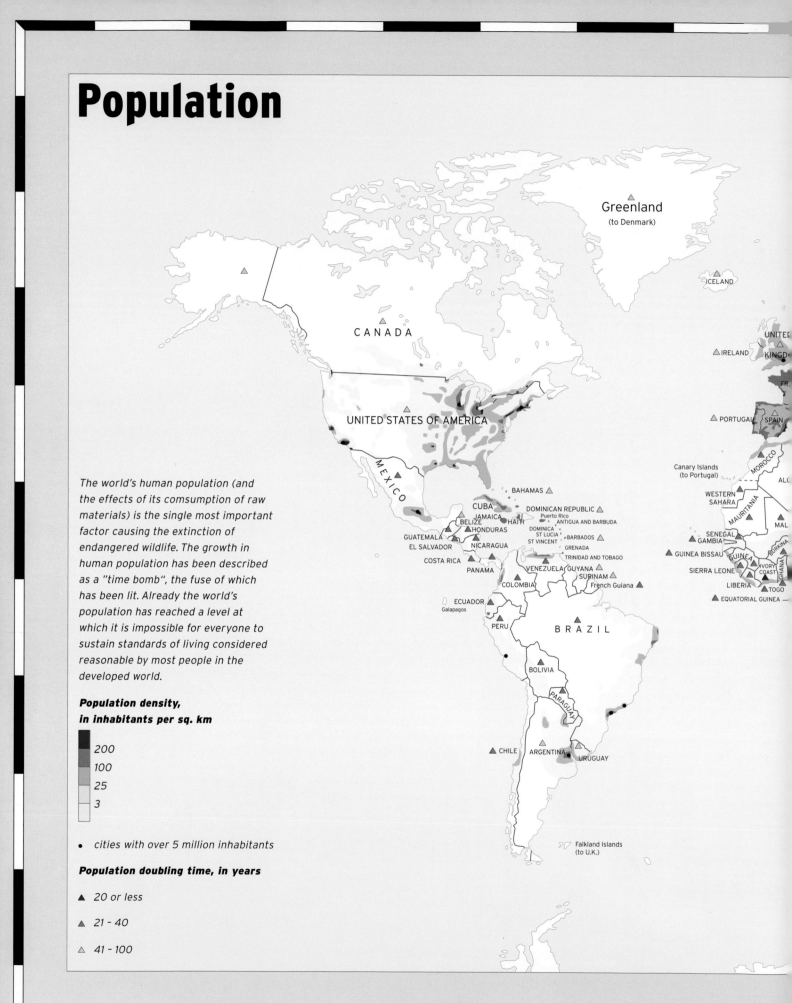

The world's human population (and
the effects of its comsumption of raw
materials) is the single most important
factor causing the extinction of
endangered wildlife. The growth in
human population has been described
as a "time bomb", the fuse of which
has been lit. Already the world's
population has reached a level at
which it is impossible for everyone to
sustain standards of living considered
reasonable by most people in the
developed world.

Population density,
in inhabitants per sq. km

200
100
25
3

• cities with over 5 million inhabitants

Population doubling time, in years

▲ 20 or less

▲ 21 - 40

△ 41 - 100

Greenland
(to Denmark)

ICELAND

CANADA

IRELAND

UNITED
KINGD

FR

PORTUGAL   SPAIN

UNITED STATES OF AMERICA

Canary Islands
(to Portugal)

MOROCCO

AL

MEXICO

WESTERN
SAHARA

MAURITANIA

MAL

BAHAMAS

CUBA
JAMAICA
BELIZE   HAITI   DOMINICAN REPUBLIC
HONDURAS   Puerto Rico
GUATEMALA   ANTIGUA AND BARBUDA
EL SALVADOR   NICARAGUA   DOMINICA
              ST LUCIA   BARBADOS
COSTA RICA   ST VINCENT
PANAMA   GRENADA
         VENEZUELA GUYANA   TRINIDAD AND TOBAGO
COLOMBIA   SURINAM
         French Guiana

SENEGAL
GAMBIA
GUINEA BISSAU   GUINEA
SIERRA LEONE   IVORY   GHANA
LIBERIA   COAST
              TOGO
EQUATORIAL GUINEA

BURKINA

ECUADOR
Galapagos

PERU   B R A Z I L

BOLIVIA

PARAGUAY

CHILE   ARGENTINA   URUGUAY

Falkland Islands
(to U.K.)

Species
AT RISK

The Palearctic Region

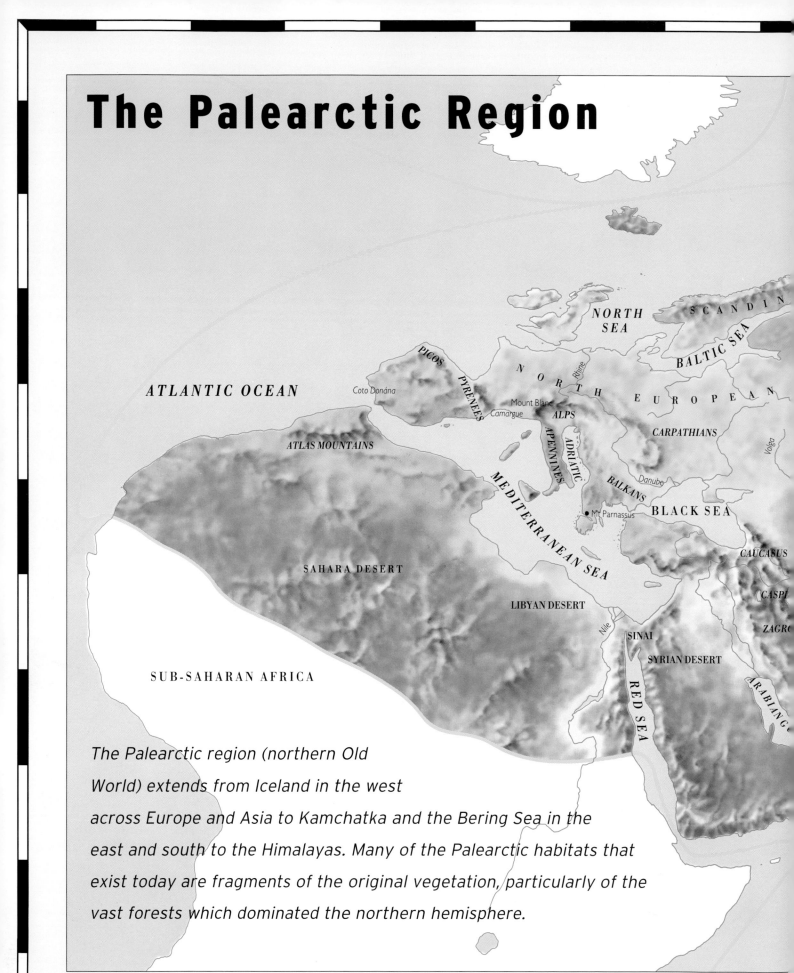

The Palearctic region (northern Old World) extends from Iceland in the west across Europe and Asia to Kamchatka and the Bering Sea in the east and south to the Himalayas. Many of the Palearctic habitats that exist today are fragments of the original vegetation, particularly of the vast forests which dominated the northern hemisphere.

Habitat & Plants

John Akeroyd graduated in botany from the University of St. Andrews, followed by a Ph.D. from Cambridge University and research fellowships at Trinity College, Dublin, and the University of Reading, including the revision of Vol. 1 of *Flora Europaea*. He is the joint founder and editor of *Plant Talk*, the first international magazine devoted to plant conservation. He has written numerous scientific papers and popular articles, and contributed to many books.

The Palearctic region covers a wide range of climates and habitats in Europe, temperate Asia, and North Africa. These range from the cold deserts of the tundra of northern Europe and Siberia, through zones of coniferous and deciduous forests, and dry grasslands or steppes, to the hot deserts of central and southwestern Asia and north Africa. Within these zones are coastlands, wetlands and mountains, each with a further zonation that creates a graded and variable mosaic of vegetation and habitat. Comparatively recently many of these habitats have been eroded or have disappeared through human activity. Their loss threatens the region's rich resources of plants and animals.

Many of the Palearctic habitats that exist today are fragments of the once extensive tracts of natural vegetation, much of them dominated by forest, that formerly girded the northern hemisphere. The basic pattern of vegetation zonation was established some 100 million years ago, when the continental masses were assuming their present configurations. Since that time there have been countless episodes of migration, adaptation, and extinction of plants in response to climatic and other changes. These have given rise to today's complex patterns of distribution, often with isolated populations of individuals spread over a large area. One of the main factors influencing distribution has been successive cold periods, known as Ice Ages, during which glaciers spread out from arctic and mountainous regions. The other main factor has been the evolution and advancement of humans.

There are few records to show what plant species may have become extinct during historical times. Large mammals or birds such as the Lion or the Ostrich were recorded by writers in classical times, whereas the rarer plants were not. In more recent times, however, botanists have become increasingly concerned about the loss of valuable plant species, especially from the more populous areas of Europe and the Mediterranean. Many have disappeared through urbanization and road construction, intensive grazing and arable

Right A managed woodland in the Cotswolds, England. Humans have been managing European woodlands for centuries, the tended wood or coppices being used to produce wood for charcoal, as well as poles and laths. In Britain coppicing is a common practice, and the open woodland created is an important habitat for many flowering plants.

cultivation, forest plantation, drainage, fire, and pollution. Others are endangered by over-exploitation, either for particular products that they yield, such as medical drugs, or for their use in an expanding horticultural industry. Above all, however, it is habitat destruction and disturbance that threatens plants.

FORESTS: A SURVIVING NATIVE VEGETATION

Provided there is enough water and a reasonably fertile soil, vegetation will in time come to be dominated by trees. Native forests or wildwood once covered much of the Palearctic between the tundra and the grassland of the steppes. Forests do still cover extensive areas of Eurasia and the higher mountains of parts of north Africa, but they have been severely reduced in extent and fragmented over the last 10,000 years through human activity. Fortunately, the mixed landscape of woodland and agriculture that covers much of the populated Palearctic often provides as valuable a habitat for plants and animals as the wildwood that preceded it.

Temperate deciduous forest is characteristic of, and largely confined to the Palearctic, from western and central Europe through into Russia, and over much of China and Japan. This type of vegetation has been especially reduced in area by human clearance for agriculture, as it tends to grow on better soils in areas of adequate rainfall. Some areas were set aside for forestry, but much forestry practice has been and continues to be destructive. Across the region, huge tracts of woodland have been cleared for lumber, charcoal-burning, and bark for tanning as well as to make way for grazing animals or farmland. Forests of conifers, often growing on poorer soils or in rugged or mountainous terrain, survived longer. However, these resinous trees are susceptible to fire, and the safety match has represented their greatest threat, as it has to the evergreen Mediterranean oak forests.

Above Coppicing is one of the traditional methods of managing a deciduous woodland. Each year the trees in a different section of the wood are cut down and trimmed to ground level. The stumps are cut at an angle to prevent water from settling on them and to allow the trees to regenerate. Over a period of years, the wood will contain areas of trees at various stages of regrowth, each of which will be a home for a particular group of plants and animals. The overall result is a dramatic increase in the variety of species present in a wood. The cut wood is used for a variety of purposes such as firewood, wattle fencing, stools, broomsticks, and other wood products.

Left Much of the Mediterranean has been replaced with second-growth forest, either as plantations or after fire-damage. The pines in this view of the Bucaco Forest, Portugal are all the same size; an indication that they are probably second growth.

The habitats that the native deciduous wildwood supported have now mostly disappeared, with just a few areas of lowland primeval forest surviving, notably in parts of Poland and Lithuania. Happily, the trees themselves will regenerate locally and many of them occur widely in leisure areas and forestry plantations.

Plants have a remarkable ability to survive in small remnants of their native environment, far more so than the mammals and birds that need to forage for food. Patches of Wood Anemone, a widespread plant but one characteristic of ancient woodland, can often be found in hedge-banks, fields, or mountain-ledges. Their presence in an area suggests that it used to be covered by native deciduous forest. The Wild Service Tree, another indicator of ancient woodlands, survives in copses in some parts of London. A forest species that used to occur over the whole of Europe is the large, handsome Ladies-slipper Orchid. It is still present in reasonable numbers in a few parts of Scandinavia and the Alps, but elsewhere is extinct or decimated. Forest clearance started its decline, which has been hastened by over-collection.

Evergreen forests of coniferous trees occupy vast areas of the Palearctic. The taiga of Siberia is a forest mostly of pines, spruces and larches, mixed locally with birch and aspen, and interspersed with areas of raised bog. It still forms a belt across Russia, although it is seriously degraded in parts of the Baltic region. In the mountains of Europe, Asia, and North Africa, there are some fine forests of pines, spruces, firs, and cedars. A few coniferous trees have restricted distributions, such as the Serbian Spruce, which occurs only in a small part of Bosnia-Hercegovina. Fortunately, this elegant, spire-like tree is popular as an ornamental elsewhere in Europe and will certainly survive in cultivation. An even rarer conifer, the Sicilian Fir, once formed stands in the mountains of Sicily and now survives in just one native grove. However, it is now being actively protected and propagated.

GRASSLANDS AND HEATHLANDS: A HUMAN LANDSCAPE

Many grasses are drought-resistant, and large areas of eastern Europe and central Asia that are too dry for the growth of trees, together with drier parts of the Mediterranean area, are dominated by the grasslands known as steppes. These are mainly natural, although some have been created through the loss of tree and shrub cover by human activity. All are composed of drought-tolerant grasses, notably species of feather-grass *(Stipa)*. Much of the huge steppe region that extends from eastern Europe across the former Soviet Union is now under cultivation, which has put a great deal of pressure on the limited areas of surviving steppe, and the many species of plants and animals adapted to live in it are under threat.

When wildwood and, in wetter northern and western parts, peat covered huge areas of the Palearctic, insufficient light penetrated for the growth of grasses and other light-demanding plants, including those now known as "weeds" of cultivated land. Such plants were restricted to broken or rocky ground, or unstable or poor soil that did not allow the growth of trees. Some of these refuges still survive today, for example the astonishing plant-rich gorges of the island of Crete, and the strange mixture of Mediterranean and alpine plants in the rocky limestone pavements of the Burren region of County Clare in western Ireland.

The clearance of forests to provide pasture for grazing or meadows for hay opened up large areas of grassland. Although these are not natural environments, grassland that has been managed over successive human generations can still be very rich in species. Sadly, economic pressure has led to the abandonment of older management techniques, and modern meadows and pastures tend to be "improved" by artificial fertilizers. Britain has lost 95 per cent of its traditional colorful meadows, a terrible destruction of its heritage. The

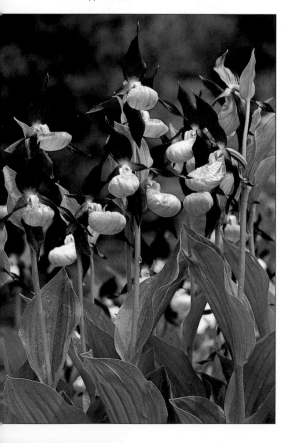

Below *Ladies-slipper Orchid* (Cypripedium calceolus) *is now extinct or rare over much of its European range. Collecting by gardeners and for the horticultural trade is largely responsible for its disappearance.*

resulting bright green sward containing just a few species is a poor habitat for both plants and animals. Elsewhere the situation is not quite so bad, but many attractive species have been lost, such as in some of the traditional hay meadows of the Picos de Europa mountains of northern Spain. Bory's Gentian, a rare member of an attractive genus of mountain grassland flowers, is threatened by changes in traditional grassland management both in the Picos and in the Sierra Nevada of southern Spain.

Heathlands are another "unnatural" or managed type of vegetation with a rich flora. As their name suggests, they are often dominated by members of the heath or heather family, small or dwarf shrubs with reduced leaves and usually tiny massed flowers. Other shrubs include peaflowers such as the gorses and brooms, and grasses too may be present. Native heathlands are largely restricted to naturally broken ground or to coastal areas. Burning and sheep or cattle grazing, together with thin or poor soils, prevent trees from growing. However,

in recent times, much heathland has been lost through encroachment of trees either naturally or by planting.

Moorland has a more peaty soil than heathland and occurs in more northern and mountainous climates. It has some affinities with the tundra of the far north, a treeless, mossy landscape with permanently frozen soil. Despite their remoteness, moorland and tundra have not escaped human disturbance. Forestry plantations have encroached on moorland and, in some parts of Russia, tundra has been disturbed by oil extraction.

MOUNTAINS: A RICH FLORA UNDER THREAT

Mountains provide a wide range of habitats, from cliffs, rocks and screes, to grassland and, on the lower slopes, forest or scrub. They are fairly undisturbed compared with the lowlands, but are increasingly threatened by development for industry and tourism. The Alps have become "the playground of Europe," coping with millions of visitors throughout the year. Feet are trampling precious plant communities and pollution is damaging forests.

Mountainous areas are often rich in minerals and the extraction of these can wreak havoc. In recent years the mountains of central Greece have been strip-mined to obtain

Above left Drystone walls, grazed meadows, and isolated groups of trees are all typical of the intensively managed landscapes of most of Britain and Europe. However, these are often old-established landscapes with a rich fauna and flora, such as this one near Chelmorton, Derbyshire, England.

Above Alpine meadows, many of which have never been sprayed with pesticides or herbicides, are often remarkably rich in flowering plants. In recent years there has been a rapid destruction of this once widespread habitat.

bauxite, the major ore of aluminum. These mountains, which include the famous Mt. Parnassus, have a rich endemic flora. Mount Iti Speedwell, found in a few wet places on Mount Iti and nowhere else in the world, is in immediate danger of extinction due to nearby bauxite mining, despite the fact that its mountain home has been designated a nature reserve.

Over the past few decades there has been an unprecedented growth in personal wealth and leisure time among sections of the region's population, and people in many parts of Europe and Asia are now flocking to their mountains for recreation, often damaging mountain habitats in the process.

WETLANDS: IN CONSTANT DANGER

Wetlands may be great expanses of water such as Lake Baikal in Siberia, large enough to have developed a whole suite of endemic wildlife, or regions such as the Camargue or the Volga delta, or they may just be small ponds or even damp hollows in an arable field. Whatever their size, they are perhaps the most threatened of all habitats. In Ireland, vast areas of bogland have been dug out to provide peat for domestic and industrial fuel, and its reserves of peat will be exhausted early in the next century. Elsewhere, wetlands have been drained on a huge scale for building or agriculture or because they harbored malaria. They are also susceptible to environmental pollution by acid rain or the run-off of fertilizer from farmland. More recently, recreational use has put pressure on inland areas of open water.

A growing problem in many areas has been the extraction of water to supply the human population, which has gradually lowered the watertables. Much of lowland Britain, for example, has become increasingly dry since the nineteenth century, when there were raised bogs even in southern England and wild Cranberries could be harvested around London. A dramatic example of threatened wetland is the enormous delta of the river Guadalquivir in southeastern Spain, forming the massive marsh and sand-dune systems of the Coto Doñana. These have a remarkable vegetation, dominated by woodland of Umbrella Pine and Cork Oak interspersed with impenetrable marshes and tidal lagoons. In the spring, a variety of rock roses and other shrubs give a blaze of color, and Wild Daffodils bloom under the pines. The area is famous for its bird life and is one of the last havens of the European Lynx. Alas, hoteliers and property developers have built indiscriminately around the reserve, and the

Threats to the mountains

■ Skiing damages habitats both through the construction and use of facilities and by opening up remote areas to large numbers of visitors.

■ Mountain walking damages the habitats of many plants and makes them more vulnerable to picking and collecting. In some areas, such as the Alps, the flora is protected by law. In other areas, such as the Balkans and Spain, there may be little protection.

■ Tourist development related to walkers is damaging formerly undeveloped areas such as the Atlas mountains, the Caucasus, and the Sierra Nevada.

■ Excessive numbers of grazing animals in the Mediterranean region and elsewhere threaten many rare plants with extinction.

■ Amateur botanists and, more seriously, the horticultural trade dig up mountain flowers and bulbs. Species under particular pressure are saxifrages, bellflowers, Snowdrops, and Cyclamen.

■ The bulb trade between Turkey and western Europe is a particular scandal. A combination of the need of poor local people to make a living and the unscrupulous behavior of some bulb dealers has denuded large areas of bulbs, particularly Snowdrop and Cyclamen. Recent initiatives have included village bulb nurseries to produce sustainable crops of bulbs.

area is now drying out through extraction of water to serve the requirements of tourists.

The threat to wetlands is reflected in the large numbers of species that have declined in recent years. All over Europe, for example, the tiny Bog Orchid which grows on hummocks of moss in raised bogs has gradually disappeared.

THE MEDITERRANEAN AREA: A VERY SPECIAL CASE

The lands that surround the Mediterranean sea are subject to four months or more of hot and rainless summer. The vegetation is consequently dominated by trees and shrubs with drought-resistant, often small and leathery leaves, such as evergreen oaks, Carob, and Wild Olive. Many are aromatic, and familiar garden herbs such as Rosemary, Sage, and Thyme have their origin here. Thousands of years of felling, burning, and grazing have reduced the forests to a remnant. However, there are still great areas of scrubland, the maquis or macchie, and on thinner soils a vegetation of often spiny hummocks less than a yard tall, the garique. Areas of formerly wooded land often have a rich flora, but are vulnerable to invasion by alien plants, and several of the rarer species are threatened with extinction. This region has been affected by human activity for so long because of the great antiquity of the civilizations around the shores of the Mediterranean and in adjacent parts of the Middle East. These civilizations grew up as a result of the richness of the flora, which included the ancestors of many of our modern crops. The basic crops were wheat, olives and grapes, but people also made use of local cabbages, lettuces, chicories, onions and cresses, and fruits such as figs, dates, plums, and cherries. The wild populations of crop plants that survive in the Mediterranean region are a valuable reservoir of material for the plant breeder – and some of them are now rare or threatened. The Egadi Cabbage, a close relative of our garden cabbages, grows only on the small Egadi islands off the western coast of Sicily, which are facing increasing tourism and building. A related cabbage grows on one tiny island between Spain and North Africa and may already be extinct in the wild.

Far left *An Irish peat bog after cutting. Peat has been cut as a source of fuel for centuries, but in recent years an enormous market has developed for horticultural peat and this has destroyed many peat bogs. Efforts are now being made by the peat industry in Ireland not to exploit the biologically important bog.*

Above *The Coto Doñana National Park relies on water that has its source outside the park. In recent years developments around the park have threatened its water supply and a toxic waste spill from a mine reservoir in 1997 may have long-term environmental consequences.*

Wildlife

Tony Hutson left the Natural History Museum, London to spend six years as Conservation Officer on a bat project set up by the Fauna and Flora Preservation Society. He is currently Senior Conservation Officer of The Bat Conservation Trust and Co-Chairman of the IUCN's Chiroptera Specialist Group.

Spotlight

■ Pheasants *(Phasianidae)*. Nine of the 15 Palearctic species are threatened by collecting for their plumage or for keeping in captivity or through loss of habitat.

■ Wolf *(Canis lupus)*. In Europe, the Gray Wolf has been subjected to unremitting persecution, resulting in a much fragmented relict population still undergoing local extinction. The wolf recently bred in Norway for the first time in 50 years.

■ Capercaillie *(Tetrao urogallus)*. Hunting, habitat loss, and other human pressures have reduced most of Europe's population to isolated pockets. Between 1980 and 1991, 80 per cent of Scottish woods holding capercaillie recorded a decrease to a population of 1,000–2,000 birds.

■ Giant Panda *(Ailuropoda melanoleuca)*. The Giant Panda's population has declined to fewer than 1,000 in three main populations, due to disturbance to it and its habitat. However, concentrated efforts mean that its population remains stable.

Right *The European Bison or Wisent* (Bison bonasus), *once extinct in the wild, is now thriving having been bred from captive animals and released into several east and central European forest reserves from the main herd in the Bialowieza forest, Poland. Some of these newer populations have been lost following the break-up of the USSR.*

Elephants, large cats, hippopotamuses, rhinoceroses and other animals that are now regarded as essentially tropical once roamed the Palearctic region. The evidence of this early fauna can be found in fossil and subfossil remains, which reveal not just these big vertebrates, but also invertebrates, including insects and molluscs. Changes in climate and land connections have considerably altered this fauna. Some of the changes came in waves, most were slow, but in recent millennia the changes have been considerably influenced by the activities of one species – humankind. People affected the environment in a wide range of ways from utilization of forest timber to management of land for agriculture, settlement and transportation. The killing of wildlife for food or as "pests" or competitors – and, more recently, for "sport" – has also had a major influence, particularly on the larger animals.

It is possible to identify only about five Palearctic mammals that have become extinct in historical times, but many have been reduced to severely threatened relict populations in isolated areas, or persist only as domestic animals or through captive breeding. Other species have lost their Palearctic populations, but persist elsewhere in the world. The African Elephant may have survived in northwest Africa until about AD 100. The Lion is believed to have been present in Greece until about the same time, and occurred in Morocco until about 1920 and in Iran until 1942.

The western Palearctic and Japan have seen the most dramatic reductions in range of many species. Small remnant populations of, for instance, the Gray Wolf and the Brown Bear only survive at all through intensive conservation effort. However, even considerable effort

Left The European Brown Bear (Ursus arctos) *once occurred throughout Europe, surviving in Scotland until the Middle Ages. Only isolated remnant populations survive in western Europe, but there are healthier populations in former Yugoslavia and other parts of central and eastern Europe.*

Below In the Palearctic, the Gray or Timber Wolf (Canis lupus) *survives in only a few places in the North and in Italy, Iberia, and central and eastern Europe after centuries of persecution. Continuing prejudice means that populations are still threatened with local extinction. However, it has recently re-established in France and possibly also in Germany.*

and protection failed to save the European populations of the Bald Ibis, which became effectively extinct in Europe in 1990. The species survives as a few, small, isolated populations in Morocco. The Wisent (European Bison), once widespread from southern Sweden to the Caucasus, persisted only in captivity until wild populations were re-established in the Bialowieza forest of Poland and Lithuania, and subsequently in other isolated areas east to the Caucasus. The Arabian Oryx was destined for extinction, but some of the remaining wild animals were trapped and taken for captive breeding. The wild population did become extinct, but the captive-bred population allowed a later successful reintroduction program in Oman. Père David's Deer, from the lowlands of north China, was similarly extinct in the wild but was widely kept in zoos and parks from a herd established in Woburn, England. It, too, has recently been re-established in the wild. Initiatives such as the EC Habitats and Species Directive and the Pan-European Biological and Landscape Diversity Strategy are designed to protect priority species and habitats as well as to maintain or restore the integrity of landscape features.

FORESTS

The land habitat that has probably been most reduced in area in historical times is forest. Huge tracts of forest were lost in exactly the same way as we are currently losing tropical forest: by extraction of the largest trees and by clearfelling for timber, for agriculture and for other development. Large programs of afforestation or reafforestation have occurred, but these have usually been with monocultures of introduced trees and frequently at the expense of other valued habitats, particularly heaths and moors.

The deforestation started in prehistoric times and was the cause of the demise of many larger mammals. In historical times, fragmentation continued and helped many local extinctions, for example of boars in Britain, but sufficient forest remains to maintain populations of these animals elsewhere in the Palearctic. However, European populations of

Right *A male Capercaillie (Tetrao urogallus) displaying in a Swedish forest. This large, extremely palatable game bird was exterminated in Scotland but successfully reintroduced from Scandinavia.*

Spotlight

■ Bustards *(Otididae)*. The two European and the two other Palearctic bustards are all threatened by hunting and habitat loss. In Britain, for example, their low dry grassland habitat has been reduced by 95 per cent.

■ Butterflies. Of Europe's 575 butterfly species, 70 are threatened, particularly in western Europe, due to land drainage, agrochemicals and mechanization of agriculture.

■ Tortoises *(Testudo)*. The three European species have been threatened by trade, and even where this is controlled, they still suffer from habitat loss.

■ Cranes *(Gruidae)*. Five of the seven Palearctic crane species are threatened by drainage of wetlands and hunting for food, sport, and their plumage.

European Lynx, Brown Bear and Gray Wolf are in a precarious state and their long-term survival relies on protected areas, since elsewhere they are still subject to persecution as pests, to hunting for sport and to loss of habitat. Small mammals may not often suffer persecution but they are vulnerable to habitat change, and the Bavarian Pine Vole, first described as recently as 1962, is probably already extinct.

The great Palearctic taiga, a forest of conifers, birch and aspen, lies south of the arctic tundra. With its equivalent in North America, it once constituted a third of the world's forested area. At its western end, in Scandinavia and the Baltic countries, it has been seriously eroded, and new forestry industry is affecting 1.6 million square kilometers (600,000 square miles) of unspoiled taiga west of the Urals. But further east in the vast and sparsely populated region of Siberia, extensive tracts persist. These maintain forest species that have suffered in the west, and also provide some shelter in the winter for many of the tundra animals. Thus the famed Sable, prized for its fur, no longer exists in Scandinavia, Finland, and western Russia, giving the former Soviet Union total control over the trade in its fur. While the geese, ducks, waders, and many of the passerines of the arctic tundra migrate as winter approaches, other animals follow the Reindeer south to winter in the great northern taiga. There the Capercaillie, the most forest-loving of the grouse, is found, in greatly reduced populations. It became extinct in Britain, Ireland and Belgium, but has been reintroduced to Scotland.

Moving south, the forests become more deciduous and diverse, until in the drier areas around the Mediterranean there is a return to a more restricted tree flora. The Mediterranean forests are very diverse in other plant and animal life. Those in northern Greece provide the last European strongholds of European Lynx, Gray Wolf and Brown Bear, but large areas have been lost and further losses are planned.

A different kind of forest altogether is found in China. Extensive high-altitude bamboo forests occur around central and southern China and up into the foothills of the Himalayas. In small remnant parts of this forest lives the Giant Panda. Taxonomists and systematists still debate this enigmatic creature's relationship to other animals. Its rarity and popularity have led to its being a prized diplomatic gift and it is both an emblem and a millstone of conservation: despite vast resources devoted to attempts to conserve the species and increase its populations, there remain serious doubts about its long-term future. In the wild it has nearly every protection people can offer, although severe disruption to its habitat continues. There have been concerted efforts to develop captive-breeding programs, but the animal remains uncooperative.

GRASSLANDS TO DESERTS . . .

Forest loss has been spread over such a long period that it is difficult to measure the declines of its fauna. In comparison, the conversion of grassland for agriculture, particularly for arable farming, has been rapid. Europe has lost about 90 per cent of its dry grassland in the last 100 years, and as a result some 30 bird species are now considered vulnerable. Several recent initiatives have been developed to help protect this habitat and its fauna. Many of these initiatives have come through European Community (EC) directives or recommendations coupled with local effort, often aimed particularly at flagship species such as the Great Bustard, Montagu's Harrier, and the Stone Curlew. But many of the steppic birds are dispersive, due to an erratic and thinly distributed food supply, and so local protection may not be enough. The grasslands may be one of the most important areas for international co-operation through, for example, EC and non-EC international treaties. While the major aims must be prevention of further losses of grasslands and even their re-creation, there is also the realization that sympathetically managed, pesticide-free cereal crops can provide good cover and feeding areas for some species.

The Arabian Bustard is probably now extinct in the Palearctic, and the other three western Palearctic bustards (the Great, Little, and Houbara Bustards) are all considered endangered or threatened, with hunting being as responsible as habitat loss in some areas. The Corncrake is still widespread, but in very fragmented populations due to pressure of agriculture. The mixture of forest and grassland is particularly important for a number of mammals, including deer, Wisent, Wolverine, and wild horses. Przewalski's Horse was once widespread around the northern and western borders of the Gobi desert. Discovered in the

DISTRIBUTION
GREAT BUSTARD

■ *Current range*

Great Bustard (Otis tarda). *Toward the end of the eighteenth century the Great Bustard reached the maximum extent of its range, encouraged by clearance of forest areas in central and western Europe. However, as steppes and dry meadows were replaced by arable land its range diminished. Hunting pressures, pesticides and further habitat changes mean that its current range is severely fragmented.*

1870s, it is now only known from captive-bred stock and has been reintroduced to a number of places within its former range. Another wild horse, the Tarpan, occurred throughout much of Europe and eastward, probably to China. It was last seen in Europe in about 1850 and is now also extinct. The Tarpan is the origin of the domestic horse and efforts have been made to recreate it by selective breeding, with some recent success in Poland.

The wild ass of Asiatic lowlands, the Onager, includes the Syrian Wild Ass, the smallest and most distinctive form. Only 1 meter (3¼ feet) high, this was the wild ass of the Bible, but it, too, is extinct. Its range took it into the deserts shared with gazelle, antelope, camel, oryx, and Arabian Tahr. Despite living in habitats that are apparently inhospitable to people, most of the Palearctic populations of these animals are at least threatened, with the Arabian Oryx only existing in the wild as a result of the reintroduction of captive-bred animals. Dromedary (one-humped) Camels only survive as domestic animals – indeed, the largest wild population is now in Australia! – while the wild population of the Bactrian (two-humped) Camel is reduced to a few hundred, mainly in protected areas of the Gobi desert. The bustards and the larger mammals have long been hunters' prey, but in some instances, human activity has helped species. The "greening" of Israel for food production has encouraged one gazelle species to the extent that it is now regarded as a pest and controlled by culling.

The large cats – Caracal, leopards, and Cheetah – are found from southwest Asia through Arabia to Africa. They are principally arid zone species, but the first two at least do occur in

Above Domesticated Bactrian or Two-humped Camels (Camelus bactrianus). Their wild ancestors roamed the deserts of central Asia. They are now confined to a small area of the Gobi desert, but are strictly protected and may be increasing in number.

Above right The Snow Leopard (Panthera uncia) is found only at high altitudes in and around the Himalayas. Although it is probably the rarest of the big cats, its skins are still regularly seen on sale in Kashmir.

forests. Although they have a wide distribution and versatility of behavior, their Palearctic populations are nowhere healthy and some of the more eastern ones are seriously threatened. The Snow Leopard occurs from western Mongolia down to the Himalayas and eastwards. Mongolia is the only country within its range that is not party to an international treaty to protect the species, and it allows foreign hunters to stalk and kill in exchange for very high trophy fees. The Caucasian race of the Tiger is extinct, and the population of the Amur or Siberian Tiger is only a few hundred. It has been suggested that there is now not enough wild game to sustain even this limited population and that the Tigers should be culled to prevent them turning to domestic animals.

Changes to the arid zones pose an equal threat to smaller birds and mammals. Various partridges and some of the larger birds of prey that soar over the plains in search of food are affected, and so is their prey, including some of the variety of snakes, lizards, and tortoises that are adapted to the dry regions. Europe is surprisingly rich in reptiles and some, such as the Meadow Viper, have been identified as species of international importance in the conservation of European grasslands. The status of tortoises has also excited interest, leading to the establishment of a tortoise "village" in the Massif des Maures of southern France. This is developing programs for tortoise breeding and rehabilitation, and forms a center for research and education, especially for the endangered Hermann's Tortoise of southern Europe. Rodents are a large and diverse group of mammals with their stronghold in the dry and arid zones, so it is pleasing to note that relatively few species from this habitat are threatened – Menzbier's Marmot, from southeast Kazakhstan, a poorly known rodent with an extremely limited population, is an example.

The dry grasslands also support many invertebrates. One eighth (or 70) of Europe's 575 butterfly species are regarded as threatened, including 13 in danger of extinction. The Alcon Large Blue Butterfly is the most endangered in a genus of eight species, all threatened, and including the Large Blue, which was lost in Britain, but has now been re-established.

Swallowtail (Papilio machaon)

Apollo (Parnassius apollo)

Large Blue (Maculinea arion)

. . . AND WETLANDS

In some areas the plains give way to desert, in some to wetlands, another habitat so threatened that an international convention has been established for its conservation. Overall the greatest problems are peat digging for fuel, and drainage. Grazing, hunting, and over-exploitation are also significant, while afforestation, as proposed for the unique flow country of northern Scotland, is being resisted by a determined conservation lobby. There are still spectacular freshwater wetlands, coastal wetlands, and salt marshes scattered through the Palearctic, but few do not face some threats.

Of particular concern are birds such as pelicans, herons, storks, and cranes, while wildfowl, waders and other birds are also threatened. For many species, the wetlands are only temporary homes – not their breeding grounds. But studies of birds using wetlands as wintering areas or stopover points on migration may give the first indications of population problems. Action is now being developed through the African-Eurasian Migratory Waterbird Agreement. The Slender-billed Curlew is regarded as Europe's rarest migrant, and major efforts are being made to study it both on its wintering grounds in Europe and North Africa, and on its breeding grounds in the vast marshes of southwest Siberia. It is hoped that the wide-ranging international effort will establish the reasons for this bird's decline and improve its status.

Interest in the more spectacular cranes was also provoked by declines noted at migration points or wintering grounds. The two species of the western Palearctic, the Crane and the Demoiselle Crane, have disappeared from considerable parts of their former range, but are in no immediate danger. However, four species in the eastern Palearctic are giving grave cause for concern, with populations now limited and fragmented, and their habitats threatened. At least for the beautiful Siberian White Crane, an outstanding international conservation effort has resulted in a major success story. It is now protected at its known breeding grounds and along its migration routes, wild populations have been bolstered by captive-breeding programs, and significant previously unknown populations have been discovered. As mentioned earlier, the Bald Ibis was not so fortunate and became extinct in Europe. Strenuous efforts are being made to monitor, study, and protect the few remaining wild Crested Ibis, backed up by a captive-breeding program in China. The species is already extinct in Japan and North Korea.

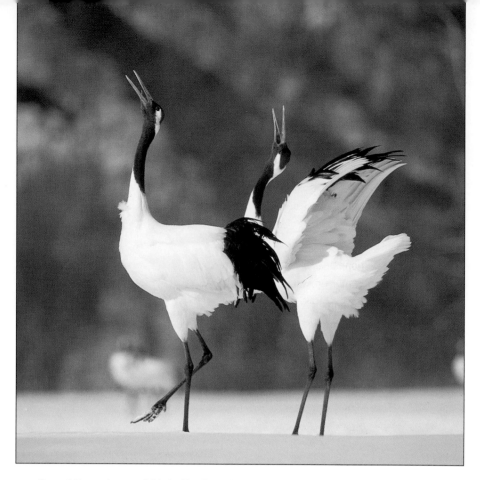

Right *Japanese Cranes* (Grus japonensis) *displaying. The elegant "dancing" displays of cranes have inspired many Japanese artists.*

Spotlight

■ Eurasian River Otter *(Lutra lutra)*. River Otters are endangered throughout Europe due to a complex of problems, including drainage, dam construction, pollution, pesticides, persecution, and incidental trapping. The country where they most recently became extinct is Switzerland in 1989.

■ Pelicans *(Pelecanus)*. Two European species, formerly widespread through most of Europe, are now restricted to the extreme southeast, where they suffer persecution by fishermen, and drainage and development of their habitat.

■ Valencia Toothcarp *(Valencia hispanica)*. Formerly occurring all along the Mediterranean coast of Spain and France, it is now restricted to two localities due to competition with an introduced fish and habitat loss.

■ Dragonflies. Nearly a quarter of British dragonfly species are threatened. Species are also declining throughout Europe, particularly in the south where intensification of agriculture is causing desiccation and pollution. Species depending on shallow well-vegetated water are especially at risk.

One of Europe's rarest birds, the Greenland White-fronted Goose, faces major problems in its wintering grounds. It is being monitored with concern in Ireland, Wales, and Scotland, including the island of Islay where nearly half the world population winters. Threats of peat digging of the raised bogs of Duich Moss on Islay and persecution on crop fields there have been resolved. All the wintering range is fully protected, farmers are compensated, and the population has increased.

While many coastal wetlands have been lost or spoiled, some good areas have been created. The new polder lands of the Netherlands include extensive marshland, providing an important haven for waders, wildfowl, and reedland birds. Many human-made reservoirs, gravelpits, and sandpits have also provided wonderful wildlife areas. For example, birdwatchers flock to near Reims, France, to see the migrant cranes, sea eagles, and a great number and variety of other birds at reservoirs that were completed only about 40 years ago.

LAKES AND RIVERS

The extremes of the wetland habitats are, of course, the lakes and rivers. An indication of the scale of the conservation problems facing this habitat is the fact that over half of the 200 European freshwater fish species are endangered. This is mainly due to pollution and over-fishing, although the problem of probably the most threatened European fish, the Valencia Toothcarp, is competition with alien species such as the Mosquito Fish, introduced (as its name suggests) to control mosquitoes. A Red Data Book of European vertebrates being prepared by the Council of Europe recognizes and aims to address the threats to fish. There has also been a surge of interest in dragonflies with the realization that many species are in trouble.

Rivers are an obvious example of a habitat that does not recognize political boundaries, and there is continual complaint by one country of pollution of its rivers by another. Nevertheless, there is hardly a country through which they flow that cannot take part of the blame for the troubled state of some of Europe's greatest rivers, such as the Danube and the Rhine. Some rivers have improved, for example the River Thames has much higher levels of oxygen than 40 years ago, and over 100 fish species, including the Salmon, have been recorded in its waters. But this is still a far cry from the distant days when dockworkers on the Thames went on strike, refusing to eat salmon and oysters every day! Even the most highly protected and best funded fishing, that for game fish such as Salmon, has its own lobby for conservation of stocks, which are declining due to its own activities and commercial, non-sporting, fishing in river mouths and at sea.

Lakes and rivers have also been affected by the increase in boating activities of various kinds, causing pollution, damage to banks and bankside vegetation, and considerably reducing the amount of undisturbed water available to birds. Of particular concern have been pelicans, the Pygmy Cormorant and ducks, such as the White-headed Duck, in the west, and inland gulls (Relict and Saunder's Gulls) in the east of the region. The establishment of spectacular reserves for the shooting of waterfowl has had the side effect of poisoning birds, for example swans, which take in the lead pellets during feeding. While there has been considerable success in getting fishermen to change lead weights for weights of more acceptable materials, finding an alternative to lead shot is proving more difficult. Steel shot has been tried but it seems to be less effective than lead shot at killing birds and so may not be the best answer.

The mammals arousing most concern in the aquatic environment have been the Eurasian River Otter and the Beaver. The Beaver has long disappeared from much of its former range, and forestry interests and fear of flooding caused by the dams it builds have frequently deterred its reintroduction. Its current decline in Norway has encouraged only limited activity to protect it, but it has been reintroduced recently to Sweden, Finland, Czechoslovakia, and the Netherlands. The decline of the River Otter, on the other hand, has been widely regretted and there are major conservation programs to meet a variety of causes. These include recovery plans, reintroductions, pressure to reduce pollution, provision of havens, and the development of devices to avoid its accidental capture in nets and traps. The range and

DISTRIBUTION
EUROPEAN BEAVER

 Current distribution

Range of the European Beaver (Castor fiber). Formerly found throughout the forested areas of Eurasia, its current natural distribution is severely reduced. However, beavers have been reintroduced to France, Netherlands, Germany, Austria, Switzerland, Poland, Finland, Norway, and Sweden. Its reintroduction to Scotland is under discussion.

Left *A Beaver (Castor fiber) lodge in Finland. Beavers are the only mammals that can modify the landscape on a large scale to suit their own specialized requirements. They do this by felling trees and damming rivers to form shallow swamps. The huge lodges are used for breeding and for storing supplies of food for the winter.*

populations of the Pyrenean Desman are also declining. This is a remarkable little insectivore of montane streams in the Pyrenees and other areas of northwest Spain and Portugal. Even in such mountain streams there is pollution, and afforestation causes shading and acidification of the waterways. The desman also suffers predation by feral American Mink, a scourge of European waterways which thrives even at the expense of indigenous European Mink.

The declines of some invertebrates have aroused considerable interest, such as that of the Medicinal Leech. Although no longer of much medical importance, the Medicinal Leech is a familiar, if not household, animal and its disappearance from much of its former range has led to high levels of protection for it. Many of the invertebrates are at least as sensitive to pollution as fish and ducks, and their diversity is being used increasingly as a biological indicator of pollution. This is important since even regular analysis of water samples can fail to detect major incidents of effluent pollution.

MOUNTAINS

As might be expected, the mountains are probably the least disturbed habitat. Apart from providing refuge for animals such as bear and wolf, they also have their own large mammal fauna, including the Ibex, Chamois, Mouflon, Markhor, and Goral. Nevertheless, forestry and farming have gradually encroached on wild territory, and the populations of these animals have become fragmented and reduced. The Pyrenean race of Spanish Ibex is almost extinct, and the rest of its populations need continual support. The Mouflon and Chamois are experiencing mixed fortunes. Thought to be the origin of domestic sheep, the Mouflon is losing ground in some areas but increasing in, for instance, Poland. Until recently the Chamois population of Abruzzo National Park in northern Italy was considered endangered, while now

Above *A ram Mouflon* (Ovis musimon). *This animal may represent the wild form of an early domesticated sheep. Once endangered, it has been introduced in many parts of Europe as far north as Germany.*

Top *The Alpine Ibex* (Capra ibex ibex) *was nearly exterminated, having been extensively hunted in the nineteenth century for its horns, gall bladder, and other parts which were used in Europe as medicine and aphrodisiacs.*

it has recovered sufficiently for some animals to be used as founder stock for a reintroduction to another park. The Markhor, with its spectacular spiral horns, has been a much sought-after hunting trophy. It lives on lower slopes than the Ibex and, although still occupying most of its former range in Afghanistan, India, Pakistan, Tadjikistan, Turkmenistan, and Uzbekistan, many populations are reduced or extinct.

For many of the larger birds of prey, which breed in the rocky mountaintops and range over large areas for food, persecution and disturbance are the main problems. In some areas, the placing of poisoned baits for pest species, such as foxes, or even for the birds themselves, has caused many deaths. The Lammergeier (or Bearded Vulture) hangs on in mountain areas of southern Europe and north Africa and has even been recently reintroduced to Austria, but its status is still precarious. The same is true for other vultures, such as the Griffon and Black, and eagles such as the Imperial Eagle. The Black Vulture is distributed from Spain to China but is believed to have a world population of fewer than 2,000 pairs, about 400 of which are in Spain. The largest colony occurs in an extensive hunting estate with a broadly sympathetic owner, and has survived a threat from a proposed airforce shooting range. However, its survival remains precarious.

The mountain forests and bare tops also provide habitat for a range of pheasants, partridges, and grouse. Encroaching farmland can affect these birds by reducing feeding areas and forcing them into unsympathetic areas when they move down to lower altitudes in winter. The five species of snowcock are all restricted to small mountain areas and the Altai Snowcock is believed to be particularly at risk, as is the Caucasian Black Grouse. The spectacular pheasants of Asian mountain forests have been widely hunted for food, for sport, and for their beautiful plumage. Among the most threatened in the wild are Cabot's Tragopan, Chinese and Slater's Monals, and Brown-eared, Blue-eared, Elliot's, Reeve's, and Lady Amherst's Pheasants. Perhaps fortunately, their beauty makes them popular captive birds, but the genetic stock of some captive collections is unclear.

While afforestation may be a threat in some areas, deforestation is affecting the wildlife elsewhere. The growth of skiing has brought a range of problems, including the clearing of woodland that provided winter cover for a range of animals, compaction and scarification of heavily used ground leading to denuding of the soil, and increased disturbance. Extending the skiing season has a particularly bad effect on the flora upon which many special upland insects rely, as well as on the breeding of birds and mammals.

CAVES

Caves provide an important refuge, notably for bats, but also for a range of other animals (including humans). While temperate caves do not contain the diversity of fauna found in tropical caves, a number of animals have become specialized for this type of environment.

Traditionally, certain species of bat, particularly horseshoe bats, some "mouse-eared" bats, and bent-winged bats, have used caves as their major breeding site, forming large summer colonies for the birth and rearing of their young. Northern European breeding colonies, especially those of horseshoe bats, have deserted underground sites and sought the extra warmth of surface structures, principally the roofs of buildings. It is speculated that this move followed disturbance and declines in populations, so that there were no longer sufficient numbers of these bats to maintain in caves the temperatures required for the successful rearing of young. In southern Europe, caves are still important for maternity colonies of bats. Throughout Europe, these underground structures provide hibernating sites

Right A cluster of roosting Greater Horseshoe Bats (Rhinolophus ferrumequinum). *Many species of bat need to roost in large, closely packed clusters to conserve energy. When their populations become reduced they may have to use up energy maintaining the temperature of the cluster.*

Spotlight

■ Horseshoe bats *(Rhinolophus).* All five European species are threatened by disturbance of breeding sites and damage to feeding sites. The two most widespread species, the Greater and Lesser Horseshoe Bats, are disappearing in the north and west of their range, and the UK population of the former is estimated to have declined by over 95 per cent in the last 100 years.

■ Bechstein's Bat *(Myotis bechsteinii).* Cave deposits show that this bat was very common 3,000 to 10,000 years ago. It is now extremely rare throughout Europe, probably due to loss of forest for feeding and roost sites.

■ Egyptian Fruit Bat *(Rousettusaegyptiacus).* Having expanded in range following the increased cultivation of fruit, it is now under pressure from fruit growers and townspeople. Control campaigns in Israel resulted in the extinction of three insectivorous bat species and the near extinction of a further five species.

■ Pond Bat *(Myotis dasycneme).* This bat is still widespread through northern Europe to western Russia, but has only about three healthy centers of population. It has declined due to disturbance of its roost sites, particularly wood treatment of buildings housing summer roosts, and pollution of the waterways over which it feeds.

– cool, undisturbed environments where bats can eke out reserves of fat through the winter period when their insect food is scarce.

To what extent the cave salamanders of Sardinia and of north and central Italy rely on this habitat is uncertain, but there are some exclusively cave-dwelling animals. The permanent association with the dark, stable environment of caves leads to adaptations, such as loss of color and loss of eyes, and their replacement with the increased development of other sensory organs, such as antennae. One specialist, a salamander known as the Orm, has reduced eyes, is almost translucent, and retains its aquatic larval form (with gills) throughout its life. It occurs in caves in a small area around the north end of the Adriatic Sea. Fish of various groups have cave specialists, mainly in the tropics, but also in Iran, Iraq and Japan. There are also a number of invertebrate cave specialists, including freshwater crustaceans and insects – and certain fungi are specialist parasites of these insects.

Caves are like islands, where a restricted and specialized fauna can develop, frequently lacking a "normal" complement of species. Predators and decomposers are few, and pure herbivores are virtually absent. Whether the specialists have arisen separately for each cave system is unknown, but in some groups it is possible to differentiate between populations in individual caves, suggesting long isolation. Both the unique fauna of (perhaps even individual) caves and the other animals, such as bats, which rely on this stable environment, are particularly vulnerable to disturbance. Quarrying for minerals, blocking for safety purposes, tourism or sport, conversion to other uses (such as stores or dumps), and alterations in water tables, have all resulted in the loss of or damage to a vast number of caves and their specialist fauna. Unwarranted campaigns against fruit bats in Israel included the fumigation of large numbers of caves. While the fruit bats survived, this campaign resulted in the extinction or near extinction of many of Israel's insectivorous bat species.

Many caves also have intrinsic value as places of unusual beauty or historical interest, such as those with cave paintings. Careful management of use and observance of agreed codes of conduct is helping to preserve many important caves and their associated fauna. Europe-wide treaties have been developed for the conservation of caves and their fauna, and for the conservation of bats.

Left *A Puffin (Fratercula arctica) with a beakful of sand eels. Seabirds once nested in vast colonies on most of the coasts of northwestern Europe. In addition to threats from oil spills and entanglement in fishing nets, they are now threatened by competition for declining fish resources. Even small fish such as sand eels are fished commercially.*

Below *Monk Seals (Monachus monachus) swimming off Mauretania. Once widespread in the Mediterranean, they are now among the most endangered mammals in the world, only breeding in sea caves or on remote beaches.*

DISTRIBUTION
MONK SEAL

▨ *Current distribution*

The Monk Seal (Monachus monachus) has a world population of about 500 individuals. Large-scale mortalities recently occurred off the coast of Western Sahara and were attributed to a morbillivirus. Later investigations suggested that algal toxins were a more likely cause of death. The mortality affected mainly adults and was responsible for the loss of about one third of the remanant population.

THE SEAS AND OCEANS . . .

The fauna of this habitat suffers mainly from over-exploitation, dumping and spillage. Increasingly, limitations on pollution and exploitation are agreed, but quotas are hard won and difficult to enforce. Despite pressure through the International Whaling Commission and independent conservation bodies, Japan and Norway continue to hunt whales "for scientific purposes" and have increasingly turned to stocks of smaller whales. Even the small dolphins and porpoises are now being carefully monitored, having suffered from pollution, over-exploitation and accidental catch during tuna fishing. Subsistence hunting by Eskimos has also affected cetaceans, particularly the Narwhal and Beluga. Efforts to stop the traditional rounding up and slaughter of Pilot Whales in the Faeroe Islands have met considerable resistance. International treaties have been developed for the conservation of small cetaceans in European waters.

Steller's Sea Cow was barely known to science before it was wiped out in about 1770 through over-exploitation. Other large animals suffering over-exploitation or persecution include the Walrus, the Polar Bear, and Seals. Of three monk seal species, the Caribbean Monk Seal is thought to be extinct, and the Hawaiian and Mediterranean Monk Seals are considered critically endangered. Once widespread in the Mediterranean and down part of the west African coast, hunting, disturbance, and pollution have drastically reduced populations of the Mediterranean Monk seal. Even these reduced populations have been persecuted by fishermen for alleged damage to fishing nets, despite local protection and education campaigns about the seal and its habitat. In some areas compensation for net damage has replaced culling, but few viable populations remain. While not generally thought to have had a major impact on populations, culls of North Atlantic Gray Seals have been a very emotive issue. In contrast, a recent viral epidemic gave rise to major concern for Common or Harbor Seals around the North Sea. The virus killed over 17,000 seals and was similar to one that had already seriously affected the Baikal Seal. The recent epidemics have been linked with pollution, which has also seriously affected landlocked populations of Ringed Seal in Lake Saimaa, Finland, and Common Seal in the north Pacific Ocean.

Marine pollution, a particular problem in the Mediterranean, Baltic, and North Sea, also

Below The seas of Europe are among the most polluted in the world. Oil pollution poses a major threat to marine life, killing millions of seabirds every year. In addition to the damage caused by the oil, many of the chemicals used to "clean" the beaches can be harmful to wildlife and the environment.

takes its toll on marine invertebrates. The most obvious pollutant is oil, and wide coverage has been given to major accidents involving oil tankers. Starting with the *Torrey Canyon*, which sank off Cornwall in 1967, such incidents have been a frequent feature of recent years and have been responsible for the deaths of many thousands of seabirds, as well as otters and marine invertebrates. But, in fact, these major accidents contribute only a small proportion of the oil released through spillage and dumping. In addition, the importance of other pollutants, such as "waste" chemicals and sewage, is now beginning to be appreciated.

Over-exploitation of corals for trophies, and lobsters and sea urchins for food, has led to local extinctions. To reduce the harvesting of the Channel Islands' Ormer, benefactors were invited to "adopt" an Ormer and so raise money for a marine conservation area. The establishment of marine reserves has been slow, but the situation is improving and there are now major reserves in Mauritania, Madeira, and the Red Sea. Although a few have been set up in Britain and around the North Sea, it is hard to augment them in the face of increasingly serious pollution problems.

. . . AND THEIR ISLANDS AND COASTLINES

The islands of the Mediterranean Sea and the northern oceans carry their own unique fauna. Most of them offered limited opportunity for human settlement, but tourism has had profound impacts. In the North Atlantic, the Canary Islands, Madeira, and, to a lesser extent, the Azores have all suffered from tourism and associated development. The Canary Islands subspecies of the Black Oystercatcher is extinct, the Madeiran and Gon-gon Petrels, and land birds such as the Fuerteventura Stonechat, laurel pigeons, and the Blue (Canary Island) Chaffinch, have all been considered threatened, mostly by habitat loss and hunting. In some cases the problems have been or are being addressed, but certainly the Fuerteventura Stonechat and Madeiran Petrel (Freira) are endangered. The stonechat has healthy populations in some areas, and researchers have been investigating why it is present in such low densities in other apparently suitable areas. Conservation efforts for the petrel have concentrated on excluding from breeding areas the introduced rats which prey on eggs and young.

Most of the indigenous mammals on these islands are bats, none of which seems to be particularly threatened at present. Some endemic bats with limited populations need care, as do other mammals such as the Canaries White-toothed Shrew. The Hierro Giant Lizard of the Canaries is considered endangered, and Madeira has a threatened land nemertine worm and a number of endangered molluscs. Firmly including the fauna of these islands in European protective legislation could improve their conservation status.

Similar problems affect the fauna of Mediterranean islands, including land birds, such as the Barbary Falcon and Corsican Nuthatch, a range of reptiles, such as the Filfola Lizard of Malta, and possibly amphibians, such as the Mallorcan Midwife Toad. This toad was described only in 1977 from subfossil remains and it was not until 1980 that the first specimen was found alive. Mallorca lost several endemic species long ago and the evidence of subfossils suggests

Spotlight

■ Sea Turtles (Cheloniidae and Dermochelyidae). Persecution and accidental trapping have taken their toll. Two nests of Loggerhead Turtle (Caretta caretta) were found along 250 kilometers (155 miles) of beach in Israel where 30 years ago it is estimated there were 15 nests per kilometer (24 nests per mile).

■ Terns/gulls (Laridae). Many gulls and terns that nest on beaches and islands have declined due to disturbance and predation. The Arctic Tern (Sterna paradisaea) in Scotland declined by 70 per cent between 1980 and 1991, and the remaining birds are showing very poor breeding success in some years. The British Roseate Tern (S. dougalli) population has declined by 85 per cent but is doing well in Ireland.

■ Seals (Phocidae). The Monk Seal (Monachus monachus) has retreated from nearly all its former breeding grounds, and the already depleted population of 40 years ago has been reduced by up to 90 per cent. Up to 70 per cent of many North Sea populations of Common Seal (Phoca vitulina) were killed by a virus in 1988.

■ Fuerteventura Stonechat (Saxicola dacotiae). The population of 750–850 pairs on Fuerteventura is threatened by introduced predators, development and long-term desiccation.

Right Audouin's Gull (Larus audouinii) *is one of the rarest gulls in the world. It breeds only on a few Mediterranean islands where competition from the much more adaptable Herring Gull is a major cause of its decline.*

DISTRIBUTION
AUDOUIN'S GULL

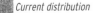
Current distribution

Audouin's gull (Larus audouinii) *usually nests on exposed rocky islands and islets, but may also nest on uninhabited islands with gentle rocky slopes to the sea. In 1981 a colony established in the Ebro Delta, Spain. By 1993 the colony had grown to 9,000 pairs. Despite this and recent discovery of additional colonies in Greece, Audouin"s gull remains a globally threatened species.*

that the toad's distribution has been drastically reduced, probably through droughts and introduced predators. As a safety net, a captive-breeding program has been established.

Audouin's Gull, with only a few limited colonies on Mediterranean islands, is one of the world's rarest gulls. One of its major breeding sites is the Spanish possession of the Chafarinas islands, just off the Moroccan coast. The islands have been declared a national game reserve, but their protection status needs to be upgraded and enforced. Apart from current problems of human disturbance, Audouin's Gulls are affected by Herring Gulls, which compete for nesting space and prey on the smaller gull and its eggs.

Larger mammals often get preferential treatment in conservation nowadays. Although the Corsican Red Deer became extinct recently, the limited populations of Sardinian Red Deer and Sardinian and Cyprus Mouflon will probably survive, helped by captive breeding. Red Deer were reintroduced to Corsica from Sardinia in 1985 and this was supported by an education program, including a film shown to all schoolchildren. Less charismatic mammals, such as the endemic subspecies of the Genet on the Balearic islands, may not be so lucky. On the other hand, these islands can act as the last refuge for mainland animals − for example, a now extinct group of European rodents hung on until historic times only on Sardinia.

In the north Pacific, the Short-tailed or Steller's Albatross breeds on Japanese islands. It was brought to the verge of extinction by plume hunters in the late nineteenth and early twentieth centuries, with about ten pairs left in 1953. Since then it has recovered, but is still very rare. Also on Japan's islands is the rare Crested or Japanese Murrelet. With a small population and a very limited breeding distribution, it is a vulnerable species − and was especially so when the US Air Force began using one of its major breeding islands for bombing practice! Advised of the conservation problem, the Air Force quickly stopped its activities.

Gibraltar is famous for its Barbary Macaque (Barbery Ape), which was probably introduced from Morocco about 250 years ago. The relics of north African populations, which had dwindled to a few isolated colonies in Algeria and Morocco, have been supplemented from captive-bred animals. The population on Gibraltar is small but stable and well looked after. In view of the "ape's" popularity it has been proposed that at least one troop should be incorporated into a "monkey" park for education and fundraising.

Tourism has affected coasts as well as islands. Rocky coastlines still provide sanctuary for breeding seals and birds, including sea eagles, but the development of beach resorts has had an enormous impact. While this has been marked in northern Europe, it is nowhere more obvious than in the Mediterranean Sea. The rapid development of the coastlines of Spain, Portugal, and southern France continues apace. Now attention has turned to Greece and Turkey, and turtles are in the forefront of battles to save these beaches. Intense efforts are being made through national organizations, a pan-Mediterranean organization and other bodies, to conserve beaches important for Loggerhead and Green Turtles. The resultant clash of interests has been most apparent on the Greek island of Zakynthos, home to Europe's largest breeding population of Loggerhead Turtles. Tourism is deemed so important for the local economy that the efforts to restrict development have met strong local opposition and even violence. The fauna of many Japanese islands is poorly known. Current studies are finding additional, even undescribed, species in mammal groups such as bats, but the natural habitat on many of these islands is threatened by such factors as increased demand for agricultural land.

Below *A Loggerhead Turtle* (Caretta caretta) *arriving at its nesting beaches. Many of the beaches in the Mediterranean have become holiday resorts, and turtles returning to nests have little chance of success.*

R. I. Vane-Wright started his long career in the Entomology Department of London's famous Natural History Museum as an "assistant (scientific)." This led on to a zoology degree and a deep interest in the relationship between animal classification and evolutionary biology. For the last decade he has been involved with international research programs combining his four main interests – butterflies, evolution, systematics, and conservation. In 1998 he became Keeper (head of department), and now holds responsibility for the most important insect collection in the world.

Above Eastern Tailed Blue (Everes comyntas), from North and Central America. Many "blues" have complex ecological needs and are very vulnerable to change.

Above The Red Admiral (Vanessa atalanta), a familiar butterfly found throughout the Nearctic and Palearctic regions, is relatively adaptable to changing conditions.

Right This map of the Malay archipelago shows the number of butterfly species found on main islands. To set effective conservation priorities, we also need to know the distribution of every one.

Butterflies

The total number of animal and plant species on Earth is between 5 million and 50 million, and each has special needs for its survival. We can try to conserve some, such as the Loggerhead Turtle or Channel Islands' Ormer, by careful habitat management, or in zoos or gardens. But a significant proportion of the millions of species now seem to be at risk, and it would be impractical to make individual provision for them all. Instead, we need to plan how to save priority areas which between them will conserve the greatest possible variety of the planet's life. This section looks at the need for a plan, and how we might go about setting priorities, by examining the problems presented by one of the best-known groups – the butterflies.

VULNERABLE BUTTERFLIES

Of the 18,000 species of butterflies in the world, almost half are found in South and Central America. These include the brilliant *Morpho* butterflies with wings like blue mirrors – "little pieces of the sky come down" according to Amerindian folklore – which can be seen up to half a mile away. Africa accounts for another 3,600 butterflies, including many of the spectacular *Charaxes*. The Australasian region has more than 4,000 species, including all the birdwings, the largest butterflies on Earth. The whole of the Palearctic and North America are relatively poor, containing less than 2,000 species, including the Peacock and the Corsican Swallowtail.

The exotic-looking Peacock, with a color pattern like no other butterfly in the world, can be found throughout most of the Palearctic region, from Britain to Japan. Several hundred butterflies live only within the boundaries of this huge area. But, unlike the ubiquitous Peacock, many of them have very limited distributions, such as the Corsican Swallowtail. Found only on the Mediterranean islands of Corsica and Sardinia, this handsome insect is now considered to be endangered.

Many of the world's butterflies are known only from particular habitats, such as certain mountain ranges, forests, swamps, or islands, because they depend on particular plants for

● Luzon 380	● Buru 190
● Palawan 350	● Seram 225
● Mindenao 490	● Timor 110
● Malaya Peninsula 1,000	New Guinea 800
● Sumatra 910	● New Britain 170
● Java 640	● Bougainville 160
Borneo 940	● Guadalcanal 140
● Sulawesi 475	● Australia 390
● Halmahera 200	

their caterpillars to feed on, or have other precise needs. Their specific requirements make these butterflies very vulnerable to change. For instance, draining the wetlands of East Anglia for agriculture wiped out most of the water dock and fenland habitat on which the English Large Copper depended, and this beautiful butterfly became extinct in Britain during the mid-nineteenth century.

Queen Alexandra's Birdwing, the largest butterfly in the world, is found only in northern Papua New Guinea, in one small area of lowland rainforest now extensively cleared for agriculture. Its caterpillars feed exclusively on one special type of vine. Such is the interest in this magnificent species that it is protected by international law – but its habitat is not. The Queen Alexandra's Birdwing could well become the first tropical insect to survive in captivity long after it has disappeared from the wild.

Because of their special appeal, this giant and a handful of other species may perhaps be preserved in insect zoos. But for the great majority of the 18,000 butterflies, let alone the many millions of other insects, it is inconceivable that individual care could be lavished on them. Those that remain to delight future generations will be those, like the Peacock, that can survive despite us – unless we make some provision for vulnerable species.

There are two major ways in which we can help butterflies on a global scale. The first is by managing agricultural and recreational land and wastelands so as to maintain natural and semi-natural habitats within them. This would not only preserve species but would also help

Above *A male Rajah Brooke's Birdwing* (Trogonoptera brookiana). *The caterpillars of this spectacular insect, which lives only in parts of the Malay archipelago (including Malaysia, Sumatra and Borneo), can only feed on particular vines.*

Below *The Paris Peacock* (Papilio paris), *was once voted the most beautiful butterfly in the world. Many of its natural habitats in China, India, and Indonesia are vulnerable.*

Two butterflies from the island of Sulawesi. Vindula dejone **(above)** is widespread, occurring throughout most of the Malay archipelago. In contrast, Lamasia lyncides **(below)** is one of some 200 butterfly species only found on Sulawesi and small islands nearby.

to maintain a healthy enough environment for our own survival. The second method is to set up nature reserves in wilderness and other areas. Reserves must be safeguarded from interference, and managed to ensure the survival of species within them. Funds to buy or set aside areas and manage them effectively are very limited, so the areas need to be carefully chosen. We must aim to identify a series of priority areas which will form a worldwide network of reserves, protecting as great a variety of living things as possible. Looking at butterflies which live on islands can give us ideas on how to set about this complex task.

ISLAND BUTTERFLIES

Throughout the world, islands vary remarkably in the number of native breeding butterflies they support. Hawaii has only two, New Zealand about a dozen, Great Britain less than 60, Hispaniola 196, Sri Lanka 242 and Trinidad over 600. Islands also vary in endemism – the proportion of species not found elsewhere. Both of the native butterflies of Hawaii and most of the native butterflies of New Zealand are endemics, while almost all of the Trinidadian species occur on the South American mainland, and not one British butterfly species is an endemic. Levels of endemism are of profound importance in identifying priority areas to preserve.

All the major islands of the Malay archipelago have a wealth of butterflies. The richest is Borneo, with an estimated 900 species, including the fabulous Rajah Brooke's Birdwing. This may seem to suggest that Borneo should be the top priority in the archipelago for

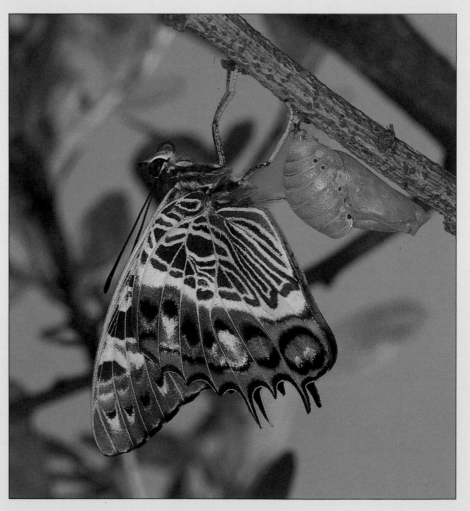

Right Africa is home to over 160 species of Charaxes. Some of these fast-flying butterflies live in the savannas, but many are restricted to forests. This Black-bordered Charaxes (C. pollux) has just emerged from its chrysalis.

conservation action. Yet only a handful of these species are restricted to Borneo, with Java, Sumatra, and the Malay Peninsula sharing much the same set of butterflies. In contrast, of the roughly 600 butterflies in the Philippine Islands to the east of Borneo, more than 40 per cent cannot be found in any other country and many are restricted to particular islands within the Philippines. Similarly, 43 per cent of the 470 or so species on Sulawesi only occur on this curiously shaped island. A high proportion of the butterflies of New Guinea are also endemics, including the Queen Alexandra and a number of other remarkable birdwings.

To plan a network of reserves to protect as many of the butterflies of the archipelago as possible, it is essential to have accurate knowledge of all the species and their distributions. Such knowledge is now being assembled for this purpose. Inevitably, high on the list will come the major islands of the Philippines, Borneo, New Guinea, and Sulawesi. Regrettably, the plan may be too late to save many of the Philippine species because so many of the islands have been completely stripped of their native vegetation.

But the task cannot stop there. For example, not all the 470 species on Sulawesi occur

Below left The Peacock (Inachisio) *is closely related to the Red Admiral, Small Tortoiseshell and other familiar north-temperate species. From Britain to Japan, its unique color pattern is constant.*

Below A female Archduke (Lexias pardalis), *one of many species distributed from Assam through parts of the Malay archipelago. The male looks very different, but both sexes enjoy feeding from rotting fruit on the forest floor.*

throughout the entire island. Kuekenthal's Tiger is a striking primrose-tinted milkweed butterfly known only from montane areas near Manado, in the far north of the island. Bedford-Russell's Idea, a huge black and white milkweed butterfly discovered just a few years ago, is restricted to a few of the central mountains. The Bonthain Tiger, another endemic milkwood species, flies only on the volcanic peak of Mount Lompobatang, at the island's southern tip. Today these butterflies remain on sale by dealers and, unless their particular habitats are adequately protected, they will soon disappear forever.

They could be saved by identifying a set of sites that between them cater for all the butterflies of Sulawesi, in all their different habitats and communities. Similarly, we could identify priority islands or regions in other parts of the world, and then set up networks of well-managed reserves within each of these areas. In this way it would be possible to make provision for the majority of the world's butterflies – and, in a similar way, for the widest possible variety of other animals and plants.

It has taken 2,300 million years for butterflies, and all the other forms of life, to evolve on our planet. It would take about ten years to make a plan to save most of the thousands and millions that still remain. If we devoted the resources, the strength, and the will, we could put that plan into action. If we fail to do this, the Earth will be forever impoverished.

Above Bush-browns of the genus Lohora *form the largest group of butterfly species entirely confined to the Sulawesi region. They will only survive if the dense forests survive too.*

ARCTIC

GREENLAND

BERING STRAIT

BROOKS RANGE

Yukon

Banks Island

DAVIS STRAIT

ALASKA RANGE MACKENZIE MOUNTAINS

Mount McKinley

Victoria Island

Baffin Island

Mackenzie

Great Bear Lake

R O C K Y   M O U N T A I N S

Great Slave Lake

Southampton Island

HUDSON BAY

LABRADOR

Churchill

Saskatchewan

CASCADES RANGE

Mount Rainier

Columbia

Lake Winnipeg

Newfoundland

Mount St Helens

WHITE MOUNTAINS

NOVA SCOTIA

SIERRA NEVADA

Snake

Lake Superior

Lake Huron

Mt Washington

Great Salt Lake

Missouri

Lake Michigan

Lake Ontario

Mount Whitney

Colorado

Platte

GREAT PLAINS

Lake Erie

San Andreas

OZARK PLATEAUS

Ohio

APPALACHIAN MOUNTAINS

BLACK RANGE

Arkansas

Mississippi

BLUE RIDGE MOUNTAINS

Red River

Bermuda

VIZCAINO DESERT

GULF OF CALIFORNIA

CHIHUAHUAN DESERT

Rio Grande

EVERGLADES

Bahamas

GULF OF

WEST INDIES

MEXICO

MEXICO

CARIBBEAN SEA

PACIFIC OCEAN

SOUTH AMERICA

The Nearctic Region

The Nearctic region (northern New World) embraces
Canada, Greenland, the USA and parts of Mexico.
Deciduous forests, swamplands, prairies, mountains,
deserts, coniferous forests, and arctic tundra combine
to form a wonderfully varied landscape, despite the
extensive alterations brought about by the spread of
European settlement.

Steller's Sea Lion (Eumetopias jubatus), Vancouver Island, BC.

Habitat & Plants

Peter Alden of Concord, Mass., USA graduated from the University of Arizona, Tuscson. He led dozens of Mexican bird and nature trips in the 1960s and wrote *Finding Birds in Western Mexico*. From 1968 to 1982 he led birding tours worldwide for the Massachusetts Audubon Society and co-wrote (with John Gooders) *Finding Birds around the World*. From 1982 to 1989 Peter was a vice president and naturalist guide for Lindblad Travel. He wrote the *Peterson First Guide to Mammals* and *Peterson's Western Birds*, and has been a major contributor to field guides on birds of the USSR, Mexico, Colombia and Venezuela. In the 1990s he has been principal author of field guides to African Wildlife, and Wildlife in New England, Florida, California, and the Pacific Northwest.

This region encompasses Canada, the United States of America or the USA (minus Hawaii) and parts of Mexico north of the tropical zone. Flanked by the Atlantic and Pacific Oceans, it is a mosaic of extensive deciduous and mixed forests, swamplands, prairies, mountains, deserts and great coniferous forests, with arctic tundra to the north bordering the Arctic Ocean.

Settlers from Europe and elsewhere wrought major changes in these habitats, felling virgin forests, putting prairies to the plough and draining swamplands. Within only a few hundred years, vast areas of wilderness vanished and with them went a number of animals and plants. A few of these extinctions were well publicized and public attitudes gradually started to shift. In the late 1800s, the first national parks were created and private nature groups began to form. Progress in setting aside reserves and protecting species by law continued into the 1900s. Then in the 1960s and 1970s, public outrage, provoked mainly by the effects of DDT and rampant pollution, resulted in various endangered species Acts. Inventories of long-neglected species began, and these took note not just of mammals, birds, and trees, but of the entire range of animals and plants. Even subspecies were studied, and the presence of one tiny fish or flower could suddenly stop a dam, move a highway or close an offending industrial plant. Many classrooms focus on endangered species, and as a result some rare creatures are better known than common everyday species. Yet pressures on vulnerable flora and fauna continue, and much work remains to be done.

While loss of habitat, over-exploitation, and invasive species are frequent threats, other diverse and sometimes subtle factors may affect species. Identifying these is essential if conservation work is to be effective. The following sections outline case histories of particular interest which, between them, illustrate a wide range of the problems being faced by plants and animals and how these are being tackled.

NEARCTIC PLANTS

Among the first areas of the Nearctic region to receive settlers from Europe, eastern Canada and northeastern USA were covered with vast tracts of great virgin forests. These have long been felled and replaced by second-growth woodland, and by farms and towns. Along with the majestic trees went much of the smaller flora, virtually unremarked. An increase in awareness has taken place since then, and is illustrated by the efforts made in recent times to conserve even tiny threatened plants.

Only 13 square miles of alpine habitat exist in the eastern US, and it is heavily used by hikers and mountain bikers. Thirty-three species are at risk in New England's alpine zone. The Dwarf (Robbin's) Cinquefoil of the rose family sports solitary yellow flowers at two sites in the alpine zone of New England's mountains. One of the sites straddled the Appalachian Trail near Mount Washington, New Hampshire and the plants were being trampled, so this famous trail was rerouted. This action has resulted in a modest rebound and the plant may soon be taken off the endangered species list. Another tiny plant even helped stop a dam. Listed as endangered, the Furbish Lousewort is a perennial snapdragon with spikes of greenish-yellow flowers. It once grew along terraces above the St. John river on the Maine-New Brunswick border. In 1976, a plan to build a huge dam which would flood a large area was being opposed

Left Bald Cypress (Taxodium distichum) *swamps once covered huge areas of the southeastern USA. Although they have been extensively logged, some are now protected, including stands in the Okefenokee swamp in southern Georgia and the Corkscrew Swamp Wildlife Sanctuary in southern Florida.*

Venus fly trap

Pitcher plant

by many people. Then the lousewort, last seen in 1943, was rediscovered in the area to be flooded – and was a factor in killing the plan.

Further south, most of the original trees were also cut, including the Bald Cypress which once grew along the great rivers and swamplands of the southeastern USA. This deciduous conifer, with buttress roots and protruding "knees," dominated many swamps and anchored valuable wildlife habitat. Its wood is excellent, and nearly all the virgin stands were exploited. However, ancient, massive specimens still survive in a few preserves, while younger trees are common.

American Ginseng grows in the understory of the vast deciduous forests of the Appalachian mountains. Its health benefits are such that escalating demand has caused prices to rise, and it is now grossly overcollected in rural areas.

Areas of the southeast with impoverished soil are home to some of the region's most fascinating plants – the carnivorous (or insectivorous) plants, including sundews, bladder-worts, Venus flytraps and pitcher plants. All have developed ways to lure and trap insects for food. The great Green Swamp area of North Carolina has been stripped of all its insect-eating plants, as have many other sites. The attractive pitcher plants have been particularly sought by collectors and, while all may be in trouble, some have suffered a drastic decline. The first to make the endangered species list was the Green Pitcher Plant which survived at just four sites. Then a commercial dealer made a wholesale raid at the DeSoto State Park in Alabama, and the number is now down to three.

Even rarer in the wild is a long-leaved tree with showy white flowers discovered by John and William Bartram in 1765 by the Altahama river in Georgia. It was last seen in the wild in 1803, but fortunately the Bartrams had cultivated some, and the Lost Franklinia is now grown in a number of gardens. Another tree with problems is the Virginia Roundleaf Birch, discovered in 1914 at an altitude of 850 meters (2,800 feet) near Sugar Grove Station, Virginia, growing among Sweet Birch. It was not found again until 1975, when a local biology teacher spent the whole summer searching for it and eventually found 12 trees and 16 seedlings. Although high fences were erected around the plants, in 1983 vandals destroyed all but five of them. Today, it survives in arboretums and has been successfully found at or transplanted to secret sites on national forest lands.

The Mountain Golden Heather, a dwarf rockrose which produces solitary yellow flowers in early summer, has also "reappeared." Described by Thomas Nuttall in 1818, it was thought to be extinct by the 1960s and then 2,000 individuals were recently found. Unfortunately, they grow in areas of the Blue Ridge Mountains of North Carolina attractive to campers – and one camper was noted building a fire on top of a colony of these threatened plants.

While rare plants often survive in an isolated area among commoner species, in northwest Florida there is a concentration of a dozen or so rare and endangered plants restricted to the vicinity of the Apalachicola river. Various members of the yew family are common ornamentals, but two small trees of this family are found only there, the Florida Torreva and Florida Yew. Chapman's Rhododendron grows at only three sites in this area and is the rarest member of its genus in North America. Clumps of it have been dug up for the nursery trade, and large areas of the bogs in which it lives have been "improved" for commercial pine plantations. Harper's Beauty is restricted to ten individuals at two sites by the river. This yellow-flowering lily, and many other rare plants and animals, depend on sound management of the Apalachicola National Forest and the efforts of the Nature Conservancy to save them. Further south, the Everglades area of south Florida is partly protected by the Everglades

periphyton (algae and one-celled animals)

dead leaves and stems

limestone

marl (deposit of mixed limestone and clay)

peat

Above *Periphyton is the basis of the complex web of life in the Everglades. Not only is it the beginning of the many food chains in the marsh, it also removes calcium from water flowing over the limestone and converts it to marl. Sawgrass roots in the marl; dead sawgrass forms peat; other marsh plants grow in the peat; acid from the peat and from decaying plant matter dissolves some of the marl and bedrock – and the cycle is complete. Damage to any part of this cycle or to the many food chains – pollution, lowering the water table, elimination of alligators – could destroy the glades.*

Right *Florida Slash Pine* (Pinus elliottii) *and Saw Palmetto* (Serenoa repens) *in the Florida Everglades. The core of the Everglades is the shallow outflowing of Lake Okeechobee (the Sea of Grass). In the drier, slightly elevated areas, pines and tropical hardwood hummocks occur.*

National Park. However, the majority of its life-giving water flows down a wide river of grass and marsh from central Florida, and much of this has been diverted to supply cities, industry, and agriculture, reducing the Everglades to a shadow of its former richness. Some progress has been made in the late 1990s to redirect some of this water back into the park.

Extending from the Canadian Prairie provinces south to Texas is the area known as the Great Plains. Before cultivation, fencing and urbanization, there was a sea of grass from the eastern forests west to the Rockies. Over 99 per cent of the long-grass prairie growing in the eastern half of the Great Plains has been destroyed. Tiny plots have been found in Illinois and elsewhere, while somewhat larger tracts in the Flint hills of eastern Kansas and parts of northeastern Oklahoma may gain national park status. The larger remnants of the drier short-grass plains to the west are protected in a number of provincial and national grasslands. One of the most beautiful wildflowers of the southern plains area is the Texas Poppy Mallow, which produces showy white-purple, cup-shaped flowers in May and June. Today its only known site is an area of deep sandy soil along the "other" Colorado river in Texas.

The Antioch dunes, California
The first land to be bought by the US government from private landowners to protect habitat for endangered plants was a remnant of the Antioch dunes above the San Joaquin river in California. Once reaching 35 meters (115 feet) in height and stretching for miles, these dunes have been mined to supply pottery works, brickyards and mix for asphalt and concrete. The remaining 22 hectares (55 acres) with dunes only 9 meters (30 feet) tall were purchased in 1980. The dunes' flora includes the Contra Costa Wallflower, a member of the mustard family with showy yellow flowers, and the Antioch Dunes Evening Primrose.

Above left The tallgrass prairie is defined by a predominance of big bluestem grass. Tallgrass prairie used to cover more than 400,000 square miles over 12 states of the USA. Now only a few nature reserves and isolated pockets remain.

Left Mammillaria pectinifera *cacti from the higher altitudes of Mexico's Sierra Madre. It is a relatively small species, less than 5 centimeters (2 inches) across, and like several other species with a restricted range, very easily wiped out by commercial collectors.*

While cattle rustling in Texas has almost ceased, cactus rustling is booming. In a recent year, over 500,000 small, globular cacti were harvested by illegal aliens working for dealers who shipped the cacti out nationwide and around the world. Rare species commanded high prices in the USA, Japan and Europe, and many buyers insist on wild specimens. One of the smallest and rarest cacti in the world is the 25-millimeter (1-inch) Nellie Cory Cactus which usually grows under clubmoss. One of its two remaining colonies was wiped out by cactus rustlers in the 1960s. A small button cactus *Epithelantha micromeris* var. *bokei*, has even been poached from the remotest corner of Big Bend National Park in southwest Texas.

The eastern, southern and western flanks of the dry Mexican plateau are known as the Sierra Madre mountains. These edges were covered with great virgin forests of long-needled pines, short-needle firs, oaks and many other hardwood trees, while vast freshwater lakes and marshes filled the valleys. Now, the old-growth trees are essentially gone and the swamps largely drained. Two trees there are considered endangered. The wood of the Guatemalan Fir

Right *Saguaro Cacti* (Cereus gigantea) *seen here through Ocotillo flowers, are popular with gardeners in the southwest USA and have been dug up in large numbers in many areas. They are also frequently damaged by trigger-happy gunmen.*

Ancistrocactus tubuschii

Epithelantha micromeris *var. Bokei*

Coryphantha minima

or Pinabete is used for making hand looms, saplings were cut for Christmas trees (now illegal, but unenforced), and seedlings are eaten by sheep. The Ayuque only grows to 7 meters (23 feet) and, with its pyramidal shape and brilliant red flowers in season, made a good substitute. The Ayuque has now been virtually eliminated from its home area in Michoacan state.

Two endangered wildflowers of New Mexico are linked with gypsum layers. The Gypsum Wild Buckwheat, with large clusters of bright yellow flowers, lives only on one limestone hill near Artesia. A proposed lake which would have covered its only home has been stopped, and it now only has to contend with cattle, off-road vehicles and botanists. Todsen's Pennyroyal, a mint with solitary red flowers, escapes these threats – all 750 individuals occur on steep gypsum slopes of the San Andreas mountains in the White Sands missile range.

The Channel Islands off the coast of California are a botanical treasure, with 76 flowering plants not found on the mainland and 18 that are restricted to just one island. Many of these islands have never had major herbivores. Their flora has now been devastated by introduced grazers, browsers and plants. On the relatively large San Clemente Island, the main problem is feral goats which have eaten most of the plants, causing erosion and wreaking ecological havoc. Four of the island's 14 endemic plants were the first plants to be listed as federally endangered – the San Clemente Broom, Bushmallow, Larkspur, and Paintbrush. The only way to save the island's plants and birds was to remove the goats. As many as possible were trapped and it was decided to shoot the rest. Then animal rights activists heard about it and took legal action to delay the killing. So the goats ate and bred, and entire species of plants came closer to being lost from the planet. There is a major conflict between animal rights extremists and those wishing to preserve biodiversity.

On the mainland, the west-facing slopes of the majestic Sierra Nevada south of Lake Tahoe are home to the largest living organism in the world – the Giant Sequoia, which can weigh up to 2,000 tons and live for thousands of years. Large numbers were cut, but national parks created in the 1890s saved many virgin stands from plunder. Until recently, it seemed that another great tree, the Coastal Redwood, would not be so fortunate. In the hills and valleys that absorb the coastal fogs, this redwood can reach 110 meters (360 feet) high and takes about 500 years to mature. Its lumber is straight-grained, free of knots, resistant to termites and easily worked – and so, of course, the trees were chopped down. After a messy battle, some of the last great stands have been saved in the new Redwoods National Park.

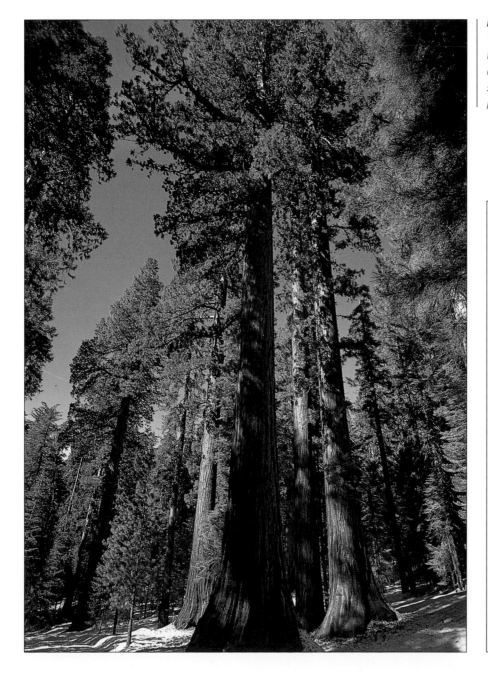

Left *Giant Sequoias* (Sequoiadendron giganteum) *in Yosemite National Park, California. Large numbers of these trees were felled in the late nineteenth and early twentieth centuries and the majority of the survivors occur within national parks and other protected areas.*

DISTRIBUTION
COASTAL REDWOOD

■ *Current range*

The Coastal Redwood (Sequoia sempervirens) grows from Santa Cruz to southwest Oregon. The Redwoods National Park in northwestern California preserves some of the last stands.

Wildlife

In this overview of endangered and threatened Nearctic animals, the region is divided into twelve areas. Some species range (or used to range) over several areas and these are described in just one major part of their range.

EASTERN CANADA AND THE NORTHEAST USA

When Europeans began whaling off these shores in the late 1400s, numerous North Atlantic Right Whales lived near the coast. These slow surface swimmers were so-named because they floated rather than sank when harpooned and so were the "right" whales to catch. While whales are protected off North America today, only about 350 of these carry on the ancient ritual of summering off New England and the Maritimes and swimming to Florida for the winter. Great attention is now focused on keeping ship captains apprised of Right Whale

Right Throughout the early exploration and colonization of North America by Europeans, the Canadian (or American) Beaver (Castor canadensis) was one of the most important exports and was systematically exterminated over much of the continent. Under conservation and management programs it has now recolonized or been reintroduced to much of its former range. However, in some suburban areas its activities and numbers are causing economic losses.

whereabouts day by day. It is a slow breeder with dangerously low numbers. Humpback Whale are viewed by thousands of people on the popular whale-watching day cruises off New England. Once numbering in the hundreds of thousands worldwide, it became the prime target for whalers in the early 1900s and its numbers dropped to 4,000.

On land, the American (or Canadian) Beaver lured the early explorers into every stream in every quarter throughout North America. Beaver pelts had a market that never dropped and the animals were hunted and trapped ruthlessly, causing them to vanish from much of their range. In recent years they have been reintroduced in many areas for their value in creating wetlands and increasing the diversity of plant life within the forests. Unfortunately, the anti-trapping lobby has denied game managers the ability to remove individuals that in some areas are flooding homes and roads, causing huge losses, and thus causing a backlash against wildlife conservation.

Fiercer mammals were persecuted through fear or because they were viewed as competitors. Wolves are long extinct in the US part of this area, while the Newfoundland White Wolf continued to hunt caribou (reindeer) until the last of these wolves was shot in 1911. The eastern race of the Cougar (or Puma or Mountain Lion) was also killed on sight, being the subject of bounties. The last American bounty was paid in 1890 in the Adirondacks of New York. Several dozen survived in northern New Brunswick, however, and today these animals appear to be re-occupying their range, feeding on healthy numbers of White-tailed Deer.

Birds as well as mammals were decimated by the settlers. A race of the Prairie "Grouse" called the Heath Hen was abundant on salt marshes and open heathland from New England to the Carolinas. It was a major source of food for European colonists, and by 1791 had become rare. Then its heaths were turned into farms, cats and rats raided its nests, and it succumbed to diseases spread from chickens. By 1830 it was extinct on the mainland, and by 1896 there

Below left The Piping Plover (Charadrius melodus) *is a small shorebird that breeds on sandy beaches, where it and its eggs are extremely well camouflaged. Its populations have suffered from human disturbance and off-road vehicles.*

Below After dramatic declines in the 1950s and 1960s due to pesticide poisonings, the Peregrine Falcon (Falco peregrinus) *has made a remarkable comeback and can even be seen in some city centers where it preys on feral pigeons.*

were only 100 left on its last stronghold of Martha's Vineyard Island, Massachusetts. A reserve was established there, and its numbers rebounded to 2,000. Then in 1916, fire swept the island, burning the bird's cover, an influx of hawks arrived, and a turkey disease swept through the population. In 1927, 13 survived; and on 11 March, 1932, the last one died. This shows the vulnerability of a healthy population reduced to just one locality.

A newcomer to the endangered species list, the Piping Plover, nearly suffered a similar fate. Like so many shorebirds, it was a target of market gunners in the late 1800s, but recovered after 1900 when the hunting of shorebirds was banned. It nests only on beaches, both inland in the Great Lakes and Plains, and on Atlantic beaches from Virginia to Newfoundland. Ever-increasing numbers of beach users and off-road vehicles caused serious disturbance, and many eggs and young were crushed under oversized wheels. By 1987 there were only 17 pairs in the Great Lakes and 475 pairs on its US Atlantic coast range. Eventually the bird was listed, and government agencies had to close many prime beaches during the early summer. This resulted in great cries of protest from beach users, but marked improvements in the numbers of plovers fledged.

The Peregrine Falcon had to contend with rather different threats. It is the world's fastest bird, reaching nearly 240 kilometers an hour (150 miles per hour) as it dives on prey, usually a flying bird. A local race of this falcon bred on many cliffs in the forested mountains of the northeast and west to Alaska south of the tundra. At one time it suffered from capture by falconers, but more recently it was severely affected by the widespread use of DDT on crops. This insecticide, accumulated in the falcon's prey, caused the falcon's eggshells to become so thin they broke easily. The resultant extinction of the bird in the US and its great decline in Canada were instrumental in getting DDT banned. Today the public watches with great interest the reintroduction of captive-bred Peregrine Falcons into many cities and reserves.

Lost in all the commotion over the rare bigger creatures is the story of many a small invertebrate. Giant Carrion Beetles are fascinating insects that look after their young as carefully as many "higher" animals. They locate a small dead rodent or bird, bury it, lay their eggs on the carcass, and then cover it up. The parents communicate with the larvae by buzzing sounds and tend them until they pupate. The Giant Carrion Beetle lived in virgin forests from Nova Scotia to Louisiana and was once found in 33 states and provinces. Today it is known only in Rhode Island – one of the largest reductions in an insect's range ever recorded.

THE SOUTHEAST USA AND BERMUDA

Overfishing, with long lines, has killed off about 70 per cent of breeding age Swordfish since the 1960s. A coalition of top US chefs and several cruise lines has stopped buying or serving Swordfish in 1998 due to its overharvest.

Sharks are also grossly overharvested for both meat and just for their fins. While people have long had a fear of sharks, fisheries' biologists now fear that sharks are crashing in numbers, with unknown consequences for the ocean's ecology.

Bermuda, a British colony off the Carolinas, has many endangered animals and plants, but none is more famous than the Cahow or Bermuda Petrel. Vast numbers of these shearwaters used to nest there free of humans and their animals. Shakespeare described the birds in *The Tempest* as millions of shrieking, winged shapes swirling round the masts of a Spanish galleon riding out a storm in the lee of one of these islands in 1603. The Spanish sailors left pigs as a source of meat for the next ship and by the time English settlers arrived in 1612, there were few Cahows left on the main island. Cats, dogs, and accidentally introduced rats killed the rest. In 1616, the Cahows received protection from the first game law in the New World but they never recovered. A few must have returned secretly to uninhabited rocks over the centuries, because they were rediscovered there in 1951. This led to a rescue attempt by David Wingate, which included building baffles around each burrow. Despite losses due to DDT in the 1960s and disturbance from the nearby NASA station and airport, 36 pairs had fledged 22 young by 1982, and numbers have gradually increased since.

One of the characteristic sights along the shores of the Gulf of Mexico and the Atlantic coast is the huge, aerial-diving, Eastern race of Brown Pelican. It nested by the thousands in coastal Texas and Louisiana, but by 1968 it had vanished from both states. As with the Peregrine Falcon, the main culprit was DDT. After the banning of this pesticide, 50 birds taken from healthy Florida colonies were placed on Grand Terre Island, Louisiana, and did well. Then in 1975, 300 died from Endrin, a pesticide used on boll weevils and sugar-cane borers, which had washed down the rivers from hundreds of miles away. Fortunately the birds recovered

Above *The Bald Eagle* (Haliaeetus leucocephalus), *despite being the national bird and depicted on the great seal of the USA, was once widely persecuted. Populations also crashed during the 1950s and 1960s due to pesticide poisoning. However, their recovery is another success story and they are now quite widespread, locally abundant, and no longer endangered.*

from this set-back, and by 1987 there were 6,000 pelicans in Louisiana, and 300 pairs in Texas raised 500 young.

Another success story is provided by the American Alligator, once found from New Jersey south to Texas. Trade in its skin became so lucrative that it declined in most areas and had to be protected in the 1960s. This allowed its numbers to increase so much that it is no longer considered endangered, although commerce in its skin is still strictly regulated.

In the cypress swamps of the southeast, the Ivory-billed Woodpecker once lived. Many were killed for sport, food, and to supply private collections of birds, but it was the systematic logging of virtually all the old-growth timber that doomed it. Its last major stronghold, the Singer tract in Louisiana, was logged and turned into soybean fields in 1934. Despite a few sightings into the 1950s, the American race is now extinct. The Cuban race survived in eastern Cuba until the early 1990s, and may now be gone. Now another southeastern woodpecker is in trouble. The Red-cockaded Woodpecker lives in fire-climax pines, and requires trees at least 65 years old for nesting. Modern forestry practices on 90 per cent of its range include cutting trees of age 30–45 years, and the woodpecker's population has become very scattered and is declining rapidly. When some land-developers heard that these endangered woodpeckers were inhabiting an area due for development, they instructed employees to chop down all nesting trees and shoot the woodpeckers so that they would not have to abide by endangered species laws, since none lived on their property (any more)! But word got out, and the developers were prosecuted and fined hundreds of thousands of dollars.

The most endangered of the southeastern mammals is the Red Wolf. Weighing up to 34 kilograms (75 pounds), it is smaller than the Gray Wolf, with a narrower face, longer ears and

DISTRIBUTION
AMERICAN ALLIGATOR

Current range

The American Alligator (*Alligator mississippiensis*) was exterminated over a large part of its range. With protection, populations are increasing and it is spreading to the south of Texas and is even becoming too common and bold in a few Florida regions.

longer legs. It occurred from Pennsylvania to Texas in the southern swamps and woods until people started killing it off. By the early 1970s, pure-blooded individuals existed only at a few spots from southwest Louisiana west to southeast Texas. With this species virtually exterminated, Coyotes moved east and interbred with the scattered remaining Red Wolves. In an extensive program to rescue the species, the few surviving pure Red Wolves were captured and bred. By 1977 the species was extinct in the wild, but radio-collared individuals have since been released at Coyote-free sites in North and South Carolina, Florida and Mississippi. A pair released at Horn Island, Mississippi, produced a litter of seven, and the Red Wolf became one of the first mammal species, extinct in the wild, to raise young in the wild again. Despite the fact that these animals hunt alone and seldom prey on large mammals, there is local opposition at release sites.

Among the endangered reptiles of the southeast is the Gopher Tortoise. Formerly very common, it inhabits sunny sand ridges with pine and oak, and digs deep burrows of great value to many other animals. Commercial forestry practices have excluded fire from its homes, and the herbs it feeds on cannot grow in the shade of the heavy brush. In addition, people have killed many for food, it is frequently run over on highways and farms, and housing and agriculture have taken over much of its habitat.

In the rivers of the southeast, 14 of the 18 freshwater mussels are endangered due to coal mining in the basins of the Cumberland and Tennessee rivers. Silt containing coal particles has washed into many streams, and chemical pollutants have added to the damage. Fish have suffered as well, including the darters. While the Snail Darter became famous for stopping a dam in the 1970s, and later was found in several other Tennessee streams, its cousins the

Below *A Florida Keys White-tailed Deer* (Odocoileus virginianus clavium) *being followed by a Cattle Egret. The Key Deer is exceptionally small and its population is considered to be endangered.*

Sharphead and the Trispot Darters have been lost due to reservoirs, and the Niangua Darter is in trouble.

FLORIDA

This state has truly tropical habitats and a number of unique animals of concern. Most of the thousand or so remaining West Indian (Caribbean) Manatees live there, swimming slowly at the surface, clearing vegetation from the waterways. They once occurred from the Carolinas to Texas, but hunting, and pollution, dredging and filling-in of waterways have greatly restricted their range. The propellers of the rapidly increasing numbers of motorboats have caused many deaths and injuries among the survivors. Boat speeds are now regulated in many manatee areas in Florida, and the whole state has been declared a manatee refuge. Many of these animals congregate during cold spells at the warm-water outflows of powerplants – the same plants that are fuelling the loss of the manatee's habitat.

The Key Deer (a subspecies of the White-tailed Deer) used to occur over much of the Florida Keys but is now found on only a few. The size of a large dog with small antlers, it has a low birthrate, like most animals in the tropics (other than humans). By 1947, numbers had dropped to 30 and the deer were given a refuge. Although they have since increased to 600 and inhabit 18 islands, the Key Deer still face threats. In dry spells they have to swim back to Big Pine and No-Name Keys to find permanent fresh water. Development continues rapidly in their range, stray dogs and poachers still hunt them, and many are killed by traffic.

Key Largo is the only home of the Key Largo (Eastern) Woodrat and a race of the Cotton Mouse. It is also one of the last homes of the Schaus' Swallowtail Butterfly, which is at risk due to urbanization, aerial mosquito spraying and overcollecting. The state of Florida is trying to protect parts of Key Largo in the face of land developers.

Among the reptiles, only a few hundred American Crocodiles survive in the Florida Keys and the Everglades coastal fringe, having been shot for their valuable skin, for sport, and as nuisances around marinas. Sea Turtles have also suffered greatly, sought for their meat and shells, while their eggs are considered a delicacy. Now the turtles face new dangers. It is estimated that 11,000 drowned annually in shrimp nets off Florida and the southeastern states in the 1980s. Hatching turtles, instead of crossing the sand to the sea, are attracted to the lights of nearby highways and hotels, often fatally. The increase in offshore oil drilling and tanker traffic has led to more turtles eating tarballs – and they eat plastic bags because these resemble the jellyfish they feed on. Efforts are now under way to force shrimpers to use

Famous extinctions

■ The flightless Great Auk, which stood 80 centimeters (30 inches) tall. Clubbed for food and feathers, it was extinct in the mid-1800s.

■ The Sea Mink hunted for its fur, which was even more luxuriant and valuable than that of the American Mink. The last was killed near Jonesport, Maine, in 1880.

■ The Eastern Wapiti (Elk), doomed by the demand for its canines from every member of the fraternal Order of the Elks. It was extinct by 1877.

■ The Labrador Duck, the first purely North American bird to become extinct in historical times. The last was shot in 1878 by a young boy and served by his family for dinner.

Below left The Florida Panther (Felis concolor coryi) is a small race of the Mountain Lion. It is critically endangered, and, due to the many killed by vehicles, it may not recover.

Below The Green Turtle (Felis concolor coryi) has fewer than 1,000 breeding females in Florida today, although it formerly nested in much larger numbers.

Above *American Bison* (Bison bison) *in Yellowstone National Park, Wyoming. Once occurring in herds numbering millions, by the end of the nineteenth century they were virtually extinct (see p.70). Thanks to farsighted conservation measures introduced by a few enthusiasts, a small herd was protected in Yellowstone and this has been used to found herds elsewhere.*

Sea Lamprey

Lake Sturgeon (Acipenser fulvescens)

turtle-excluding devices in their nets, and massive publicity campaigns have resulted in urban lights being turned down on hatching nights.

Much of the water which used to flow to the famous Everglades area of south Florida has been diverted, and this has shrunk the marshes where Apple Snails live. The Florida Everglade (Snail) Kite feeds chiefly on these snails, and its numbers now average about 500. Special nest baskets for the kite have been introduced into prime breeding areas with good results. Water drainage and diversion have also affected the Florida population of the Wood Stork. So few young could fledge that the population declined from 20,000 to 6,000 pairs, and the bird was declared endangered in 1984. Its breeding range is shifting northwards and it is making a slow comeback.

By this time, the Dusky race of the Seaside Sparrow was virtually extinct. Prior to 1956, this heavily black-striped saltmarsh sparrow lived by the thousands around Merritt Island. Much of the bunchgrass-dominated saltmarsh that the sparrow lived in was altered to control mosquitoes and enhance the area for waterfowl. Then drainage of land for housing, pastures and highways wiped out the last of its habitat in the shadow of America's space center. In 1979, the five survivors were captured and all turned out to be males. These were bred in captivity with females of other races, but the last Dusky died on 16 June, 1987 in a modest cage beside the glitz and glitter of Disney World.

THE GREAT LAKES AND THE MIDWEST

Overfishing, massive pollution, and the completion of the St. Lawrence Seaway doomed the Great Lakes fishery. The canals and locks of the seaway allowed some ocean fish to get above Niagara Falls, in particular Sea Lampreys. These invaded the lakes and attached themselves to many fish that had no strategies to thwart them. Three ciscos were major components of the Great Lakes fisheries until the invasion of Sea Lampreys, and fish competing for food, such as the Alewife and Small Bloater. The Deepwater Cisco was last taken in 1951, the Blackfin Cisco was last seen in 1955, while the Longjaw Cisco was declared extinct in 1983.

The Lake Sturgeon is the largest fish in the Great Lakes, exceeding 2.1 meters (7 feet) and 130 kilograms (300 pounds). As far back as 1885, millions of kilograms of this fish were sold commercially. Today it is greatly reduced in numbers and range, its last stronghold being Lake Winnebego, Wisconsin. Before its swift decline in the 1950s, the Blue Pike produced catches of 9 million kilograms (20 million pounds) a year from Lake Erie and a fraction of this a year from Lake Ontario. Now it is virtually absent from both lakes. In an attempt to save the species, a pair was captured and 9,000 fry were placed in isolated clean lakes.

Overexploitation and alteration to habitat have also devastated species on land. In the great forests of the Midwest (and eastwards) there once lived the commonest bird in the world, the Passenger Pigeon. This large blue pigeon with a long pointed tail easily numbered

Left Gray Wolves (Canis lupus) *feeding. Because they will prey on people's domestic stock, wolves have been extirpated from all but the most remote and inaccessible parts of the USA (see p.70). Proposals to reintroduce them into the Yellowstone region met with strong opposition.*

five billion. Vast flocks roamed the forests, nesting together in areas with heavy crops of nuts. Extensive lumbering destroyed their habitat in many areas, and they were shot by local residents for food, but it was the coming of the railroads and the telegraph that wiped them out. Railroads pushed into most corners of the pigeon's range in the mid-1800s, and through these and the telegraph lines joining towns, news of mass nesting sites was sent out far and wide. Professional market gunners came every year along with amateur sportsmen to capture the prized fat nestlings, and to trap and shoot the adults. By the mid-1880s, only a few scattered lonely groups remained. The Passenger Pigeon has not been seen in the wild since 1906, and the last captive bird died at the Cincinnati zoo in 1914.

Today, the Midwest is the only breeding area of the endangered Kirtland's Warbler, the entire world population of which would fit in a suitcase. A gray and yellow warbler with black streaks, it breeds only in young jack-pine areas in central Michigan, ignoring other similar territory around the Great Lakes. Never common, its numbers dropped from 500 pairs in 1951 to 167 in 1974 and this provoked major conservation efforts. Attempts were made to improve the quality and size of its habitat. The Brown-headed Cowbird, which has increased enormously in recent decades and parasitizes the warbler's nests, was trapped and removed from breeding areas. Birders can only see the warblers on strictly regulated tours, and are not allowed to take tape-recordings or other devices to lure them closer. Despite all these steps, there were only 212 pairs in 1989, and it was thought that the bird might have been experiencing problems in its wintering grounds in the Bahamas. However, by 1997, they had rebounded to over 700 pairs!

Many larger mammals, such as the Bison, Wapiti (Elk) and Cougar have lost their Midwest populations. The Gray Wolf continues to hang on at Michigan's Isle Royale National Park in Lake Superior, and there are a number of packs in the north woods of Minnesota. A smaller mammal, the Indiana Bat, illustrates the damage that can be caused by even well-intentioned humans. The bat's population has dropped from 900,000 to 450,000 in recent years. The bats hibernate chiefly in seven cold caves in Indiana, Kentucky, and Missouri, and human disturbance in just one of them caused 60,000 to die. The entrance to another cave was blocked to keep people out. However, this also prevented cold air from entering, and 80,000 bats died as the temperature mounted.

THE GREAT PLAINS

Before humans arrived this area was home to an aggregation of large mammals that would rival today's Serengeti plains in Tanzania. Most were killed off by the early hunters and gatherers that streamed south from the Bering Strait landbridge. But the Plains race of American Bison still numbered around 75 million when European settlers arrived. Then in about 1830, the US government urged the extermination of this animal as a way to decimate the native Americans of the plains, who stood between the colonizers and the Pacific Ocean. The coming of the railroads and waves of settlers led to a great slaughter, and only about 800 animals remained by the late 1880s. A rescue attempt saved them from extinction, and today about 30,000 live on private ranches and in various parks and reserves.

The Great Plains race of Wolf, often called the Buffalo Runner, lived with the vast herds of plains animals. As the big game vanished, the incoming ranchers of sheep and cattle shot and poisoned the wolves, the last one perishing in 1926. Coyotes were also persecuted but remain widespread. Unfortunately, the poisoned bait put down for them was often taken by Swift Foxes, and the northern race of this species may be extinct in the Canadian prairies. Restrictions on poisons in the 1970s have revived populations, at least in the southern part of their range, but it remains scarce.

A much smaller animal brought to the brink by poisons is Wiest's Sphinx Moth. This small, diurnal moth was badly affected by sprays used to kill grasshoppers. In its last home in Weld County in the plains of eastern Colorado 300 were counted in 1979, and only 25 in 1981 after a spraying program in 1980. County officials, scientists and landowners have agreed to try using parasitic protozoans to kill grasshoppers instead of insecticide sprays.

TEXAS

This enormous state harbors more species of bird than any other in the United States. The endangered Whooping Crane winters only in the middle of the Texan Gulf coast, and the Red-cockaded Woodpecker inhabits the eastern pinewoods. The colorful Golden-cheeked Warbler breeds only on the Edward's Plateau, and the Black-capped Vireo breeds there and northwards into central Oklahoma. Both the warbler and vireo are declining fast due to habitat destruction in Texas and on their wintering grounds in Mexico.

In the 1800s, the coastal prairies of Texas and Louisiana resounded with the booming calls of millions of Attwater's Prairie Chickens (a subspecies of the Greater Prairie Chicken).

DISTRIBUTION
BISON

■ *Extent in 1650*

American Bison (Bison bison). *The vast expanse of the North American plains was once the migration route for huge herds of buffalo. Although buffalo numbers have slowly rebuilt, the plains are now plowed, built on and crisscrossed with roads, making it unlikely that buffalo will ever again roam in a truly wild state.*

Since then, much of their prairie home has been converted into fields of crops, rice paddies, and pasture for cattle, and the birds have been heavily hunted. Their decline was evident in 1903, when the state of Texas established a bag limit of 25 birds a day. Today, fewer than 100 remain, scattered over a few refuges between Houston and Corpus Christi, and its days appear numbered.

Two cats which also occur in Latin America are endangered in south Texas, the only US part of their ranges. The Texas race of Ocelot is a beautiful spotted nocturnal cat that was once found as far north as Arkansas. It has suffered from habitat clearance, and has been trapped for its pelt, and for its meat and blood which were said to aid stamina. The small dark weasel-like Jaguarundi formerly inhabited the bottomland forests of the lower Rio Grande valley and 99 per cent of these forests have been destroyed. A recent survey of 1,500 trappers

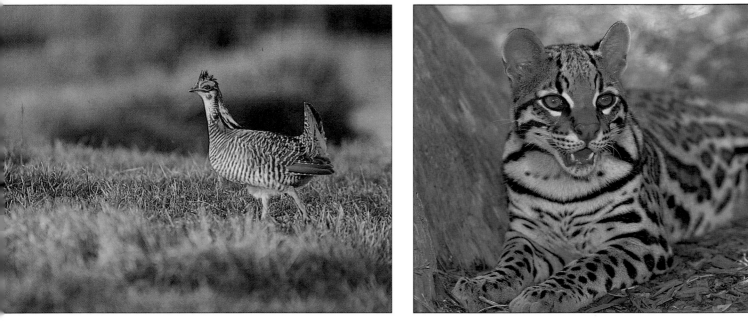

revealed that none had caught or seen a Jaguarundi recently – and with so many trappers around, a comeback seems unlikely!

Texas is also home to some endemic animals with very restricted distributions. The Houston Toad, for example, is found in just a few areas of Loblolly Pine in east Texas. Alterations to its habitat have brought it into contact with other toads, and it is being genetically swamped by them. The Texas Blind Salamander occurs in caves and underground streams in Hayes County. In one cave, it ate invertebrates which were nourished by guano from roosting bats. When a door was put on the cave, the trapped bats starved and the rest went elsewhere. Although the door was later removed the bats have not returned, and with no new bat guano, the salamanders have dropped in numbers.

Some species of small fish live only in certain springs in west Texas. All these fish have suffered due to water being pumped away for use in agriculture, which lowered water tables, and from the introduction of exotic competitors. The Comanche Springs Pupfish and the Pecos Gambusia survive only at Phantom Lake spring near Toyahvale, while the Leon Springs Pupfish was last seen in 1851. The struggle of another fish, the Big Bend Gambusia, illustrates how active intervention can pay off. This tiny fish with orange and yellow pigments was discovered in 1928 at Boquillas springs. When these dried up, the fish was feared extinct. Then in 1954 more were found at another spring, but they were threatened by competition from the closely related *Gambusia affinis.* So the 19 surviving Big Bend Gambusias were removed, their

Above left *Attwater's Prairie Chicken* (Tympanuchus cupido attwateri) *is another animal that once numbered in millions. By 1989 it had been reduced to about 500, and in 1998 it is below 100. There seems little hope for the species unless sufficient unmodified prairie can be protected in Texas.*

Above *The range of the Ocelot (*Panthera pardalis*) once extended as far as Arkansas, but is now restricted to Texas. It is no longer hunted, but its habitat is subject to clearance.*

Right *The Mexican Axolotl (Ambystoma mexicanum) is a popular aquarium pet, often bred from an albino strain. It can remain in its larval form with gills throughout its life. This salamander used to be common in highland lakes of Mexico, but has been hunted for food and eaten by introduced trout.*

DISTRIBUTION
MONARCH BUTTERFLY

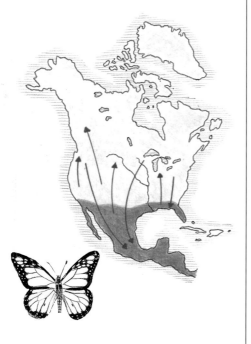

■ *Winter hibernation ground.*

The Monarch (Danaus plexippus) is the only butterfly that makes birdlike migrations on a regular basis. Although they migrate both north and south, no single individual makes the entire round-trip. In spring the butterflies head north and breed along the way. Their offspring return south in the autumn.

relatives were killed off and the Big Bends were returned to the springs. They did well until *G. affinis* somehow re-infested Boquillas springs. The four surviving Big Bends were then placed in a specially created new pool where they thrived free from competition. They have since been placed in Croton springs in Big Bend National Park and elsewhere, and their numbers have reached 1,000.

MEXICO

The Nearctic region includes the non-tropical areas of northern and plateau Mexico. There, as in other parts of Mexico, a handful of scientists and government agencies are involved in conservation, but they are not backed up by the powerful private organizations and millions of amateur naturalists that are active in the north. This is partly due to a paucity of field guides. However, the government can and does call on the help of the military!

Since 1967, military units have been protecting the nesting females and eggs of the Kemp's Ridley Sea-turtle at Rancho Nuevo on the Gulf of Mexico in Tamaulipas. In the 1940s, tens of thousands of the turtles came ashore each year on a single day, attracting locals who slaughtered them for meat and leather, and gathered all the eggs. By 1963, only a few thousand were coming ashore, and in the 1970s, sometimes only a few hundred. It is hoped that the protection, and the hatchery programs that have been initiated, will show good results when the youngsters are old enough to return to their ancestral beaches. Unfortunately in the meantime many are being killed in shrimp nets, because the turtles feed on crabs near the sea bottom where shrimp congregate.

Inland, in the mountains of Nuevo León and Coahuila states, pressure from logging and other human activities is increasing. The number of cliff-nesting Maroon-fronted Parrots is now less than 2,000 because of the removal of the trees on which they feed. Below these mountains stretches a vast desert containing scattered springs. Many of these harbor fish, turtles and invertebrates that are endangered due to the use of these springs by industry, and for recreation and washing clothes. The Parras Pupfish and the Sharptooth Minnow are already extinct, while the Mexican Blindcat and the Checkered Killifish are each restricted to single springs. The Aquatic Box-turtle lives only in the Cuatrociénagas basin in Coahuila. In addition to overuse of its marshes, this turtle is being over-collected by amateur naturalists.

The future of the largest surviving ground-living reptile in North America, the Bolson Tortoise, also looked bleak. It occurs on the gentle slopes above the seasonal flood plains in the Bolson de Mapini in the Chihuahuan desert. The Tobosa Grass on which it feeds was severely overgrazed by cattle, and the tortoise was overcollected for food and the pet trade. Now a major campaign has been instituted and the tortoise is protected by law and given refuge by concerned ranchers and in the new Mapimi biosphere reserve.

Further south, the mountain forests of Michoacan and Mexico states are the winter home of most of the Monarch Butterflies of North America. Some 15 million come here from all over eastern and central North America, beating their orange and black wings to accomplish the most notable migration of any insect. The threats to these butterflies include logging, cattle which eat them, and insensitive tourists who flush them to enjoy the spectacle they create – and force them to use up their precious fat reserves. A private Mexican organization has now been formed to save the Monarchs and it pays local people to guard them.

Three aquatic salamanders are in trouble in the remnants of the highland lakes of the area. The famous Mexican Axolotl, which can retain its larval form throughout its life, is commonly bred in laboratories around the world. In its home, though, in Lake Xochimilco east of Mexico City, it is rare and threatened by introduced predatory fish and pollution. The Lake Lerma Salamander is prized as food, and its lake has been largely drained. Michoacan's Lake Patzcuaro Salamander is another local delicacy, and is suffering from the introduction of bass, silting, pollution, and the pumping of water for agriculture.

Below *American Monarch Butterflies* (Danaus plexippus) *migrate to Mexico and coastal California where they hibernate in huge clusters which may number several million. The butterflies accumulate poisons from their food plants and these ward off most birds that prey on insects.*

The Sierra Madre Occidental along the western side of the Mexican mainland is a lightly populated wonderland of deep canyons, cliffs and vast pine-oak forests. Nevertheless, loggers, trappers, and hunters penetrated the remotest areas, wiping out the silver-colored race of the Grizzly, the Mexican Grizzly. The Mexican Gray Wolf was also persecuted, but a few survive in remote areas and may be saved by a captive breeding program near Tucson.

The peninsula of Baja California, separated from the mainland by the Gulf of California, is home to the Baja California race of Pronghorn. It has been driven by local and North American hunters out of most of its former range, and less than 100 now roam the Vizcaino desert near Scammon's Lagoon. These few survivors have to compete for forage with domestic animals, and fences restrict their movements.

Surrounded by dry deserts and lonely mountains, the Gulf of California's waters are rich in marine life. A large fish of the Gulf, the Totoaba, has been so overexploited that it was declared endangered in 1975. Gill nets set for this fish also killed many of the endemic Gulf of California Porpoise. Only discovered in 1958, this is the smallest and rarest cetacean in the world. Unfortunately, illegal gill-netting continues and reports of these porpoises are decreasing.

In contrast, healthy Gray Whale populations now calve in the quiet warm lagoons around this gulf and on the west side of Baja. Once numbering up to 50,000, they had been reduced by hunting to only 100 by 1937, when they were protected. Mexico set up the world's first whale sanctuary at Scammon's Lagoon, and its numbers have increased to about 11,000.

CALIFORNIA

Flying into Los Angeles airport on the Pacific Ocean, you might notice a small area of sand dunes and brush among the vast urban sprawl. This is the El Segundo sand dunes, the last remnants of many miles of dunes, and the last home of the El Segundo Blue Butterfly and many other specialized insects. Elsewhere along southern California's famous beaches, human activities have affected wildlife. The formerly widespread California race of Least Tern, for example, was forced to abandon most of its nesting colonies, and its numbers sank to about 600 pairs. Since being listed as endangered, its nesting sites have been fenced and new

Above The Gulf Porpoise (Phocoena sinus) *is the smallest of its kind and may be the smallest of all cetaceans. It is very like the Common Porpoise (bottom) in shape but, on average, is about 30 centimeters (12 inches) shorter and 5 kilograms (10 pounds) lighter.*

Right A Gray Whale (Eschrichtius robustus) *surfacing to breathe off the coast of British Columbia, Canada. Under strict protection its numbers are slowly increasing, and a major industry has developed taking tourists whale watching.*

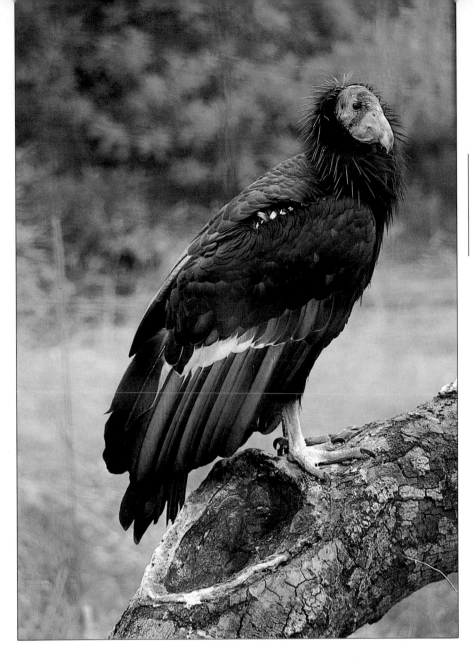

Left *The California Condor* (Gymnogyps californianus) *became extinct in the wild in 1987 when the last one was captured to join 26 others in a captive breeding program. Andean Condors* (Vultur gryphus) *have been released into the wild in the USA as part of long-term research before reintroducing California Condors.*

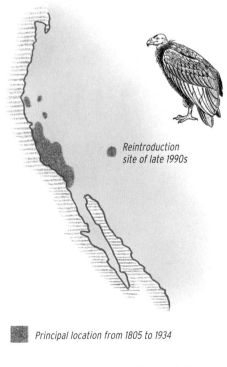

DISTRIBUTION
CALIFORNIA CONDOR

Reintroduction site of late 1990s

■ *Principal location from 1805 to 1934*

California Condor (Gymnogyps californianus). *By the time Europeans reached California and Oregon, the California Condor was already a rare bird. Collecting for museums, as well as poisoning, played a part in their demise.*

ones created, with papier mâché decoys placed to attract the terns. Spirits rose when an early arriving male offered a fish to one of these decoys!

The coastal salt marshes of southern California have been largely filled in for marinas and housing. As a result, a small, dark race of Clapper Rail, the Light-footed Clapper Rail, only survives in disjunct populations. Some marshes have only males, some only females, and 65 per cent of apparently suitable marshes have no rails at all. In 1986, only 143 pairs bred in six marshes, and half the birds were restricted to Upper Newport Bay in heavily populated Orange County. Their situation remains perilous.

Mountains soar above the coastal cities of California. Unfortunately the California Condor no longer soars above the mountains. These giant birds once ranged east to the Great Plains and Florida, and in historical times they flew from British Columbia down to Baja California. When the gold rush began, their last strongholds in California were overrun with people who shot them and most of the larger mammals on which they relied. In later decades they ingested the poisons left for Coyotes by ranchers, and the lead left in deer by hunters. By the mid-1970s, only about 50 remained in the wild and many of these were unhealthy and not fledging young. So it was decided to capture the remaining birds, and all are now in the

San Diego and Los Angeles zoos. In 1989, four healthy young hatched, and the population stood at 32. In the late 1990s captive-bred condors have been reintroduced to the wild on the north rim of the Grand Canyon in northern Arizona. Part of their historic range, this area has far fewer people and poison problems than California. Fingers are crossed in hopes that they will succeed and breed here.

The little gray and white Least race of Bell's Vireo is also under severe threat. Once common in streamside willows throughout much of California, this bird is down to about 355 pairs, most of them in San Diego County. Everyone wants to take water from the streams – farmers, municipalities, industry – and many of the waterways have been channeled, diverted, or gone dry. The vast increase in farmland, feed lots and cattle has greatly benefited the parasitic Brown-headed Cowbird, and many vireo nests are now full of cowbird eggs.

The cold waters of central California are well known for the richness and variety of their marine life. One of the most sought-after animals there was the Southern race of Sea Otter, valued for its pelt. This southern race of the Sea Otter ranged from Washington state to Baja California, before Russian and American sealers began harvesting them. By 1910, the southern race was thought extinct, but in 1914, a group of 14 was located near Monterey. To protect them, their existence was kept secret until 1938 when they numbered 100. Although the

Above The largest herds of the Tule race of Wapiti or Elk (Cervus canadensis nannodes) *occur in the Owens Valley of California. Other herds have been established south of San Francisco. Under protection, most of these are slowly increasing.*

Above right *The San Joaquin race of Kit Fox* (Vulpes macrotis mutica) *survives in only a few relict populations in central California. Intensive agriculture in the San Joaquin Valley has reduced the available habitat.*

population is now nearing 2,000, their habitat is sliced by oil tankers and they are being killed by people harvesting abalone, so a new colony has been started in the Channel Islands.

A greater recovery has taken place among Northern Elephant Seals. So many were slaughtered for oil on the beaches of California and Baja that by 1892 only 100 survived at their last stronghold on Guadalupe Island. Protected in Mexico, these 3-ton deep-sea divers staged a comeback. By the 1930s, they had recolonized some of the Channel Islands, and in 1979, they started a mainland colony at Ano Nuevo Point near Santa Cruz in California. Today they number 70,000, and are proving a major tourist attraction for Santa Cruz.

Less of an attraction is the Santa Cruz race of Long-toed Salamander which lives nearby in an area of ponds and woods. Unfortunately its rarity has caused it to be heavily collected by amateur biologists. To try to save the salamander, its breeding ponds have been made into reserves and additional ponds have been created for it.

To the north, San Bruno mountain divides San Francisco from its peninsula communities, and between the mountain's two ridges lies an industrial park. While it is protected to some degree, invasive exotic plants, recreational activities, and fire suppression are altering the natural vegetation. This is the last home of two grassland butterflies, the Mission Blue Butterfly and the Callipe Silverspot, while the endangered Bay Checkerspot, a black butterfly with red and yellow markings, is found here and at a few other sites down the peninsula. Another vividly colored creature, the yellow-, red-, and black-striped San Francisco race of Garter Snake, survives in just a few reservoir and pond edges from San Bruno mountain southward on the peninsula.

At least three-quarters of the saltmarshes around San Francisco and San Pablo bays have been filled in and dyked. As a result, the docile, cinnamon-colored Salt Marsh Harvest Mouse has been "on the list" since 1970. The vulnerable California race of Clapper Rail and two sub-species of the Song Sparrow (*Melospiza melodia pusilla* and *samuelis*) also rely on the remaining bits of marsh.

The great central valleys of California, once covered in vast forests, grasslands and marshes, are now under the plow. Half a million of the smallest race of Wapiti (Elk), the Tule Wapiti, used to roam these valleys and the coastal hills from Santa Barbara to the Russian River. They were slaughtered for meat until only one herd remained, in the tule swamps of Kern County. There they were, at last, protected and have since been released at new sites in the Owens valley, Cache Creek in the coast range, and elsewhere. Today they number over 2,000.

Rivers in the valley once hosted the abundant Thicktail Chub, last seen in 1957. Other fish barely hang on in undrained areas where pools collect in the spring. These pools have a hardpan of compacted clay underneath preventing winter rain water from seeping away. To add to the problems of conserving fish species, fishermen seem to care little about the purity of stock of fish grown and released from hatcheries. Two trout subspecies of the Sierra Nevada are endangered due to these sloppy practices. All the rivers of the Kern race of Rainbow Trout, with golden-yellow sides and orange on the ventral regions, have been invaded by hatchery hybrids and the last pure-bloods occur only in the Little Kern river. The Paiute race of Cut-throat Trout, which lacks spots, has probably been wiped out by the introduction of the wrong trout stock into its last home on Silver King creek.

THE AMERICAN SOUTHWEST

The dominant plant in southern Arizona is the tallest cactus in the world, the Saguaro Cactus, and one of its most important pollinators, Sanborn's Long-nosed Bat, has disappeared from most of its roosts. The 20,000 that once roosted in Colossal cave near Tucson are gone, and the other caves these bats rely on are subject to destruction, disturbance and vandalism. In addition, locals in Mexico kill all bats in an attempt to eradicate the Vampire Bats which do cause losses in cattle. The related Mexican Long-nosed Bat has dropped in numbers from over 10,000 in 1967 to about 1,000 in 1983 at its chief US roost in Big Bend National Park in Texas, and it is also crashing in Mexico. As these long-tongued bats decline, the reproductive success of the Saguaro, other cacti and the night-blooming agaves could suffer, sending these plants into a related downward spiral.

These deserts are home to many reptiles, including the sought-after Gila Monster and Desert Tortoise. A large poisonous lizard covered with black and orange beads, the Gila Monster is vulnerable through overcollecting for sale in Europe and elsewhere. The Desert

Above *The Gila Monster* (Heloderma suspectum) *is the only poisonous lizard found in the USA. Although its poison is rarely fatal to humans, it has been persecuted and is also collected for the pet trade.*

Tortoise is threatened by habitat degradation, capture for the pet trade, and off-road vehicles which cause its dens to collapse. State laws made it illegal to catch or kill the tortoise and it now receives national protection.

Mammals of the desert have also suffered. The Arizona Jaguar used to live from California east to Arkansas and southward into Mexico. The last Californian individual was killed near Palm Springs in 1860, and New Mexico's last one in 1905. But some still wander north from Mexico, including one sighted in Arizona in 1971. Another overhunted animal, the Sonoran race of Pronghorn, has in addition to compete with domestic animals for forage. Perhaps 1,000 now survive in the deserts of northwest Sonora and southwest Arizona.

A luxuriant grassland covered wide valleys at the edges of the Sonoran desert north-wards into Arizona. Massive herds of cattle were driven there to feed in the late 1800s, and a drought in 1892 forced them to devour every last blade of grass. The soil turned to cement, and deep-rooted mesquite bushes took over the grasslands. This greatly reduced the range of a very distinct race of the Bobwhite quail. Well isolated from other races to the east, the Masked Bobwhite has a black head and an entirely orange breast. By the mid-1900s only one good population of this quail could be found, in the Benjamin Hill-Carbo area. Some birds were taken to Arizona but the reintroduction attempt failed and the Masked Bobwhite's survival rests on keeping cattle out of large enough reserves in Sonora. Reintroductions continue at the Buenos Aires National Wildlife Refuge southwest of Tucson, Arizona.

Many people think of Arizona as an area of deserts and canyons, not realizing that the mountains in the center and southeast are verdant with forests and flowers nurtured by over 100 millimeters (40 inches) of rain in the summer and winter months. Naturalists flock there to see many animals from the Sierra Madre that occur virtually nowhere else in the US.

While birders enjoyed views of trogons, Painted Whitestarts (Redstarts), and a dozen kinds of hummingbird, the cone-eating Thick-billed Parrot was absent for many years. These

DISTRIBUTION
DESERTS IN THE USA

■ Great Basin Desert

□ Sonoran Desert

▨ Mohave Desert

▨ Chihuahuan Desert

Right *The Masked Bobwhite* (Colinus virginianus ridgwayi) *is a distinctive subspecies of the Northern Bobwhite. It is confined to the Mexican state of Sonora, where it occurs in thickly grassed desert among shrubs and cacti; it is being reintroduced to southern Arizona.*

huge green parrots, with red forehead and yellow stripes under the wing, were shot by early miners and loggers, and disappeared from the Chiricahua mountains in the 1930s. In the Sierra Madre Occidental of Mexico, their numbers are dropping, partly due to capture for the cage-bird trade. In the 1980s, 30 Thick-billed Parrots being illegally imported into the US were confiscated. Since they are threatened in Mexico, it was decided to attempt a reintroduction into their former range in the Chiricahuas. Some dispersed up to the Tonto National Forest in central Arizona, where they bred in the wild, and the parrots were being seen regularly in the Chiricahuas in southeast Arizona. But in the 1990s they vanished again.

The Chiricahuas are also home to the Arizona Ridge-nosed Rattlesnake. This small species is at risk due to an active trade in live specimens by private collectors.

The removal of areas of forest has silted up the rivers which supported two forms of trout, the Gila and Apache Trouts. These fish have also suffered from having exotic trout released in their waters. The last strongholds of the Gila Trout were in the Black Range of New Mexico, while the Apache Trout may still survive in streams of the White Mountains of Arizona.

THE ROCKY MOUNTAINS AND GREAT BASIN

This vast area of snow-capped peaks, wide valleys and sculptured rocks has not escaped the ravages of humans. The Wood Bison is now gone and the Plains Bison's numbers are a shadow of its former abundance. The Southern Rocky Mountain race of Gray Wolf was last seen in 1940, and the Northern Rocky Mountain race of Gray Wolf, once abundant from Oregon to the Dakotas, is down to about 35 individuals around Glacier National Park in Montana. Wolves have been reintroduced to Yellowstone National Park, despite some opposition from ranchers outside the park. Formerly found across many of the northern states, the Selkirk herd of the Woodland Caribou barely hangs on as loggers invade its last home in the old-growth coniferous forests of northern Idaho.

A brighter story can be told of the northern race of Pronghorn. Its numbers had dropped to about 20,000 in 1900 due to hunting and fencing of its range. Now fences are used which restrict the movements of sheep but not Pronghorns. This and good management have raised its numbers to more than 500,000. The Utah Prairiedog has also bounced back from 3,000 in 1979 to 10,000 today. While other species of prairiedog continue to be shot, gassed, and poisoned, the persecution of the Utah Prairiedog has been stopped. To overcome the additional problem of habitat loss caused by overgrazing and farming, colonies were started at new sites where artificial holes had been dug and some predators were removed.

Below left The Thick-billed Parrot (Rhynchopsitta pachyrhyncha) *only occurs in the Sierra Madre Occidental, Mexico, where it is endangered through trapping for the cage-bird trade, and destruction of the old growth pine forest. A population released recently in Arizona has failed to survive.*

Below The Ridge-nosed Rattlesnake (Crotalus willardi) *is confined to the extreme south of Arizona, New Mexico and adjacent Mexico. It lives in scattered populations in pine-oak woodlands at altitudes of over 1,700 meters (5,500 feet).*

Right *The Pronghorn "Antelope"* (Antilocapra americana) *is one of the fastest animals on land. The subspecies resident in Baja, California, Sonora, and Arizona have become very rare. The northern race is doing very well.*

Some of the animals that depend on the waters of the Colorado river basin are in trouble. The demands on this water made by farmers and water authorities in Mexico, Los Angeles, and Phoenix increase daily. Dams have been built for hydroelectricity, canals divert the water, and overgrazing, logging, and agricultural runoff cause pollution and siltation. The poor native fish have experienced blockage of their migration routes, massive changes in stream flow and temperatures, and the stocking of new lakes with exotic fish that compete for food and prey on them. The Colorado River Squawfish used to reach 35 kilograms (80 pounds) and was a major source of food for native Americans and early settlers throughout the basin down to Mexico. Today it survives in just a few reaches of the upper Green and Colorado rivers. The Humpback Chub, a minnow highly specialized for life in fast streams, is gone from all areas below the dams and reservoirs. A recovery agreement on the native fish of the basin signed in 1988 may revive these and other inhabitants.

The growth of Las Vegas in Nevada caused local water authorities to take over springs and seepages in the area. Along with the introduction of Bull Frogs, this action caused the first known extinction of an amphibian in historical times in North America – the Vegas Valley race of Leopard Frog, last seen in 1942. Water usage and competition from introduced fish also killed the last of the Pahrangat Spinedace in 1959.

A now-protected area to the west of Las Vegas, Ash Meadows, is the only home of many plants and fish which are endangered due to earlier habitat disturbance and introduced predatory fish. One of the endangered fish, the Devil's Hole Pupfish, may have the most restricted range of any vertebrate on Earth, being found at only one pool in Ash Meadows. The 125 adults there are protected by a high fence and a locked gate.

THE PACIFIC NORTHWEST

Vast virgin coniferous forest once blanketed the Cascades and the Pacific slope of the northwest. Today perhaps 75 per cent of it has been cut, and instead younger trees, farms, and scrubland cover the land. Over 200 species of wildlife live in the old forests, including Marbled Murrelets nesting on the mossy limbs of the great trees, Black-tailed Deer (a race of Mule Deer) and Roosevelt Wapiti (Elk) grazing below, and many species of salamander inhabiting the forest floor. But most of the native wildlife is doing poorly in the managed

Left Trumpeter Swans (Cygnus buccinator) on the National Elk Refuge, Wyoming. Heavily hunted, they were protected only at Red Rock Lakes, Montana in the "lower 48." Stock from there was transplanted to other lakes in the west in recent years.

plantations that sprang up in place of the irreplaceable old-growth forests.

The Cascade Wolf, a brown race of the Gray Wolf, is gone from this area and survives only in coastal British Columbia. Oregon Giant Earthworms grow up to 58 centimeters (23 inches) long in the deep soil of little-disturbed old-growth forests. Such forests in the Wilmette valley of Oregon have been cut down to such an extent that these giants are now found in only four scattered patches of forest. However, the animal that has become the central figure in the heated battle between loggers and environmentalists is the northern race of Spotted Owl. This endangered subspecies needs large areas of old-growth forest to survive, and is suffering from competition with other owls in the forest fragments that remain.

The first areas cleared for farms were the willow thickets and meadows by the Columbia river. This was the habitat of the Columbian race of the White-tailed Deer. They can no longer be hunted and a reserve protects some of them. Once down to a few hundred, with protection they have increased to over 1,000 and will soon be off the endangered list.

WESTERN CANADA AND ALASKA

This huge area has extensive boreal forests, great mountain ranges, most of North America's tundra, and cold ocean waters teeming with life. Extending from northeast Alberta into Northwest Territories lies Wood "Buffalo" National Park, named for its resident population of Wood Bison. This race differs from Plains Bison in being larger and having a longer neck, longer hair on the forehead, hairy horns, darker color, and a square hump. It was once found in meadows and forests of the Rocky mountains, but was killed off virtually everywhere. Now animals from this park have been used to start up new herds in a number of other Canadian parks.

The Wood "Buffalo" Park is the only nesting ground of the Whooping Crane. This huge white crane with bare red skin on the head once lived over much of the continent. A long decline due to overhunting, nest disturbance and habitat clearance brought the population down to only 15 birds in 1941, and their last breeding grounds were discovered in this park in 1954. The birds had to pass an army of hunters in the Great Plains on migration to their wintering grounds in Texas. A massive education campaign reduced this threat and the crane's numbers reached 43 in 1964. The Whooping Crane lays two eggs, but only the stronger

DISTRIBUTION
TRUMPETER SWAN

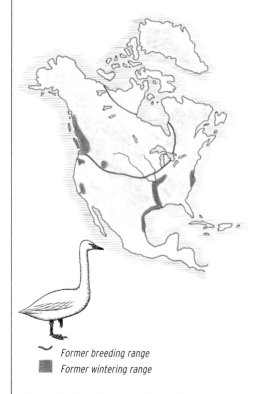

~ Former breeding range
▬ Former wintering range

Trumpeter Swans (Cygnus buccinator). These birds used to winter on both the west and east coasts, and bred as far east as the Great Lakes. By the turn of the century they were confined to the Rockies, but are now spreading once more.

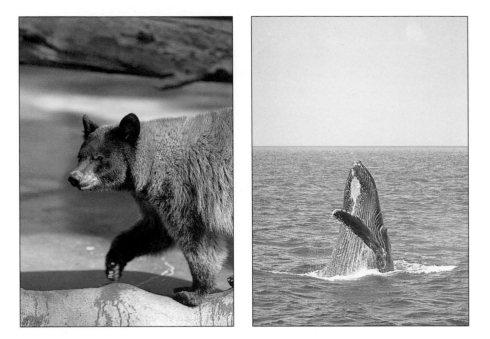

Right The Black Bear (Ursus americanus) from Yukata Bay, Alaska, also known as Blue or Glacier Bears. The population is small but apparently stable.

Far right A Humpback Whale (Megaptera novaengliae) breaching. They are among the most spectacular of whales, often leaping almost clear of the sea and slapping the surface with their huge bodies. Under protection their numbers have increased and they are now a major tourist attraction.

Bowhead Whale
(Balaena mysticetus)

Gray Whale
(Eschrichtius robustus)

Humpback Whale
(Megaptera novaengliae)

Blue Whale
(Balaenoptera musculus)

one survives. Starting in 1964, spare eggs from many nests were removed in the hope of building a captive flock. This succeeded, and there are now close to 200 wild birds and over 100 in captivity. In the 1970s, some Whooping Crane eggs were placed in the nests of foster-parent Sandhill Cranes in Idaho. The young followed their "parents" to their wintering grounds in New Mexico, but they have not done well and have not bred on their own. Efforts now focus on starting a non-migratory flock in Florida or in Georgia using resident Sandhill Cranes as foster parents.

The Copper river delta near Cordova, Alaska, is the main breeding ground of a more numerous but still threatened creature, the Dusky race of Canada Goose. This dark, medium-sized race numbered about 25,000 before an earthquake in 1964. The quake uplifted the delta and much of the marshland became a dry bluff. The goose's numbers increased at first as there was less flood damage to nests, but alder and willow thickets soon took root, providing bears and other nest predators with good cover. The geese winter in Oregon's Wilmette valley, and hunters there funded a program to remove bears from the goose's Alaskan breeding range. Despite this, the population has dropped to 12,000 and the Dusky race is in trouble.

An emergency decree in 1990 focused attention on the huge Steller's (or Northern) Sea Lion. In the late 1950s, there were 140,000 in southwest Alaska, but a census in 1989 found only 25,000. The decline is thought to be due to the reduction in its favorite fish prey caused by commercial fishing, and many thousands being killed in trawls or dying tangled in marine debris. This sea lion is now being studied closely, and people are being kept well away from all known breeding grounds.

Alaska is a major summering area for many whales including the California Gray, the Blue and the Humpback, viewed by tourists from dozens of cruise ships. Less often seen are the Bowhead Whales of the Arctic Ocean. These whales help the Arctic seals and smaller cetaceans by breaking a way through thick ice. They have been hunted by the Inuit for centuries, but suffered a steep decline when commercial whalers arrived in the late 1800s. By 1977, only 3,000 survived and populations are being monitored while the Inuit continue to hunt them.

The vast tundra is the breeding ground of many of the New World's shorebirds and waterfowl. Huge numbers of Eskimo Curlew used to breed there before flying south to winter in Argentina. Market gunners then turned their sights onto migrating shorebirds, and the Eskimo Curlew was thought to have been shot to extinction. Recently, though, it has been spotted occasionally on migration, and it may be nesting somewhere in the Northwest Territories. Another migratory bird, the Tundra race of Peregrine Falcon, is suffering from a very different threat. Although its far northern breeding grounds are relatively free of DDT, this chemical is still in use in its Latin American wintering grounds.

Some of the larger mammals of the tundra and further north remain at risk from hunters. With the arrival of the rifle, the Musk Ox was exterminated from much of its high Arctic range, and was extinct in Alaska by 1865. It has been reintroduced to protected islands in the Bering Sea, such as Nunivak Island where descendants of 31 pioneers now number about 750. Some of these have been placed elsewhere in Alaska. Only about 500 Barren-ground Grizzly Bears are thought to survive and, although they are protected, illegal kills may number 30 or more a year. The Polar Bear is not yet endangered but is being watched closely. It is absent or reduced in many areas, shot for the high price of its hide by hunters in their new snowmobiles or from small planes and boats.

However, in the long-term the wildlife of the far north and the Canadian islands is probably less threatened by hunters than by impending global warming and the effects of haze and soot from industrial centers far away.

DISTRIBUTION
ESKIMO CURLEW

- - - *Migration route*

Breeding

Wintering

The Eskimo Curlew (Numenius borealis). *Once one of the most abundant birds in North America, it now teeters on the brink of extinction. The map shows the migration routes between its Arctic breeding grounds and its wintering grounds in South America.*

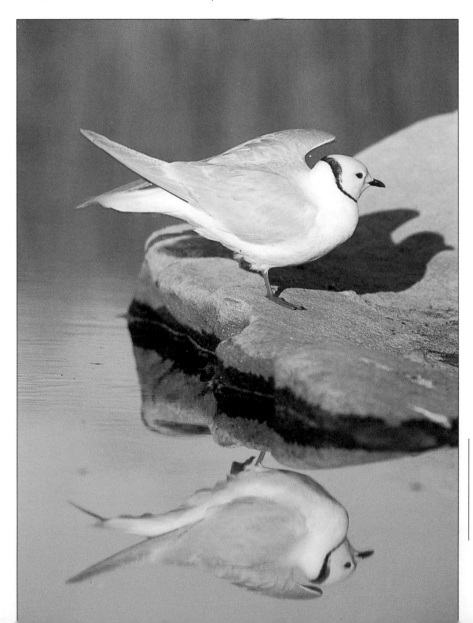

Left *Ross's Gull* (Larus rosea) *near Churchill, Manitoba. The world population of this gull is probably low, but its status is uncertain because its main breeding colonies are in remote parts of Siberia. However, small colonies have recently been found near Churchill and other parts of the Canadian Arctic.*

Tobias Salathé studied biology at Basle University, Switzerland. He then worked on the ecology and conservation of waterbirds at the Biological Station of Tour du Valat, southern France. Moving to Cambridge, UK, he coordinated the Migratory Birds Conservation Program for the International Council for Bird Preservation. Moving back to Tour du Valat, in the 1990s he became a consultant to the European Commission in Brussels on conservation problems of migratory birds and the natural wetlands, on which they depend. Currently, he is helping his fellow researchers at Tour du Valat to develop a Mediterranean-wide research program for the conservation of wetlands and colonial waterbirds.

Migrating Birds

The annual migration of millions of birds has fascinated people since the beginning of history, being first recorded in magnificent paintings in 4,000-year-old Egyptian tombs. Weird theories to account for these movements, such as swallows vanishing in the muddy bottom of lakes and cuckoos turning into sparrowhawks in winter, persisted until recently. They have now disappeared, thanks to modern research including records from bird-ringing stations, and direct, radar and satellite observations of migrating birds.

As days in higher latitudes become shorter, heralding a harsh season with scant food supplies, migrants leave their breeding sites in temperate regions to spend the winter in milder climates. Long-distance migrants may have to fly over large, inhospitable areas with little or no suitable food. There are ecological barriers several hundred miles across, such as the Gulf of Mexico (traversed by the globally threatened Blackburnian Warbler), the Mediterranean Sea, the Sahara desert, and the western Pacific. So the birds have to start their journey well prepared.

Migrants deposit fat reserves mainly under their skin by increasing their food intake up to 40 per cent prior to departure. Small warblers like Kirtland's Warbler, now nearly extinct, may accumulate deposits up to half of their lean bodyweight, which they can restore by only a few days' stopover in an area with abundant food. Such refueling sites at either end of ecological barriers along international flyways are of great strategic importance. Outstanding among these are the wetlands in northern Africa situated between the sea and the desert like El Kala in Algeria or Lake Ichkeul in Tunisia, while the Waddensee mudflats of Germany, Denmark, and the Netherlands are also significant.

Whooping Crane (Grus americana)

Right *A female Arctic Tern* (Sterna paradisaea) *begs food from the male on an ice floe in Churchill, Canada. After breeding in the Arctic, they will journey to the Antarctic, undertaking the longest annual migration of any bird.*

Far right *This map shows the main migration routes for birds.*

The journey of long-distance migrants may be many thousand miles – up to 30,000 kilometers (18,600 miles) or more for some waders and the Arctic Tern, migrating back and forth between the Arctic circle and the Antarctic pack ice. Bad weather, storms, predators, and competition for scarce food and shelter encountered during migration may levy a heavy toll. What percentage of the migrants that set off accomplish their journey is largely unknown.

THE FLYWAYS

The phenomenon of bird migration involves movements between northern and southern continents, and also shorter journeys within single continents and regions. The current routes or flyways evolved some 10,000 years ago after the retreat of ice age glaciers. Since then, some birds originating in the tropics have migrated to breed in temperate regions where they can take advantage of abundant food supplies during the summer months.

For example, the Mexican tropical forests harbor an extreme variety of migratory warblers breeding in the eastern USA. In the Americas, there are four important flyways used by birds breeding in North America and wintering mainly in Central America and northern South America, with some species migrating as far as Tierra del Fuego at the southern tip of the South American continent. The most eastern, the Atlantic flyway, follows the east coast south to Florida. Birds breeding further west in Canada and Alaska use the Mississippi flyway with its many wetlands, on which some 8 million ducks, geese, swans and coots spend the winter, among them the endangered Piping Plover. The Central flyway runs east of the Rocky Mountains to the coastal wetlands of Texas and Louisiana. The Pacific flyway leads birds along the Rocky Mountains and the Pacific east coast to Central America.

Migrants cross the European continent flying south and southwest on a wide front. Many Siberian birds start migrating westwards to Europe and then partly follow a south-southwesterly route. The Slender-billed Curlew, of which only a hundred or so may survive, breeds in Siberia and crosses southeastern Europe to winter in North Africa. Important

Above *Waterfowl, including large numbers of Snow Geese* (Anser caerulescens), *wintering in the Tule Lake National Wildlife Refuge in northern California.*

Flyways and the hunters' toll

The fixed routes followed by migrating birds (see map, **left**) make them extremely vulnerable. Along many of the Mediterranean, Caribbean and south-east Asian flyways in particular, bottleneck areas enable people to shoot and catch migratory birds with decoys, nets and limesticks. With the widespread availability of shotguns and mistnets, this "sport" has been taken up by many who cannot claim "tradition" as an excuse for their destructive pastime. It is estimated that in the Mediterranean region alone, 1,000 million birds are killed annually by 10 million shooters and an additional 1 million trappers. This means that up to a fifth of all birds crossing the Mediterranean may be falling prey to humans. A detailed analysis of birds ringed in Europe and later found dead reveals that the chances of a bird population surviving decrease significantly with increasing hunting pressure. Hunting is believed to be one of the main reasons for the near extinction of the Eskimo and Slender-billed Curlews in America and the Mediterranean respectively.

Main migration routes

Barn Swallow (Hirundo rustica)

Below *The Dalmatian Pelican* (Pelecanus crispus) *breeds from Yugoslavia east to China, wintering in Greece, Turkey, the Middle East, and India. Over the past century it has declined dramatically. However, recent, coordinated conservation efforts have slowed down this trend. Currently there remains a vulnerable population of about 4,000 pairs breeding at a few key sites in the Palearctic.*

Below right *The Red Kite* (Milvus milvus), *still widespread in some parts of mainland Europe, has declined dramatically in the British Isles and now only a small population survives in Wales. Recently a reintroduction program was initiated.*

concentrations occur during fall migration and throughout winter on the northern coast of the Mediterranean at wetlands and maquis with abundant food sources in the Camargue (France), Coto Doñana (Spanish Atlantic coast), the Evros delta (Greece), and the Danube delta (Romanian/Ukrainian Black Sea coast). Some soaring species like storks, pelicans (including the endangered Dalmatian Pelican), and many raptors choose narrow sea crossings at the Straits of Gibraltar and Messina, or follow the eastern Mediterranean flyway over the Bosphorus and along the Levant coast. Birds taking the western Mediterranean flyway cross the western Sahara and tend to winter in the Sahel countries, some going as far south as Angola. Birds using the eastern Mediterranean flyway follow the Nile valley or the Red Sea coast and the Rift valley, and winter in eastern and southern Africa. The White Stork is the most conspicuous bird on this route. Many breeding birds from Siberia and central Asia migrate instead over the Arab peninsula to southeastern Africa.

Important wintering areas of Palearctic birds in Asia, including the threatened Siberian Crane, are located south of the Caspian Sea, on the Indian subcontinent, in Japan, and in the Asian tropics. Some species migrate west of the central Asian mountains, others on the eastern side. But a large number cross the Himalayas over a wide front. Important flyways follow the Asian Pacific coast, through eastern Indonesia and the Philippines to Australia. The Mekong delta in Vietnam and the Sumatran coastal swamps are the most important refueling stops.

STOPOVER AND WINTERING SITES

Migrants concentrate at favorable stopover and wintering sites in enormous numbers. Hawk mountain in the USA, the Bosphorus near Istanbul, and the Sinai peninsula in Egypt are famous places for gatherings of thousands of raptors. Refueling and wintering sites for several million waders and other waterbirds include the Banc d'Arguin in Mauritania, the Copper river delta in Alaska, and the Waddensee in Europe. At such bottlenecks, migrants have traditionally been captured in large numbers for human consumption. Quails and, to a lesser extent, Corncrake are netted by the thousands when they arrive exhausted at the north coast of Sinai after crossing the Mediterranean. With the advent of shotguns the numbers of hunters and birds killed increased drastically. The large-scale netting or capture with limesticks, clapnets, and blinded decoys of thrushes, warblers, robins, and other migrating birds has become a jealously preserved pastime in many areas of the Mediterranean, Caribbean and southeast Asia.

HABITAT DESTRUCTION

But the most important threats which face migrants are the alteration and destruction of the habitats they visit in the course of their annual cycle. In the highly industrialized and populated northern countries, traditionally used farmland, natural grassland, woodland, and many wetlands are disappearing because of urban, industrial and agricultural developments. Consequently Whooping Crane, Red Kite, and Marbled Teal have shown marked declines. The widespread fragmentation of forests in North America poses a particular threat to species like the Worm-eating Warbler, adapted to the conditions of the interior of large unbroken stretches of boreal forest. Habitat destruction is no less a conservation problem in the wintering areas. Wetland drainage, landslides on cleared forest slopes, and deforestation of primary and secondary tropical forests in Central America and southeast Asia directly affect many migrants. Recent extreme drought conditions in the African savannas have substantially contributed to the decline of many Palearctic migrants. The droughts also led to overgrazing, overuse of firewoods and overfishing of remaining wetlands, such as in the Senegal valley and the inner Niger delta in Mali. This increased human pressure on the fragile lands degraded the migrants' habitats even more. Key stopover and wintering sites are being lost through tourist developments, such as those along the coasts of Amvrakikos gulf in Greece and Chesapeake Bay in the USA. Large-scale water management schemes, including huge dams and reservoirs, are destroying important wintering sites in South America, Sahelian Africa, and south and southeast Asia.

A few countries alone cannot avert these threats. Migratory birds are the common property and responsibility of many nations and, as such, they act as flagships for wider conservation issues. They form bonds of interest between countries, emphasizing the need for international cooperation, and establishing major educational and institutional connections through which many other kinds of conservation can follow. Since its foundation in 1922 (under the name of International Committee for Bird Preservation), Bird Life International, a global partnership of conservation organizations, has been particularly active in promoting the conservation of migrants through its Migratory Birds Programs. From 1993 onwards, enthusiastic birdwatchers and the general public have been given the opportunity of enjoying the magnificent spectacle of bird migration in early October, on World Birdwatch day, when bird observation and awareness activities are organized world wide, in 91 countries. In 1997, there was a record participation of over 200,000 people.

Above At each stage in the food chain, pesticides accumulate and become more and more concentrated. Predators such as hawks and stoats are more likely to eat contaminated prey, because poison makes animals weaker and easier to kill.

Left The Barn Swallow (Hirundo rustica), *found in both the Old and New Worlds, is perhaps the best known of all migrants. Until the eighteenth century it was widely believed that swallows spent the winter at the bottom of a pond.*

UNITED STATES OF AMERICA

NORTH

ATLANTIC

GULF
OF MEXICO

BAHAMAS

WEST INDIES

Puerto Rico

SIERRA MADRE ORIENTAL

Popocatépetl

Cuba

Jamaica

Hispaniola

SIERRA MADRE DEL SUR

YUCATAN

CARIBBEAN SEA

LESSER

ANTILLES

Trinidad

OCEAN

CORDILLERA ORIENTAL

Cauca

Magdalena

Orinoco

Roraima •

GUIANA HIGHLANDS

Mouths
of the Amazon

Cotopaxi

Chimborazo

Negro

Branco

Galapagos Islands

Putumayo

Japurá

Amazon

Marañón

Juruá

Purus

Madeira

Tapajós

Xingu

Tocantins

Ucayali

PACIFIC

Huascarán

Madre de Dios

N

D

Lake Titicaca

MATO GROSSO

BRAZILIAN HIGHLANDS

São Francisco

Parnaíba

Araguaia

E

Lake Poopó

PANTANAL

Pilcomayo

Paraguay

Paraná

ATACAMA DESERT

S

Bermejo

Salado

OCEAN

Uruguay

Colorado

A

Aconcagua

Plate

N

PAMPAS

D

PATAGONIA

Negro

E

S

TIERRA DEL
FUEGO

Falkland Islands

CAPE HORN

The Neotropic Region

The Neotropic region is all of South America and Central America as far north as coastal Mexico, and the Caribbean. The two dominant physical features of the region – the massive ridge of the Andes mountains and the vast Amazon river – have dramatic effects on the climate, vegetation, and wildlife. Landscapes vary from tropical forest to the wastes of Patagonia.

Monkey Puzzles (Araucaria araucana), Chile.

Habitat & Plants

Sabina Knees is a botanical consultant and writer with a special interest in the floras and vegetation of Central and South America. After reading botany at University College North Wales, Bangor, and the University of Reading, she was appointed assistant botanist to the Royal Horticultural Society, Wisley. Sabina then moved to Kew as conservation officer, dealing with international conservation legislation and research into the effects of trade on endangered or vulnerable species of plants. She is currently working at the Royal Botanic Garden, Edinburgh.

DISTRIBUTION
FLORISTIC REGIONS

1 Caribbean
2 Venezuela and Guiana
3 Amazon
4 South Brazilian
5 Andean
6 Pampas
7 Patagonian
8 Juan Fernandez

The countries of Central and South America contain a variety of biogeographical areas, from the very wet to the very dry. The climate ranges from tropical in the north, where the equator passes through the continent, to subarctic at the southern tip. Two massive physical features have dramatic effects on climate and conditions: the long ridge of the Andes mountains runs along almost the entire length of the western (Pacific) coast, influencing climate and wildlife in seven countries, while the mighty River Amazon and its many tributaries dominate an area in the north that includes much of Brazil and parts of five other countries.

Away from the Andes and Amazonia, vast tracts of tropical grasslands (or savanna), and tropical deciduous forest, cover the hotter northern regions, giving way to treeless temperate grassland (the pampas) further south. As the climate becomes cooler in southern Argentina, the pampas changes to a scrub of thorn and parched grasses, with the vegetation dwindling through Patagonia to the cold, windy wastes of Tierra del Fuego.

The eastern coast receives moist winds from the Atlantic Ocean, supplying rain to a strip of tropical forest that follows much of Brazil's coast. Although no more than a few miles wide in places, this region supports a rich flora and fauna. The western coast from Ecuador to Santiago in Chile is a virtual desert, since the rain that comes from Amazonia to the north-east is extracted by the Andes and returned to the Amazon system. Further south, prevailing winds from the Pacific Ocean bring moisture to support a temperate deciduous woodland, until the bitter winters of the far south impose their own limitations on the landscape.

Within the Neotropic region, then, are many distinctly different types of landscape. Each main type contains a number of variations, depending on latitude and topography, in some places giving rise to virtually unique habitats, where precisely adapted plants and animals occupy narrowly defined niches. Some of the endangered species of the region inhabit such places. Other more widely distributed species are threatened by large-scale alterations made by people.

TROPICAL RAINFOREST

The Neotropic region is divided into eight regions of flora (floristic regions): the Caribbean, Venezuela and Guiana, Amazon, South Brazilian, Andean, Juan Fernandez, Pampas, and Patagonian. The first four of these are largely covered by rainforest, giving the Neotropics probably the greatest species diversity in the world. Unlike its counterparts in Africa and southeast Asia, the extensive area of tropical rainforest covering much of Brazil and adjacent

Left Rainforest in the Serra dos Carajas, Pará State, Brazil, shrouded in early morning mist. The tree in the center has a termite's nest hanging from it.

Above Patagonian pampas near Valdez, Argentina. Like many temperate habitats it lacks the rich diversity of tropical areas.

countries in South America had remained more or less intact until the rapid destruction in the latter part of the twentieth century. The greater the area of tropical rainforest, the greater the number of species likely to be found inhabiting it. The Amazonian rainforest is no exception with an estimated 80,000 species of seed-bearing plants, about one third of the world's total, making it the most species-rich area in the world. By comparison, the rainforests of Africa and southeast Asia each contain about 30,000 seed-bearing plant species. It is mainly their favorable climates that allow rainforests to support such a great number of species and, for comparison, Britain has just 1,800 while the states of North and South Carolina combined contain some 3,360 species.

Much of the area covered with tropical rainforest in the Neotropics is flat or rolling, with mountainous areas rarely exceeding 1,200 meters (4,000 feet). The annual rainfall varies from

Above *A mahogany tree* (Swietenia) *shrouded with climbers in the botanic gardens on the island of St. Vincent. Throughout Central America and the Caribbean, large mahoganies are now found only in protected or remote areas.*

Above right *The dense cover of creepers and epiphytes in a Costa Rican tropical forest. The rich flora at the canopy level is almost invisible from the ground, except when an occasional plant or flowerhead falls to the forest floor.*

2–4 meters (80–160 inches) per year, and the temperature is relatively high and quite uniform, usually around 24–26°C (75–79°F). There is no regular seasonal change affecting the whole vegetation as in temperate parts of the world. The component plants may lose their foliage on an annual basis, but the timing of this varies from species to species, and flowering and fruiting is a year-round event.

Forest trees are the most obvious structural component of the rainforest, forming the canopy or "roof" of the forest. Some familiar and everyday woods as well as fine cabinet woods come from the Amazonian forests, including rubber *(Hevea brasiliensis)* and mahoganies. Among the endangered trees of the Ecuadorian lowland rainforest is the Caoba *(Persea theobromifolia)*. Described as new to science as recently as 1977, this tree is a relative of the Avocado and has commercially important lumber with properties similar to mahogany. However, the main cause of the Caoba's demise is the rapid conversion of forests to banana and oil palm plantations.

With so many species concentrated together in the rainforest, it may seem surprising that the forest floor is often no more colorful than that of a northern beech or pine forest. This is because in undisturbed or primeval rainforest, little light reaches the ground except in clearings where a tree has fallen. All the color and much of the life and activity of a tropical rainforest are concentrated in the canopy. The herbaceous plants, including gingers, ferns, grasses and sedges, only occur where sufficient light penetrates the tree strata. There they may become large, often growing to 5 meters (16 feet) or more.

Unlike the trees and herbaceous plants, the lianas, vines and other climbers are dependent on external mechanical support. With the support of large trees, climbers can grow to 200 meters (650 feet) or more. The larger climbing palms and rattans are prominent examples of climbers greatly exploited by humans. *Dicliptera dodsonii*, an orange-flowered vine of lowland forest is, like the Caoba, a recently described species threatened with extinction through forest conversion.

EPIPHYTES AND COLLECTORS

On tree trunks and branches, and on the climbers, grow the epiphytes, well known outside their natural habitat as house or conservatory plants. It is probably this group which contains the greatest number of endangered or vulnerable plants. Among the epiphytes often collected for specialist growers around the world are the air plants or bromeliads. Many of the 411 species of the genus *Tillandsia* are endangered through overcollecting. *Glomeropitcairnia erectiflora* is vulnerable in the cloud forests of Trinidad for a different reason – because of disturbance by visitors climbing to the summit of Mount Tucuche. Many of the rainforest orchids are epiphytes and these highly specialized plants occur in greatest numbers in the tropical rainforests. Ecuador, for example, boasts 2,670 species out of a world total of about 25,000. In contrast, the whole of the USA has a mere 200. Sadly, there is now only 6 percent of the original coastal rainforest left in Ecuador, the rest having been converted into farmland since 1970.

THE ANDEAN FLORISTIC REGION

Much of western South America is included in the Andean floristic region. Traveling south from Colombia on the western side of the Andes, the tropical rainforest soon gives way to dry forest, then to a Mediterranean-type vegetation and eventually to true desert, with less than

Bromelia serra

Vriesea hieroglyphica

Orthophytum burle-marxi

Left *An air plant or epiphyte* (Tillandsia) *from Mexico. Several species of these bromeliads are extremely rare and yet are collected for the houseplant trade.*

Right *The Chilean False Larch* (Fitzroya cupressoides) *may take up to 500 years to mature and live for over 4,000 years. Only a few forests now survive, the rest having fallen to loggers or been consumed by fire.*

Below *The Monkey Puzzle Tree* (Araucaria araucana) *in its natural habitat in the Chilean Andes looks very different from the familiar straggling garden specimens.*

2 millimeters (0.08 inch) annual rainfall in the Atacama region of Chile. Among the most vulnerable plants there are the succulents, particularly the Chilean barrel cacti. The threat to these is overcollecting for commercial purposes rather than habitat destruction.

Chile is the longest country in the world, spanning some 4,000 kilometers (2,600 miles) from the Atacama desert to Tierra del Fuego and encompassing many vegetation types. At latitudes greater than about 38 degrees south, the annual rainfall is actually higher than in tropical South America, the average often exceeding 5 meters (200 inches) per annum. Chile does not include any tropical rainforest, but an equally valuable temperate rainforest has developed over thousands of years on the windward side of the Andes. Covering a much smaller area than its tropical equivalent, this unique forest is very vulnerable.

Rare conifers such as the Chilean False Larch *(Fitzroya cupressoides)* and the curious Monkey Puzzle *(Araucaria araucana)* are characteristic of the temperate rainforest. The False Larch has been described by the Chileans as a cornerstone of their culture and civilization, needed throughout life from the cradle to the grave. Large tracts of native forest have been felled to obtain its lumber, which is used in building and construction as well as in smaller items, such as musical instruments. The threat to this remarkable tree is heightened by the fact that it is extremely slow-growing, often taking up to 500 years to reach maturity. Nearly all the really fine specimens, believed to be up to 4,000 years old, have been removed. Even if replanting programs were to be considered, who would invest in an afforestation program with a 500-year cycle? Furthermore, once felled, temperate and tropical rainforests cannot be recreated and, like the tropical mahoganies, the False Larch is unable to grow in monocultural stands. Despite CITES listing, which bans international trade, and internal protection, the trees are still being felled.

The Monkey Puzzle is also threatened, mainly because of the central role it has played in the lives of the original inhabitants of the Andes, the Araucarian Indians. They traditionally used the tree's seeds as a source of food and now also use it to make buttons and other artefacts to supplement their basic income. As a result, the Monkey Puzzle's gene pool has been severely depleted. More recently, large areas of the forests have succumbed to the chainsaw in a futile attempt to clear land either for cattle ranching or, even worse, reforestation with alien species.

JUAN FERNANDEZ

Juan Fernandez is a small group of Pacific islands, lying some 640 kilometers (400 miles) west of Santiago, Chile (see also p.212). They form a separate floristic region because they are even more isolated botanically than the Galapagos islands. Their endemic flora includes about 98 flowering plants and 17 ferns, the vast majority of which are threatened by forest destruction caused by introduced grazing animals.

Crusoe's Mayu-monte *(Sophora fernandeziana)*, scattered through the montane forests of Isla Robinson Crusoe, is described as vulnerable. Another species of the same genus, Selkirk's Mayu-monte *(Sophora masafuerana)*, is considered to be endangered. It occurs only on the neighboring Isla Alejandro Selkirk, where it is found on cliff ledges and in the forest covering the walls of deep canyons. These two species are particularly important as they represent a vital link between other species of the genus found in Easter Island, New Zealand, Hawaii, and Chile.

PAMPAS AND PATAGONIA

The floristic region described as Pampas covers a large area in temperate South America, including Uruguay, southeastern Brazil, western Argentina, and the Argentine pampas. Large parts of this region have been modified by humans over many centuries, and cattle ranching maintains the area in a way comparable with the savannas of east Africa, where grazing by herds of large herbivores and natural fires prevent the growth of secondary forest.

The Patagonian region comprises Patagonia and Tierra del Fuego, the southern Andes and the Falkland Islands. These areas have not suffered the phenomenal population explosions experienced in the tropical north and so the threats to their native flora and fauna are much less significant. However, tourist development since the 1980s could have an adverse effect on the wildlife of the Falkland Islands. Felton's Flower is now considered extinct in the wild, although it survives in cultivation close to its original locality on West Point Island. Three other species are considered rare and another *(Arabis macloviana)* is endangered, all as a result of overgrazing.

***Below** The steppes of Patagonia are bleak and inhospitable, rendering them fairly safe from most forms of exploitation. However, overgrazing by sheep has occurred in some areas.*

Wildlife

Chris Madsen is a professional writer and editor. Having graduated in zoology from Oxford University, UK, and after a spell as demonstrator in zoology at Reading University, she went into natural history, science and educational publishing, eventually turning freelance. Chris is author of more than 40 natural history and conservation titles, many of them for children, and has contributed to a number of other books.

Much of South America's wildlife is unique. Whole families of birds, such as ovenbirds, ant-birds, cotingas, manakins, tinamous, and toucans, live nowhere else on earth. Guinea pigs, hutias, pacas and agoutis, spiny rats, leaf-nosed bats, and the prehensile-tailed woolly monkeys and spider monkeys are all totally neotropic families, as are marmosets and tamarins. This is mainly because, after South America separated from Africa, about 100 million years ago, its wildlife evolved in isolation. The Panama land bridge reconnected South America and North America a mere two million years ago. The many marsupial mammals occupying South America at that time were outclassed by invading placental mammals from the north, and are now represented only by opossums. Anteaters, armadillos, sloths, and the New World monkeys are also relics of pre-Panama fauna. Parrots go further back, to the days – perhaps 200 million years ago – when South America, Africa, India, and Australia formed a single continent.

TROPICAL RAINFOREST

Tropical moist forest contains the richest and most varied flora and fauna in the world. In sheer quantity of material, or biomass, the world's tropical moist forests account for four-fifths of the planet's terrestrial vegetation, although they occupy barely seven per cent of the land's surface.

Below Despite the amazing color, variety and richness of life in a tropical forest, most tropical soils are relatively shallow and often poor in nutrients. If the forest is cleared, the soil quickly deteriorates. This makes it unsuitable for farming and means that the forest, once destroyed, has little capacity for regeneration.

Above left *The Vinaceous Parrot* (Amazona vinacea) *formerly occurred in forests from southeast Brazil through Paraguay to northeastern Argentina. It has suffered a dramatic decline through loss of habitat. An isolated population in Misiones, Argentina, a region susceptible to climatic disturbance, is particularly at risk.*

Above *The Resplendent Trogon or Quetzal* (Pharomachrus mocino) *is confined to cloud forests of Central America. Although still locally abundant in more remote areas, it has disappeared over much of its range, which remains unprotected. The Quetzal is both the national bird of Guatemala and the name of its currency.*

Rainforest is disappearing at an alarming rate. Throughout the region, the annual toll is approximately 6.5 million hectares (16 million acres). In Brazil alone, nearly 30,000 square kilometers (approximately 11,583 square miles) is lost each year, and the rate of deforestation there appears to be increasing. Mexico once contained 22 million hectares (54 million acres) of forest, and barely eight per cent of this remains. The two main reasons for this wholesale destruction are logging and farming. Hardwood timber is often obtained by demolishing whole tracts of trees so that heavy machines can move in to haul away the few commercially valuable trunks, leaving behind 60 felled giants for each timber tree that is taken. Farmland may be flattened and bulldozed clear to provide pasturage for beef cattle, or burned to open up a patch of ground for cultivation. The land thus obtained is of astonishingly low fertility, which means that new patches have to be cleared every few years. Poor soil fertility is typical of tropical moist forest, where practically all the available resources are locked up in the living trees. In this warm, humid climate anything that falls to the ground is either eaten by scavengers or decays in a matter of days, leaving little to fertilize the shallow, light soil. Cleared forest has only a small capacity for regrowth, especially if all the timber is bulldozed away, and it soon loses what little soil it had to erosion by wind and water. The forest is a self-maintaining system that, once broken, cannot be put back together again.

Throughout Central America, animals are in danger from forest clearance. Troops of Central American Squirrel Monkeys once flourished in the forests of Panama and Costa Rica, feeding on fruit and insects in their small home ranges. Most of their home has now been cleared for growing rice, sugar cane, and bananas, and their only chance of survival may be a single reserve in Costa Rica. The islands, too, are losing rainforests. Puerto Rico and Dominica have some left, but it is rapidly diminishing. The Puerto Rico Parrot has been on the verge of extinction for at least a quarter of a century. A population of 200 in 1950 fell to just 24 by 1968, due to a shortage of trees in which to nest. Desperate efforts to save the species raised the numbers to 47 in 1989, which were then cut to 14 by Hurricane Hugo. The population rose again to 41 by 1993, but dramatic climatic events are not uncommon in this region and could eventually tip the balance fatally.

Black-handed Spider Monkeys, widely distributed from Mexico to Panama, are vulnerable to forest clearance and suffer the added problems of being killed for food and captured as pets. Spider monkeys spend up to four years becoming mature, and then only produce a single offspring once in two or three years. Four of the five known species are on the danger list and the status of the fifth is unknown. A related species, the Yellow-tailed Woolly Monkey of Peruvian montane forest, also suffers from hunting, and its home forests are being cut on the slopes where most figs grow. Deforestation is partly caused by roadbuilding, and road construction crews need food, so the monkeys suffer further losses. In the north of Colombia, the little Cotton-top Tamarin is endangered by its popularity as a pet. Between 1960 and 1975 as many as 40,000 were exported to the USA, but half as many again would probably have died to supply this number. Deforestation adds to the pressure on this monkey, and on the vulnerable, closely related White-footed Tamarin from the same region.

Tapirs are hoofed mammals that live near water in lowland and montane forests, foraging on the ground for leaves and fruit. They reproduce slowly, producing only a single offspring after more than a year's gestation. The striped and spotted baby can travel with its mother almost as soon as it is born, but must suckle for another year before it becomes independent. Tapirs are shy, secretive, and easily disturbed. They are also very good to eat and it is therefore not surprising that their numbers are rapidly declining. The Central American (or Baird's) Tapir is probably already extinct in El Salvador and Mexico, and practically extinct in Panama.

Forest cats are also hunted, in their case for the fur trade. In 1975 nearly 77,000 skins went from the region to Britain alone. Ten years later, legislation and falling demand had reduced this annual number by more than half, but this still means that 34,500 skins went to

Below *The Cotton-top Tamarin* (Saguinus oedipus), *once widespread in Panama and Colombia, was collected extensively for use in biomedical research. Trade in wild specimens is now controlled and it is being bred in captivity.*

Below right *Baird's Tapir* (Tapirus bairdii) *has extremely palatable flesh and has consequently been hunted to extinction over much of its range in Central and northern South America.*

Britain in 1985. Jaguars, the largest neotropical cats with the most prized fur, have been ruthlessly hunted – often with traps baited with "protected" species of monkey. They were once fairly common from California to Argentina, but are now extinct from all of North and most of Central America – with the notable exception of Belize, where unspoiled rainforest has survived and is being actively conserved. Their numbers continue to decline throughout the region, along with many smaller cats such as the Margay and Tiger Cat, which are under similar pressure from fur hunters as well as being more vulnerable to forest clearance than wider-ranging Jaguars. Ironically, information about the status of a species is much easier to obtain when the species is consistently hunted. The number of Jaguarundi still surviving in the rainforest is not known, and even the habits of this exotic cat are a mystery, as it is neither good to eat nor the possessor of a desirable skin.

We remain ignorant of much of the flora and fauna of the tropical forest, particularly species for which no "use" has been found. "New" species are constantly being discovered, sometimes on the brink of extinction in a rapidly dwindling patch of forest. One such new-to-science species is a lion tamarin that was recently found on a small island off the Paraná coast of Brazil. No more than 200 individuals of this beautiful primate remain. It has been named the Black-faced Lion Tamarin just in time to join the list of other lion tamarins already known to be endangered in Brazil's dwindling Atlantic forest. Three other species, the Golden, Golden-headed, and Golden-rumped Lion Tamarins exist in distinct areas of this coastal rainforest, with populations of over 100, under 600, and about 100, respectively. All four species like to live in the privacy of tangled vines between 3 and 10 meters (10 to 30 feet) above ground level in dense primary forest, where they feed in small groups on fruit and insects. They have probably always been rare, and it has been their misfortune to have evolved in a region destined to become one of the most densely populated in Brazil, close to the conurbation of Rio de Janeiro.

Brazil's unique Atlantic coastal forest has been reduced to no more than 2 per cent of its original area. Plantations of sugar cane, cocoa, coffee, rubber and bananas replace the giant forest trees by a further 0.5 per cent each year. This region was also hard hit by climatic

Jaguar

Margay

Mountain Cat

Tiger Cat

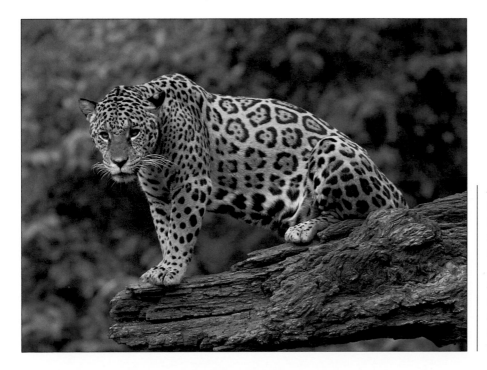

Above *The beautiful skins of the spotted cats have made them vulnerable to hunting for the fur trade. Despite legislation and reduced demand, skins are still being exported to the developed world. As a result, all species are becoming increasingly rare.*

Left *A young male Jaguar (Panthera onca). Jaguars once ranged from the southern states of the USA south over almost the entire South American continent, but are now extinct in almost all areas close to human settlements.*

Above *The Seven-colored Tanager* (Tangara fastuosa) *now has an extremely limited range in forest and secondary growth of northeastern Brazil. It has declined due to habitat destruction and collection for the caged-bird trade.*

Above right *Like most other curassows and guans, the turkey-sized Red-billed Curassow* (Crax blumenbachii) *is threatened by hunting and habitat loss. It is now restricted to a few areas of primary forest in southeast Brazil.*

Below *Natterer's Longwing* (Heliconius nattereri) *from Esperito Santo, Brazil, is one of many threatened species in the area.*

events in 1998 and the consequences of exceptional rains and floods, accompanied by human hardship, might not be known for some years. Besides the lion tamarins, other primates known to be in danger in this beleaguered habitat include the Buffy-headed Marmoset, the Buffy Tufted-eared Marmoset, the Masked Titi, and the Woolly Spider Monkey. The endemic Three-toed Sloth and Thin-spined Porcupine are also vulnerable to loss of territory.

Of the 115 species of birds that inhabit the Atlantic coast forest, 94 exist nowhere else on Earth. Endangered species range in size from the little Hook-billed Hermit Hummingbird to the White-necked Hawk. Hunting and trapping for the pet trade has driven Spix's Macaw to the brink of extinction. The very last wild male was provided with a captive-bred mate in 1994. Roughly 30 more survive in zoos around the world, but they do not breed well in captivity and the gene pool may now be too impoverished for long-term success. Another bird that probably only exists now in a private zoo is the Alagoas Curassow, a grouse-like gamebird. About 40 species of related gamebirds – curassows, guans, and chacalacas – inhabit woods, forests, grasslands, and even mountainsides, throughout the Neotropics, and at least 15 of them are considered to be in danger. Loss of habitat has added extra pressure to the intense hunting with which these large, tasty birds already have to cope. They have never been domesticated, but will happily associate with domestic fowl and breed well in zoos. Perhaps, instead of being annihilated from the wild, this group might be exploited in captivity to provide a valuable source of food in the future.

AMAZONIA

In the forests of Amazonia, as elsewhere, the species known to be at risk are those that are actively sought. Vulnerable primates include two marmosets, the White (or Silvery) and the Tassel-eared. Already much depleted by the pet trade, their home ranges are being lost to ranching and road building. The Bearded (or Red-backed) Saki is endangered by two highways cutting through its home range as well as a hydroelectric plant. This small primate has the added misfortune of owning a tail that is traditionally used as a duster. Woolly monkeys and spider monkeys are hunted for meat, as well as being captured for the pet trade. They live high in the tree canopy, which makes capture difficult. The most common method is to shoot a mother carrying a baby on her back and then hope that, when they both fall to the ground, the baby is not killed in the fall. If it survives the baby is sold, and if it dies it is eaten: the mother is eaten in any case. The Black Spider Monkey is endangered, and the Long-haired Spider Monkey and woolly monkey are also vulnerable. Like all woolly and spider monkeys, they breed very slowly, maturing at four to five years and producing a single infant only once in two or three years.

Among the few large animals living on the ground in the deep forest are two dogs. The Small-eared Dog, a middle-sized, short-legged animal, is so secretive that it is hardly ever

DISTRIBUTION
NEOTROPIC FORESTS

Forest destroyed since early 1940s

Extent in mid 1990s

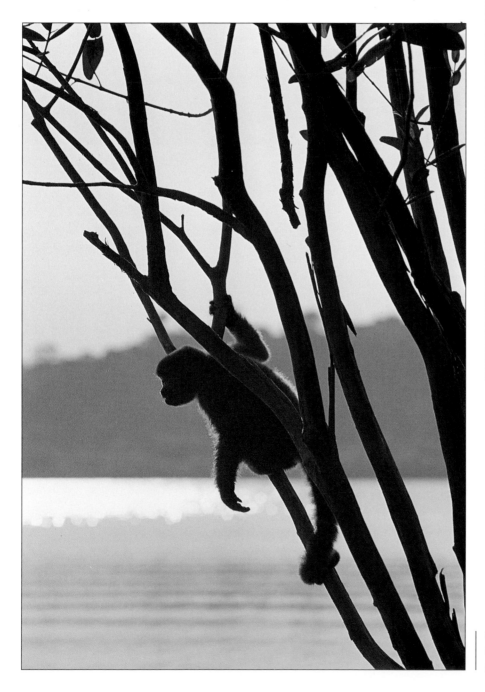

Left A woolly monkey on the edge of the Amazon. Like most South American primates, it has a prehensile tail that can act as a fifth limb.

Right *Although the Harpy Eagle* (Harpia harpyja) *has a vast range, extending from southern Mexico to northern Argentina, it is extremely rare, surviving only in large areas of undisturbed forest.*

Amazonian variety

■ At least 50,000 species of flowering plant, amounting to possibly half of all the flowering plants in the Neotropics, are found here.

■ One acre may contain 235 species of tree, supporting 100,000 species of insect.

■ An adjoining acre may contain 100 tree varieties not found in the first acre.

■ A temperate forest may have 25 different tree species in one acre, and an adjoining acre may not differ at all.

■ Some trees are so rare that single specimens found over 50 years ago are still the only ones of their kind known to science.

■ Many tree species still have no scientific name.

■ Nearly a quarter of all medicines known to the West have been derived from rainforest plants.

■ The Amerindians utilize many of the plants and animals of the forest, such as this male Arrow Poison Frog *(Dendrobates pumilio)*. As the name suggests, they tip their arrows in the poisons the frogs secrete to protect themselves against predators.

seen. While little is known of its lifestyle and less still of its numbers, it must be seriously disturbed by any encroachment on deep forest, such as roadbuilding. The smaller Bush Dogs are found in many forested regions, but are rare everywhere. Their relationship with people is ambivalent: they are sometimes kept as pets, but are often shot on sight by hunters. These ground-dwellers are also vulnerable to fire, especially in a region where natural fire would be a rare event.

Another carnivore that suffers from human activity is the Giant Otter, a goliath among otters measuring about 2 meters (6½ feet) from nose to tail-tip and weighing up to 40 kilograms (88 pounds). Giant Otters live in sociable family groups, playing and hunting by day in the lakes and rivers of the Amazon basin. Being tied to water, they are less able to escape from hunters looking for fur than some other targets such as the spotted cats. They are also easy to locate and approach because they are noisy, practically fearless (even hunting small caimans), and insatiably curious. Pollution adds another level of pressure, so that they are now rare or extinct in many regions and only survive in remote or protected locations.

The rivers of the region also contain two species of dolphin and the South American Manatee (see also p.221). Manatees are entirely aquatic and live in herds, floating in the warm water and browsing on underwater vegetation. Each cow produces only one calf in about four years, which takes seven to ten years to mature. The calf is born in the water after a gestation period of about a year, and suckles from a mammary gland under the mother's front flipper. When water levels fall in the dry season toward November, manatees migrate to lakes, where there is little to eat, and virtually fast until the rainy season begins in May or June. Then they go with the floodwater into the forest and feast on flooded vegetation. Manatees are easy prey for hunters, and are readily threatened by disturbance or pollution of the waters where they live. Their numbers at one time declined steeply due to the demand for hard-wearing manatee leather. This has now been superseded by synthetic materials and manatees are officially protected, but they still remain a valuable and vulnerable source of meat.

Above *A male Arrow Poison Frog* (Dendrobates pumilio). *The poisons secreted by this and related frogs to protect themselves against predators were used by the Amerindians to tip their arrows. Some species have been popular in the pet trade.*

Highly sociable animals such as manatees probably need a higher level of population to ensure their survival than do solitary creatures. On the other hand, solitary hunters may require a large territory and may be more vulnerable to habitat loss over a wide area. The magnificent Harpy Eagle is a huge bird that needs vast tracts of tall primary forest in order to survive. Its relative, the Crested Eagle, has similar requirements.

Where broad rivers cut through the forest, light and air flood in to produce a ribbon development, and a further variation in conditions is provided when the rivers flood in the rainy season. Forest regions that are seasonally inundated by small lowland blackwater rivers are called igapo. The floodplains of large whitewater rivers, running swiftly down from the Andes, are called varzea. Floodplain forest is the home of a rare primate, the Uakari. White Uakaris inhabit varzea forest, and Red Uakaris are found in igapo forest. Both subspecies feed on seeds and nuts, especially those with really hard shells, such as Brazil nuts, and forage over a wide area. They reproduce only slowly and are clearly dependent on the contrasting seasons of the flood cycle – like so many other animals and plants whose existence we are only now beginning to notice, and whose ways of life are still a mystery.

DECIDUOUS FORESTS

Not all Neotropical forests – nor even equatorial ones – are evergreen rainforest. Outside the tropical belt, and on higher ground within it, are deciduous broad-leaf, coniferous, mixed, and bamboo forests. Although less dramatically diverse and biologically concentrated than the tropical moist forests of Amazonia, they support many endemic species, including birds, amphibians and larger mammals. Being more accessible than dense rainforest, they are heavily exploited for timber, fuel and agriculture, and so are damaged by roads and mines. They receive less attention from conservation organizations than Amazonia, and are at great risk of destruction.

The endangered parrots of the Neotropics – macaws, parakeets, parrotlets and the

Forest fish

■ There are possibly as many as 2,000 in-digenous species of freshwater fish in the Amazon system, compared with about 300 species in the whole of Europe.

■ During floods, millions of fishes are carried into the igapo forest to feed on fallen leaves and fruits, returning to the rivers when the waters subside.

■ Specializations include a species with teeth and jaws capable of cracking rock-hard rubber-tree seeds, while another leaps into tree branches to glean insects, and even hummingbirds.

amazones – occupy a variety of niches in tropical and subtropical forests. Hunting for export to the pet trade has brought many near extinction. The largest parrot (aside from the flightless Kakapo of New Zealand) in the world is the Hyacinth Macaw, which lives in dry forests and on the edges of wet forests in Brazil, Bolivia and Paraguay. Total numbers of surviving Hyacinth Macaws are now estimated at around 3,000, with very few outside Brazil. Additional pressures on parrots come from habitat loss and being shot to protect crops. Pearly Parakeets are losing their home forests in northeast Brazil, and many other species of parakeet have been reduced to estimated populations as small as 2,000. Since as many as 20,000 Gray-cheeked Parakeets have been exported from Peru in a single year, such small populations are clearly in grave danger.

Hummingbirds are mostly forest birds with very exact requirements, each occupying a narrow niche that must have the right climate and contain a particular food plant and nest site. They are found almost anywhere there are trees, and some even manage to live high above the treeline in the Andes. Almost incessantly active during the day, tiny hummingbirds need a great deal of carbohydrate food. At night their body temperature falls, thus enabling

Above *The large and spectacularly colored Hyacinth Macaw* (Anodorhynchus hyacinthinus) *is extremely popular in the zoo and pet trade. By the mid-1990s, it was estimated that there were fewer than 3,000 left in the wild.*

Right *The Red Siskin* (Carduelis cucullata) *once ranged across northern Venezuela to Colombia, with isolated populations elsewhere. It produces red-plumaged hybrids with domestic canaries, and so has been extensively exploited.*

Far right *The Purple-winged Ground Dove* (Claravis godefrida) *is confined to wooded country in southeastern Brazil and Paraguay where it is dependent on flowering bamboo, and consequently vulnerable to any change in its habitat.*

them to survive without food while they roost. The relationship between a hummingbird and its foodplant can be so intimate that loss of the hummingbird causes the plant's pollination system to fail. These jewel-like creatures also fall prey to the pet trade. At least 50 species of Neotropic hummingbirds are known to be at risk, out of a total of around 320.

Ovenbirds and antbirds are also highly specialized, requiring particular nest sites and specific insect food. About 56 birds in these two groups are thought to be threatened, mostly due to habitat disturbance. Other endemic bird families with members at risk include the cotingas, a group that contains many extraordinarily eccentric species; tyrant flycatchers, a large group with species in every habitat where there are insects to be caught; and three out of five known species of potoo. Also called wood nightjars, potoos are secretive nocturnal birds that are hardly ever seen but emit horrible screams in the forest at night which sound like a person being murdered. Ground-nesting birds are especially vulnerable, and four nightjars, from Costa Rica to Argentina, are also endangered. The White-winged Nightjar may only survive in a single national park in Brazil, where its future prospects are still unclear. Several species of ground dove in various regions are also becoming very scarce. The Purple-

Vinaceous Parrot
(Amazona vinacea)

winged Ground Dove, which is dependent on flowering bamboo, is now considered to be critically endangered.

Two species of woodpecker have been hit hard by habitat loss. The Mexican Imperial Woodpecker, which once occurred in high pine forests that have now been extensively felled, may already be extinct. The Helmeted Woodpecker occurs in scattered populations in south Brazil, Paraguay, and Argentina, and two species of piculet from Brazil are also considered vulnerable.

A new threat to highland moist-forest dwellers may presently be developing. Many species of frog and other amphibians are believed to be in serious trouble, but as yet the exact cause is unknown. The Golden Toad of Costa Rican cloud forest was last recorded in the wild in 1987, and dozens more amphibians are now in critical decline.

Throughout the forests of the region, mammals such as the Ocelot are becoming rarer. The fur hunters have taken their toll, and this beautiful cat is further threatened by habitat loss. It is adaptable, however, in both the type of country it can cope with and the prey it will

Amphibians in crisis

Since 1974, two-thirds of Puerto Rico's 18 endemic amphibian species have declined. Four of these may even have become extinct. Between 1995 and 1997, the number of amphibian species observed at a single reserve in Panama fell from 55 to 24. A similar story is emerging from Honduras. The species most severely affected in the Neotropic region inhabit montane or sub-montane forest and the streams that run down from them. Theoretical reasons for these alarming mortalities include airborne pollutants in mist and fog, ultra-violet solar radiation, and disease.

Upland rice

Cassava

Sorghum

Maize

Amazon Basin ☐
Savanna ☐

Right In an attempt to accommodate the demand for farmland and prevent rainforest clearance, studies are being carried out on the agricultural potential of savannas. Savanna soil, with its high acidity, low nutrient content and potential for erosion, restricts many types of farming. However, properly managed combinations of certain crops and pasture grasses can be both ecologically and economically successful. Cultivars of crops such as upland rice, cassava, soybeans, sorghum, and maize, have been developed specifically for farming the savannas.

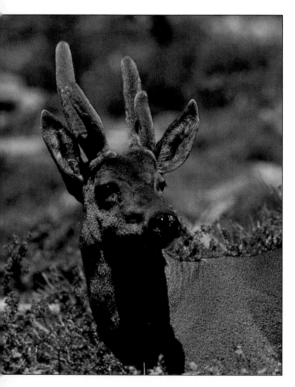

Above Although protected by law, the Chilean Huemul, or Southern Atlantic Deer (Hippocamelus bisulcus) is still hunted. By the early 1980s it was thought to number fewer than 2,000, confined to the southern Andes and perhaps a few islands.

take, and could recover if hunting were properly controlled. Although officially classified as being at low risk of extinction, the level of hunting that Ocelots and other small cats might safely tolerate without decline is not known, so even the authorized cull is arbitrarily set. Unfortunately, as with so many furriers' favorites, the high price of Ocelot skins stimulates illicit trading.

The only South American bear is the Spectacled Bear. It is probably now the only Neotropic bear, since no Mexican Grizzly has been seen since 1962. Spectacled Bears are catholic in diet, though mainly vegetarian, and inhabit forest, mountain, desert and scrub from Venezuela to Bolivia. They seem to prosper only in remote regions or reserves. Captive breeding has so far largely failed, and disturbance, hunting and habitat loss are inexorably taking their toll. This bear is one of many creatures whose future rests on a combination of environmental measures and individual protection.

A mammal that depends even more heavily on habitat conservation is the Volcano Rabbit, whose precise lifestyle is finely tuned to a combination of pine forest, zacoton grass, and altitude found only on the slopes of four volcanoes in Mexico. Agriculture, property development and forestry all contribute to the risk of extinction for this vulnerable little creature, but – paradoxically for a volcano-dweller – one of its main enemies is fire that spreads to the zacoton zone from burning pastureland.

GRASSLANDS

Large tracts of natural grassland occur in parts of the region. The highlands of Eastern Brazil, rising from the Amazon basin, grow deciduous forest on their lower slopes, which gives way to hot, dry savanna higher up. Grassland of a different sort – both temperate and fertile – is found around Uruguay. The plateau of the Mato Grosso, between the Plata and Amazon river systems, provides pasture for cattle, while poorer scrubby grassland extends southward into Argentina. Grassland tends to support relatively small numbers of species, although their numbers may be high. The two main enemies of natural grassland fauna are fire and the cattle ranch.

There are no indigenous sheep, goats, antelope, or gazelles in the Neotropics. The native grazers are deer, Llamas and their kin, peccaries, tapirs, and various rodents. Some large rodents like the Mara and Capybara fit into niches that might be occupied by hoofed mammals in the Old World. Rodents have a talent for breeding that enables them to survive heavy losses, but many other grazers have difficulty competing with humans and their domestic livestock.

The native deer of South America are vulnerable to the diseases and parasites of domestic cattle. In the southern Andes of Chile and Argentina, the South Andean Huemul has probably always been hunted for food. Now its habitat is shrinking, and it is ravaged by foot-and-mouth disease, coccidiosis, nematodes and tapeworms from domestic cattle, together with bladder-worms from the dogs that also harass it. There are probably fewer than 2,000 of these huemuls left. North Andean huemuls face their own problems. In Bolivia, they are killed to make dried salt meat called charque; in Chile they are killed to protect fields of lucerne, and they also lose tree cover due to charcoal burning; in Peru, mining brings both hungry people and charcoal burners. Almost everywhere, cattle, sheep and Llamas compete for forage.

Argentinian Pampas Deer once flourished throughout 647,000 square kilometers (250,000 square miles) of pampas from the Andes to the Atlantic coast. They are now reduced

__Below__ The 1-meter (3¼-foot) long Pampas Deer (Ozotoceros bezoarticus) lives in small herds in open habitats from Brazil to central Argentina. It has declined through loss of habitat and uncontrolled hunting.

to two small populations on the Argentinian coast and a few scattered groups in San Luis Province. Hunted mercilessly for skins and for sport during the eighteenth and nineteenth centuries, their ground was also taken for ranching. By 1980, there was hardly any stretch of pampas large enough to support deer. Diseases of cattle add to their problems, and their future existence is seriously in doubt.

Wolves are traditionally persecuted almost everywhere in the world, and the Maned Wolf of Brazilian open forest and grassland is no exception. It appears to have survived the conversion of its savanna home into agricultural and grazing land, but in farming regions where the wolf's usual mixed diet of wild birds, rodents, lizards and small armadillos is supplemented with chickens, it is shot on sight. Annual grass burning to improve pastures probably kills wolf pups along with many other breeding mammals and birds.

The Giant Anteater and Giant Armadillo are very widely distributed mammals with highly specialized feeding requirements. Solitary and secretive animals, both species dig for ants and termites in open woodland and savanna. Armadillos have been hunted for food, while anteaters, though of little value as game, are occasionally killed out of curiosity. Both species are losing ground to plantations, ranching and other human manipulations of natural grass and scrub. The Brazilian Three-banded Armadillo and the Fairy Armadillo of Argentina are also in some danger, although no accurate estimates of the numbers of these shy creatures have been made.

Among the grassland birds that are affected by human activities, four species of tinamous are thought to be threatened. These ground-nesting birds rely on camouflage for safety. Their chief means of defence is to keep very still. If this fails, they will fly up explosively at the last possible moment. Nothing a tinamou can do will keep it safe from machines or fire. Nightjars, too, must be at risk here.

THE ANDES

The Andes system runs for about 7,200 kilometers (4,500 miles) from the isthmus of Panama to Cape Horn, reaching 7,000 meters (23,000 feet) at the highest peak. Rising from tropical land in the north and extending southwards into the subarctic, the system encompasses an

Below *Giant Anteaters* (Myrmecophaga tridactyla) *are found mostly in open grassy areas, where they use their powerful claws to tear open termite mounds in order to feed on the grubs.*

Below right *The long legs of the Maned Wolf* (Chrysocyon brachyurus) *may give it a better view in the tall grass of its swamp and savanna habitat. While its numbers have declined, its range has extended in the west.*

enormous variety of habitats and conditions, from desert to cloud forest. The main human activities there are mining, agriculture, including extensive vineyards, and herding animals. Mining brings roads, people and machinery together with increased demand for fuel, wood and meat. Domestic animals compete with wild ones for forage and space, and may pass parasites and diseases to related wild species.

Four species of camel live in the Andes. Two – Llamas and Alpacas – have been domesticated and do not exist any longer in the wild. The other two have lost ground for contrasting reasons. Guanacos, the largest animals of the group, are of little value to people except for food. They range along the western side of the mountains, from the coastal desert up to 4,000 meters (13,000 feet) in small herds of females led by a male. Their numbers are not known, though there can be little doubt that habitat loss, competition from domestic animals, and hunting are taking a toll. Vicunas are the smallest animals of the group. Their pale golden-brown wool, evolved for warmth in the high, cold lands where they live, has always been prized and is still considered the finest in the world, but Vicuna have proved impossible to domesticate. The Incas – whose laws forbade anyone other than royalty to wear Vicuna-wool robes – rounded up wild herds every three to five years to shear them. There

Above *A herd of Vicuna* (Vicugna vicugna) *in the High Andes of Peru. Once threatened by overhunting for their exceptionally fine and valuable wool, they have increased dramatically and have even been reintroduced into areas from which they had been extirpated.*

Right *The Long-tailed Chinchilla* (Chinchilla laniger) *from the Andes of northern Chile was brought to the brink of extinction by hunting for the fur trade. Since the 1920s, the fur industry has depended on captive-bred Chinchillas, and the animal's current status in the wild is critical.*

DISTRIBUTION
VICUNA

■ Former distribution

■ Current distribution

Vicuna (Vecugna vicugna). It is estimated that during the Inca period there were up to two million vicuna. By 1965 there were around 6,000. Strict conservation methods have allowed numbers to rebuild to approximately 80,000 in the wild.

were probably more than two million roaming the flat rangeland (puna zone) of the Andes in Inca times. After the Spanish conquest, Vicuna were simply killed for their wool. Tens of thousands a year were slaughtered for 500 years. By 1965, only 6,000 animals remained. Strict regulation and protection pulled them back from the brink of extinction, and now their numbers have risen to over 80,000. The Vicuna is a precious resource, especially for Peru, but the best management method has not yet been established. Most of the surviving animals are presently concentrated in reserves, where drought, overgrazing, or epidemic could cause disaster, and so the Vicuna's future is by no means secure. However, new herds are being established in other parts of this former range.

Two rodents are also protected from the chill of the high Andes by wonderfully soft warm coats. Chinchillas have been mercilessly hunted for their fur and hardly any now survive in the wild. But for the establishment of chinchilla farms in the 1920s, they would probably have become extinct. The better-known Long-tailed Chinchillas live sociably in dens among rocks on shrubby north-facing slopes feeding on leaves, seeds and fruit. They are not as prolific as many rodents, producing two young once (sometimes twice) a year, and are only known to survive in the wild in a small area of Chile's coastal cordillera. Short-tailed or Royal Chinchillas are even more scarce – they are believed to exist in the wild although none has been located in recent years. Living higher in the mountains than the long-tailed species, they were kept in semi-captivity by the Incas. Although their long-tailed relatives are commonly bred in captivity, it has proved difficult to keep short-tailed chinchillas outside their natural high-altitude range. Chinchillas have been protected in Chile since 1929. Despite this and captive

Left *The Andean Flamingo (Phoenicoparus andinus) is confined to the Altiplano of southern Peru, northern Chile, western Bolivia, and northwestern Argentina, where it nests in a few high-altitude salt lakes. With a population possibly as low as 50,000, it may be the rarest flamingo in the world.*

Llama

Alpaca

Guanaco

breeding, the commercial value of wild pelts is so high that poaching still occurs and chinchillas, now probably already extinct from Peru, may soon no longer exist as wild creatures of the Andes.

The demand for firewood and grazing land is rapidly reducing tree cover and scrub in the mountains, driving away shy creatures like the Northern Pudu and Mountain Tapir. Neither of these animals is normally abundant, and both are hunted for meat. Where mines are in operation, the quest for firewood and food intensifies and such species are put under even more pressure. The Tamarugo Conebill, a New World warbler of the high scrub zone of south Peru and north Chile, is another species whose habitat is going up in smoke. Tamarugos trees *(prosopis)* make good firewood for mines, and it is thought that this bird depends on the trees in some way. In addition, it is only known to breed in scrub containing a particular combination of plants. Like many other small species with no great commercial value, little is known about this bird's numbers, and by the time its ecology and behavior are understood it may have ceased to exist. However, Tamarugos also occurs in large plantations in Pampa del Tamarugal National Reserve, and a healthy population survives there.

Other bird populations have declined dramatically as a result of abstraction of water from lakes to supply towns and cities, and by pollution from mines. High, remote lakes in the Andes were once private places where many species lived in anonymous isolation. They are home to the rare Andean Flamingo and Puna Flamingo of Peru, Bolivia, Chile, and Argentina. Other rare waterbirds disappearing from mountain lakes include three grebes and a coot. The Columbian Grebe is now thought to be extinct; the Junin Grebe appears to be declining in its single home lake by 50 per cent each year and is critically endangered; the Horned Coot is also declining; and the flightless Atitlan Grebe finally became extinct due to hybridization with (or being ousted by) the closely related Pied-billed Grebe.

WETLANDS

The Pantanal is an area of seasonally flooded wetland, outstanding in its size and importance to wildlife. Its name is Spanish for "large swamp" and it covers 130,000 square kilometers (50,000 square miles) of western Brazil, bordering Bolivia and Uruguay. The Pantanal is a refuge for the Marsh (or Swamp) Deer, which is scarce and scattered elsewhere. A solitary creature, this deer likes to have its feet wet while it browses and grazes on swamp vegetation. It has been seriously affected by hunting, by loss of habitat through drainage of marshes for pasture and cultivation, and by competition with domestic cattle during the rainy season, when deer and cattle are driven together onto limited patches of high ground above the floodwaters. Within the Pantanal, disease is probably the greatest threat. The Marsh Deer is susceptible to brucellosis, foot-and-mouth disease, and other ailments carried by domestic cattle, and the virtually captive population is very vulnerable to an epidemic.

Whether the Pantanal continues to offer sanctuary to these deer and other beleaguered wetlands animals depends on future plans for the area. There is already concern about raised levels of mercury due to goldmining. Forest destruction higher up the Paraguay river, where much of the Pantanal's water comes from, is causing erosion that may reduce water flow to the swamps. Another problem highlights the interdependence of different species: piranhas

Below *The Orinoco Crocodile* (Crocodylus intermedius) *is an endangered freshwater species restricted to Venezuela and eastern Colombia. It was hunted excessively for its skin from the 1920s, and since the 1950s has been too rare to be regularly used by the hide trade.*

Above *The Warbling Antibird* (Hypocnemis cantator) *is characteristic of the Amazonian region, where it is usually seen in dense undergrowth.*

Above left *The Swamp Deer or Guasupucu* (Blastocerus dichotomus) *is the largest South American deer, weighing up to 150 kilograms (330 pounds). Its numbers have declined drastically due to loss of habitat to agriculture and through drainage, as well as hunting.*

are increasing in number dramatically because the caimans, which normally eat them, have been reduced by hunting. Drainage to improve pastures in the savanna of the region also threatens the swamp.

Localized wetlands are steadily succumbing to drainage and pollution, and not in small measure. An estimated 20 per cent is already lost to drainage and 30 per cent to pollution. A New World warbler called the Altamira Yellowthroat draws attention to the loss of marshes in Mexico where it is declining, and two rare rails reflect the situation further south. The Austral Rail has not been recorded in Chile since 1959 and is critically endangered in Argentina, and the Bogota Rail of Colombia is restricted to a few isolated populations.

Swamps can offer some protection, but humans have always used rivers as highways through remote and sparsely populated regions, making aquatic creatures vulnerable to hunters. Such disturbance was almost certainly responsible for the extinction of the riverside cliff-nesting Glaucous Macaw. Even some of the crocodiles of the region, in spite of (or perhaps because of) being apparently well able to defend themselves, are now under threat. The large Black Caiman, once considered so dangerous to livestock that it was regularly slaughtered on the island of Marajo at the mouth of the Amazon, is now recovering slowly due to active conservation. At least three other crocodiles – the Cuban Crocodile, Morelet's Crocodile of Mexico, Belize and Guatemala, and the Orinoco Crocodile, a large creature that lives only in the Orinoco river – are endangered, and most of the closely related caimans are also threatened.

Turtles, on the other hand, have little defence. The South American River Turtle gathers on a few islands in the Amazon and Orinoco rivers each year to lay its eggs. The eggs have traditionally been harvested by local people to be turned into turtle-egg oil, while many adult

---

Trade in animal skins

Spotted cats are not the only animals endangered by the trade in skins. Reptiles are also hunted mercilessly, the Black Caiman, Spectacled Caiman, and Yacare Caiman all being pursued for their desirable skin. Manatees were once hunted for their skins, which made thick, hard-wearing leather. Now they are killed for meat.

Above The Argentine Pearl Fish (Cynolebias nigripinnis) *is a killifish, many species of which are popular with aquarists. It breeds in temporary pools and puddles and is particularly susceptible to habitat changes and to pollution from pesticides in the run-off from rain and rivers.*

turtles were killed as they returned to the water. In the mid-nineteenth century, an estimated 48 million eggs a year were being taken. Even then, it was apparent that the turtles could not sustain such losses. Today, the few turtles that miraculously remain also have to contend with habitat loss and dams flooding their egg-laying islets.

One of the world's rarest ducks, the Brazilian Merganser, a tree-nesting duck that spends the whole of its life in a small section of a small stream, is critically endangered by deforestation and pollution. The only known population in the province of Misiones in Argentina has dwindled to perhaps a single pair, and its future existence now seems extremely doubtful.

Species with habitat requirements so exact that they have always been rare are all too easily swept away. Annual fishes *(Cynolebias)* are tiny topminnows which hatch and breed in the puddles and streams that collect during the rainy season. When the waters dry up the adult fishes die, leaving their eggs buried in the ground waiting to hatch with the coming of the next rainy season. Wherever land reclamation improves drainage, these little fishes and their precise lifestyle are lost.

DESERT AND SHORE

The two main desert areas of the region lie in Mexico and along the Pacific coast of Peru and northern Chile. Although human presence in desert lands is not great, species living there are already so close to the limits of survival that any extra pressure can tip them into extinction. Tortoises of semidesert are threatened by agriculture, by the pet trade, and by off-road vehicles.

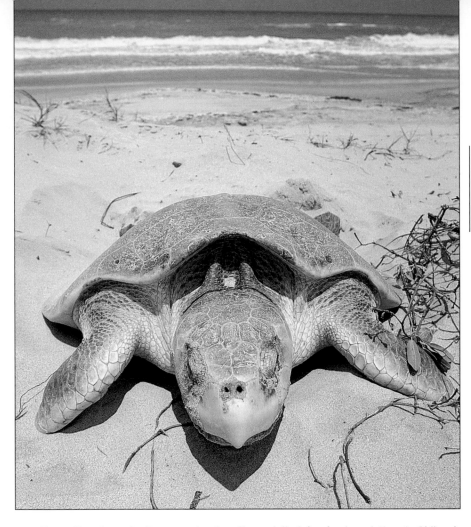

Along the shore, turtles are also heavily exploited for food, and Kemp's Ridley is gradually succumbing to extra pressures from pollution and shrimp trawl nets in the Gulf of Mexico (see p.72). The turtles feed near the sea bottom and become entangled in the nets. Prawn fisheries and seaweed harvesting on the coast of Peru and ocean pollution on Chile's coast threaten very different animals – Marine Otters, very like the Sea Otters of North America, and similarly vulnerable to sustained hunting.

It is important to bear in mind that not all the losses suffered by wild animals and plants come from human activities. Natural events can have devastating effects on an entire ecosystem or a single species. Central America has always been touched by hurricanes. In 1988, a hurricane cut down one of the last unspoiled rainforests of Central America – an area only recently marked for preservation – in Nicaragua. A year later, another hurricane hit a carefully nurtured colony of Puerto Rico Amazon Parrots. The Peruvian Penguin, after declining for over a century along the coasts of Peru and Chile, lost more than half of its population to an aberration of El Niño in 1982/83, and the consequences of the most recent El Niño aberration, that of 1997/8, have yet to be assessed. This event caused floods in western deserts and then parched, burned, and finally flooded an enormous area of permanently wet rainforest in northeastern Amazonia. Up to 5,180 square kilometers (2,000 square miles) of tinder-dry forest in Central America may have been lost to fire. The effects of the 1998 El Niño on ocean life, and on species such as seabirds that depend on seafood, must also have been serious. Disasters such as these serve to remind us that pushing survival to the limits is a dreadful risk to take with so much of the world's wildlife at stake in the Neotropic region.

Sue Wells is the Marine Program Coordinator at WWF International, based in Switzerland. She has a zoology degree from Cambridge University. She previously worked at IUCN for ten years where, among other things, she compiled and edited the three-volume reference work *Coral Reefs of the World*. Prior to joining WWF, she worked freelance as a consultant on coral reef conservation for a number of organizations including IUCN, Greenpeace, the European Union and the Universities of Newcastle in the UK, and Rhode Island in the USA.

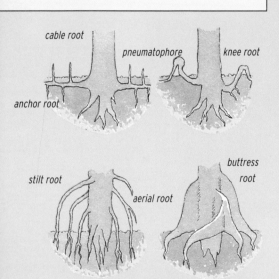

Above *Types of mangrove root.*

Right *Mudskippers are characteristic fish of mangroves. When the tide retreats they are able to survive in the muddy creeks, and some species even clamber among the trees. Out of water, they hold water and air in their gill chambers and also breathe through their skin and fins. They move by levering themselves forward on their pectoral fins. The different species have very differing diets, ranging from algae to crabs.*

Mangroves

Sometimes referred to as "forests of the sea," mangroves are marine tidal forests, growing in areas periodically flushed by salt- and freshwater. As well as black mangroves (*Avicennia*) and red mangroves (*Rhizophora*), these forests contain other bushes and trees such as the palm-like Nypa, creepers and vines, ferns, lichens, and even orchids.

The mangroves have special adaptations to help them survive in their harsh tidal environment. They grow best in sheltered areas where the waves and winds do not uproot seedlings, but their unusual root systems help them to cope with strong currents and tides. Shallow "cable" roots spread out over a wide area just below the surface of the mud, while smaller vertical roots descend deeper. The muddy soils lack oxygen but chimney-like roots protruding from the soil or descending from higher up the trunk are covered with pores through which oxygen can enter.

ANIMALS OF THE MANGROVE FOREST

Some 400 species of fish and many more invertebrates are dependent on mangroves for all or part of their life cycles. Other animals spend some time in the forest, feeding, roosting or breeding, particularly birds and reptiles. Fallen mangrove leaves are the basis of the food chain that supports all these animals. The leaves, partially broken down by fungi and bacteria, are an ideal food for small animals which in turn provide food for fish, birds and other vertebrates, including humans.

Enormous numbers of molluscs, such as oysters and ark shells, and crabs live in the mangroves, and are harvested by local people. But it is as a nursery habitat for prawns, shrimps, and fish that the forests are most important to commercial fisheries. The densities of fish and prawns may be up to an order of magnitude greater in mangroves than in other adjacent nearshore habitats.

Mangroves harbor reptiles and amphibians, although these are not generally dependent

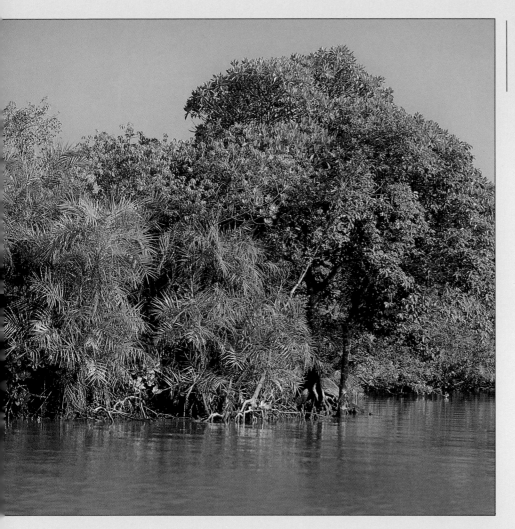

Left *Mangrove forest in the Sundarbans Tiger Reserve, West Bengal, India. Soil accumulates around the mangroves* (Bruguiera gymnorhiza) *eventually allowing other species such as the palm* (Phoenix paludosa) *to colonize.*

on them. The threatened and increasingly rare Mugger Crocodile and Estuarine Crocodile can be found in mangroves in Asia. Several turtles and terrapins, such as the endangered River Terrapin, known only from one river system in the Bangladesh Sundarbans, seek the shelter provided by mangroves.

A variety of birds use mangroves, such as the beautiful Scarlet Ibis and other migratory and resident waterfowl and waders, including herons, egrets, and spoonbills viewed by thousands of tourists at the Caroni Swamp in Trinidad. The threatened Mangrove Humming-bird is found only on the Caribbean coast of Costa Rica. The Masked Finfoot, a strange coot-like bird dependent on secluded streams in mangrove forests, and a stork, the Lesser Adjutant, are threatened throughout their southeast Asian ranges.

Rather few mammals are found in mangroves, but these are becoming of increasing concern as their habitat shrinks. While the Crab-eating Macaque *(Macaca fascicularis)* is still common throughout much of coastal South Asia, some populations are under threat. The Bengal Tiger, a subspecies of the Tiger, is found only in the Sundarbans mangroves and its presence there has ensured protection for these mangroves at least. Some estuarine and

Above *Often disparaged as swamps and wastelands, mangroves are among the richest habitats in the world. At the bottom of the food chain are fish and invertebrates, which in turn provide nourishment for birds and reptiles. Humans can either benefit from or destroy this interdependence.*

river dolphins spend time in the river and creek systems of mangroves, and populations of Ganges River Dolphin have been drastically reduced by the same dams and irrigation schemes that are damaging the mangroves of India and Bangladesh.

THREATS

Mangroves are now seriously at risk throughout much of their range. In developed countries, their destruction to build marinas, ports, factories, and houses is perhaps the major problem. In developing countries, where the major stands of mangroves remain, many factors contribute. One of the most damaging may be clearfelling for lumber and wood chips. For example, this is affecting about half the existing mangrove area in southeast Asia. In addition, uncontrolled exploitation of mangroves for firewood and charcoal is a widespread practice in southeast Asia, India, and Africa. Diversion of rivers or reduction in flow arising from irrigation schemes or dam construction is probably the second most serious threat. A drop in freshwater inflow has caused the decline of the commercial mangrove tree *Heritiera fomes* in the Ganges delta. In the Indus delta, the mangroves are sparse and stunted because dams upstream cut off fresh water for nine months of the year.

The biggest threat now is culture of shrimps which has affected vast areas. In some countries, shrimp farming has accounted for 20 per cent of the mangrove loss; in Asia about 40 per cent of shrimp farms have resulted in mangrove clearance. Such aquaculture is also often counter-productive. In Ecuador, nearly all the mangrove has been converted into shrimp ponds. This almost certainly caused the decline in wild shrimp larvae that has forced shrimp farmers to go to Peru in search of larvae to stock their ponds. Since the Peruvians are now also destroying their mangroves in order to start shrimp farms, the Ecuadorean farmers may have to set up expensive hatchery operations to produce the larvae. Similarly, the clearing of mangroves for agriculture, practiced in many parts of the world, is rarely successful in the long term. In the Rufiji delta in Tanzania, for example, the yield in areas converted to rice cultivation drops rapidly and farmers have to move on and clear new areas.

Mangroves are also vulnerable to pollution. Oil spills kill the trees by smothering the roots, and cause high mortalities in the molluscs attached to them. A year after a spill of more than 8 million liters (1.8 million gallons) of crude oil on the Caribbean coast of Panama in 1986, mangroves had died along 27 kilometers (17 miles) of coast, along with their associated invertebrates.

Exploitation of mangroves

The forests provide, for example:
- firewood and charcoal
- Nypa for roofing and shingles, and a sugar which can be converted into alcohol fuel for vehicles
- traditional medicines
- lumber for local houses and boats
- commercial lumber and wood chips
- molluscs, crustaceans and fish for food
- nursery grounds for commercial fisheries
- honey from wild bees
- protection of shorelines from erosion and storm damage

Above A boatload of mangrove wood cut for fuel in Brazil. The value of mangroves for fuel, lumber and the woodchip industry has led to overexploitation.

Right Mangroves are most luxuriant around the mouths of large rivers and in sheltered bays, in regions where rainfall is at least 1,500 millimeters (60 inches) a year and the temperature does not fall below 20° Centigrade (68° Fahrenheit). Mangroves cover about 180,000 square kilometers (69,500 square miles) worldwide. About 7,500 square kilometers (2,900 square miles) – or 4 per cent of the current total – has been lost in the last century, and probably one half of the original world cover has been lost altogether.

Distribution of mangroves

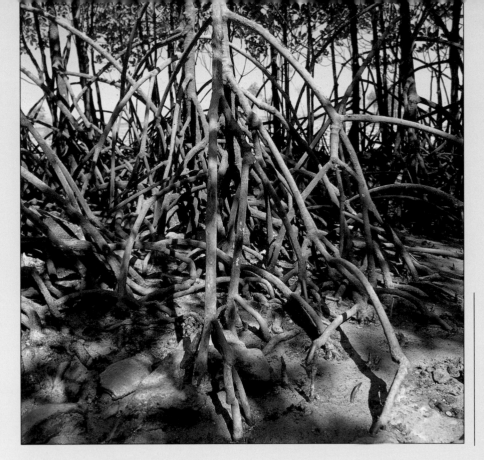

Left *Mangroves have evolved several different rooting systems to help support them in their unstable environment and to enable them to breathe. The* Rhizophora *species have stilt-like roots.*

Below *Mangrove seedlings are being planted in many countries, as here in Vietnam, either to encourage and speed recovery of damaged mangrove forest or even to recreate forest that has been totally destroyed.*

CONSERVATION

Although long viewed as wastelands, mangroves have an enormous commercial value and this provides a strong incentive for their wise management. In several countries, such as Thailand, Venezuela, and Malaysia, some of the large mangrove forests have been managed for many years, with trees cut in rotation and regeneration encouraged by the planting of seedlings. In Indonesia, mangroves are managed simultaneously for forestry and fishery by villagers under a system known as *tumpang-sari*.

In many developing countries, regulating the exploitation of mangroves is difficult because of their economic importance locally. Efforts are therefore being made to involve local people in management and to return to traditional systems of sustainable multiple use. Replanting schemes are being initiated in many countries. This can be done on mudflats, in abandoned aquaculture areas, and in degraded forests. An added incentive for reafforestation is the fact that mangroves stablize shorelines and protect them from erosion and storms. In India and Bangladesh, loss of life and property from cyclones has been found to be noticeably lower in the Ganges-Brahmaputra delta behind the mangroves than in the unprotected areas to the east and west. This role of mangroves will become increasingly significant if sea levels rise in response to global warming.

In most management schemes, the emphasis is on exploitation rather than protection, and over time, exploited mangroves may lose some of their associated wildlife. It is therefore very important to retain some areas of undisturbed mangroves. There are now about 625 parks and reserves that contain mangroves, one of the largest of which is the 100,000 hectares (250,000 acres) of mangrove in the Everglades National Park in Florida. Several of the most important mangroves are protected under the Convention on Wetlands of International Importance or Ramsar Convention, an international treaty which encourages countries to cooperate over issues such as the management of shared water systems.

The economic value of mangroves

■ Subsistence fisheries in the mangroves yield each year an estimated 9 tons per square kilometer (0.4 square mile).

■ Honey production in Florida's *Avicennia germanis* forest is estimated at 213–567 g (7½–20 ounces) per hectare (2½ acres).

■ In the Chanthaburi mangroves of Thailand, charcoal, fish and shrimp production bring in an estimated 160 dollars per hectare (2½ acres).

The Ethiopian Region

The Afro-tropical or Ethiopian region consists of Africa south of the Sahara, and Madagascar. From savannas and grasslands to tropical forests and from thorny thickets to deserts and glaciers, the main threat to this region is the fast growing human populations and their exploitation of the land for crops, live-stock and firewood.

African Elephant (Loxodonta africana)*, Tanzania.*

Habitat & Plants

Stephen Droop is a phycologist at the Royal Botanic Garden Edinburgh (RBGE), where he specializes in the systematics of diatoms. After training as a plant taxonomist, he worked at the IUCN Conservation Monitoring Centre, Kew, where he collected information on threatened plants and habitats of Africa and its associated islands. He contributed to IUCN's *Plants in Danger: What Do We Know?* and Anthony Huxley's *Green Inheritance*.

Michael Möller is a Research Associate at RBGE, where his work concerns the systematics and evolution of plants. Initially he was in the horticultural side and plant trade, but he became involved in the genetic aspects of plant development and evolution and has contributed to the molecular systematics of threatened southeast African and Madagascan plant species.

The vast herds of wildebeest, antelope, and zebra of the African savanna are world famous, yet the backdrop of grass and scattered trees that make up their habitat receives little attention. To take plants for granted is to be blind to an immense variety of form and lifestyle, and sheer breathtaking beauty. In addition, of course, the savanna herds – and virtually all the animals on our planet – are dependent on plants for the air they breathe and the food they eat.

As well as the familiar savannas and grasslands, Africa's habitats range from rain-drenched forests and impenetrable thickets to deserts and glaciers. Almost everywhere, the plants have found some way of making a living – until human actions led to the destruction of huge areas of Africa's wilderness. As the diversity of habitats is lost, so too are large numbers of the species living within them, many disappearing even before they have been discovered. The cause of much of this destruction is a lack of foresight on the part of developers, miners, and so on. But by far the largest losses are due to the use of the land for collecting firewood, grazing livestock and growing crops needed by the region's fast-growing human populations. And so the loss has been described as the tragedy without a villain.

The plants of Africa are well known compared with those in some other parts of the tropics, but most of the knowledge comes from collections made up to 250 years ago. Information is available on the present status of some groups of special interest to horti-culturists, and others such as succulents, bulbs, cycads, timber species and palms, and most

Right By 1967 the Socotran Fig (Dorstenia gigas) *was confined to an area inaccessible to goats on the island of Socotra. The particular cliff where it survived was also home to a number of other endangered plants. Socotra, which is part of the Yemen Republic, has been visited only rarely by botanists. When recently investigated it had 281 endemics, an enormous number, 34 of which are endangered.*

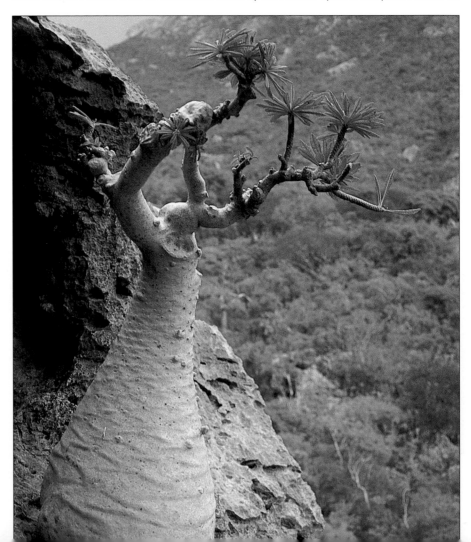

of the ericaceous species from South Africa. Others groups have been largely undersampled, and no one is really sure how well many of the rest of the plants are surviving in the face of such massive loss of habitat. In a recently finished compilation of threatened plants, the IUCN Red List catalogs 9.6 per cent of vascular plants in South Africa alone as threatened, with 53 species already extinct. In particular, little is known about the status or even the botany of the "lower" plants in tropical Africa.

We can get to know habitats better, since there are fewer of them and they are much bigger. Most scientists now agree that the key to species conservation is the protection of as wide a range of habitats as possible, on as large a scale as possible. If a habitat is protected, then so too are all the species that live within it – plants and animals – whether or not we know them all by name.

FOREST

The tropical rainforests of the world have received a lot of attention recently, and many people are now aware of the great diversity of life which exists within them. People are also aware of the pressing need to protect them, both to conserve species and to maintain the overall health of the planet and its weather systems.

The forests of tropical Africa are somewhat less rich in flora than their Amazonian counterparts, but nevertheless harbor an enormous variety of wildlife. There are two main areas where rainforests are the natural habitat: the huge Congo basin in central Africa around Gabon and Congo and extending into Cameroon, and a broad coastal band in west Africa extending from Ghana westward to Senegal. The central African forests are the more intact, being very much less accessible. The west African forests have almost completely disappeared as a result of indiscriminate logging and shifting agriculture, and most of what remains is in the Ivory Coast.

Below The bark of Prunus africana *contains chemicals which are used for certain ailments of the prostate gland. As a result, Europe imports huge amounts of bark and, without some kind of management program, this formerly common species could easily face rapid extinction.*

Below left Thonningia sanguinea *is a root parasite from the Cameroon. Because it is totally dependent on its host and cannot be cultivated, its survival is inextricably linked to that of its rainforest habitat.*

One species at risk is *Prunus africana.* Its bark contains chemicals which help in the treatment of certain ailments of the prostate gland. Huge quantities of bark are shipped to Europe each year, resulting in the death of thousands of trees. If the demand continues and no control is exercised, this formerly common species could soon face extinction.

Thonningia sanguinea is a root parasite found in the rainforests of Cameroon. It has no photosynthetic tissue of its own, and therefore is totally dependent on its host. If the forests go, so will this plant for it cannot survive in cultivation. Rainforest is also the home of *Strophanthus thollonii.* The chemicals it contains are used as an arrow poison in Cameroon, and as heart drugs in Western medicine. Its habitat is now threatened.

WOODLAND AND GRASSLAND

By far the greatest part of Africa south of the Sahara is occupied by deciduous woodland or grassland, either naturally or as a result of degradation of forest. The vegetation ranges from the moist *miombo* woodland covering huge parts of southern tropical Africa, to the very dry, near-desert steppes south of the Sahara. In between is a range of drier woodland types including the *mopane* woodland named after the dominant species, *Colphospermum mopane.* *Mopane* is the Bantu word for butterfly, and this tree's leaves look rather like butterflies.

Loss of habitat due mainly to population pressure and burning is so severe that widespread extinctions can be expected in the foreseeable future. There is no easy way to

Above Strophanthus thollonii *from korup forest in Cameroon has been found to contain cardiac glycosides used in Western heart drugs. However, it is doubtful whether its discovery will contribute to the economy of the Cameroon or the preservation of the forest where it was found.*

Right *Desertification in Africa commenced tens of thousands of years ago, but since the introduction of agriculture it has been steadily accelerating. The Sahara desert spread rapidly following the introduction of grain crops by the Romans, and elsewhere overgrazing by introduced cattle, sheep, and goats over the past 2,000 years has caused desertification. However, deserts and arid environments are not devoid of wildlife and many species are adapted to survive in these harsh habitats.*

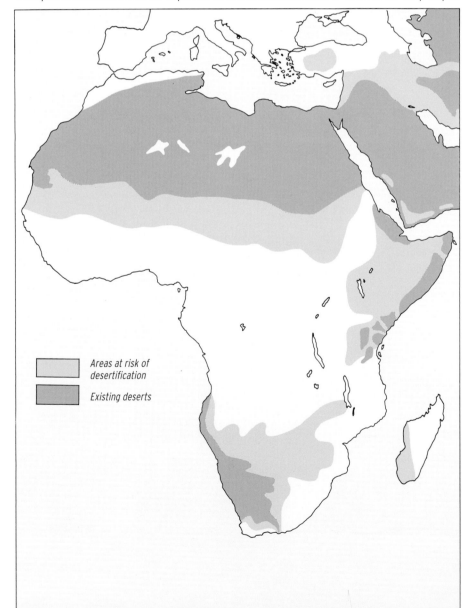

Areas at risk of desertification

Existing deserts

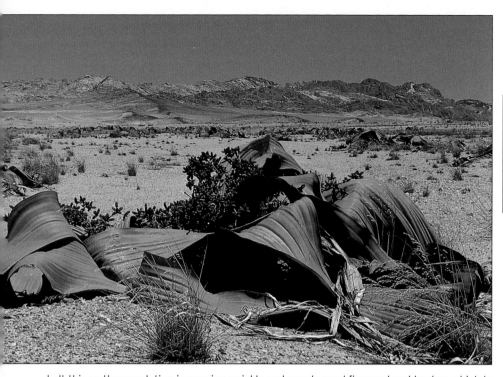

Left One of the oddest plants of all grows in the Namib desert – Welwitschia bainesii. *Its turnip-like stem can reach a width of over 1 meter (3¼ feet) but seldom projects more than a few centimeters above ground, while its tap root can be as deep as 20 meters (65 feet). The Welwitschia produces its first flowers after about 20 years and may live for over 1,000 years.*

halt this as the population is growing quickly and people need firewood and land on which to grow crops. Long-term investments and survival strategies mean nothing when you have to feed your family this week and next.

Among the species suffering is the African Blackwood, *Dalbergia melanoxylon*, highly sought after for making musical instruments. This tree is also very prone to fire, and so most of the specimens left are small, rather contorted – and of no use for clarinets.

DESERT

There are two main areas of desert or semidesert in mainland Africa apart from the great Sahara desert: parts of lowland Ethiopia and Somalia in the northeast, and the Namib and Kalahari deserts in the southwest.

The northeastern desert, which stretches across the Red Sea to the Arabian peninsula, is quite separate from the Sahara, and the plants it contains are related to those from tropical Africa rather than the Mediterranean. The vegetation is mostly deciduous bushland and thicket, with large areas of semidesert. Many of the species are succulents, and a good proportion are found nowhere else. The problem facing these plants is desertification and its associated climatic changes. The local population needs firewood and grazing for its flocks, and the resulting denudation and erosion lead to a change in the rainfall pattern and desert.

The Yeheb Nut, *Cordeauxia edulis*, is a valuable food crop in arid lands because of its ability to survive in very low-rainfall areas. Uncontrolled exploitation combined with habitat deterioration and overgrazing have reduced the plant to seriously low numbers in the wild. Trials are underway to cultivate it, but it remains to be seen if these will be successful. The Nubian Dragon Tree, a relative of Sisal, has been exploited, probably beyond redemption, for firewood and for its fibrous leaves which are woven into mats and baskets. The Socotran Pomegranate, *Punica protopunica*, was also thought to be on the verge of extinction; however, this may have been a case of incomplete recording or even recovery, as it is now known to grow in hundreds in several places on the island of Socotra off the Horn of Africa.

Right Senecio dendrosenecio. *There are several species of giant senecio growing near the tops of east Africa's highest peaks. Related to grounsels, they have huge rosettes of leaves at the ends of branches which help to protect its buds and stems from temperature extremes.*

Socotra

The island of Socotra off the horn of Africa has about 850 species of flowering plants, of which 281 are endemic, found nowhere else. Of these, 34 are believed to be threatened with extinction. However, a presumed extinct species, *Tavernieria sericophylla*, a leguminous plant, was re-discovered recently there. The climate is predominantly dry, and so many of the species are succulent. The main problem facing them seems to be overgrazing by introduced goats – a common problem on islands. Many of the rare plants only survive at all because they can grow on inaccessible cliffs.

The desert areas in the southwest cover much of Namibia and extend east to northern South Africa and Botswana. Their isolation from other areas of low rainfall means that many of their plants are unique. The largest single threat to the flora seems to be the same as that facing the South American pampas: huge areas of Botswana are being used for the ranching of cattle to supply the beefburger trade.

Parts of this region are so dry that they only receive rain once every 10 or 20 years. When rain does come the plants must make full use of it, resulting in the formation of single-age stands. One plant which continues to grow between the rains is *Welwitschia bainesii*. A relative of the conifers, it inhabits the Namib desert and is among the oddest plants in the world. It has no trunk to speak of, and bears only two leaves which keep on growing for hundreds of years. Although not in immediate danger, it is difficult to cultivate and so we could lose it if anything damaged or destroyed its desert home.

MOUNTAINS

The mountains in the west and south are of great botanical interest. But it is in the east that most of Africa's highest mountains occur, associated with a rift valley system created by great Earth movements over millions of years. The chain of high ground they form is almost like an archipelago of islands in the sea.

The climate on a mountain is so different from that of the surrounding lowlands that its species are as isolated as on an island, often not found anywhere else or only on other mountains. The combination of high altitude and low latitude means that the ground gets very hot during the day and very cold at night. The plants that have succeeded in adapting to this problem include several species of giant senecio *(Dendrosenecio)* growing near the top of east Africa's highest peaks. Huge rosettes of leaves at the ends of the branches, and a thick layer of decaying leaves over the rest of the plant protect the vulnerable buds and stem from temperature extremes. Other mountain plants have come up with different solutions, some so bizarre that plants like them are found virtually nowhere else on Earth with the exception of the Andes in South America.

Species on the upper slopes of mountains are relatively safe from human interference – except, perhaps, from overenthusiastic botanists! Unfortunately, the highest numbers of species are found on the lower slopes, where the montane habitats merge into lower-altitude woodlands and grasslands, and where species are subject to the pressures of human populations and habitat loss.

The very attractive Spiral Aloe, *Aloe polyphylla*, of the Drakensberg mountains in Lesotho has been decimated by uprooting for the horticulture trade. It is now officially protected, but will undoubtedly continue to suffer at the hands of poachers. This is particularly pointless since it almost never survives transplanting, and has to be grown from seed.

The well-known African Violets of the horticulture trade are all derived from *Saintpaulia ionantha* from Tanzania. This grows mainly on limestone cliffs shaded by dry evergreen forest; there are around 20 related species described, all of them vulnerable to habitat loss. The forests are threatened by encroaching agriculture, especially on the accessible lower slopes of mountains, and when these go, so too will the African Violets, leaving as their only memorial a multimillion dollar houseplant trade.

THE CAPE

The Cape of South Africa is rather like a florist's – only it is outdoors! It harbors an incredible number of species crammed into a small area, including 8,500 or so flowering plant species. This is nearly as many as can be found in the whole of Argentina, which is about 30 times as

Below *The Mulanje Cedar* (Widdringtonia cupressoides) *grows in South Africa as well as Malawi, but reaches its greatest size only on Mt. Mulanje, Malawi.*

Right The Giant Protea (Protea cynaroides) *has the largest flowerhead of the protea family – up to 30 centimeters (11 inches). It became South Africa's national emblem in 1976 – official endorsement for the growing public awareness of the country's unique flora.*

Far right Erica verticillata *is extinct in the wild, and is now found only in cultivation.*

extent of fynbos

Fynbos

The southernmost tip of Africa has one of the world's highest concentrations of plant species, with 8,550 vascular plant species, occupying an area of only 89,000 square kilometers (34,000 square miles). Of these plants, 73 per cent grow nowhere else.

The natural vegetation of most of the area is a type of scrub called *fynbos*. The area is highly populated and already about a third of all the fynbos has been destroyed. This has put many species at risk: 46 are already known to be extinct, another 214 are endangered, on the verge of extinction, and a further 1,473 have become rare or vulnerable. Scientists fear that the greatest numbers of plant species' extinctions could occur in this area.

large, or nearly five times as many as in Britain, which is nearly three times the size. About three-quarters of the Cape's flowering plants grow nowhere else.

Such richness is remarkable because the Cape does not contain any tropical forest habitat, where the highest levels of diversity are usually expected. Whereas most of Africa south of the Sahara has rain in the summer months, the summers in the southwest corner of Cape Province are very dry and windy and rain falls only in the winter. The main natural vegetation is *fynbos*, a shrubby habitat containing mainly plants with small, hard leaves, such as heathers and proteas, and also a lot of bulbs.

Unfortunately, the Cape is highly populated, and the natural vegetation is rapidly being eroded by agriculture and other development, and by the uncontrolled spread of alien species. Another problem is that many of the plants are very showy and so are attractive to the horticulture trade. The combination of high species diversity and high human population in the Cape has led scientists to predict that the greatest numbers of plant species' extinctions could occur there. Fifty-three of its species are already known to be extinct, with another 226 endangered.

Official endorsement for the growing public awareness of the Cape's unique flora came in 1976 when the Giant Protea, *Protea cynaroides*, became the country's national emblem. One of the most famous Cape species, it is a highly sought-after garden plant. In contrast, the Bluebearded Iris was only discovered in 1973, restricted to a small granite hill. It was nearly wiped out a few years later by a quarrying company, and dynamiting was stopped just in time to save the species. The shrub *Erica verticillata* was not so fortunate. Along with five other species it became extinct in the wild and is now found only in cultivation.

MADAGASCAR

Almost as amazing is the island of Madagascar with between 10,000 and 12,000 species of flowering plant, of which perhaps as many as 80 per cent grow nowhere else on Earth. It contains three main types of vegetation: rainforest in the east, dry deciduous forest in the west, and spiny thicket in the south of the island. Sadly only about one-fifth of the island's original vegetation survives, much of the remainder having been converted to a uniform grassland through slash-and-burn farming, especially on the central plateau. Very little rain-forest is now left in the east, although some of this is in good condition, where about three-quarters of Madagascar's plant species occur – or occurred.

The spiny thicket in the south must be one of the oddest-looking habitats in the world. Most of the plants are adapted to keep in as much water as they can, and have developed some very unusual shapes to achieve this. As with succulent species around the world, their unusual and attractive life forms have made them targets for the horticulture trade. This has, in some cases, been a threat to their continued existence in the wild. No plants or seeds may be exported without permission.

The recently discovered *Didierea trollii* is very rare in its spiny Madagascan home. The distinctive entire-leafed palm *Marojejya darianii*, discovered only in 1983, is one of the most sought-after palms in Madagascar. It may be close to extinction as it only occurs in one small population in the northeast of Madagascar, and is subject to the unrestricted collection of its seeds for the horticulture trade in California and Australia.

The Madagascan Periwinkle, commonly cultivated around the world, is known to produce about 70 chemicals of great medicinal value, including some used in treatments for cancer. Its close relative, *Catharanthus coriaceus*, is rare and locally endangered in the dry forests of Madagascar. Although it was first recorded as long ago as 1946, no one has collected enough material from it to assess its undoubted chemical and medicinal importance.

Wildlife

For many people, Africa is *the* wildlife continent, full of teeming herds of "big game." In fact, these occur mainly on the eastern and southern savannas, and spectacular as they are, form only a small fraction of the biological riches of this vast continent. Africa is a land of many parts, and each has its own complement of unique and distinctive species, as well as a share of the continent's more widespread fauna. Each of these parts is also subject to pressure from human activities, and the degree of this pressure is reflected in the status of the animals found there. In some areas, environmental destruction and disturbance are as yet so limited that most species are still relatively secure. In others, human impact has been far-reaching and a high proportion of the fauna is under some degree of threat, or (as in some Indian Ocean islands) has already been exterminated. Sadly, in most parts of the continent, the loss of natural habitats is proceeding at an ever-accelerating pace and the number of species being driven toward extinction is bound to increase. This is true even in apparently inhospitable areas, such as the Sahara desert and the high Ethiopian mountains.

THE SAHARA AND THE SAHEL

The great Sahara desert and the arid semidesert Sahel area to the south harbor some of the most critically endangered of all African animals, notably several species of desert antelope. The two largest, the spiral-horned Addax and the elegant Scimitar-horned Oryx, were formerly abundant in the dry steppe-lands of the Sahel, the oryx also occurring in semidesert regions north of the Sahara proper. But competition with domestic livestock, especially in periods of drought, progressive desertification, and hunting with rifles from desert-ranging vehicles have brought them both to the very brink of extinction in the wild. It is possible that a few Scimitar-horned Oryx survive in the vast Ouadi Rime-Ouadi Achim Reserve in Chad – a stronghold where conservation activities ceased in the late 1970s owing to civil disturbance – but even if they do, their long-term prospects are poor. Similarly, although a very few Addax are believed to persist in the Air and Ténéré region of Niger and possibly other inaccessible areas in Mali, Mauritania and Chad, it is unlikely that the population is viable. Fortunately both species breed well in captivity and reintroductions have begun within their former range, notably in Tunisia. Also reduced in numbers and range, although less imminently endangered, is the Dama Gazelle, the largest true gazelle. Several hundred survive in the wild, mainly in Chad, and the species breeds well in zoos.

Least known of all the desert antelopes is undoubtedly the Slender-horned Gazelle. This rarely seen species is the most desert-going of all the region's antelopes, and has specially adapted splayed hooves to enable it to walk over the soft desert sand without sinking into it. Its population density will be naturally low in such an inhospitable habitat, making it vulnerable to hunting and other pressures. However, living in some of the least visited parts of the whole African continent may also protect it to some extent from humans.

The mountain massifs of the Sahara are home to the Aoudad or Barbary Sheep. Despite its name, this animal is thought to be halfway between the sheep and the goat. It has been heavily hunted and suffers from competition with domestic sheep and goats, although the harshness of its terrain affords it a measure of protection.

Martin Jenkins worked at the World Conservation Monitoring Centre for ten years after graduating in zoology from Cambridge University. He co-authored Part 1 of the IUCN *Mammal Red Data Book*, and went on to produce an Environmental Profile of Madagascar, covering all aspects of its ecology and conservation. He has also worked on a variety of other topics, including the wildlife of the Sahel and Ethiopia, and the Pacific Ocean coral reefs. He is now a freelance writer and researcher in conservation and wildlife issues.

Below *Although superbly adapted to life in the desert and able to survive without drinking water, the Addax (Addax nasomaculatus) tires easily when pursued. People hunting with high velocity rifles from cars were easily able to kill them, and in the past half century have reduced herds numbering thousands to the brink of extinction.*

Spotlight

■ Scimitar-horned Oryx *(Oryx dammah)*. This oryx, once widespread, is now virtually extinct in the wild. A few dozen may survive in Chad.

■ Addax *(Addax nasomaculatus)*. It has been reduced from a population of tens of thousands spread across north Africa to a few dozen at most in Niger, and possibly scattered individuals elsewhere.

■ Dama Gazelle *(Gazella dama)*. Only a few hundred Dama survive, mainly in Niger and Chad, having declined drastically in the last few years.

■ Slender-horned Gazelle *(Gazella leptoceros)*. This is one of the least known of all antelope. Possibly only a few hundred survive in remote parts of the Sahara desert.

The Sahel is, paradoxically, inhabited by a distinctly un-desert like species. The vast inland delta of the Niger river in Mali in the heart of the Sahel harbors an important population of the wholly aquatic West African Manatee. This placid, sluggish creature also occurs in rivers through much of the rest of western Africa as far south as northern Angola. Reputed to make very good eating, it is widely hunted and its very low reproductive rate means that populations are slow to recover from overhunting. So despite still being widespread, it is vulnerable.

North of the Sahara desert is found one of the most threatened and, to many eyes, one of the ugliest of all birds, the Waldrapp or Northern Bald Ibix. Once widespread in central Europe, North Africa and the Middle East, the population has plummeted, for reasons that are

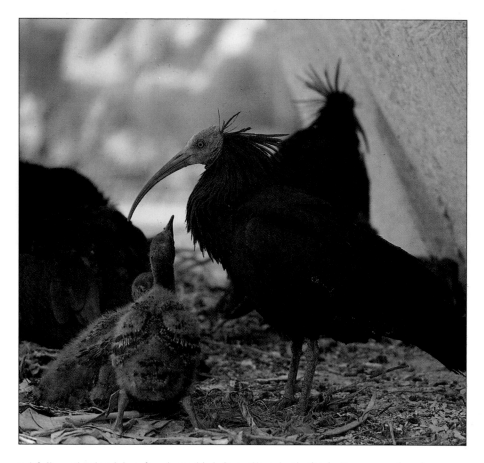

Right *The Bald Ibix* (Geronticus eremita) *is now virtually extinct. However, captive breeding seems to be successful and may save the species.*

not fully understood, to a few dozen birds in scattered colonies in Morocco and perhaps one or two in Algeria. The decline is apparently continuing, and the only real hope for the survival of the species seems to rest with captive breeding, which has luckily proved uncomplicated.

THE ETHIOPIAN HIGHLANDS

This is by far the largest high montane area in Africa, with some of the most spectacular scenery anywhere in the world. The mountains support a rich and varied wildlife, much of which is found nowhere else. They also support an ever-growing human population, and each year people clear more and more of the mid-altitude forest for cultivation and firewood, and graze increasing numbers of livestock in the high alpine moorlands and grasslands. The resultant erosion and progressive shrinkage of habitat threatens species whose entire world range is already perilously small. One of the most spectacular and rarest of these is the Walia Ibex, which leads a precipitous existence on some of the steepest and highest crags of the Simēn mountains, north of the great Rift valley.

Formerly quite widespread, the Walia Ibex has been drastically reduced over the past century by hunting and human encroachment on its habitat. It is now confined to a mere 30-kilometer (19-mile) stretch of cliffs at around 3,000 meters (9,000 feet) where it numbers perhaps 300–500 individuals. The entire range of the Walia lies within the Simēn National Park, which should theoretically help safeguard its future. Indeed, by the late 1970s, poaching and habitat destruction in the park had been brought under control and prospects seemed good. However, the prolonged civil war in the region led to the cessation of conservation activities and to serious concerns for the species' future. Fortunately it seems to have survived remarkably unscathed.

The Walia shares its range with the world's most terrestrial monkey, the shaggy, herbivorous Gelada Baboon. Similarly confined to mountains north of the Rift valley, the Gelada is much more widespread and abundant than the Walia, and is not considered immediately endangered. But it, too, suffers from progressive encroachment of its habitat by human settlers and is certainly declining in numbers.

The Simēn mountains have given their name to what is almost certainly the rarest living member of the dog family, the Ethiopian Wolf or Simēn Jackal. This stocky, tawny-colored animal lives in the high-altitude moorlands and grasslands where it feeds mainly on small mammals, in particular the abundant molerats of the family Spalacidae, several of which are themselves endemic to Ethiopia. As well as occurring in the Simēn mountains, the Ethiopian Wolf is found in the much smaller Bale mountains in the southeast of the highland region. The species is believed to number fewer than 400 individuals and the population is slowly but inexorably declining. However, the wolf derives some benefit from the fact that 2,200 square kilometers (850 square miles) of the Bale mountains are protected in a national park. This park is also home to virtually the entire world population of the Mountain Nyala, one of the most attractive of African antelopes. It holds the distinction of being the most recent large African mammal to be made known to science, having been described only in 1919. Although locally common and not apparently declining rapidly in numbers, its total world population and range are very small for such a large animal, and as a result, it must be considered permanently under threat.

The Ethiopian highlands are inhabited by around 30 endemic bird species. Fortunately most are widespread and not considered threatened at present, but some have a very limited range and are definitely at risk. For ornithologists, the most remarkable is certainly the Ethiopian Bush Crow, a species not discovered until 1938. It has proven almost impossible to classify – it may be related to the crows, the starlings or neither. Whatever its affinities, it is known to be confined to a very small area of about 6,000 square kilometers (2,300 square miles) in southern Ethiopia. Although none of its habitat is formally protected, this bird does not appear to be under immediate threat. The situation may be worse for another restricted species, Prince Ruspoli's Turaco. This also occurs in southern Ethiopia in a few scattered

Below left A male Gelada Baboon (Theropithecus gelada). *This baboon is confined to northeast Africa at altitudes of up to 5,000 meters (16,500 feet) where it lives in gorges, alpine meadows and other largely treeless areas. An old male leads the troops, which sometimes gather into packs of up to 600.*

Below The Walia Ibex (Capra walie) *is found only in the Simēn mountains of Ethiopia at altitudes of 2,500–4,500 meters (7,600–13,000 feet). Reduced to perhaps 300-500 individuals, its future is precarious.*

localities in juniper forests (at around 1,800 meters/5,900 feet), which were largely undisturbed until recently. It now appears that these forests are being cleared rapidly by settlers from drought-affected parts of Ethiopia, and their future, and the Turaco's, looks far from secure.

THE SOMALI-MASAI

Apart from the Ethiopian highlands, most of the Horn of Africa is taken up by an area known as the Somali-Masai which includes much of lowland Ethiopia, all of Djibouti and Somalia, and northern Kenya. The area supports a large number of arid land species, including a wide diversity of antelopes. Least known, and almost certainly one of the rarest, is the diminutive, rock-haunting Beira of the hills of northern Somalia and adjacent Ethiopia. It is very seldom recorded and its total world population remains unknown but is undoubtedly small. This species is believed to have declined as a result of drought and competition for food with domestic livestock, particularly goats. An antelope which is definitely known to have decreased in number and is now thought to be seriously endangered is the Hirola or Hunter's Antelope. In the late 1970s there were an estimated 18,000 surviving in a small range on the Somali–Kenya border, while recent surveys could find no more than 350. If this alarming decline continues, the species will soon become extinct. Grevy's Zebra is rather more widespread, but is still declining rapidly in numbers. The most elegant of all the zebras, it has suffered markedly from droughts, competition for grazing with domestic livestock and, formerly, hunting for its beautiful skin. Unlike Hunter's Antelope, which does not occur in any protected area, Grevy's

Below Grevy's Zebra (Equus grevyi) *in the Samburu, northern Kenya. This zebra is thought to have particularly attractive striping, and so it has been hunted for its hide. There may be as few as 15,000 left in the wild.*

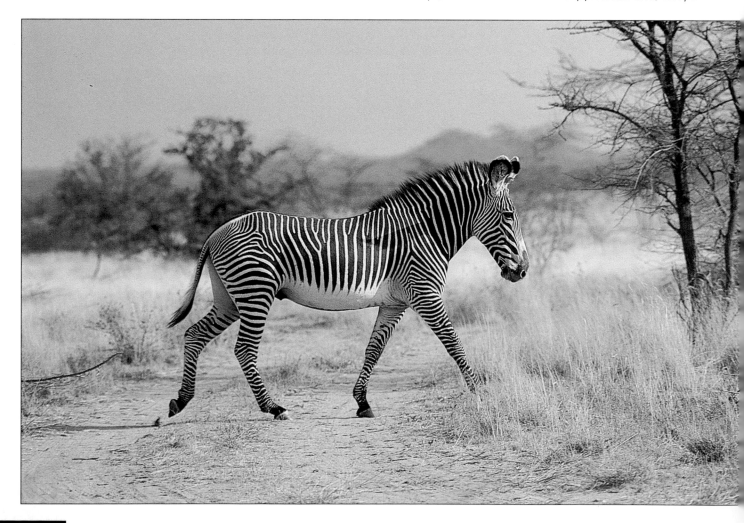

Zebra is found in at least one game reserve, Samburu in northern Kenya, but is still regarded as seriously threatened. Closely related to Grevy's Zebra, and at least as endangered, is the African Wild Ass. Once widespread in the Somali-Masai and Sahel, it is now confined to northern Ethiopia and possibly Sudan. Less immediately endangered, but nevertheless still threatened, are Speke's Gazelle and the Dibatag or Clarke's Gazelle. The former is confined to coastal lowland Somalia and northeastern Ethiopia, and, although still locally common, is declining rapidly. The elegant, long-necked Dibatag is mainly found in the low-lying Ogaden region of eastern Ethiopia and adjacent Somalia. Its overall population remains unknown, but it is undoubtedly rare and decreasing in number.

Several bird species are also confined to the Somali-Masai. The most threatened of these is the Djibouti Francolin, restricted to two small areas of juniper forest in Djibouti. These forests are being cleared for firewood and pasture at such a rate that they, and the francolin, are likely to disappear in a very few years unless action is soon taken.

THE WEST AFRICAN RAINFORESTS

Rainforests are the richest habitats on Earth, with an astonishing variety of animal and plant species. The African rainforests are no exception, although they generally have slightly fewer species than equivalent areas in South America and Asia. There are two major blocks: the vast central African forests and the much less extensive west African forests, now largely confined to the Ivory Coast, Liberia, Guinea, and Sierra Leone. The two blocks have many species in common, and each also has its own complement of unique plants and animals.

Many of the west African species are considered threatened to some degree, mainly because the forests themselves are seriously threatened. A large and growing human population has cleared so much forest for logging, agriculture, and mining that undisturbed rainforest now only occupies a tiny, and decreasing, fraction of the area it once covered. While some rainforest species can survive in disturbed or logged-over habitats, others seem dependent on primary or virtually undisturbed forests. Moreover, forest animals are a major source of protein in most west African countries and many species are under intense hunting pressure.

One of the most sought-after animals is the Pygmy Hippopotamus. This retiring, pig-sized cousin of the widespread Hippopotamus is found near water-courses and lakes in lowland rainforest. Its solitary habits and secretive nature make it very hard to estimate numbers, but it is thought that several thousand still survive. However, Pygmy Hippo populations invariably decline as human population levels rise and it is undoubtedly becoming rarer.

Scarcer and less well known even than the Pygmy Hippo is the strikingly colored gray and chestnut Jentink's Duiker, one of the largest of this widespread genus of forest antelopes. Previously only known from a few specimens in Liberia and the Ivory Coast, it has recently been discovered on the Freetown peninsula in Sierra Leone. There, as elsewhere in its range, it is hunted for its meat and skin, and it is unclear how long populations will be able to survive. Also under threat, although apparently rather more numerous at present, is the closely related but smaller Zebra Duiker. The Liberian Mongoose, the least known of all mongooses, occupies a range very similar to these two antelopes. A specialist feeder on earthworms, it is also intensively hunted for its meat and is reported by villagers to be declining in numbers.

Relatively few primates are confined to these forests, exceptions being the attractive Diana Monkey and the Olive Colobus. Both are subject to the twin threats of hunting and habitat loss, but appear more resistant to these than many of the larger terrestrial mammals.

Above *Hunter's Antelope* (Damaliscus hunteri) *is confined to a 100-kilometer (60-mile) wide strip north of the Tana River, Kenya, where it is declining due to competition from cattle.*

So, although both give cause for concern, neither is regarded as imminently endangered.

Several threatened bird species are confined to these forests, including the little-known Rufous Fishing-owl *(Scotopelia ussheri)*, the White-breasted Guineafowl *(Agelastes meleagrides)* and the Gola Malimbe *(Malimbus ballmanni)*. Fortunately, populations of much of the threatened fauna of the west African rainforests are present in protected areas. Most notable of these are the Tai National Park in the Ivory Coast, and the Sapo National Park in Liberia. Both parks are, however, subject to encroachment and poaching, and whether they will be adequate to conserve populations in the long term remains to be seen.

THE CENTRAL AFRICAN RAINFORESTS

These are far more extensive than the west African rainforests and are under less immediate threat. Many of their inhabitants are still widespread and relatively abundant, and are considered reasonably secure, at least in the short or medium term. There are, however, notable exceptions to this, including several primates. The most endangered is probably the Drill, an imposing, gregarious relative of the baboons. This species occupies a small range in lowland rainforest in Cameroon, extreme southeastern Nigeria, the island of Bioko and possibly part of Gabon. It is hunted extensively for its meat and as a crop pest, and its noisy and social nature make it easy for hunters to track groups down and kill large numbers at once. In addition, the forests it depends on are being rapidly cleared. The only protected population is that in Korup National Park in Cameroon, and it is not known whether the numbers there are large enough to enable the species to survive in the long term.

Closely related to the Drill is the Mandrill, the males of which are among the most flamboyant of all monkeys, with multicolored faces and hindquarters. Although it is subject to the same threats as the Drill and is declining rapidly in numbers, it is regarded as less immediately threatened. The Mandrill occupies a range to the south of the Drill's and is rather more widespread. Occupying a similar range to the Mandrill is the highly arboreal Black Colobus. This species was regarded as rare in much of its range as long ago as the 1930s, and appears to be especially vulnerable because it reportedly cannot survive in disturbed or logged-over forests.

The forests of Cameroon and neighboring Nigeria and Gabon are very important for bird species. The mountain forests of the Cameroon highlands, for example, harbor no fewer than 22 species found nowhere else, seven of which are definitely threatened with extinction. Most

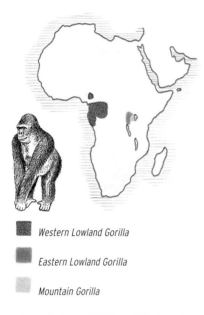

DISTRIBUTION
GORILLA

■ Western Lowland Gorilla

■ Eastern Lowland Gorilla

■ Mountain Gorilla

Gorilla (Gorilla gorilla). Three distinct populations survive. The western lowland form is still relatively abundant, numbering around 100,000; the eastern lowland form is much rarer with only 10,000 surviving; and the highland race is rarer still with a population of around 400 in the central African highlands.

Right *A Pygmy Hippopotamus (Choeropsis liberiensis) with its young. They are normally solitary and nocturnal, and are found in wet forests and swamps in a small area of west Africa. They have probably always been thinly populated, but are becoming increasingly rare due to hunting and destruction of their habitat.*

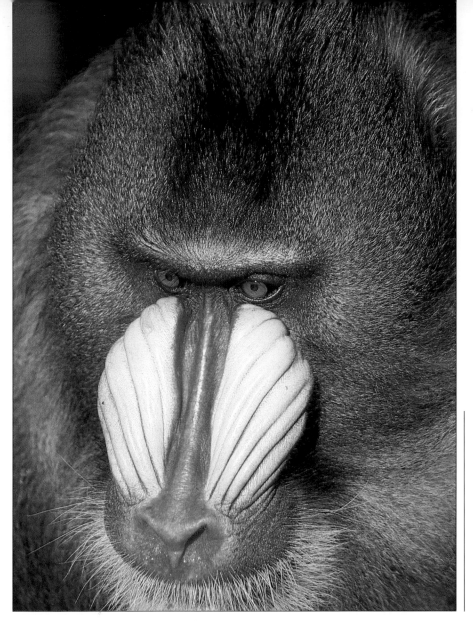

Left Only the male Mandrill (Mandrillus sphinx) has the spectacular facial coloration. These monkeys live in groups of up to 250, each of which ranges over an area of 5,000 hectares (12,400 acres). Due to extensive hunting and trapping, they are now among the rarest monkeys in Africa.

Below The White-necked Picathartes (Picathartes gymnocephalus) nests in small colonies in rock clefts and caves. It is confined to forests in west Africa where it is seriously threatened by habitat destruction. In the past it was collected extensively for exhibition in zoos.

mysterious, and undoubtedly the rarest, is the Mount Kupe Bush-shrike. Known only from Mount Kupe, it had not been seen since 1951 until rediscovered in 1989. The remnant forest in which it occurs is now the subject of a major conservation program. Two other highly threatened species are the Banded Wattle-eye and Bannerman's Turaco. Both these birds are likely to disappear unless the last few remnants of their forest home on Mount Oku in the Bamenda highlands are preserved.

Also giving cause for concern is the extraordinary, bare-headed Gray-necked Rockfowl or Picathartes, an inhabitant of lowland rainforests of southern Cameroon and northeast Gabon. Like the similarly threatened west African White-necked Picathartes, the bird has very precise habitat requirements – caves and rocky cliffs under a rainforest canopy. This makes it naturally rare and particularly vulnerable to habitat destruction. These forests are also home to the world's largest frog, the Goliath Frog, which is avidly hunted for food and considered vulnerable.

Further east lie the forests of the great Zaire river basin and the eastern Zaire highlands. Notable species found here include the remarkable, velvet-skinned Okapi. This close relative of the Giraffe was first discovered by Westerners only in 1900. It is not regarded as immediately endangered, but it has a relatively limited range in eastern Zaire, occurring particularly in the Ituri forest east of the Zaire river. Similarly confined to Zaire is the Dwarf Chimpanzee or Bonobo. Although extensive tracts of forest persist within its range, Bonobo populations seem to be very scattered and it is absent from many apparently suitable areas. No sizable population is protected in a national park or reserve at present.

The most noteworthy avian inhabitant of these forests is undoubtedly the Congo Peacock. The only true pheasant found in Africa, this spectacular bird was not described until the 1930s. Like the Dwarf Chimpanzee, it occurs over a wide area but is nowhere common. It is extensively hunted and seems to have disappeared from the vicinity of most villages and settlements within its range.

Two of the Dwarf Chimpanzee's larger and better-known relatives are considered under some degree of threat, despite both being still widespread and relatively numerous. These are the Gorilla, largest of all primates, and the Chimpanzee. Three separate populations of Gorilla exist, all within the general area of the central African rainforests. The western population is the most abundant, with perhaps as many as 100,000 surviving, the majority in Gabon. A population estimated at 10,000 inhabits lowland eastern Zaire, where it is highly threatened by forest clearance. Then a further 300–400 are found in the Virunga volcano region of Rwanda and Zaire and in the Bwindi forest in Uganda: these are Mountain Gorillas – their population is fairly stable at present but a few are lost to poaching, and both they and their habitat will have to be subject to constant vigilance if they are to survive.

The Chimpanzee is probably somewhat more abundant than the Gorilla, with between 100,000 and 200,000 surviving. It ranges through the west African forests as well as much of the central African rainforests, and is also found in a variety of more open, wooded habitats. It remains under threat, however, from hunting for food and habitat loss. In west Africa it also suffers from hunting for export, particularly for biomedical research, although this has decreased considerably in recent years.

Also found in both the west African and central African forests is one of the smallest of

Below *An old male Chimpanzee (Pan troglodytes) photographed in Liberia. In addition to loss of habitat, Chimpanzees have been seriously threatened by the trade for biomedical research. Captive breeding programs are now partially satisfying this demand.*

crocodilians, the African Dwarf Crocodile. This inoffensive reptile has been heavily hunted for its hide and has declined in many parts of its range, although reasonable populations may survive in remote areas. The African Giant Swallowtail Butterfly has not been persecuted but appears to be naturally rare throughout its range in central and west Africa, and to be vulnerable to loss of its forest habitat.

THE EAST AFRICAN FORESTS

While less rich than the rainforests further west, the forests of Kenya and Tanzania – particularly those of the Kenyan coast and those on the scattered low mountain ranges of Tanzania – support a number of rare and localized species, especially birds. Six threatened bird species occur in the 100-square kilometer (40-square mile) Sokoke forest in Kenya, and one of these, Clarke's Weaver, is found nowhere else. The forest is under considerable pressure from logging and firewood collection but is now the focus of a long-term conservation and development project. Two other threatened species there, the Amani Sunbird and the Sokoke Scops Owl, are slightly more secure since they also occur in a similar-sized area of forest in the East Usambara mountains, some 320 kilometers (200 miles) south of Sokoke. However, this forest, which supports several other threatened birds, is also shrinking and is in urgent need of increased conservation efforts.

A reptile causing concern is the appropriately named Pancake Tortoise which looks as if it has been flattened by a steamroller. A small rock-dwelling tortoise, it is less dependent on the forests than the birds, but it has been seriously affected by collection for the pet trade and is generally rare, with no population known to be protected in a national park or reserve.

SOUTHERN AFRICA

The varied habitats of southern Africa support an equally varied assemblage of species, many of them unique to the area. Much of the area has been heavily settled for many years and some habitats have been drastically reduced in extent by intensive agriculture and urbanization. The only two large mammals to have become extinct in sub-Saharan Africa in

Above left A captive Broadfronted or African Dwarf Crocodile (Osteolaemus tetraspis). *Little is known about the status of this species in the wild, but small numbers are being bred in captivity.*

Above The Pancake Tortoise (Malachochersus tournieri) *lives in rocky areas of southern Kenya and northeast Tanzania. It is a slow breeder, laying a single egg once or twice a year.*

Spotlight

■ Drill *(Mandrillus leucophaeus)*. The total population is unknown, but it is certainly declining rapidly in its small range of less than 10,000 square kilometers (3,900 square miles) in western central Africa.

■ Okapi *(Okapia johnstoni)*. A few thousand Okapis survive in a small area of the eastern Zairean rainforests, where they remain at risk from habitat destruction.

■ Congo Peacock *(Afropavo conogensis)*. This pheasant is widely but patchily distributed in the Zairean rainforest. Its total numbers are unknown, but it has certainly become progressively rarer over the past few decades.

Right *The Brown Hyena* (Hyaena brunnea) *is confined to southern Africa. It is extinct over much of the Cape, but is still widespread in Botswana and Namibia, particularly in the Kalahari and Gemsbok National Parks.*

Far right *A Black Rhinoceros* (Diceros bicornis) *in Amboseli National Park. In the 1950s this animal was still found over most suitable habitats in Africa south of the Sahara. By the 1970s poaching had reduced its population to about 30,000, and by the late 1980s there were possibly less than 5,000.*

DISTRIBUTION
AFRICAN ELEPHANT

Probable range 1600

Range in 1995

African Elephant (Loxodonta africana). *An original population of several million had been reduced to just over 1,200,000 by the early 1980s and now stands at under 500,000.*

the past 200 years – the Quagga and Blaubok – lived in this area. The last surviving Quagga, a partially striped zebra, died in the Amsterdam Zoo in 1874. The Blaubok, an antelope of the veld region of Cape Province in South Africa, was exterminated around 1800. In more recent times, concerted conservation efforts have prevented several other species following suit.

The Mountain Zebra of Namibia, southern Angola and the southern part of Cape Province in South Africa at one time looked likely to suffer the same fate as its cousin, the Quagga. It was ruthlessly persecuted by farmers as an alleged competitor with livestock, and the population plummeted from an estimated 50,000–70,000 in the early 1950s to fewer than 7,000 by the late 1960s. Most of these are now protected in game reserves and national parks, and the population is relatively stable. Also unjustly persecuted, this time as a stock-killer, is the carrion-eating Brown Hyena, an inhabitant of the arid semidesert parts of southern Africa. Like the Mountain Zebra, reasonable numbers of Brown Hyenas are protected in national parks and reserves, but outside these areas it has become very scarce. In 1882 the southern White Rhinoceros was believed to be extinct, but then a small population was found in Zululand. Breeding and translocation have increased their numbers to about 7,000, which are now well protected in a number of areas in southern Africa. In addition to this relatively stable southern population, the last vestiges of a once-common northern population cling on in Garamba National Park in northern Zaire, but their prospects are poor. There are probably no White Rinoceros outside protected areas or zoos.

Some southern African species are particularly threatened by habitat destruction in their already tiny ranges. This is the case for the Giant Golden Mole, confined to small and rapidly disappearing forest patches in eastern Cape Province. Similarly the tiny, star-patterned Geometric Tortoise has had its range reduced by an estimated 90 per cent to a few square miles in southwest Cape Province, and numbers at most a few thousand individuals. The Cape Platana Frog is found in the same area and has been similarly depleted as the ponds it inhabits have been polluted or drained for building and farmland. The only known protected populations are in three small ponds in the Cape of Good Hope Nature Reserve.

WIDESPREAD SPECIES

Some of the best known of all African threatened species have ranges which span – or spanned – a large proportion of the continent. Many of these suffer primarily from persecution by people. The Black Rhinoceros is perhaps the most notable example. Formerly widespread in woodlands and savannas in sub-Saharan Africa, the population has plunged from an estimated 20,000–30,000 in the early 1970s to around 2,400 today. This decline can be virtually entirely ascribed to poaching for the rhino's horn, which is used in medicine in the Far East and for dagger handles in Yemen. The only hope of halting the decline lies in the vigorous protection of the last few viable populations, such as that in the Zambesi valley in Zimbabwe.

Although the African Elephant is still far more numerous and widespread than the Black Rhino, it is evidently declining at almost as fast a rate. It is notoriously difficult to count elephants, particularly those in the dense central and west African rainforests, but the best estimates indicate that the population has dropped from around 1,200,000 in 1981 to around 500,000 today. A major cause of this has been hunting for ivory. Also, as more land is converted to agriculture, elephants inevitably destroy crops in their constant search for food, bringing them into conflict with people. The long-term survival of elephants outside a few well-protected reserves will depend not only on maintaining control of the ivory trade, but also on the full involvement of local people in management plans.

Never abundant, and apparently declining as rapidly as the elephant and Black Rhinoceros, is the nomadic African Hunting Dog. It was previously found in open plains and savannas in most of sub-Saharan Africa, but has died out in much of its former range. This is largely due to its persecution as an alleged predator of livestock, and diseases, such as

DISTRIBUTION
BLACK RHINO

Range in 1700

Range in 1995

Range of the Black Rhinoceros (Diceros bicornis). Fewer than 2,400 now exist compared with at least 25,000 in the early 1970s.

canine distemper, anthrax and rabies, to which it appears to be particularly susceptible. Conservation of this species is problematic because few existing protected areas are large enough to hold viable populations. The Cheetah is less threatened than the Hunting Dog but is still declining in many areas. Like the Hunting Dog, this cat requires very large areas of suitable habitat if it is to thrive.

Africa's expanses of wetlands, such as the vast Sudd swampland in southern Sudan and the inland Okavango delta in Botswana, support a number of distinctive species which will become increasingly threatened as these areas are drained and developed. One of the most aquatic of all antelope, the Lechwe, is found in marshes and floodplains in southern central Africa, mostly in Zambia and Botswana. It has been heavily hunted and some populations have been badly affected by hydroelectric schemes. The striking Wattled Crane occupies much the same range as the Lechwe, with an outlying population far north of this, in Ethiopia. The population densities of this bird are always very low and it appears to be particularly susceptible to disturbance, so it is likely to be threatened by any development of its habitat. The same is true of one of the most extraordinary of all birds, the Shoebill Stork, which inhabits marshes and swamps from Sudan and Ethiopia south to Zambia.

MADAGASCAR

Although it is included in the Afrotropical realm, Madagascar truly is a world apart. This enormous island, roughly the size of France, has been separated from the mainland for at least 100 million years, allowing a unique flora and fauna to evolve. Such is the richness and diversity of wildlife on the island that it has been described as a paradise for naturalists. Sadly it is a paradise very much under threat as its forests are being destroyed at a terrifying rate, mostly for slash-and-burn cultivation, and to produce pasture for cattle in the west and on the central highlands.

The best known of all Madagascar's animals are surely the lemurs, a group of primates which evolved on the island. They are found nowhere else in the world, except for the nearby Comoro islands where the highly threatened Mongoose Lemur and the commoner Brown Lemur occur. These two species were almost certainly introduced to the Comoros by people some time in the past few hundred years. When humans first arrived on Madagascar, between

DISTRIBUTION
MADAGASCAN FORESTS

Original extent

Extent in 1995

Madagascar

■ Of the island's 106 endemic breeding birds, 27 are threatened with extinction and one is extinct.

■ It has 30 surviving lemur species, of which 28 are found only on Madagascar, the other two also occurring on the Comoros. Eight species are currently considered endangered or critically endangered, and over half of all species are considered threatened.

■ Madagascar is home to 260 reptiles, including two-thirds of the world's chameleons. Around 90 per cent of the reptiles are endemic and among these are four threatened tortoises, including the rare Angonoka (Geochelone yniphora).

1,500 and 2,000 years ago, there were at least 45 species of lemur. The largest, *Megaladapis edwardsi*, was roughly the size of an adult male Orang Utan. This and 14 other species of lemur, including all the largest ones, are now extinct. Some of the remaining 30 or so species are hanging on so precariously that it is unlikely to be long before they follow their larger cousins.

One of the more threatened is the largest surviving lemur, the Indri. This splendid beast looks like a cross between a gibbon and a piebald teddy bear. Like all Madagascar's forest species, its habitat is inexorably shrinking, and it is now confined to a stretch of around 500 kilometers (300 miles) of the north and central eastern rainforests of Madagascar – a much smaller area than it was found in even a few decades ago. In addition it has a slow reproductive rate, with females not breeding until they are at least seven years old. Its large size and diurnal habitats make it very vulnerable to hunting – although fortunately in many areas Indris are protected by local taboos as they are thought to represent the ghosts of departed ancestors.

In contrast, the extraordinary Aye-aye, with its pop eyes, shaggy coat, rodent-like teeth, long, bony fingers, and nocturnal habits, is often regarded by the Malagasy people with suspicion. In some areas it is considered a harbinger of evil and is killed on sight. This, and the infrequency with which it was recorded, led many people to conclude that it was on the very brink of extinction. So in 1966/67, nine Aye-ayes were released on the island of Nosy Mangabe, off the eastern coast of Madagascar, in a last-ditch attempt to save the species. Although Aye-ayes certainly still survive on this island, in fact the species is now known to be much more widely distributed on the Madagascan mainland than was previously thought. They are extremely elusive, and certainly not common anywhere, but may be no more threatened than many other Madagascan species. Similarly the Hairy-eared Dwarf Lemur may be commoner than has been thought. This diminutive creature had not been seen since the 1960s until 1989, when a population was discovered in northeast Madagascar near the original collecting site. Its size and arboreal habits mean that it is easy to overlook.

Two species which are definitely threatened are the Greater Bamboo Lemur and the recently discovered Golden Bamboo Lemur. As their names suggest, both species are specialized feeders on bamboo and are apparently confined to the same small area of

DISTRIBUTION
AFRICAN WILD DOG

☐ *Former distribution*

☐ *Current distribution*

Range of the African Wild Dog (Lycaon pictus). Total numbers are unknown but there are probably no more than a couple of thousand, and it is thought likely that this dog will become extinct in 20–30 years if present trends continue.

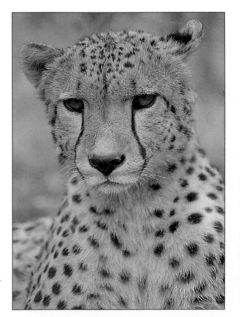

Opposite *A pack of Hunting Dogs (Lycaon pictus), each one of which has its own unique pattern and coloring. Earlier this century they were killed as vermin even in national parks and game reserves. They are now one of the most endangered mammals in Africa.*

Far left *The Cheetah (Acinonyx jubatus) once occurred in the more open habitats of eastern and southern Africa, and in southern Asia. Its range is now fragmented and it is only numerous in Namibia and a few areas of adjacent South Africa.*

Left *The Mongoose Lemur (Lemur mongoz) inhabits a wide variety of mostly forested habitats on Madagascar, where it is declining with the destruction of the forests. It also occurs on the Comoro islands.*

Right *The Aldabra Tortoise* (Geochelone gigantea) *is restricted to the atoll of Aldabra in the Indian Ocean. Although they number well over 150,000 at present, their dependence on a single island leaves them vulnerable to both human-made and natural disasters.*

Below *The Madagascar Tree Boa* (Sanzinia madagascariensis). *Like the majority of the island's fauna, this snake is only found there. It lives in trees, where it is particularly well camouflaged.*

southeastern Madagascar, although there are unconfirmed reports of the former much further north around Maroantsetra. Both species occur in the 31,000-hectare (76,000-acre) Andringira Nature Reserve and the recently established 41,600-hectare (102,800-acre) Ranomafana National Park, where the population of each is estimated at around 1,000. The latter also offers a refuge to a variety of other threatened lemurs, including the beautiful Diademed Sifaka, the Red-bellied Lemur and the striking Ruffed Lemur. The Fossa, the largest of Madagascar's unique carnivores, is also found there.

Madagascar's 250 or so bird species include over 100 that are unique to the island. Unfortunately, at least 30 birds are currently considered threatened, some of them seriously so. In addition, the Snail-eating Coua, a relative of the Cuckoos, is almost certainly extinct, having last been seen in 1834 on the island of Nosy Borah off the eastern coast of Madagascar. There is a faint possibility that it survives deep in rainforest somewhere on the mainland.

The spectacular Madagascar Serpent Eagle was, until recently, also feared extinct. This bird of deep forest had not been seen for 58 years when, in 1988, one was found in the mountainous, inaccessible Marojejy Reserve in the northern part of the island. Although evidently surviving, it must be very rare and, like most tropical forest birds of prey, is likely to require large areas of undisturbed habitat to feed and breed in, so its future seems bleak. Somewhat better known, but also apparently on the brink of extinction, is the Madagascar Fish Eagle. Around 100 of these are believed to survive along the coast of northwest Madagascar where they breed mainly on small offshore islands. The extraordinary, ground-dwelling Long-tailed Ground Roller is another bird of very restricted range. Its entire population in southwest Madagascar may number less than 1,000. The species seems stable at present, but with none of its habitat protected it remains permanently at risk.

Madagascar is also home to an astonishing variety of reptiles, including two-thirds of the world's chameleons and the world's rarest tortoise – the Angonoka. This tortoise is found in one small area of northwest Madagascar where fewer than 400 are believed to survive. A captive breeding program in Madagascar has had considerable success (despite the theft of around 100 young by unscrupulous reptile-collectors in 1997) and reintroductions are in progress. More widespread but still threatened is the beautiful Radiated Tortoise of southwest Madagascar. This species has been extensively collected for the pet trade, and its habitat is being rapidly cleared for crop cultivation and charcoal production. The Madagascar Tree Boa mainly inhabits the moist forests of the north and east where it is at risk from habitat loss.

THE MASCARENES AND SEYCHELLES

The Mascarene islands – Réunion, Rodrigues and Mauritius – lie to the east of Madagascar, and the Seychelles to the north. While far less rich in species than Madagascar or mainland Africa, their fauna is bizarre and exotic. Sadly, it has also been thoroughly devastated by humans. Since the first Europeans visited these islands in the sixteenth century, more species (mainly of birds and reptiles) have become extinct here than in the whole of mainland Africa and Madagascar combined. Those that have gone include probably the most famous of all extinct animals, the Dodo of Mauritius. This giant, flightless relative of the pigeons was exterminated by 1665, a few decades after its discovery. The Rodrigues and Réunion equivalents of the Dodo, the solitaires, survived into the eighteenth century. Also gone are at least eight species of giant tortoise *(Cylindraspis)*, and only one species from another genus remains in the Indian Ocean to remind us of what we have lost. The Aldabra Giant Tortoise, whose shell may be over 1 meter (3¼ feet) long, exists in good numbers on the Aldabra atoll in the Seychelles group. The species seems reasonably secure at present but is permanently at risk from natural disasters affecting the atoll.

The catalog of extinctions on the Indian Ocean islands is probably far from complete (see p.212). Several of the surviving species exist in critically low numbers, although concerted efforts are being made to rescue some of them. One spectacular success story is the Mauritius Kestrel, whose wild population has been increased, mainly by release of captive-bred individuals, from six in 1974 to around 300 today. Also back from the brink, though increasing somewhat more slowly, is the Pink Pigeon of Mauritius. Protection of the last wild breeding colony and reintroduction to suitable sites has increased the wild population from fewer than 20 in the mid-1980s to around 100 today. One of the few native mammals of the Mascarenes, the Rodrigues Flying Fox, has also increased in number, from a low of around 70 in 1979 to perhaps 300–400 today. It remains permanently at risk, however, from cyclones, habitat loss through deforestation, and illegal hunting.

The fate of the Mascarene fauna – with many species already extinct and others keeping a precarious toehold on survival in the wild, or reduced entirely to captive populations – provides a sobering warning of the possible, or even probable, future for much of the fauna of Madagascar and continental Africa. Many of the species discussed above are confined to small patches of suitable habitat which are the continental equivalent of islands like the Mascarenes. However, these habitat "islands" are shrinking in size year by year. Local conservation activities have sometimes helped slow down, or even halt for a while, the tide of destruction. But the long-term future for most of these species, and many others not yet considered threatened, will only fully be assured when we realize that our future wellbeing depends on the maintenance of a healthy biosphere, and that the conservation of natural habitats and the wildlife they contain is an integral part of this.

Above *The Mauritius Kestrel* (Falco punctatus) *was once one of the rarest birds in the world, with only six surviving in 1974. It has been rescued from the brink of extinction by a combination of protection in the wild and captive breeding.*

Tropical Timbers

Sara Oldfield graduated in botany and geography at London University. Since then she has worked for many conservation organizations. Her knowledge of rare plants around the world developed while she was employed by the Royal Botanic Gardens, Kew, working on international conservation issues. Sara is currently employed by the World Conservation Monitoring Centre and has recently completed a global survey of the conservation status of tree species.

Tropical forests harbor the greatest diversity of plant and animal species in the world, including plants of great economic value which occur only there. Hardwood timber is the main economic product derived from this rich and rapidly disappearing habitat. The current volume of the trade is approximately 80 million cubic yards with an annual value of over six billion dollars. If the tropical forests were properly managed they could provide a much needed and sustainable source of income for developing countries. At present, however, only a tiny fraction of the forests are managed successfully for lumber production. Selective felling of tropical hardwoods has damaged the forests over the centuries and is leading to scarcity of many valuable species.

Exploitation in historical times led to the virtual disappearance of certain island timbers: *Diospyros hemiteles*, a species of ebony found only on Mauritius, has been reduced to a single tree remaining in the wild; two endemic species of St. Helena, the St. Helena Ebony and the Redwood, are on the brink of extinction. The pace of destruction has increased dramatically during the present century, with many more tropical timbers becoming threatened by international trade. Export of the so-called African mahoganies (species of *Khaya* and *Entangdrophragma*) began in Ghana about 100 years ago, while the French developed an interest in the mahoganies of the Ivory Coast around the same time. Malaysia's wood export industry developed to supply Britain's demand for timber early in the present century. In west Africa, Malaysia, and other parts of the tropics, exploitation for the export market has concentrated on a very limited number of species, leading to their depletion, and has ignored the wide range of other timbers which could be brought into commercial use.

AFRICAN TIMBERS

African "mahoganies" are still highly sought after and in west Africa supplies are now very restricted. Of the eleven species of *Entandrophragma*, four were found to be vulnerable because of exploitation and habitat destruction, in a recent survey carried out by the World

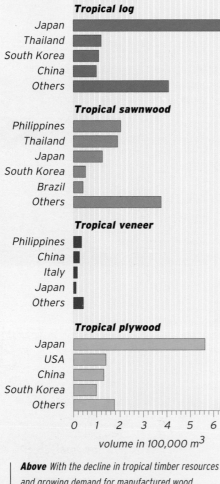

Major importers in 1997

Tropical log

Tropical sawnwood

Tropical veneer

Tropical plywood

volume in 100,000 m³

Above With the decline in tropical timber resources and growing demand for manufactured wood products, many former exporters are now importing supplies to maintain their manufacturing industries.

Right The main importers of tropical timbers in recent years have been Australia, Europe, USA, Saudi Arabia, China, Japan, and South Korea.

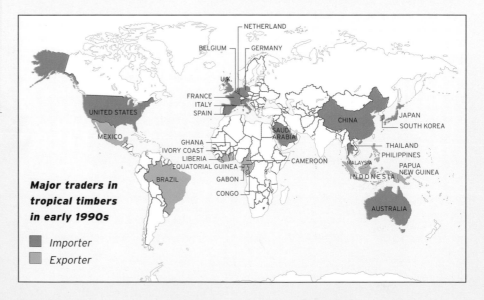

Major traders in tropical timbers in early 1990s

- Importer
- Exporter

Conservation Monitoring Centre. Three species of *Khaya* are recorded as vulnerable by the centre, and the Madagascan species of *Khaya* is considered to be endangered. Acajou *(Khaya ivorensis)* was the main timber species exported from the Ivory Coast in the first half of this century. It is now included in a national list of protected species.

The main commercial timbers of *Entandrophragma* are Tiama *(E. angolense)*, Sapele *(E. cylindricum)*, and Sipo *(E. utile)*. As stocks of these species have declined in west Africa, the timber is being increasingly sought from central Africa. Sapele is one of the most important commercial timbers of Cameroon and is one of the few species logged for export from the remote eastern forests It is also logged in the relatively intact northern forests of the Congo.

Along with Sapele, Afrormosia is one of the very few timbers exploited commercially in the virgin forests of northern Congo and eastern Cameroon. One of the world's most valuable hardwoods, it was little known to the trade before the Second World War but over the past 50 years its decline in the wild has been rapid. It also occurs in pockets of forest in Ghana and the Ivory Coast. In both countries it is under threat and, although still exported from Ghana, it is considered to be on the point of commercial extinction there. Congo and Zaire are now major suppliers of this species. Afrormosia is similar in appearance to teak. Unfortunately, unlike teak, it has not been developed as a plantation timber. In 1992, Afrormosia was added to Appendix II of CITES. This means that international trade in the timber is subject to licencing, and the levels of trade are monitored. Only a few timber species are protected by CITES, and proposals to add additional species have been strongly resisted by trade interests.

In total, Africa exports around 35 principal timber species. In southeast Asia logging concentrates on just under 100 species, with members of the dipterocarp family accounting for around 60 per cent of the trade. There are about 500 species within this family and their wood is marketed under broad trade names on the basis of timber characteristics. The main commercial groups are Meranti (species of *Shorea*), Keruing (species of *Dipterocarpus*), and Kapur (species of *Dryobalanops*). Many trees within these groups are threatened.

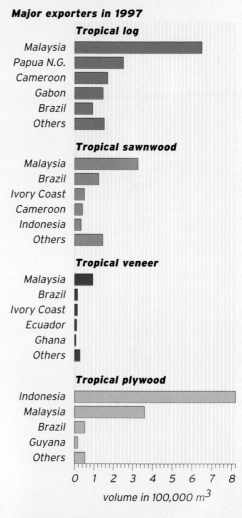

Major exporters in 1997

Tropical log
Malaysia
Papua N.G.
Cameroon
Gabon
Brazil
Others

Tropical sawnwood
Malaysia
Brazil
Ivory Coast
Cameroon
Indonesia
Others

Tropical veneer
Malaysia
Brazil
Ivory Coast
Ecuador
Ghana
Others

Tropical plywood
Indonesia
Malaysia
Brazil
Guyana
Others

0 1 2 3 4 5 6 7 8
volume in 100,000 m³

Above *Increasingly, tropical countries are producing and exporting "value-added" manufactured wood products, which provide increased revenue and jobs. Log export bans are one means of promoting this trend and encouraging timber species conservation.*

Left *Wood exports remain a major source of income for both temperate and tropical countries. Sustainable forest management and certification of forest products is important to maintain the trade.*

Forestry's share of trade in 1995, in per cent

- 30 and over
- 15 to 29
- 9 to 14

Above Mahoganies have been severely depleted worldwide for their very valuable lumber.

CRISIS IN THE PHILIPPINES

The situation is particularly acute in the Philippines where around 40 dipterocarp species occur. Commercial exploitation of the dipterocarp forests has reduced their area from 11 million hectares (27 million acres) to less than 1 million hectares (2.4 million acres), over the past 50 years. The most important commercial timber is Philippine "mahogany" (species of *Shorea* and *Parashorea*), and Britain has been one of the main importers of this wood. Large-scale logging expanded after the Second World War, mainly to supply the US market. Japanes demand starting in 1961 led to a dramatic increase in destructive logging and deforestation. The timber boom of the 1960s was a time of vast profits for logging companies, and the government was unable to enforce effective logging regulations. The decline of the forests and improved conservation measures have reduced logging by 90 per cent over the past 20 years, and the Philippines now bans the export of logs and lumber. Some species of dipterocarp are, however, already believed to be extinct, and most others are vulnerable. Dipterocarps are also under severe threat in other parts of southeast Asia. In Borneo and Sumatra the recent forest fires have destroyed the soil seedbanks for trees so that natural regeneration cannot take place. In Sumatra nearly 100 species of dipterocarp are threatened with extinction, and nine of these grow nowhere else.

LATIN AMERICAN TIMBER

In Latin America, high-value timbers are also under pressure from logging. Trees of true mahogany (species of *Swietenia*) are felled wherever they are found. *Swietenia mahogani*,

Right Mature dipterocarp trees growing along a riverbank in the Taman Negara National Park, Malaysia. In the past, areas such as this were particularly vulnerable. Most logging was done within easy reach of rivers because they were the main form of transport to the sea.

native to central America and the Caribbean, has been traded around the world since the sixteenth century. The level of exploitation has led to the exhaustion of supplies, particularly in the northern parts of its range. The ecology of populations in Mexico and central America is relatively well understood, whereas virtually nothing is known about Amazonian populations. Basic inventories are lacking for most of the range of *Swietenia macrophylla*. Good stands apparently still remain in parts of Brazil and Bolivia, but there has been illegal felling in the Bazilian states of Acre and Rondonia, where even Indian reserves and nature reserves have been pillaged. Regeneration of the species is stochastic (random), depending in nature on large-scale disturbance. This ecological strategy makes mahogany vulnerable to logging regimes. Harvesting and processing are generally only 50 per cent efficient. There is, at present, little economic incentive to manage natural stands sustainably. Trade in timber of all three species of *Swietenia* is now subject to some degree of control under CITES. Most Brazilian mahogany is destined for the US market, and Britain is also a major importer.

Selective logging or "mining" of valuable species does not in itself lead to total de-forestation, and some wildlife can survive in the forests that remain. But commercial logging operations are often the first step in the process of forest loss. Roads built to bring out the selected timbers provide access for land-hungry settlers who remove all the trees for agri-culture, often by slash-and-burn methods, which carry a high fire risk. Such clearfelling obviously causes much greater species loss.

The demand for tropical wood and wood-based products is enormous, and at present the raw materials are undervalued and squandered. New wood-processing technology has generally led to increased forest destruction rather than more efficient use of tropical timbers. In the 1960s a method was devised to make paper pulp from woodchips of tropical hardwoods and this led to clearfelling, for example, in Papua New Guinea and Colombia. Now the tide may be starting to turn, with timber consumers increasingly demanding wood from sustainably managed forests, and countries such as Thailand introducing a ban on all logging. But concerted, sustained international efforts will be necessary if the centuries of destruction are to be reversed.

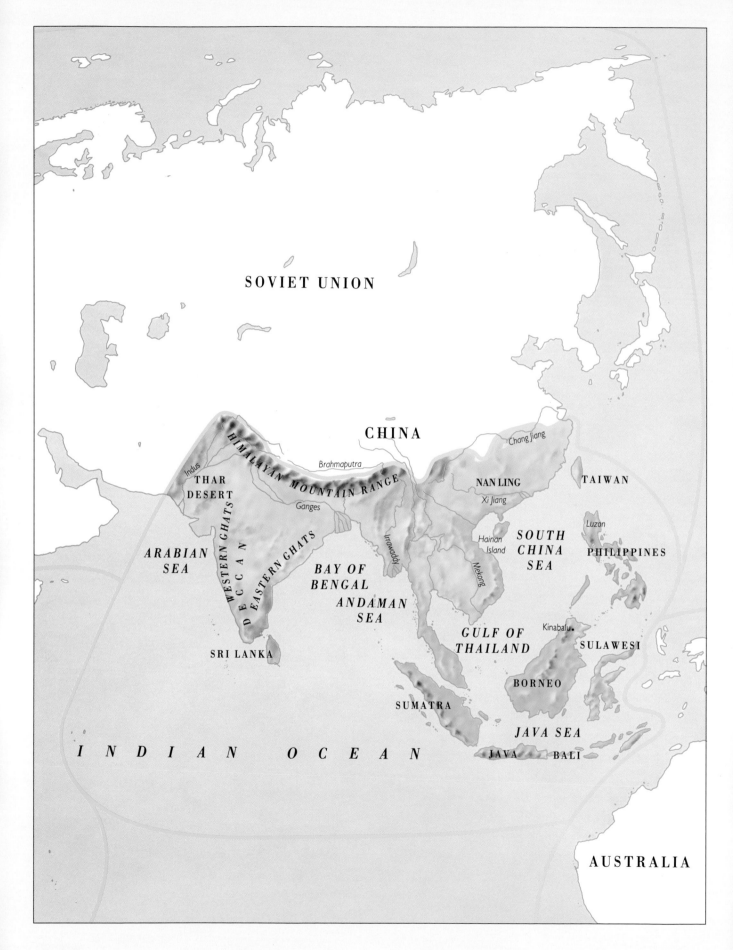

SOVIET UNION

CHINA

Chang Jiang

Brahmaputra

Indus

HIMALAYAN MOUNTAIN RANGE

THAR
DESERT

NAN LING

TAIWAN

Ganges

Xi Jiang

WESTERN GHATS

ARABIAN
SEA

DECCAN

EASTERN GHATS

Irrawaddy

Luzon

Hainan
Island

SOUTH
CHINA
SEA

PHILIPPINES

Mekong

BAY OF
BENGAL

ANDAMAN
SEA

GULF OF
THAILAND

Kinabalu

SULAWESI

SRI LANKA

BORNEO

SUMATRA

JAVA SEA

INDIAN   OCEAN

JAVA   BALI

AUSTRALIA

The Indian & Oriental Region

The Indian and Oriental region covers the lands
south of the Himalayas, through Indochina and
the Malay peninsula to the islands of southeast Asia.
Its southeastern boundary has been the subject of
much debate among biogeographers, and in this book
is taken as being between Sulawesi (Celebes) and
New Guinea.

Marsh Mugger (Crocodylus palustris), Sri Lanka.

Habitat & Plants

Ruth Taylor graduated in biology/ecology at Durham University. She has worked for a number of conservation organizations including Royal Botanic Gardens, Kew, the Nature Conservancy Council (now English Nature) and Hertfordshire and Middlesex Trust for Nature Conservation. After six years spent teaching, Ruth became education officer at the Chelsea Physic Garden, then moved on to work at The Natural History Museum. She now works for the National Trust, concentrating on interpretation and access. She is currently completing a PhD at King's College, London, investigating the possibilities of changing visitors' behavior to conservation.

Sara Oldfield graduated in botany and geography at London University. Since then she has worked for many conservation organizations. Her knowledge of rare plants around the world developed while she was employed by the Royal Botanic Gardens, Kew, working on international conservation issues. Sara is currently employed by the World Conservation Monitoring Centre, and has recently completed a global survey of the conservation status of tree species.

This vast and diverse region stretches from the Baluchistan mountains of Pakistan and the Indus valley in the west, to the hills of Yunnan and southern China and Taiwan in the east. The Himalayan chain forms the region's northern boundary. To the southeast and east lie the Philippines, the islands of Sulawesi, the Lesser Sundas and the Moluccas which comprise an important transition zone between the faunas of Asia and Australasia. These islands are included in this section. The region contains a wide range of vegetation types, and a number of floristic zones. These include the Indian zone, the southern part of the Sino-Japanese zone, the continental southeast Asiatic zone, and the Malaysian zone.

INDIAN ZONE

This zone can be divided latitudinally into three distinct parts – the sub-tropical flanks of the Himalayas, the Indian peninsula, and Sri Lanka. Essentially a meeting place of floras from the west, the north and the east, it includes an estimated 15,000 vascular plant species and about 140 endemic genera. The natural vegetation cover over much of India between the Himalayas, the Thar Desert and Western Ghats is tropical moist deciduous forest. On the Himalayan foothills of Assam and in the Western Ghats below 1,500 meters (4,900 feet), tropical semi-evergreen forests and subtropical broadleaved hill forests are found. The northeast of India up to 1,200 meters (3,900 feet), and the seaward side of the Western Ghats are covered in tropical evergreen rainforest, although it is mostly cleared below 500 meters (1,600 feet). In northern and central India at lower levels there is tropical dry deciduous forest with Teak, and tropical moist deciduous forest with Sal. Sal is one of the most important lumber trees in India and Nepal, being used for buildings and in temples for carvings and decorative beams. Much of this forest is becoming depleted, although in some places in the Terai there are areas of pure Sal forest: cool attractive forests, devoid of undergrowth and pleasant to walk in. In

Right When forests are cut in mountainous areas, such as in this Chaipur ridge region of eastern Nepal, erosion is often rapid and dramatic. The soil washed away impoverishes the mountainsides, and the excessive loads of silt carried by the rivers and streams can damage aquatic life.

the south of India large areas of bamboo forest are found. Along the south coast of West Bengal and Bangladesh, particularly in the Sundarban region at the mouth of the Ganges, mangrove forests are extensive, covering 6,000 square kilometers (2,316 square miles).

Much of India's natural vegetation has been greatly modified by various forms of agriculture, forestry, and urbanization, although certain plant species are also threatened by natural causes such as landslides, floods, and droughts. Over half of the land area is cultivated, with rice being the principal crop. The estimated rate of deforestation of closed broadleaved tropical forests is 1,320 square kilometers (510 square miles) per annum out of a total of 460,440 square kilometers (177,740 square miles), although only just over half of this can be considered adequately stocked forest lands. All forests, particularly moist forest types, are being degraded rapidly as a result of population pressure and shifting cultivation. The widespread effects of this degradation include reduction in rainfall in some areas and flooding in others. For instance, at Mahableshwar south of Bombay, where the surrounding hills have been logged, annual rainfall has decreased from 1,000 centimeters (390 inches) a year to just over 600 centimeters (240 inches).

The more fertile parts of India have been so densely inhabited by people for so long that there is probably little of the original vegetation left. But overall, the Indian flora is an important and characteristic one. It contains many plants of commercial value, including important medicinal plants, and a number of these are becoming rare through overexploitation. The root of Kuth yields an essential oil on steam distillation, and resinoids on extraction with solvents. Both these products are highly priced, being in great demand in Western countries for blending high-class perfumes. The plant grows wild in Jammu and Kashmir states, mainly occurring in the Kishanganca valley and higher elevations of the Chenab valley. Because of the threat to its survival in the wild from commercial exploitation,

Spotlight

■ *Paphiopedilum druryi.* This orchid survives in cultivation but is endangered or extinct in the wild, not having been seen there since 1972. The causes of its decline have been forest fires, and excessive collecting.

■ *Dendrobium pauciflorum.* Again endangered or possibly extinct, this orchid was recorded in the last century from two localities, but a search in 1970 revealed only a single plant. At that time attempts to bring the plant into cultivation were unsuccessful.

■ Indian Podophyllum *(Podophyllum hexandrum).* Formerly fairly widespread in India at an altitude of 2,000–3,000 meters (6,500–10,000 feet), this perennial is now under threat from commercial exploitation of its root for use in medicine.

■ Rauwolfia *(Rauvolfia serpentina).* Once widely distributed in the sub-Himalayan tract from Hamachal Pradesh eastward to Sikkim and Bhutan, the plant is now under threat due to overexploitation to obtain reserpine, a substance used in medicine.

■ Blue Vanda *(Vanda coerulea)*. A victim of its own beauty, this orchid used to be widespread in the humid evergreen forests of northeastern India and northern parts of Burma and Thailand. Massive deforestation and commercial exploitation have brought it to the brink of extinction.

■ *Merrillia caloxylon.* Solitary trees are scattered in lowland moist primary and secondary forest on stream banks and hillsides. It has been collected only once in Sabah from a stream bank in secondary forest in Sandakan. The durable, handsome wood has been used in the past in Peninsular Malaysia to make small implements. It is now presumed to be extinct in this area. The species is classified as vulnerable by IUCN.

■ *Ailanthus fordii.* This tree is rare in the wild, being originally known from only ten specimens in one locality. Recent research has found further trees in nine localities.

■ *Camellia crapnelliana.* This species is currently classified as vulnerable by IUCN. It grows in broadleaved forest, occurring along the coast in Fujian, southwest Zhejiang, southern Guangdong and southern Guangxi and also in Hong Kong. Populations are steadily diminishing with increasing habitat loss and cutting.

it is listed on appendix I of CITES, which means export cannot take place unless the plants are artificially propagated specimens. Indian Podophyllum is found in the Himalayas from Himachal Pradesh to Sikkim, and is also reported from Nepal, Afghanistan, Bhutan and China. The root was used in the past to treat intestinal worms and constipation. Now a semi-synthetic derivative from the root, Etoposide, has been found to be a first-class cytotoxic (cell-poisoning) agent and is used to treat cancer. *Podophyllum* plants in the wild are threatened by exploitation, and growth of the species is slow. Export of the plants or roots is banned under Indian law and the species is listed on appendix II of CITES. Another very important medicinal plant under threat is *Rauvolfia serpentina*, an age-old remedy in India for mental disorders. The alkaloid reserpine was isolated from it in 1952 and this is now used internationally as an effective remedy for hypertension and as a sedative or tranquillizing agent. The wild plants are protected in India by an order prohibiting export of live specimens and roots, and by listing on appendix II of CITES.

Indian plants are also threatened by over-collecting for horticulture, the orchids being particularly vulnerable. *Paphiopedilum druryi* was originally only known from a single locality in the state of Kerala in southern India and has been collected to extinction. It has not been seen in the wild since 1972, when collecting was particularly severe, but it is just possible that some rhizomes or seedlings may still remain. The orchid *Dendrobium pauciflorum*, an epiphyte reportedly found in riverine jungles, was recorded in the last century from two sites open to felling in West Bengal and Sikkim. It has not been seen in the wild since 1970 and is thought to be extinct, due to habitat destruction.

The flora of Sri Lanka has a high degree of endemism, about a third of native species being endemic. Most of Sri Lanka's best known plants are also found in India or elsewhere, but among the endemics are the Ebony, an important timber tree, and *Areca concinna*, a threatened palm. The palm occurs in a low swamp-like woodland along a backwater and there are only about 1,000 individuals in the population. The tree is at risk from changes in the drainage pattern that have occurred since the surrounding slopes were cleared of vegetation for agriculture.

Right Mangroves, seen here in the Samunsan Reserve in Sarawak, Malaysia, are among the most productive habitats in the world. The network of roots and stems traps the falling leaves and silt, providing nutrients for the fish and other wildlife sheltering there.

Far left Paphiopedilum drury *is an orchid which survives in cultivation, but is almost certainly extinct in its native habitat in southern India. A re-introduction program is now planned.*

Left Paphiopedilum micranthum *was first described in 1951. Taken from its restricted habitat in south-east Yunnan and illegally exported from China, plants sold for up to 500 dollars a growth. By mid-1985 they were widely available for a few dollars a plant and had been exploited to the verge of extinction in the wild.*

SINO-JAPANESE ZONE

This includes the elevated area of the Sino-Himalayan-Tibetan mountains and the rest of China, except the south. Its flora is almost certainly the richest in the whole of the northern temperate zone and is especially abundant in trees. The total number of endemic genera is probably 300 or more. The Sino-Himalayan mountain system is the native land of many garden plants highly prized throughout the world. Their introduction to cultivation in the West took place mainly during the first few decades of the present century. Notable garden plants originating in this region include *Anemone japonica, Paulownia tomentosa, Jasminum nudiflorum, Kerria japonica, Lonicera nitida*, and *Morus alba*. The debt which the horticulturist owes to the plants of the Himalayas is well shown by *Cotoneaster frigidus, Gentiana farreri, Magnolia campbellii*, and *Meconopsis betonicifolia*.

CONTINENTAL SOUTHEAST ASIATIC ZONE

This includes the Andaman and Nicobar islands, Myanmar, southern coastal China including Hainan and Taiwan, Thailand, and the northern part of the Malay peninsula. Its flora is comparable in luxuriance to that of Malaysia. Most of the important crop plants, rice, tea, and various citrus fruits, are believed to be natives of this region. The Nicobar islands have tropical broadleaved evergreen rainforest. Other vegetation on the Nicobars and on the Andaman islands consists of tropical evergreen rainforest, rich in *Dipterocarpus* and *Pterocarpus* species, tropical semi-evergreen rainforest and tropical moist deciduous forest. The remaining areas of rainforest are under severe pressure from logging and agriculture, particularly on the Andamans. The coastal areas of both support mangrove forests.

Over 40 per cent of Myanmar is covered by forest, mostly evergreen rainforest with some mixed deciduous forest containing teaks, and dry dipterocarp forest in central Myanmar. These forests are under increasing pressure, especially in the lowlands. Myanmar is currently the main source of teak on the world market, with wood sourced from natural forests. The demand has increased following the crisis in Indonesia which has disrupted supplies of plantation-grown teak from Java. Mangrove forests are found along the southern coasts, with

Jasminum nudiflorum

Kerria japonica

Paulownia tomentosa

temperate deciduous forests and subtropical evergreen and monsoon forest in the south. Evergreen, semi-evergreen, and mixed broadleaved deciduous forests occur on limestone in the tropical and subtropical areas of the south. The most extensive tracts of natural forest are in the northeast and southwest provinces of Sichuan and Yunnan. Probably more land has been recently afforested in China than in any other country in the world. Taiwan contains subtropical evergreen forests in the lowlands and broad-leaved evergreen forests at medium altitudes. There are mixed forests, coniferous forests and extensive grasslands at higher altitudes.

The lowland evergreen rainforest which originally covered much of central and southern Thailand is now reduced to fragments in south peninsular Thailand. Mangroves are extensive along the western coast. Semi-evergreen forests dominated by the dipterocarp family are found in the interior and north of Thailand and below 1,000 meters (3,300 feet). On hills grow evergreen forests, but the largest area is covered by dry dipterocarp forest with bamboo, and mixed deciduous forests with teak. The teak forests are extensively logged or burned.

MALAYSIAN ZONE

Probably nowhere else in the world, with the possible exception of parts of tropical America, do flowering plants attain such richness and luxuriance as in Malaysia, where conditions favor their fullest development in almost every way. The flora also contains many plants which are

Below Rafflesia arnoldii *bears the largest flower in the world. It is a rainforest parasite and this one is growing on a Teliastigma vine. Its distribution is dependent on the distribution of the lianas which it parasitizes.*

of value to people – indeed, the "Spice Islands," as part of the archipelago was called in earlier days, played a significant part in the history of many nations. The economic plants thought to have originated somewhere in Malaysia include Breadfruit, Nutmeg, and Ginger.

Climatic conditions throughout the Malay archipelago are, in general, constant. Nearly all the islands are heavily forested, tropical evergreen rainforest being the main natural vegetation. These forests are teeming with plant and animal species, being particularly rich in climbers, palms, and epiphytes, notably orchids. A major threat to the rainforests is the insatiable world hunger for wood, and forest loss is most severe in the countries with the finest lumber trees.

Other vegetation types include lowland dipterocarp forest, hill dipterocarp forest, and montane rainforest above, while semi-evergreen rainforest occurs in the far northwest of peninsular Malaysia. The rugged limestone hilltops of western Malaysia are relicts of an ancient calcareous mantle and have an extremely varied flora with numerous orchids. Many of the species are endemics with restricted distribution and are hence at great risk from habitat destruction. *Maxburretia rupicola* is a small palm confined to three limestone hilltops within 40 kilometers (25 miles) of Kuala Lumpur. It is threatened on one hand by quarrying and at risk on another from fires lit by climbers.

As the forests disappear, so too does a vast potential wealth of biological resources. On the Lesser Sunda islands, much of the original forest has been destroyed and valuable trees such as the East Indian Sandalwood have come close to extinction in the wild. Sandalwood has been used for 4,000 years to provide an aromatic oil, but with the increase in the European trade over the last century, the wild populations have become seriously threatened. Today, most of the oil to supply the perfume, cosmetic, and soap industries has to come from plantations.

The rattans are very important to the rural economy of southeast Asia, providing employment and a supplement to income from agriculture. These climbing palms with long flexible stems ascend the rainforest canopy using barbed whip-like growths on the ends of leaves. The best-quality canes for commercial use come from the genera *Calamus* and *Daemonorops*, mainly found in Malaysia and Indonesia. Rattans are usually harvested from the wild and are the second most important commercial product of the rainforest, after timber. After processing, they are made into furniture and other goods for export. If harvesting is well planned, rattans can be a renewable resource. However, overharvesting of the highest quality long canes, particularly in Indonesia, is damaging their long-term survival.

One of the most spectacular plants of Indonesia and Sumatra is *Rafflesia arnoldii*, which has the largest flower in the world, up to 1 meter (3¼ feet) or more in diameter when open. A parasitic plant, dependent on a climbing vine, it is found in mixed dipterocarp forests on moist valley bottoms or on steep but moist slopes. This plant is under threat from the destruction of nearby rainforest, and collecting by novelty hunters and for use in medicine. Nature reserves have been created to protect it.

There are believed to be 3,000 to 4,000 species of orchid – twice the number of species in the whole of Britain's flora – in the area from mainland Malaysia to New Guinea. Many of these species are vulnerable due to deafforestation and overcollecting. The *Corybas* orchids are naturally rare because they have unusual habitat requirements. *Corybas fornicatus*, for example, is found only on sharply drained, mor humus banks on ridge tops in very humid montane forest, usually among mosses. It is now seriously endangered by the illegal cutting of firewood, and forest fires.

Spotlight

■ *Abies densa*. This fir has a restricted distribution in Nepal, Bhutan, Assam, and Sikkim. It is threatened in Nepal by removal of forest for firewood and grazing land.

■ Indian Gentian (*Gentiana kurro*). Found in India and the northwest Himalayas, its population is scarce and declining due to the roots of the plants being collected for use in traditional medicine.

■ Dove Tree (*Davidia involucrata*). This plant is widely cultivated but is becoming increasingly rare in the wild.

■ Kuth (*Sausurea lappa*). The distribution of this species ranges over Indian and Sino-Japanese zones with small populations in the northwest Himalayan region. It is threatened due to collection in the wild for its roots, from which essential oils are extracted.

■ *Rafflesia arnoldii*. This rafflesia is endangered in the wild by destruction of the rainforest and collected for medicine and as a novelty.

■ Rajah Pitcher Plant (*Nepenthes rajah*). This was once so abundant at Pinasok in the Kinabalu reserve that the area was called Rajah kingdom. Now there are no pitcher plants to be seen.

■ *Maxburretia rupicola*. A vulnerable palm confined to three limestone hilltops, its total population is probably below 1,000 individuals.

■ *Corybas fornicatus*. The only known extant population is seriously endangered by fire and the cutting of firewood.

Wildlife

Tim and Carol Inskipp Tim works at the World Conservation Monitoring Centre in Cambridge, UK. Carol works in environmental education. They have a special interest in birds of the Himalayas and the Oriental region, and have visited a number of countries in the Orient studying birds and other wildlife. Together they have written a book on the distribution of birds in Nepal, and have helped to write a field guide to the birds of the Indian subcontinent.

This region is characterized by its high species richness, Indonesia, for example, supporting 17 per cent of the world's bird species. This is partly due to the Himalayas, which have acted as an effective barrier between the Orient and Palearctic for the last 10 million years, encouraging speciation. Also, the tropical climate has provided ideal conditions for the evolution of a large number of endemic species.

Oriental animals and their habitats are now under severe pressure. In 1994, for instance, BirdLife International identified over 300 Oriental bird species which are globally threatened. Habitat losses and deterioration are the most serious threats to wildlife. Other problems are poaching and hunting for food, and the wild animal trade, pollution, and introduced species.

The Oriental region is divided into the Indian subcontinent, the Indo-Chinese subregion, the Sundaic subregion and islands between the Orient and Australasia.

THE INDIAN SUBCONTINENT

A major factor helping to maintain the subcontinent's wealth of animal life is the influence of culture and religion. Most people in India, Nepal, Bhutan, and Sri Lanka are Hindus or Buddhists. Those who adhere strictly to these religions do no deliberate harm to any living creature. Animals are closely associated with Hindu gods, such as the Naga or snake with Shiva and Vishnu, and the elephant which forms the head of Ganesh, the god of wisdom. Buddhist stories frequently describe the noble qualities of animals, such as the elephant, as

Below A young female Tiger (Panthera tigris) *which has just emerged from a swim. The Tiger is now seriously endangered by poaching for its bones and other parts to supply the demands of the traditional Chinese medicine trade, as well as by loss of habitat.*

examples to people. Cows are sacred to Hindus and huge numbers of them live in every habitat in India, being allowed to forage wherever they like unharmed, and consuming vast amounts of vegetation. In addition, concern for the environment and an appreciation of the value of wildlife as a natural heritage are growing. In India, the Chipko Andolan movement protects natural forests and encourages the planting of native trees. This grassroots movement is led by women of the Chipko community and has gained widespread support.

There are numerous protected areas covering 4 per cent of India, 10.6 per cent of Nepal, and as much as 22 per cent of Bhutan. Conflicts between local people and park staff are, however, increasing and now pose serious threats to many reserves. In India, almost every protected area is surrounded by hostile people living at subsistence level. Many depend on forests for their vital daily needs, for example obtaining their food by hunting game and collecting roots, wild fruits, vegetables, and honey, or practicing shifting cultivation. It has recently been widely recognized that the long-term future of protected areas can only be assured if the people around have a vested interest in them.

The Tiger is the national animal of both India and Bangladesh. This magnificent predator occurs in most Oriental countries but the main population is in the Indian subcontinent. Aptly called "the spirit of the jungle," the Tiger inhabits all types of forest and was formerly found almost throughout India. In 1970, a census revealed that the Indian population of the species had fallen alarmingly from an estimated 40,000 in 1930 to about 1,800 animals. The causes were loss of forest, excessive hunting and the soaring prices of skins on the international market. Counts in other countries also showed serious declines, with evidence of only about 5,000 Tigers throughout its huge range. To meet this crisis, Project Tiger was launched in 1972, leading to the banning of Tiger hunting and the establishment of Tiger reserves throughout the subcontinent.

Initially Project Tiger had some success and survey estimates showed that populations had more than doubled since 1970, although some experts thought the figures were exaggerated. But by the early 1990s it became clear that the Tiger was once again fighting for survival in India. The poaching rate had rapidly increased and was believed to be equal to one Tiger a day. Poaching is driven by the demand for Tiger bones and parts for use in traditional Chinese medicines. This commercial trade is not new – Tiger bone has been used to provide health care for more than 1,000 years and perhaps longer. Its recent popularity and the demise of China's own population of Tigers and stockpile of Tiger bones have led to a marked increase in demand. The trade is supported by a highly organized network of illegal wildlife dealers.

In addition, half of the Project Tiger reserves are rapidly deteriorating due to pressures of increased human population and numerous development projects, such as mining and hydroelectric dams. After being a low government priority for many years hope for the Tiger in India was awoken again in 1997 when the then prime minister made a new political commitment to protect wildlife, the Tiger in particular. But following the collapse of his government soon afterwards, his commitment to the Tiger must be honoured by his successors if the Tiger is to be saved in India.

Above *A Golden Langur* (Presbytis geei) *high in a Flame of the Forest tree in the Manas Reserve, Bhutan. This langur was first discovered in 1953, and its range is restricted to Bhutan and adjacent Assam, India.*

The Tiger reserves created have helped to protect many other threatened animals, such as the beautiful Golden Langur at Manas. Amazingly, this large diurnal primate was not described until 1956. It has a very restricted range in the mixed deciduous forests of northwest Assam and Bhutan.

Another Assamese speciality at risk is the Great Indian Rhinoceros, the main population of which occurs in the tall grasslands of Kaziranga National Park. Since ancient times, rhinos have been highly prized as sources of traditional Chinese medicine. World rhino numbers continued to fall throughout the 1970s and 1980s, despite a 1977 ban on international trade in rhino horn. Enforcement of the ban was weak and anti-poaching efforts were very under-funded because, for many years, little was done to reduce the demand for rhino horn in consumer countries. But in recent years this has changed. One by one, long-used trade routes have been closed as a result of strong international efforts, and in the mid-1990s surveys

Right The Great Indian or One-horned Rhinoceros (Rhinoceros unicornis) *was widespread from northern Pakistan to Thailand in the Middle Ages. By the 1950s the world population had fallen to around 400, but with protection it has risen to over 1,000, mostly in India.*

showed that China had been highly successful in implementing its domestic ban on trade in rhino horn. But even a low level of use to provide health care for its population of 1.3 billion people is a great concern. The world's remaining rhino populations could not supply such a demand from China for long.

Assam's grasslands are a stronghold for the Bengal Florican, one of the world's most endangered bustards. This florican is also recorded in Nepal, Bangladesh, and Cambodia, and has recently been rediscovered in Vietnam. Its reputation of being one of the most delicious gamebirds in India must have contributed to its early decline. Also, much of its habitat has been claimed for agriculture, and most of the remaining grasslands are burned annually to encourage the growth of a new flush of grass for grazing herbivores and for thatching. Another inhabitant of these grasslands, Finn's Baya Weaver, is now extremely local with disjunct populations in northwest India and Assam.

To the north of Assam's lowland grasslands lie the Himalayas, the highest and youngest mountain chain in the world. The Himalayas are rich in species of pheasant, including two species in the western part of the range: the gorgeously plumed Western Tragopan endangered by deforestation and hunting in temperate forests, and the Cheer Pheasant mainly threatened by hunting on steep grassy slopes. The Lesser or Red Panda is another seriously

DISTRIBUTION
TIGER

Range 100 years ago

Range today

Range of the Tiger (Panthera tigris). *Formerly Tigers were very common. We do not know exactly how many there were, but 40,000 were estimated to occur in the Indian subcontinent in the early part of this century. In 1998 there are less than 3,000 in India, and its world population may be as low as 5,000.*

threatened inhabitant of temperate Himalayan forests. LIttle is known of this charming animal, mainly because of its nocturnal habits. However, a study in Langtang National Park in Nepal revealed that it is particularly susceptible to human disturbance as well as to loss of its forest habitat.

Invertebrates in the Himalayas are also suffering from deforestation. These include a dragonfly *Epiophlebia laidlawi*, a species surviving from the Mesozoic era and now known only from the eastern Himalayas in India and Nepal. One of the most spectacular of the butterflies is the Kaiser-I-Hind which has been recorded in Nepal over thickly wooded hills in the temperate zone. It also occurs in Sikkim, Arunachal Pradesh, and Burma.

The Snow Leopard (see p.38) occurs mainly north of the Himalayan range, but many people associate it with these mountains. Despite protection, it is still widely hunted for its beautiful pelt. However, the reduction in the population of its natural prey, mainly

wild sheep, is considered to be a much larger threat to its long-term survival.

The great Indian or Thar desert in northwest India and Pakistan is home to the Blackbuck. Regarded as sacred by Indians, this attractive antelope is widely illustrated in Indian paintings and sculptures and its skin is used in religious ceremonies. It was formerly common in the desert, but hunting, competition for grazing from the constantly increasing population of domestic cattle, and the spread of cultivation, have reduced its population to disjunct pockets. The most outstanding bird on the Thar desert is the stately Great Indian Bustard, the males of which stand more than a meter (3¼ feet) tall and weigh up to 14 kilograms (31 pounds). It is confined to the Indian subcontinent and is now rare. Hunting, egg collecting, loss of thorn scrub and the extension of agriculture have all contributed to its decline. Despite considerable efforts made to save it, the Great Indian Bustard continues to decline, and in 1993 there were no more than 500 to 600 left.

Wildlife is abundant in the less populated areas of the Deccan, the great plateau in peninsular India, notably at Kanha National Park. The park's speciality is the Swamp Deer or Barasingha which has suffered drastic declines, mainly because of losses of its tall, swampy grassland habitat. The Barasingha is confined to India and Nepal, and the central Indian subspecies is almost entirely restricted to Kanha. In recent years, however, grasslands have been

Above left The Lesser or Red Panda (Ailurus fulgens) *is found in temperate forests of the Himalayas above 1,500 meters (5,000 feet). They spend the day asleep high in the trees, descending at dusk to feed. They have been sought after for their rich soft pelt and were also popular as pets.*

Above A Swamp Deer or Barasingha (Cervus duvauceli) *with a Black Drongo on its rump. The Swamp Deer has large splaying hooves to enable it to walk in its swampy habitat. There are probably fewer than 4,000 in the wild, but there are substantial populations breeding in zoos.*

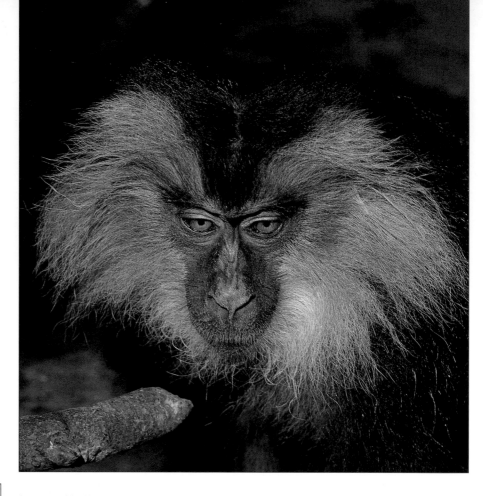

Right *A male Lion-tailed Macaque or Wanderoo (Macaca silenus). Around 3,000–4,000 survive in the tropical forests of the Western Ghats of southern India. Their habitat has been drastically reduced by encroaching agriculture, and attempts have also been made to build hydroelectric dams in the Silent valley, one of their remaining strongholds.*

DISTRIBUTION
MUGGER

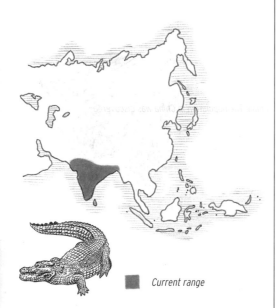

Current range

Range of the Mugger (Crocodylus palustris). *Although the range of this crocodile has not substantially changed, its numbers have been heavily depleted in most areas and it has disappeared from many of its former haunts.*

increased in the park through the relocation of villages, and the Barasingha is now steadily increasing there.

Perhaps the two most exciting ornithological events in India in recent times have been the rediscovery of two of the country's endemic bird species – Jerdon's Courser and Forest Owlet. Both birds have only been recorded rarely since their discovery, and not at all in this century. After intensive searching, the nocturnal courser was spotted one night in 1986 in Andhra Pradesh, and the owl was found in degraded forest in Maharashtra in 1997.

The humid, dense forests of the Western Ghats and the other south Indian hills support a richer fauna than the adjoining dry Deccan, including some species which are restricted to them, such as the handsome Lion-tailed Macaque. Once widely traded for zoos, this macaque is now considered endangered and given full protection. Another endemic mammal of the southern Indian hills is the Nilgiri Tahr, a wild goat restricted to rock and grass-covered slopes above the tree-line. Like the Lion-tailed Macaque, it is suffering from fragmentation and reduction of its habitat.

The island of Sri Lanka has as many as 23 endemic bird species, ten of which are considered at risk. Many of the endemic species, including the threatened Ashy-headed Laughing-thrush, are dependent on undisturbed dense forests.

The drainage of wetlands and pollution are threatening many birds in the subcontinent. The majestic Siberian Crane has only two remaining, widely separated breeding areas. The great majority of the western population once wintered at the Keoladeo Ghana National Park in northern India, but has declined from 125 birds in the winter of 1991/92 to just three individuals in the winter of 1997/98. The crane undergoes a very long, hazardous migration of over 6,000 kilometers (3,700 miles) and, in addition, faces the dangers of shooting or trapping by professional crane-hunters in Pakistan.

Several species of stork have markedly declined, notably the Greater Adjutant, the largest of India's storks. It occurred widely from India east to Vietnam but it has either disappeared or become extremely rare over much of its former range. The only known breeding populations of the species now seem to be in Assam and Cambodia. Similarly, the Spot-billed Pelican was once widespread in Asia, but has suffered severe declines and now breeds only in southeast India, Sri Lanka and Cambodia.

In large rivers in the north of the subcontinent, such as the Ganges and Brahmaputra, lives the Ganges Susu, a small dolphin about 2 meters (6½ feet) long. It is vulnerable to the construction of dams which have fragmented populations, and to accidental trapping in fishing nets. Two other threatened aquatic predators are the crocodiles, the Mugger and the Gharial. The Mugger is virtually confined to the subcontinent and can live in all types of freshwater habitats from large rivers to pools. It was once common, but hunting has reduced it to a few protected areas and rivers. The Gharial is restricted to rivers of the subcontinent where it feeds almost entirely on fish. The combined pressures of hunting and the damming of rivers nearly caused the Gharial's extinction. Fortunately, both species breed well in captivity and many hundreds have been released back into the wild.

The most extraordinary endangered species of the region must be the Sacred Mud Turtle. The entire population of up to 200 turtles lives in one large artificial pond associated with an Islamic shrine near Chittagong in southeast Bangladesh.

A number of reptiles and amphibians have suffered because of their commercial value. The Six-fingered Frog is one of several large frogs, millions of which have been caught in the

Left The Siberian Crane (Grus leucogeranus) has only two known breeding grounds, both in the USSR. It migrates to Keoladeo Ghana National Park, India, where these were photographed, and to Iran and China. The population in China was discovered comparatively recently and numbers about 2,000.

Below The Gharial (Gavialis gangeticus) is a highly specialized fish-eating crocodilian. Once on the brink of extinction, it has been saved by a comprehensive captive breeding program followed by reintroductions.

subcontinent so that their legs can be severed and exported to Europe as a delicacy. A recent export ban in India may have removed the main threat to the species. India also exported a huge number of snakeskins for many years, and this export was banned in 1976. However, the internal trade continues. Populations of several species have been depleted as a result, including the Indian Python, the Oriental Rat Snake, and the Asian Cobra.

INDO-CHINESE SUBREGION

This area extends from Burma through southern China east to Taiwan and south to Thailand, Cambodia, and Vietnam. In addition to habitat damage and losses, successive wars and hunting pressures encouraged by a proliferation of firearms have devastated wildlife in parts of Indochina.

One of the best known animals in the Orient is the now-endangered Asian Elephant, closely linked there with mythology, religion, and culture. It once had a huge range, extending as far west as the Tigris and Euphrates, north in China to the Chang Jiang river and south to Sumatra. Unlike its African counterpart, the Asian Elephant has been used extensively by people over the centuries for any jobs requiring enormous strength, such as the felling of trees and the transportation of logs. The earliest records of tame elephants in the Indian subcontinent date back to the third millenium BC. Although once abundant, its numbers are now severely reduced and all populations are fragmented to some degree. Habitat loss is the most serious threat and poaching for ivory is also a major problem.

Below An Asiatic or Indian Elephant (Elephas maximus) in the Galoya National Park, Sri Lanka. The Asiatic Elephant's tusks are small or absent, probably as a result of selection by human hunters over thousands of years.

The Leopard is another very widespread Oriental species at risk. Formerly it ranged throughout much of Africa and from the Near and Middle East to Siberia and south to Java. A highly adaptable animal, the Leopard will inhabit high mountains and coasts, tropical forests and deserts. Despite this, most of the Leopard's Asian populations are now endangered as a result of persecution over centuries for its valuable skin.

The major factor causing the decline of the Asiatic Black Bear is poaching for its gall bladder for use in Oriental medicine, and it is also affected by forest destruction. The Asiatic Black Bear had a wide range in Asia's forested hills and mountains, from the Soviet Far East south to Thailand, Vietnam, and Cambodia, and west to Pakistan. Its numbers are now greatly reduced and it no longer occurs in many parts of its former range.

The Musk Deer is also widely distributed in the montane forests of Asia. This deer is intensively hunted for musk, a secretion produced by glands of the male, and used in perfume

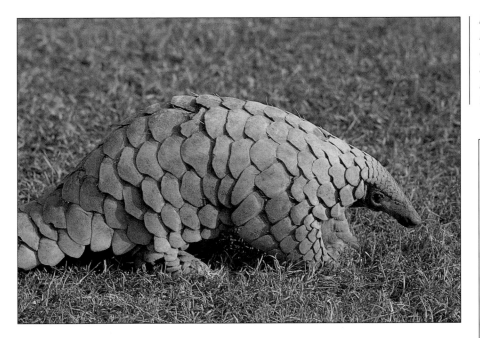

and Chinese medicine. As a result the species is rapidly diminishing, and musk has become one of the most valuable animal products in the world. Musk can, however, be extracted without killing the deer and farms have been set up in China for this purpose. Another animal of the forested mountains is the Common Goral, a goat antelope with short horns. It occurs from the Himalayas east to Burma, northern Thailand and north through eastern China to southeast Siberia, but is declining in many areas because of hunting for sport.

The three Asian species of pangolins (scaly anteaters) are threatened by heavy trapping for their scales and for their flesh, which is considered a delicacy. All occur in Indo-China: the Chinese Pangolin in forested mountains from Nepal east to southern China and Hainan, the Indian Pangolin in the Indian subcontinent and China, and the Malayan Pangolin with a range extending into the Sundaic subregion.

Deforestation is the chief threat to numerous montane forest bird species in Indochina. For example, the Giant Nuthatch, the largest of a family of small birds, now has a very restricted range. It is rare and local in Thailand, its status in Myanmar is unknown, and there are only a few recent records from China.

Below and to the south of the subregion's montane forests lie luxuriant, species-rich tropical rainforests. Hornbills are characteristic birds of these forests. They are particularly

Left *The Indian Pangolin* (Manis crassicaudata) *is hunted extensively for its scales, which consist of compressed hair and are similar in structure to the horn of rhinos. The scales are used in Oriental medicine, as is the pangolin's blood which is believed to cure internal bleeding.*

DISTRIBUTION
ASIAN ELEPHANT

▮ Present distribution

▮ Former distribution

Range of the Asian or Indian Elephant (Elephas maximas). *No early estimates were made of the population of the Asian Elephant, but it has undoubtedly suffered a dramatic decline. Only 34,000 to 51,000 Asian Elephants now survive, a significantly lower figure than the total number of African Elephants.*

vulnerable to deforestation because they feed on fruit and small animals in the canopy and so require mature trees. Also, their relatively large size makes them susceptible to hunting. The Rufous-necked Hornbill which used to occur from Nepal east to Vietnam is one of the most threatened. Although still fairly common in southern Bhutan, it is now probably extinct in Nepal, and rare and declining in the rest of its range.

One of the most impressive animals of the tropical forests is the Gaur, huge wild cattle which may have horns as long as a meter (3¼ feet) and weigh up to 1,000 kilograms (2,200 pounds). The Gaur was once found from India east to southern China and south to peninsular Malaysia but now it only survives in disjunct populations. Its numbers have been seriously diminished by extensive forest losses, indiscriminate hunting, and diseases caught from domestic cattle. Another Indo-Chinese species of wild cattle is the Kouprey, one of the world's rarest and least known mammals. The Kouprey's range is centred on Cambodia and extends into southern Laos, eastern Thailand and Vietnam. Its numbers are unknown but are believed to be very low. Prolonged warfare in much of its range, hunting for food and its horns, and a naturally low reproductive rate have all contributed to its decline.

The wetlands of Indochina harbor some fascinating endangered species. The Baiji is a river dolphin restricted to limited sections of the Chang Jiang river and its tributaries. Accidental drowning in fishing nets, collisions with ships' propellers, and water pollution are the chief causes of its decline. The same river is home to another endangered Chinese endemic, the Chinese Alligator. Local people persecute the alligator because it eats their fish

Below *A young male Gaur* (Bos gaurus) *in India. This cattle has been domesticated and there are feral as well as wild populations, including around 50,000 in Arunachal Pradesh, India. The Gaur is threatened by habitat loss and hunting, and also by cattle diseases.*

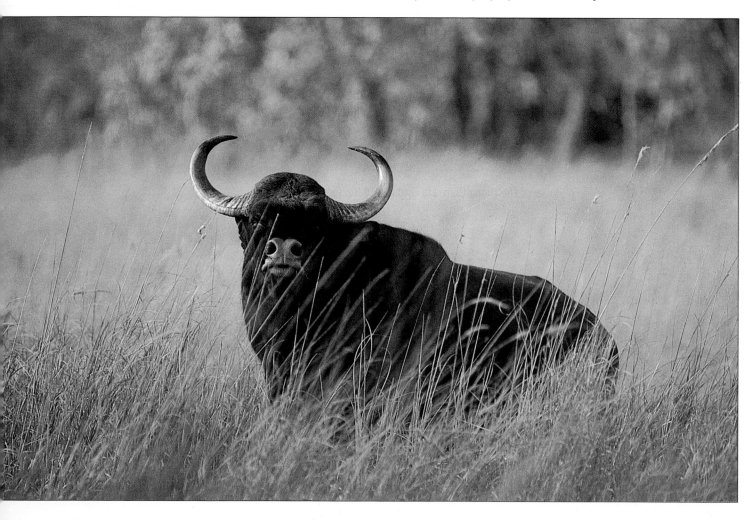

and domestic fowl. In addition, land reclamation and irrigation works seriously damage its habitat. In order to try and save the alligator a breeding center has been set up, and this has already succeeded in artificially rearing significant numbers.

Also confined to China is the Chinese Giant Salamander, which frequents mountain streams at over 1,000 meters (3,300 feet) in the center and southwest. The world's largest living salamander, growing up to 180 centimeters (71 inches) long, it is considered a great delicacy and so has become highly endangered.

The Giant Catfish is one of the world's largest catfish, reaching a length of about 3 meters (10 feet) and a weight of 300 kilograms (660 pounds). It reportedly migrates several thousand miles from Cambodia to spawning grounds in southern China and is thus seriously affected by dams which prevent it from moving upstream. In addition, it is valued for its size and high-quality flesh and so is threatened by overfishing.

Hunting also threatens the enigmatic White-eyed River Martin and may have already caused this bird's demise. It has not been recorded since 1980, despite intensive searching at its only known locality, Bung Boraphet, the largest freshwater marsh in Thailand. Also the roosting Barn Swallows, with which it associated in winter, have reduced in number from hundreds of thousands to fewer than 10,000 as a result of bird-trapping and reed-harvesting.

SUNDAIC SUBREGION

This comprises the Malay peninsula and the islands of Borneo, Bali, Java and Sumatra, and overlaps with the Indo-Chinese subregion to the north in southern Thailand, Cambodia and Vietnam. All of these territories stand on a shallow continental shelf that once formed a large peninsula known as Sundaland which had a characteristic fauna. Much of Sundaland is now flooded, but many of its animals are still confined to the remaining land masses. Unlike in India and Indo-China, there have been no long-term feelings of sympathy for wildlife based on religious beliefs. So in some of these countries animals are suffering from even more severe persecution, as well as habitat loss.

One of the animals restricted to the area is the endangered Orang Utan, Asia's great ape. It now only occurs in Sumatra and Borneo, but historically it ranged through lowland forests north to China. The gibbons, close relatives of the Orang Utan, are confined to the forests of the Orient, and all gibbon species are declining. Among those most at risk is the Siamang, a denizen of montane forests in Malaysia and Sumatra. The numbers of both it and the Orang Utan have been drastically reduced by logging and shifting cultivation. Hunting for food and, formerly, collection of live animals for trade also contributed to the decline of the Orang Utan. These apes are superbly adapted to life in trees, the gibbons swinging on their long arms and the Orang Utan climbing adeptly using its flexible toes.

Another threatened primate is the Slow Loris, which occurs from India south to Java. It spends all its time in the trees, but has adapted to a variety of habitats including tropical forests, secondary forest growth and plantations. Loss of cover and, in Indonesia, hunting for use in medicines are causing problems for this species.

The giant squirrels *(Ratufa)* are all confined to the Orient. They leap from tree to tree, hardly ever coming to the ground, and so are dependent on tall trees which are often selectively logged. Other animals are particularly vulnerable to deforestation because they require primary rainforest. One such, the Asian Tapir, is now reduced to isolated populations throughout its historical range which extends from this region into Indo-China. Overhunting and capture of live animals for trade have had additional impacts on the species. The Clouded

DISTRIBUTION
ORANG UTAN

Range of the Orang Utan (Pongo pygmaeus). Once found throughout Indo-China, Malaysia and north to China, the Orang Utan is now confined to Sumatra and Borneo.

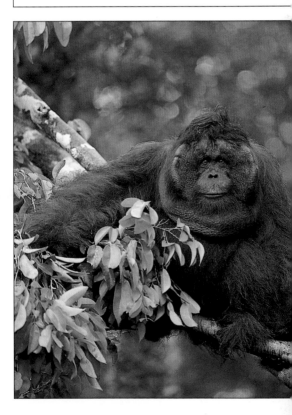

Above *An old male Orang Utan* (Pongo pygmaeus) *in Kalimantan, Borneo. They also occur on Sumatra, and once were more widespread, ranging north to China. Their decline may be due to malaria.*

Right *The Slow Loris* (Nycticebus coucang) *is a nocturnal primate found in forests over much of southeast Asia. They are threatened mainly by habitat destruction and are also hunted locally for use in traditional medicine.*

DISTRIBUTION
SUMATRAN RHINO

Borneo

Sumatra

▨ Nineteenth century distribution

■ Current distribution

Range of the Sumatran Rhinoceros (Didermocerus sumatrensis). *The numbers of the Sumatran Rhinoceros have been drastically reduced to 300 animals in total, occurring in scattered and isolated populations.*

Leopard is also vulnerable to the loss of primary forest, and hunting for its beautiful skin. It is now thought to be rare throughout its wide range, which extends from Sumatra to Nepal. Little is known about this very secretive cat.

The White-winged Wood Duck lives in primary evergreen forest ranging from lowland swamps to hill forests. However, it can survive in other forests if remnant patches of primary or old dense secondary forest are allowed to remain. It is now rare and restricted to northeast India, Bangladesh, Thailand, Indo-China, probably Myanmar and Sumatra. The largest surviving population is likely to occur in Sumatra, but much of the bird's habitat there is being converted to agriculture and settlements.

The wildlife of lowland rainforests is especially at risk because these forests are the most accessible to people and so are the first to be cleared. Gurney's Pitta, one of the rarest birds in the Orient, is probably confined to tiny pockets of lowland forest in peninsular Thailand. Following its rediscovery in 1986, 38 pairs were found the following year, but the population had declined to ten pairs by 1997.

The highly endangered Javan Rhinoceros has suffered from the extensive clearance of lowland forests combined with relentless hunting. Once it was widespread and often common, occurring from northeast India east through Indo-China and south to Java. Now there are only two known populations, in Java and Vietnam, and both are too small to be sustainable. Its relative, the Sumatran Rhinoceros (Asiatic Two-horned Rhinoceros) is threatened chiefly by the high demand for its horn and other organs. Only disjunct populations survive in this rhino's original large range from Assam east to Vietnam and south to Sumatra. Sadly, much suitable habitat remains unoccupied in protected areas.

Wetland habitats are also very vulnerable to destruction. Overfishing, river dredging and clearance of swamp forest severely threaten the Asian Arowana, a primitive fish confined to tropical freshwaters of the Orient. It apparently no longer occurs in Thailand, but still occurs in Vietnam, Cambodia, Malaya, and Sumatra. Chinese people consider that it brings good luck to their homes and large specimens are extremely valuable. Hunting for hides and live specimens is largely responsible for the decline of the Siamese Freshwater Crocodile. Formerly it occurred in Java, Borneo, and southern Indo-China, but now there is only one known surviving wild population, at Bung Boraphet in central Thailand, and that is small and decreasing.

The spectacular Milky Stork inhabits coastal mangroves in Cambodia, the Malay peninsula, Sumatra, Java, and Sulawesi. Very little was known about its status until 1984, when surveys revealed that it is suffering seriously from mangrove destruction, hunting, and disturbance at its nesting colonies.

The chief threat to the Bali Starling, the only bird endemic to Bali, is trapping for trade. By 1998 only 14 birds survived in the wild, despite conservation action since the 1980s. The remaining wild birds need to be strictly guarded, and the idea of installing alarms on nesting trees is being considered.

At the southern extremity of the subregion lies Christmas Island, the breeding site of two threatened seabirds, Abbott's Booby and the Christmas Frigatebird. Mining for phosphate destroyed a third of the known nesting areas of the booby in forest trees. Forest clearance has now stopped and some of the mined areas have been planted in a restoration program, but the booby has continued to decline because of low nesting success. Two of the three remaining colonies of the frigate bird are now protected in a national park, although birds in

Below left Until 1986, Gurney's Pitta (Pitta gurneyi) was believed to be extinct. A small population was then discovered in southern Thailand but it is critically endangered by deforestation.

Below Forest destruction and hunting have drastically reduced the numbers of the Green Peafowl (Pavo muticus). Once a common bird extending as far as northeast India, it is now rare or locally extinct throughout its range. It is similar in appearance to the more familiar Indian Peafowl but is generally green instead of blue and occurs in more dense forest.

the third colony have continued to decline due to dust fallout from the phosphate mining.

THE TRANSITION ZONE

This includes a large number of islands, in Indonesia from Lombok east to the Kai islands, and north to the Talaud islands. The Philippines are also in this account. People have had devastating effects on the big game animals in many areas, particularly in recent years when firearms have been more readily available.

Sulawesi has a fairly high percentage of forests remaining, and a reasonable system of protected areas. However, in the Philippines and the Lesser Sundas, 80 per cent of the natural vegetation has been destroyed, mainly for agricultural purposes, and many forest species are now threatened by fragmentation or complete loss of their habitat. Some of the islands that are particularly rich in endemic species, such as Sumba, have little forest remaining and virtually no protected areas. This island, in common with most islands in the Lesser Sundas, suffers frequent human-made fires and is now mainly covered by species-poor grassy hills.

The Philippines have an exceptionally high number of endemic animals, including about

60 per cent of the mammals and about 40 per cent of the resident birds. Illegal logging and hunting are the main threats throughout the majority of the inhabited islands. Most of the endemic mammals are poorly known rodents and bats. The larger species include the Tamaraw, a water buffalo confined to three montane areas in Mindoro and severely reduced by hunting and destruction of its forest habitat. Protection in recent years has allowed it to increase in numbers but habitat loss is still a threat. It has potential for domestication which could benefit the local people. The Calamian Deer, restricted mainly to Busuanga and Culion in the southwest Philippines, has also been overhunted despite complete protection.

The best known endemic bird and also one of the most threatened is the Philippine Eagle. This huge powerful bird requires extensive tracts of forest to survive and such habitat has now almost disappeared within its range. Its best hope lies in an education program which is slowly changing the local people's prejudice against birds of prey. Other threatened birds include the Philippine Cockatoo, once widespread throughout the archipelago but now rarely seen anywhere because of overcollection for the pet trade; and the brightly colored Whiskered Pitta, which has perhaps always been rare in its steep, oak-forest habitat in northern Luzon. Little is known about the status of other Philippine vertebrates, apart from the Sailfin Lizard and Gray's Monitor which are threatened by habitat loss and trapping.

Two swallowtail butterflies are listed as threatened, including the Luzon Peacock Swallowtail, a fairly large greenish-black species, the hindwings of which are margined with a striking pattern of red, purple and blue. It was first described as recently as 1965, and occurs only in a restricted montane area of northern Luzon where it is threatened by collectors. At one time it was so valuable that the sale of a few specimens in Japan paid for the costs of a return trip to Luzon!

Sulawesi also has a high level of endemism, with about 60 per cent of the mammal species, about 28 per cent of the resident birds, and approximately 30 per cent of the reptiles restricted to the area. Two of the mammal species are anoas or dwarf water buffalo. Both the Highland and Lowland Anoas are suffering from hunting pressures except in some well-protected reserves. The curious-looking Babirusa is a large pig that has declined in many areas because of hunting. The Sulawesi Palm Civet inhabits primary forests, feeding mainly on palm fruits and small mammals. Once considered extremely rare, it has recently been found to occur more widely, and its prospects are considered reasonable, given proper management.

Sulawesi

Sulawesi has an exceptionally high level of endemism. Of the 130 mammal species, comprising 70 bats and 40 rodents, around 60 per cent are confined to the area. An additional 13 mammal species have yet to be described for science. There are 265 resident bird species of which 28 per cent are endemic, including eight parrots, eight doves, six owls, six kingfishers, and a flightless rail. At least 120 species of reptiles occur there, of which about 30 are endemic, including 17 snakes and 13 lizards. There are only 25 indigenous species of amphibians but 19 of them are endemic.

Below *The Maleo (Macrocephalon maleo) is confined to Sulawesi. It breeds communally, laying its eggs in forest clearings heated by geothermal activity. The main threats are egg collectors in local villages and predation by dogs.*

Below right *The Nicobar Pigeon (Caloenas nicobarica) occurs from the Indian Nicobar and Andaman islands east through Indonesia and the Philippines to Papua New Guinea and the Solomon Islands. Little is known about its status, since most of these islands are little studied, but it is believed to have declined dramatically in many parts of its range.*

Left Komodo Dragons (Varanus komodoensis) in the national park on the island of Komodo, Indonesia. They are the largest lizards in the world, growing to nearly 3 meters (10 feet), and feed on animals up to the size of pigs and deer. Because they are confined to Komodo and a few adjacent areas, they are vulnerable to hunting, collecting and other threats.

The Maleo is an unusual bird that buries its eggs in warm sand and leaves them to hatch in the sun's heat. The large eggs are a delicacy sought after by people and dogs, and the species can now only survive with active management of its breeding areas. The Satanic Nightjar is known only from one specimen. Its name is due to a frequently heard nocturnal "plip-plop" call, believed by the local people to be the sound of the bird taking out a person's eyes. Another species known only from one individual on Indonesia is the Cerulean Paradise-flycatcher *(Eutrichomyias rowleyi)*. This bird was seen in 1978 on the forested slopes of Sangihe Island, which lies north of Sulawesi. The original vegetation of Sangihe has been almost completely replaced by coconut and nutmeg plantations and abandoned gardens. All searches to re-find the species have been unsuccessful and it is feared extinct.

The Lesser Sundas have fewer endemic species than Sulawesi, and fewer species that are considered to be threatened. Of its 18 species of threatened birds, the five that occur on Timor are perhaps most at risk as they all seem to be confined to small pockets of highly disturbed lowland forest. Sumba is another interesting island of the Lesser Sundas and has received very little attention until recently. It has eight endemic bird species, including the Sumba Hornbill *(Aceros everetti)*, one of the least known and most endangered species of Asian hornbill. The chief threat to its survival is the destruction of its forest habitat. The Komodo Monitor (or Dragon), mainly restricted to the island of Komodo, is the most spectacular threatened animal of the area. It is the world's largest lizard at about 3 meters (10 feet) long and it regularly attacks animals up to the size of water buffalo, but is not averse to carrion. It was threatened by capture for zoos until it received increased protection. The main problem remaining is fire in its savanna habitat.

Animals of the Moluccas causing concern include some of the 69 endemic birds. The majority of the nine parrots there have been heavily exploited for the pet trade. The cockatoos, particularly the Salmon-crested, are especially vulnerable because of their low reproductive rates. Up to 10,000 Salmon-crested Cockatoos were exported annually during the 1980s, despite the bird's extremely small range. International trade was banned in January 1990. The Purple-naped Lory is a small, brightly colored parrot restricted to a narrow altitudinal band on Seram and Ambon. It has been totally protected for some years but still appears in the trade in small numbers.

Spotlight

■ The Bengal Florican *(Houbaropsis bengalensis)* is the rarest bustard in the world with a current population of only 300 to 400 birds. Once fairly common over much of its range from northwest Uttar Pradesh in India, east through the lowlands of Nepal and northeast India to Bangladesh and in Cambodia and Vietnam, it is now confined to a few isolated pockets.

■ In the past, the Bali Starling *(Leucopsar rothschildi)* had a restricted distribution, only occurring on the 300-square kilometer (116-square mile) island of Bali in Indonesia. Now this has diminished to less than 50 square kilometers (19 square miles) encompassed by the Bali Barat National Park and its wild population was 14 in 1998.

■ The Musk Deer *(Moschus)* was originally widespread throughout the forested mountains of Asia including those of the USSR, Korea, China, the Himalayas, and northern Vietnam. Although its overall range is little changed, the population is reduced to disjunct pockets.

Coral Reefs

Sue Wells is the Marine Programme Co-ordinator at WWF International, based in Switzerland. She has a zoology degree from Cambridge University. She previously worked at IUCN for ten years where, among other things, she compiled and edited the three-volume reference work *Coral Reefs of the World*. Prior to joining WWF, she worked freelance as a consultant on coral reef conservation for a number of organizations including IUCN, Greenpeace, the European Union, and the Universities of Newcastle in the UK, and Rhode Island in the U.S.

Coral reefs are among the most productive ecosystems on Earth and can be thought of as the marine equivalents of tropical rainforests. They are also among the oldest ecosystems, having existed for some 450 million years. Reefs are unique in having their basic framework constructed by animals. Each tiny coral animal, called a polyp, secretes a stony cup around itself. The polyps grow and divide to form colonies, some rounded as in brain corals, others branching as in staghorn corals. The living coral colonies form a veneer on the accumulated skeletons of dead coral and so gradually build up into reefs.

Fringing reefs are the youngest type of reef, and develop along the edges of continents and islands, such as those along the coast of east Africa. When changes in sea level separate a fringing reef from the coast, it may form a barrier reef, such as the Great Barrier Reef of Australia which is so large that it is visible from the moon. If an island "sinks," its fringing reef may evolve into an atoll reef, forming a circle with a lagoon in the center. The word "atoll" originated in the Maldives of the Indian Ocean, which are made up entirely of atolls with some of the richest coral reefs in the world.

Essential to the reefs are tiny algae (plants) which live within the coral tissues and use the sun's energy to manufacture food for themselves and for the coral. The algae are responsible for the colors of many corals, but also contribute to the vulnerability of reefs. Algae need plentiful sunlight, so silty or polluted water is potentially lethal. They are also very

Above When exposed by the tide, as in Upolu, western Samoa, coral reefs look dull and stony – yet they teem with life beneath the sea.

Right Reefs are one of the most colorful ecosystems in the world, as can be seen in this general view of a reef in the Red Sea.

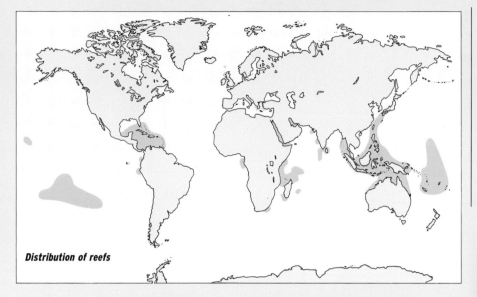

Distribution of reefs

Left Reefs cover an estimated minimum area of 255,000–600,000 square kilometers (98,400–230,000 square miles), extending out of the tropics only where there are warm currents.

Below The Copper Band Butterfly Fish (Chelmon rostratus), has the bright colors typical of many coral reef fish. Its gill covers are raised as an invitation to the cleaner shrimp (Hippolysmata grabhami) to inspect its gills and remove any parasites within them. Several species of fish are cleaned by shrimps while others have a similar relationship with smaller cleaner fish.

susceptible to changes in temperature, and a rise or fall of only a few degrees can cause the algae to die and be ejected from the coral, a phenomenon known as bleaching.

Corals grow very slowly and if they die, or are broken or removed, it may be decades before a reef recovers. Hurricanes often devastate reefs, a particularly serious problem in the Caribbean. Corals also suffer from disease, they are eaten by Crown of Thorns Starfish and other predators, and are eroded by burrowing sea urchins.

LIFE ON THE REEF

The complex, three-dimensional structure of reefs provides food and shelter for a huge range of plants and animals, the most diverse communities being found in southeast Asia and northern Australia. After corals, fish are the most conspicuous animals on a reef. There are more species of fish on a coral reef than in any other habitat in the sea, and there is no terrestrial habitat, not even a rainforest, which has a greater variety of vertebrates. Reefs are home to the smallest known vertebrate, a goby, and are visited by some of the fiercest predators, the sharks. The Hawksbill Turtle feeds on sponges and other invertebrates on the reef, while the Green Turtle is often seen near reefs, and feeds in adjacent sea-grass beds. Seabirds congregate near reefs and atolls, and remote small coral islands provide undisturbed breeding sites for boobies, frigate birds, gulls, and terns.

The reef is also home to a vast array of invertebrates, with almost all major groups represented. Molluscs occur in even greater variety than fish. Some 4,000 species are known from the Great Barrier Reef, including cowries, conchs, Giant Tritons and many others popular as marine curios. Other reef inhabitants include sponges, fan and tube worms, crustaceans, such as the valuable spiny lobster, starfish, and sea urchins.

This enormous variety and productivity mean that many people around the world can make their livelihoods from reefs through, for example, subsistence and commercial fisheries, and the tourist industry. Like rainforests, reefs are also proving to be a significant source of

The cost of reef loss

The beauty of reefs and their diverse community are priceless, but the following give some idea of their economic significance.

■ The potential world yield of fish, crustaceans and molluscs from reefs is estimated at 9 million tons a year.

■ Tourism and recreation on the Great Barrier Reef bring in each year an estimated 700–1 billion Australian dollars.

■ Destruction of the reef around Male in the Maldives necessitated the building of a 4 kilometer (2½ mile) seawall at a cost of 12 million dollars. So as a natural breakwater alone, the original reef was worth 8,000 dollars a yard.

Exploitation of reefs

Coral provides us with, for example:

- fish, molluscs and crustaceans for food
- mother-of-pearl and ornamental shells
- aquarium fish
- sites for tourism and recreation
- coastline protection
- sheltered harbors
- white sandy beaches

medicinal compounds, such as potential anti-cancer drugs, prostaglandins, and even an ultraviolet blocker, found in the tissues of corals, which acts as a "suncream" for the polyps and could be similarly useful for humans.

THREATS

The reef is constantly worn away by the action of waves and the thousands of burrowing animals that live in it. Normally, the growth of a reef keeps pace with erosion and it recovers given sufficient time. But in many areas reefs appear not to be regenerating, and it looks as if humans may be to blame. There is growing concern that the widespread bleaching of corals in the Caribbean and elsewhere may be a symptom of the "greenhouse" effect. On the Great Barrier Reef, the Crown of Thorns Starfish has caused serious damage to corals, while in Kenya and Mauritius, plagues of sea urchins are eroding reefs faster than they are growing. Although neither of these problems is fully understood, some theories suggest that they are due to overfishing by people of the natural predators of the starfish and urchins.

Damage as a result of human activities has been reported in over 90 of the 109 countries with significant coral communities and reefs. Deforestation, resulting in soil erosion and siltation, is affecting reefs in over 50 countries. For example, silt deposited by the Sabaki river in Kenya is killing corals in the reefs of Malindi Marine Park. Coastal development, including dredging, reclamation, destruction of mangroves, and the construction of harbors, airports,

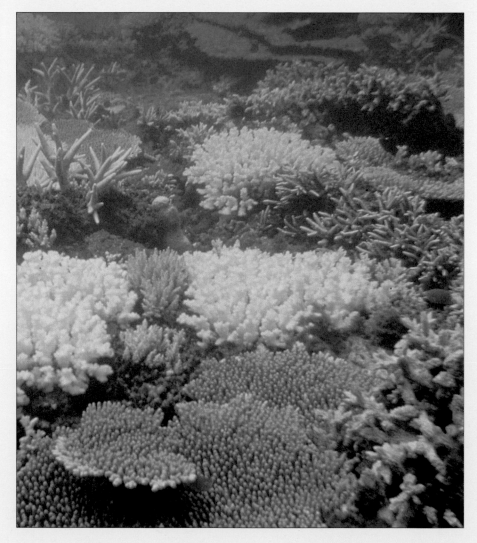

Below *Incidences of coral bleaching have increased dramatically in the last decade. Most of these have been linked to high sea-water temperatures, caused by the climate phenomenon, El Niño. Sometimes the corals recover from bleaching, but in many instances the algae are lost forever and the coral dies. This gives a strong warning of the potential impact that global climate change might have on coral reefs.*

roads, and hotels, has affected reefs in nearly 70 countries. Such activities also smother the remaining corals in silt and are often followed by high levels of sewage and other pollution.

Long appreciated as one of the most beautiful ecosystems on Earth, the reefs and the white sandy beaches formed by their erosion are major tourist attractions. Yet the tourist industry is now threatening the reefs on which it depends in nearly 60 countries. In Florida, for example, there has been a dramatic decrease in live coral cover over the last ten years, and boat groundings, anchors, and divers are clearly implicated.

The reef corals, fish, turtles, molluscs and crustaceans are also being overexploited. Giant Clams, the largest bivalve molluscs in the world reaching up to 137 centimeters (54 inches) in length, have been fished almost to extinction in Fiji and the Philippines. The trade in ornamental corals is increasing, while coral mining for building materials is stripping reefs bare. It has been calculated that in North Malé atoll in the maldives, all shallow submerged reefs could be damaged by the year 2014 if coral mining continues at the current rate. The methods used to exploit reefs are themselves often damaging. Dynamite or other explosives are used to stun reef fish in at least 40 countries, and a beer-bottle sized bomb can destroy a 7-square meter (75-square foot) patch of reef. Aquarium fish are often collected using sodium cyanide, a poison that temporarily paralyses the fish – and kills much of the other life.

CONSERVATION

There are now over 300 protected areas covering reefs in over 70 countries and many more reefs have been recommended for protection. The largest marine park in the world covers nearly 2,000 kilometers (1,250 miles) of the Great Barrier Reef. A system of zones allows one part to be strictly protected, while others are used for research, education, recreation and commercial fishing. However, marine parks alone will not stop the deterioration of reefs: it will never be possible to fence the Crown of Thorns Starfish out of the Great Barrier Reef, or the erosion-induced silt out of Malindi Marine Park. The coast has to be treated as one unit, with the shore, inland catchment area, mangroves, estuaries, and reefs being managed together.

New technology to reduce reef damage is available. Silt "curtains" erected around dredging and mining sites can prevent sediment spreading onto reefs. Sewage can be piped out into deep water or, preferably, treated fully. Mooring bouys can be installed to prevent damage to corals from boat anchors. Species such as Giant Clams can be farmed in tanks or in shallow parts of the reef. The economic importance of reefs provides enormous incentives for these and other methods of protection to be put into practice.

As with all conservation, though, success will depend on improving public understanding of the value of reefs and involving local people in their management. In many Pacific islands, traditional ways of managing reefs are being resuscitated and used in the development of marine parks and reef programs. In the Philippines, numerous small reserves are being set up by fishing villages, with the assistance of local marine scientists and government officers. These reserves usually have a central sanctuary where fishing is prohibited, within a larger area in which traditional ecologically sound fishing methods are permitted. The villagers themselves devise the regulations and are responsible for their enforcement. They often build a small visitors' center and encourage low-level tourism as an additional source of income. In the longer-established reserves, fish populations and damaged corals are starting to recover and fish catches have gone up. This sort of positive feedback will, in the long run, provide the key to the future survival of reefs.

Below Types of coral.

sea fan

pillar

antler

orange tube

Above A snorkeler in the Indian ocean with a table coral. Although generally a harmless pastime, snorkeling can damage a reef, particularly if the visitor handles the coral or kicks it with fins.

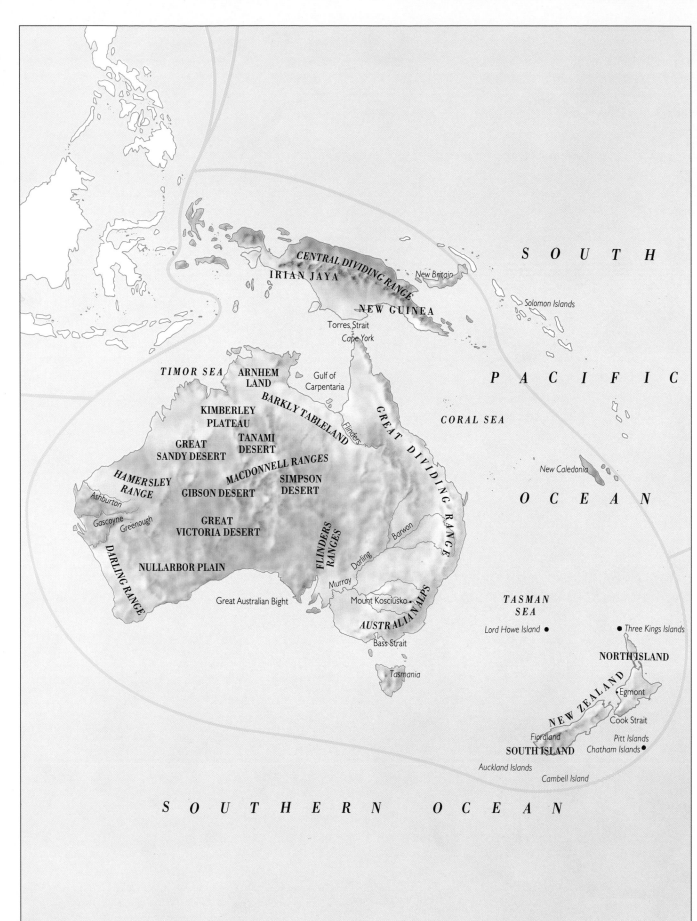

S O U T H

P A C I F I C

O C E A N

CENTRAL DIVIDING RANGE

IRIAN JAYA

New Britain

Solomon Islands

NEW GUINEA

Torres Strait

Cape York

TIMOR SEA

ARNHEM LAND

Gulf of Carpentaria

BARKLY TABLELAND

CORAL SEA

KIMBERLEY PLATEAU

TANAMI DESERT

Flinders

GREAT DIVIDING RANGE

GREAT SANDY DESERT

MACDONNELL RANGES

New Caledonia

HAMERSLEY RANGE

GIBSON DESERT

SIMPSON DESERT

Ashburton

Gascoyne

Greenough

GREAT VICTORIA DESERT

Barwon

DARLING RANGE

NULLARBOR PLAIN

FLINDERS RANGES

Darling

Murray

TASMAN SEA

Great Australian Bight

Mount Kosciusko

AUSTRALIAN ALPS

Lord Howe Island ●

● *Three Kings Islands*

NORTH ISLAND

Bass Strait

Egmont

NEW ZEALAND

Cook Strait

Tasmania

Fiordland

Pitt Islands

SOUTH ISLAND

Chatham Islands ●

Auckland Islands

Cambell Island

S O U T H E R N   O C E A N

The Australasian Region

The Australasian region includes New Guinea (Irian Jaya and Papua New Guinea), Australia and New Zealand. Some classifications put New Zealand in with Antarctica, and New Guinea in Oceania. Habitats range from rainforest to the arid areas of Australia's interior. The diversity of the region's fauna is due to millions of years of undisturbed evolutionary processes.

Erosion on Philip Island caused by rabbits.

Habitat & Plants

Stephen Davis is joint editor of *Centres of Plant Diversity*, a major WWF-IUCN project published in three volumes (1994–97) documenting sites of global importance for plant conservation. He also co-authored *Plants In Danger: What Do We Know?* published by IUCN in 1986. Stephen is now project manager for the Survey of Economic Plants for Arid and Semi-Arid Lands (SEPASAL) based at the Centre for Economic Botany, Royal Botanic Gardens, Kew.

David Given is a specialist on biological diversity based in New Zealand. As well as working as a consultant, he lectures at Lincoln University. He has published over 180 research papers and books and in 1995 authored *Principles and Practice of Plant Conservation*. In 1996 he was awarded the Loder Cup, New Zealand's premier award for plant conservation. Current projects include advising the setting-up of a government biodiversity center in Sarawak, and chairing the plant conservation program of IUCN's Species Survival Commission.

Australasia encompasses Australia, New Guinea (Irian Jaya, and Papua New Guinea) and New Zealand. (In this book, islands such as Sulawesi, the Moluccas and the Lesser Sundas are included in the Indian and Oriental section, pages 150–171.) It is one of the richest areas in the world for plants, with New Guinea alone probably having up to 20,000 vascular plant species, although only about half of these have so far been discovered and named. Both Australia and New Zealand are also among the top 25 hot-spots for overall biological diversity. The habitats range from the luxuriant evergreen and semi-evergreen rainforests of New Guinea and the Queensland coast of Australia, to the extremely arid deserts of Australia's interior and subantarctic herbfields of southern islands.

There are strong resemblances between the floras and faunas of New Guinea, Australia, and New Zealand. These can be traced back to around 135 million years ago, when the supercontinent, Gondwanaland, comprised these three island complexes with Antarctica, Madagascar, India, Africa, and South America. Between 40 and 50 million years ago, Australia and New Guinea, called the Sahul, finally broke away from Antarctica. Australia and New Guinea are now separated only by a shallow sea over the Sahul shelf. New Zealand and the Sahul continued their long, slow evolutionary development, in what was to prove to be rather splendid zoological and botanical isolation. Reminders of those very early links, however, still remain. For example, the southern beeches have a proven poor seed dispersal ability. Yet different species of southern beech (of the genus *Nothofagus*) dominate tropical montane forests in New Guinea and New Caledonia, as well as cool temperate rainforests in places as far apart as Australia, New Zealand, and Chile.

NEW GUINEA

The richest communities of the region are the tropical evergreen rainforests, which are most extensive on New Guinea. About 70 per cent of the island is still under forest cover of one sort

Right Rainforests occur extensively on the island of New Guinea. This coastal lowland rainforest is on the Gulf of Huon, northern Papua New Guinea. Small areas of rainforest also occur in northern Queensland and in the Solomons and other islands around New Guinea.

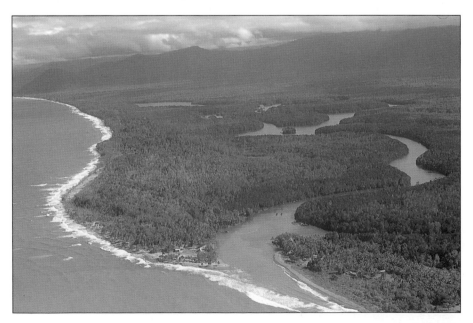

or another. In Irian Jaya (the western part of New Guinea) the figure approaches 92 per cent, giving it the largest tract of tropical evergreen forest remaining in Indonesia. Coastal mangroves and vast lowland swamps are replaced on drier ground and on alluvial plains by lowland evergreen rainforest. Some of the trees have enormous canopies of 50 meters (160 feet) or more, and *Anisoptera thurifera*, one of New Guinea's most important timber trees, reaches 60 meters (200 feet) tall with a girth of 3.6 meters (12 feet). In the forest understory are a host of tree ferns, palms, gingers, marantas, screw pines, epiphytic orchids, and ferns, together with an intertwining network of woody lianas. Rainfall patterns play an important part in governing the natural distribution of this type of forest. For example, in the drier parts of southeastern Papua New Guinea, where there is a marked dry season and annual rainfall of less than 1,800 millimeters (70 inches), rainforest gives way to woodlands containing eucalyptus species different from those found in Australia.

Mountains are a dominant feature of the New Guinea landscape, and include the highest peaks in all of southeast Asia. The backbone of the island is the Central Dividing Range, stretching for more than 650 kilometers (400 miles) and including, in the west, the four highest, permanently snow-capped peaks. A climb up the mountains is a journey through distinct vegetation zones. On mountain slopes, oaks, southern beech and conifers such as the

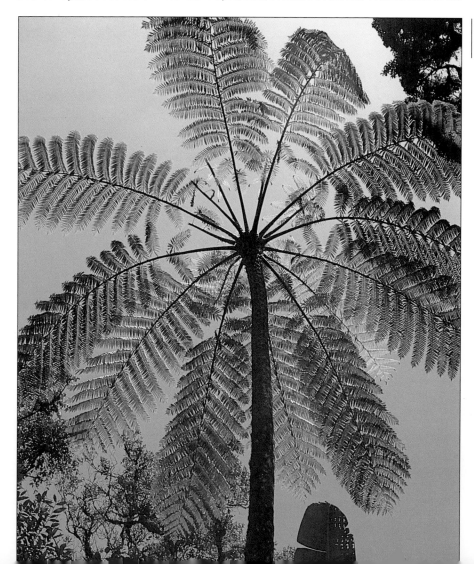

Left Tree ferns are attractive and decorative plants. This species, Cyathea contaminans, *is characteristic of the montane flora of New Guinea.*

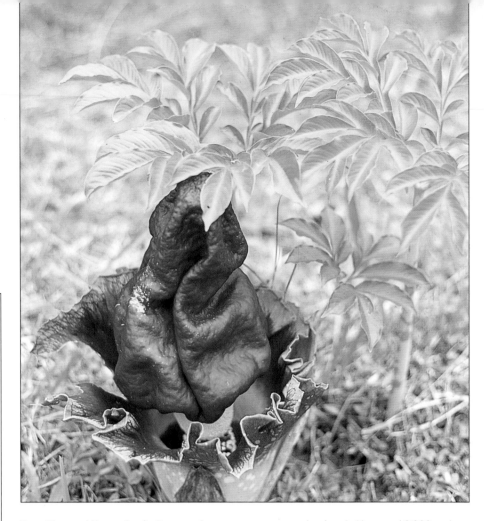

Right An arum lily (Amorphophallus campanulatus) from New Guinea, which is used by the local people to provide an infusion to cure stomach-aches. It is one of the relatively few tropical plants for which a use has been recorded, the medicinal value of the vast majority being unknown.

Medicinal plants

Plants provide us with numerous drugs for the cure and prevention of illness. About 80 per cent of the population of developing countries relies on traditional medicine, 85 per cent of which involves the use of plant extracts. In modern Western medicine, one in four medications prescribed by doctors is likely to contain one or more plant products. It is thought that as many as 1,400 tropical rainforest plants have anti-cancer properties, but less than 1 per cent of the rainforest floor has been screened. Recent research on the Moreton Bay Chestnut *(Castanospermum australe)*, a tree found only in the rainforests of Queensland and New South Wales, has revealed that it contains a compound, castanospermine, that reduces the infectivity of the AIDS virus.

Hoop Pine and the endemic *Papuacedrus papuanus* are predominant. At around 3,000 meters (9,800 feet) one enters the subalpine zone or mossy forest, in which brightly colored rhododendrons and other ericaceous plants form dense thickets, and trees take on a stunted appearance, often draped in mosses and orchids. On the Kemabu Plateau of Irian Jaya, strange-looking giant ant-house plants *(Myrmecodia brassii)* with swollen stem bases provide a home for hundreds, and sometimes thousands, of ants. There, too, grow several species of carnivorous pitcher plants, a group which is highly sought after by commercial collectors and "hobbyists" throughout south-east Asia. In other parts of the region, some species of pitcher plants have been brought close to extinction by collecting from the wild. Further up, a landscape of tree ferns and grasslands occurs on some of the high mountains. These tree fern savannas thrive in areas which have been burned, or which experience periods of drought.

Above the tree limit (at around 3,900 meters/13,000 feet) are montane grasslands and alpine communities, where plants such as buttercups, gentians, and potentillas are found. Although close relatives of these plants are familiar to temperate botanists, most of the species found in the mountains are unique to New Guinea. In fact, around 90 per cent of all the flowering plants of New Guinea may be endemic. This extraordinarily high level of endemism is a reflection of New Guinea's long isolation.

The tropical swamps and exceptionally rich rainforests of New Guinea have sustained indigenous coastal dwellers, shifting cultivators, and hunter-gatherers for thousands of years. The majority of people still rely on the forests for food, medicines, fibers and fuel. Among existing staple foods are sago (a palm of tropical Asian swamps), yams, sweet potato, taro, and breadfruit, an extremely important fruit tree occurring widely in the lowlands. A host of plants provides valuable medical treatments, including an aroid lily *(Amorphophallus campanulatus)* whose sap is used as an infusion to treat stomach-aches, and a fig *(Ficus sceptica)* used for treating fever.

Few plants from the rich rainforests of New Guinea have as yet been screened for their potential value in western medicine. The chance to do so may be slipping away as the pressures to clear the forests continue to grow. Even in remote Irian Jaya, large tracts of forest are being cleared for logging or for the resettlement of thousands of people from the overcrowded island of Java. Commercial logging and clearance for oil palm and other plantation crops is also taking place in Papua New Guinea (the eastern part of New Guinea). Mining is also a threat to forests and river systems.

In Papua New Guinea, especially, shifting cultivation accounts for significant forest losses each year. When practiced on a small scale this system of agriculture mimics the natural openings created in the forest by tree falls. Patches of forest are cleared by the cultivators on a rotational basis to grow a range of crops, and then the cultivators move on to new areas after a few years. Plants gradually invade the once-cultivated land, replenishing the soil nutrients, and a forest similar to the original develops. But as the human population increases, more land has to be cleared more often, and the forest does not have time to regenerate. With repeated burning and clearance over larger and larger areas, forests are converted to grasslands. Today in Papua New Guinea there are approximately 1.5 million people (over half the population) engaged in shifting cultivation, and vast areas which once supported rich tropical rainforest are now dominated by a single species – the Kunai Grass.

AUSTRALIA

In Queensland and New South Wales, tropical and subtropical rainforests have been severely reduced by logging and clearance for dairy cattle, sugar cane, and maize. The Cape York peninsula of Queensland and southwest Australia have the highest proportion of the 1,140 rare and threatened plants of Australia. These forests include *Idiospermum australiense*, a curious tree with primitive characteristics known only to occur in two small areas in northern Queensland. Further south, and in the uplands of New South Wales, Victoria, and Tasmania, are cool temperate rainforests dominated by southern beech and *Eucalyptus* including the giant Mountain Ash, the world's tallest flowering plant reaching over 100 meters (330 feet).

Below left Rainforest in Lamington National Park, Queensland, Australia. In addition to the oft-cited value of rainforest as a source of important medicinal plants, lumber and other plants, it has a less tangible but nonetheless important aesthetic value, as this scene demonstrates.

Below Despite the fact that Australia is a wealthy nation with numerous natural resources, remnants of tropical rainforest outside protected areas are still being destroyed and fragmented through the expansion of agriculture, building developments and road schemes. Even a road as wide as this one can be a barrier to dispersal for some rainforest plants.

The forests of Australia, dominated in many instances by the genus *Eucalyptus* (or Gum Tree) with over 600 species, are remnants of the original closed forests of Gondwanaland from which most of the present-day Australian flora has evolved. Due to the continent's isolation over the last 45 million years (since Australia separated from Africa and South America), 80 per cent of the species are endemic and there are over 500 endemic genera. Australia harbors important relics, some of which are still being discovered. A recent spectacular find has been the primitive Wollemi Pine *(Wollemia nobilis)*, known only from a single population in New South Wales. As Australia slowly drifted to the north, plants from southeast Asia were able to spread into Australia. The original temperate flora was gradually replaced by one which was adapted to the arid conditions of Australia's interior, and the tropical zone of the north. Today, the forest remnants are regarded as extremely important. Their protection was firmly placed on Australia's political agenda by vigorous national and international campaigns over the proposed damming of the Franklin river, which threatened Tasmanian temperate rainforests, and the destruction of tropical forest at Daintree River in Queensland caused by road building.

Tropical and subtropical closed forests are not the only ones under threat in Australia. Open forests and dry woodlands of acacia and eucalypts have also been extensively cleared, mainly for sheep or cattle grazing. Today, there are over 150 species of eucalypts and 160 species of acacia listed as either rare, threatened or insufficiently known. Heathlands, too, particularly in the southwestern part of Western Australia, continue to be cleared for

Below *There are more than 600 species of Eucalyptus, a genus of gum trees, ironbarks, and stringybarks, almost all of which are restricted to Australia. Although some species dominate Australia's forests and woodlands, there are over 100 species currently at risk, mainly as a result of forest clearance, grazing, and urban expansion.*

agriculture. There, 46 species out of a total heathland flora of 3,700 species are critically endangered, including orchids, such as *Drakaea jeanensis* and *Diuris purdiei*, and a number of banksias, such as *Banksia goodii*, which are also highly sought after by collectors. An orchid in Western Australia that eludes collectors (but not land developers) is *Rhizanthella gardneri*, one of two amazing Australian species with flowers below ground level. Unfortunately, the distribution of this underground orchid coincides with Western Australia's wheatbelt. Providing some areas of heathland are saved as reserves, the future of this extraordinary plant, along with other endemic heathland plants, can be secured.

NEW ZEALAND

When the first Europeans began to settle in New Zealand during the early nineteenth century, they found a remarkable land of mountains and forests dominated by birds and insects. Forest cover is now reduced to about 27 per cent of the land area and many of the animals are threatened. The changes, which began with the arrival of the Polynesians some 800 years ago, have accelerated as forests have been cleared, wetlands drained, and coasts developed. The once extensive rainforests of Kauri and ancient podocarps were prime targets for timber, although they are now mostly protected.

New Zealand's flora, like that of Australia and New Guinea, has evolved for millions of years in isolation, and over 80 per cent of its flowering plants are unique to the two main islands. Today over 10 per cent of New Zealand's 2,300 native vascular plants are threatened

Below left *Heathlands similar to this one near Mount Chudilup, Western Australia, are still being cleared for agriculture. As in Britain and the rest of Europe, they are considered wastelands. The rich and diverse flora of Australia's heathlands includes the famous underground orchid* (Rhizanthella gardneri).

Below *The Philip Island Hibiscus* (Hibiscus insularis) *is confined to Philip Island between New Zealand and Australia, where its continuing survival depends on the effective control of rabbits.*

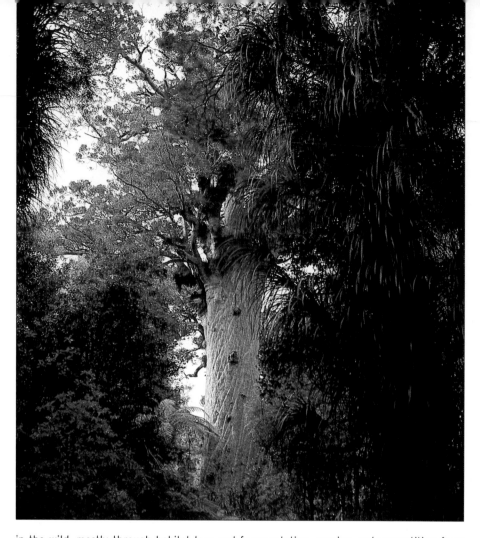

Right *Tanemahuta – an example of the New Zealand Kauri* (Agathis australis) *in Waipoua forest, New Zealand. Once widely exploited for timber, these massive trees up to 55 meters (180 feet) are now largely protected.*

Tecomanthe speciosa

Hebe speciosa

in the wild, mostly through habitat loss and fragmentation, grazing and competition from introduced weeds. This includes such remarkable plants as *Helichrysum dimorphum*, an endangered climbing daisy which is unique in changing its leaf shape to combat drought, and the living fossil, *Loxoma cunninghamii*, a relict from the Gondwanan forests.

Many of New Zealand's offshore islands have their own unique species. On some of these islands such as the Chatham archipelago east of New Zealand, where there are about 40 endemic species and two endemic genera, some plants are still threatened by grazing and land clearance. The vegetation here includes swamp forests, peat domes, unique rushlands and coastal dunelands. More than half the Chatham Island endemic plants are under threat, including the remarkable Chatham Island Forget-me-not (the monotypic genus *Myosotidium*). At one time this succulent herb with giant leaves and flowerheads was said to form an unbroken line along the shores of the Chatham Islands, but it is now greatly reduced in abundance. Other outlying islands are mostly protected nature reserves. An outstanding example is the Three Kings Islands with 12 endemic species, including *Tecomanthe speciosa*, an attractive vine known in the wild from only a single plant. In the far south of New Zealand a unique "megaherb" flora of giant-leaved colorful flowering plants is protected on the wave-lashed New Zealand subantarctic islands.

New Zealand has an extensive and largely endemic alpine flora including such notable genera as *Celmisia* (mountain daisy), *Aciphylla* (speargrass) and the mountain snowgrass *(Chionochloa)*. Although much of this is now protected, introduced herbivores such as thar, chamois and goats are a continuing threat, and mountain recreation and tourism development can provide local threats. A long-term threat to both mountain and lowland forests throughout New Zealand is the exploding population of Australian brush-tailed possum, now estimated at 70 million individuals. The possum was originally introduced to provide a fur trade, but browses on many of the important forest trees.

Coastal regions are a particular focal point for human disturbance and many lowland plants and coastal habitats are at risk. Coastal wetlands are reduced in extent by over 90 per cent, and sand-dune systems cover only a small fraction of their former extent. Plants such as the Golden Sand Sedge or Pingao *(Desmoschoemus spiralis)*, an important source of weaving material for the Maori, have disappeared from many parts of the New Zealand coast. This species is now being replanted to provide a source of craft materials. Species such as *Hebe speciosa*, a parent of many widely grown horticultural hybrids, have become increasingly rare in the wild.

There is, however, much cause for optimism. Over 25 per cent of New Zealand is under government protection. Over 2,000 private land protection agreements are in place. The Department of Conservation has an active program for assessment of risk to species, and is starting to develop recovery plans for threatened plants. Recently, the Department launched the concept of "mainland islands," large areas which will be managed intensively for predator control and species recovery. A large number of New Zealand plants are attractive to gardeners so that increasing numbers are being grown in botanical collections. An important current issue is that of the claim of ownership of New Zealand plants by the Maori, the indigenous Polynesian people.

As elsewhere, the long-term survival of the diverse flora of the Australasian region depends on the continued monitoring and protection of areas and habitats that have important concentrations of plant species, especially those which are endemic to the region. It also depends increasingly on managing production land in ways which allow native species to survive. Gardens and protected wild areas such as nature reserves and national parks also provide opportunities for the ongoing education of people in New Zealand about their unique native plants, and for generating the public support that is so vital to the success of conservation efforts.

Clianthus puniceus

Helichrysum dimorphum

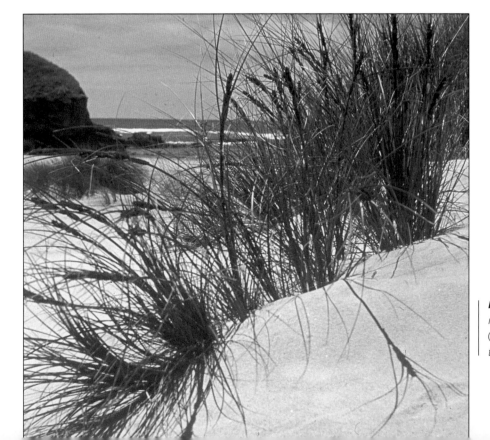

Left *Once widespread in coastal sand dunes but now rare in many parts of New Zealand, Pingao* (Desmoschoemus spiralis) *is a plant highly valued by the Maori who use it as a weaving material.*

Wildlife

Michael Kennedy became the coordinator of Friends of the Earth New South Wales in 1978, and in 1981 took up the position of Campaign Director for The Fund for Animals Ltd., Australia, one of the country's largest membership conservation organizations. Michael also jointly established a TRAFFIC office in Australia in 1983, and in 1986 became personal environmental adviser to the Australian Federal Minister for the Environment. He was the past Senior Project Officer for World Wide Fund for Nature Australia and coordinated the threatened species networks. Michael is currently the director of Humane Society International in Australia.

The diversity and beauty of wildlife species to be found in the Australasian region is immense. This is due both to millions of years of isolated and undisturbed evolutionary processes, and to the extremely broad range of ecosystems and habitat types that still exist today. Australia, for example, has the most desert reptiles of any nation in the world, and has an overall national reptile count of some 765 species, one of the highest in the world.

Vast tracts of tropical rainforests, thousands of square miles of perhaps the most inhospitable deserts known to mankind, untouched expanses of precious wetland and mangrove stands, alpine habitats, temperate forests resplendent with numerous wild and untamed rivers, grasslands, heathlands, and many other discrete biogeographic provinces, provide a species variety to please the most ardent wildlife watcher.

The risks that face these ecosystems and species are unfortunately significant. As the following pages will show, Australasia has suffered more than, or at least as much as, any other region of the globe. The process of halting such a loss of biological diversity has become one of the most urgent issues of our time.

NEW GUINEA'S TROPICAL WILDERNESS

The island of New Guinea, comprising Irian Jaya in the west and Papua New Guinea in the east, has been described as one of the six major tropical wilderness areas left on Earth. It is a

AUSTRALIA

Below This graphic representation of the status of Australasia's extinct and threatened wildlife does not include whales, dolphins, or marine turtles. It is also important to remember that it only represents species whose status is known; question marks indicate that the status of a particular group is still to be determined.

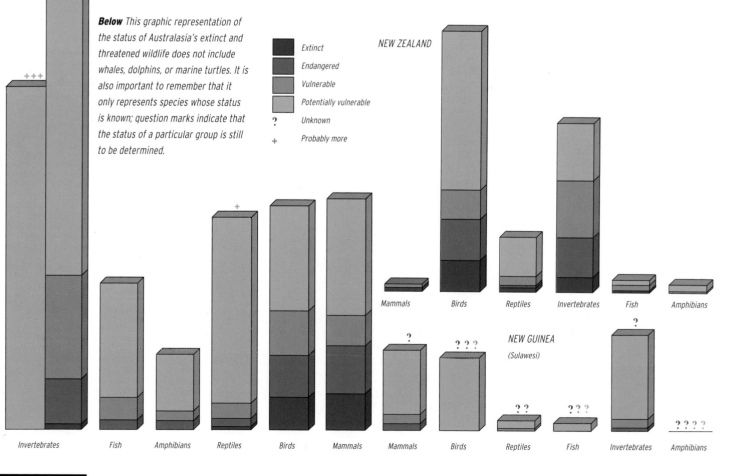

Extinct
Endangered
Vulnerable
Potentially vulnerable
? Unknown
+ Probably more

NEW ZEALAND

Mammals Birds Reptiles Invertebrates Fish Amphibians

NEW GUINEA
(Sulawesi)

Invertebrates Fish Amphibians Reptiles Birds Mammals Mammals Birds Reptiles Fish Invertebrates Amphibians "good news" area according to one well-known scientist, where unusual species' concentrations exist and where the threats are not so imminent, though pressures are now clearly increasing. Vertebrates abound, including over 200 mammals, over 700 birds, over 300 reptiles and over 200 amphibians. There is an unknown number of freshwater fish, although 103 species have been identified in the Fly river alone. The estimates for invertebrates range well into the hundreds of thousands of species, but these are based on scant scientific knowledge and the true figure is probably much higher.

The threats facing the wildlife of New Guinea are many and varied. Agricultural land and settlements for the ever-increasing human populations continue to encroach upon wildlife habitats. Industry is also taking its toll. A scandal in Papua New Guinea over government corruption in the logging industry revealed that rates of forest destruction due to timber extraction are far higher than had previously been thought, and things have not improved in subsequent years. Mining, with its destructive and polluting history, is becoming a major growth area (the Fly river for example has been very seriously polluted by foreign mining activities, with obvious implications for its unique freshwater fauna and flora). Trade in wildlife and traditional hunting play their role in reducing populations, too. There is a flourishing trade (legal and illegal) in Irian Jaya, and hunting in Papua New Guinea also has an effect on wildlife, especially when modern weapons are used and traditional practices ignored.

All these factors are putting pressure on New Guinea's largely endemic fauna. So far no confirmed vertebrate extinction can be attributed to the activities, but it seems likely that many invertebrate and plant species were swept away with the rainforests that have been cleared to date. The next decade will be a critical period for the precious fauna of New Guinea and islands to the west. In Papua New Guinea alone, for example, over 120 species of vertebrates and invertebrates are threatened to some degree. Again, these figures reflect our lack of knowledge about the region and are probably gross underestimations.

Below *The Ornate or Goodfellow's Tree-Kangaroo (Dendrolagus goodfellowi) is under pressure from hunting in its forest home in the central highlands of Papua New Guinea. Although it is believed to have declined, little is known of its precise status.*

THE MARSUPIALS

New Guinea and Australia are the only two countries in the world that are home to both the marsupials (pouched mammals) and monotremes (egg-laying mammals). In Irian Jaya (and undoubtedly throughout New Guinea) approximately 50 per cent of the endemic marsupials are montane species, highlighting the importance of the rainforests covering the Central Dividing Range.

Little is known about some of the threatened marsupials, particularly the tree-kangaroos. New Guinea has the largest number of these amazing animals, with 15 species in all, including the Golden-mantled Tree-kangaroo. Of all the tree-kangaroos, the Golden-mantled, along with the Tenkile, is the most threatened, described as "critical" by Tim Flannery, curator of mammals at the Australian Museum. The Golden-mantled Tree-kangaroo lives at the eastern edge of the Torricelli Mountains, probably limited to an area of a mere 20 square kilometers (7.7 square miles). Hunting appears to be one of the continuing threats to its survival. The other species over which there is concern include Goodfellow's, Tenkile, Timboyok, Ifola, Finsch's, Vogelkop, Seri's Dingiso, Fiwo, and Matschie's Tree-kangaroo.

Among other threatened members of the kangaroo and wallaby family are two beautiful wallabies, the vulnerable Macleay's Dorcopsis and the endangered Black Dorcopsis. Macleay's Dorcopsis is an extremely rare animal, known only from a few specimens. It is found in mid-montane forests in the eastern part of New Guinea, and is considered vulnerable to any disturbance in its very restricted range. The Black Dorcopsis, another montane marsupial, is restricted to one, possibly two, islands off the northeast coast of New Guinea. Its very dense and luxuriant black fur, suiting its cold habitat, distinguishes this wallaby from its distant mainland relatives, most of which inhabit lowland forests.

The staggering variety among New Guinea's marsupials is exemplified by carnivorous marsupials like the Bronze Quoll, long-nosed bandicoots such as the Dimorphic or Clara's Bandicoot, the beautiful Woodlark Cuscus, the endangered Black-spotted Cuscus, and the many gliders and possums, including the vulnerable Torricelli or Northern Glider and D'Albertis Ringtail. Most of these are rare species with highly restricted distributions.

AMAZING MONOTREMES

Of even more concern is one of New Guinea's two monotremes. The Short-beaked Echidna also inhabits Australia and its status in New Guinea is uncertain. The Long-beaked Echidna only occurs in New Guinea and is one of the most biologically important and threatened animals there. It is the largest of all monotremes, and also differs from its short-beaked relative in having a tongue uniquely adapted to feeding on earthworms. It is found over most of New Guinea, but with increasing rarity, and it seems that wherever human populations are high, the species is unlikely to be found. It is extremely hard to locate in the field, and is becoming locally extinct in large areas of the central highlands. Hunting pressures appear to have seriously affected population levels, and the species is endangered throughout New Guinea.

Above *The Long-beaked Echidna* (Zaglossus bruijni) *is confined to humid montane forests at altitudes of up to 4,150 meters (13,600 feet) in New Guinea. These egg-laying mammals only occur where human populations are low, and have recently become extinct in large areas of the central highlands. They have also declined in other areas where traditional taboos against eating them have broken down under the influence of missionaries.*

Right *A female Blue Bird of Paradise* (Paradisaea rudolphi) *feeding on a pandanus fruit. One of the most spectacularly beautiful of all the birds of paradise, the male has long blue, purple and cinnamon plumes on the flanks and two very long black-tailed streamers.*

Far right *A male Lesser Bird of Paradise* (Paradisaea minor). *After being brought back to Spain by Magellan's crew in 1521, this bird was systematically hunted for its plumes until it finally received protection in the 1920s when the world-wide trade in bird plumes was stopped.*

BATS AND BIRDS

New Guinea's bat fauna has not escaped the depredation of a growing human society, for example, the Lesser Bare-backed Fruit Bat, and Bulmer's Fruit Bat, both rainforest inhabitants. New Guinea's long list of threatened vertebrates is unfortunately well represented by the birds. Perhaps as many as 50 New Guinea birds may be at risk, including the Black Honey

Buzzard. A very rare endemic from New Britain, it inhabits lowland forest that is continually being logged and destroyed for oil-palm plantations. Other threatened birds of prey include the New Britain Sparrow Hawk, the Imitator Sparrow Hawk, and the New Guinea Eagle.

It is the region's birds of paradise that are simultaneously the most spectacular and the most sought after. These magnificent birds are highly prized for their extremely long and often iridescent plumes, both by indigenous peoples and overseas collectors. Fortunately, only six of the 40 or so species are actually threatened, and those that are, suffer from habitat destruction rather than collection for feathers. Species of concern include Goldie's Birds of Paradise, the Ribbon-tailed Astrapia and the Long-tailed Paradigalla.

REPTILES AND FISH

Reptile species officially recorded as threatened in New Guinea include most of the world's endangered sea turtles, the Pig-nosed Turtle, and the Estuarine Crocodile. The vulnerable Pig-

Duck-billed Platypus
(Ornithorhynchus anatinus)

Short-beaked Echidna
(Tachyglossus aculeatus)

Left A New Guinea Crocodile (Crocodylus novaeguinea) being reared on a crocodile farm in Papua New Guinea.

nosed Turtle (which also occurs in Australia) is under pressure from local hunting. The Estuarine Crocodile (recognized world wide as vulnerable to extinction) was extensively exploited in the past but is now managed under internationally approved ranching programs. The marine turtles continue to suffer from direct utilization, including egg collection and by catch in fisheries operations.

New Guinea has increasing numbers of threatened freshwater fish, including at least 12 species of "Goby," such as the Robert's, Irian and Fly River Gobies. Papua New Guinea has one of the highest numbers of threatened fish in the world.

AUSTRALIAN MEGADIVERSITY

Australia is acknowledged by scientists as being one of a dozen "megadiversity" countries on Earth today. The criteria for achieving this lofty status include a nation's total number of species, and the proportion of species, genera, families and so on that are endemic. Australia has far more endemic families than any other country in the world, including seven endemic families of mammals. The (Short-beaked) Echidna and the Platypus occur together only in

Australia. Of the marsupial species, 89 per cent are endemic, as are 73 per cent of other mammals. At least 70 per cent of Australia's bird species are endemic, along with 88 per cent of the reptiles and over 95 per cent of the amphibians.

In terms of sheer species, Australia can claim the second largest reptile count in the world (756 species), the third highest number of amphibians in Asia (208 species), over 1,000 bird species, and over 260 species of mammal. With the inclusion of over 200 freshwater fish species, a "guesstimate" of around 100,000 insect species, and tens of thousands of molluscs, the continent deserves its place on the global role of biological honor. Moreover, Australia has wilderness areas spread across a far wider range of habitats than in any other country.

THREATS AND LOSSES

The bad news is that much of this staggering diversity has been severely affected by the activities of settlers from Europe. Since they first colonized Australia over 200 years ago, Australians have cleared about 75 per cent of the rainforests, 66 per cent of the country's original tree cover, and chronically degraded well over 50 per cent of the arid lands. As a result, Australia also holds some more unfortunate world records. It has the worst mammal extinction rate of any country in the world, 18 mammals having become extinct – approximately half of all the mammal species that have been lost globally in recent historical times. In addition, over 100 mammals, 100 birds, 100 reptiles, 40 frogs, 70 fish, and over 400 invertebrate species are now considered to be at some degree of risk.

Australia is home to only 18 million people and most of its vast lands are uninhabited, the southeastern and southwestern coastal areas supporting the bulk of urban and rural life. Yet

Right *The Bridled Nailtail Wallaby or Flashjack* (Onychogalea fraenata) *was believed to have become extinct by the 1930s. It was rediscovered in 1973 near Dingo, eastern Queensland, and the area is now protected. A captive colony has also been established.*

it is in the central and arid zones with sparse human populations that species' extinctions have been highest. A third of desert mammals have become extinct, and an alarming 90 per cent of all small to medium-sized mammals in the arid zones are now considered to be either extinct or endangered. What caused this biological catastrophe?

The affected mammals fall within the weight range 35–5,500 grams (1¼–194 ounces), and have been described as "critical weight range species." It is believed that these species were susceptible to subtle changes in climate conditions. Living on a harsh arid zone, survival was difficult enough at the best of times. When droughts came, their distribution contracted to smaller "refugia" with suitable vegetation, where they were prone to natural local extinctions. When the Europeans brought their stock animals to the central arid zones, the smaller mammals simply could not compete and the "refugia" became virtual prisons.

Scientists have also suggested that it was frequent burning of large areas of desert by Aboriginal communities over the past 60,000 years that had created suitable habitats for a large range of mammals. When the Aboriginals were forcibly moved from their lands by invading Europeans, many thousands of years of land management expertise were lost. Wildfires became the norm and conditions radically changed. Unable to disperse from their "refugia" when good rains fell, the remaining mammals were probably particularly vulnerable to predation by introduced foxes, animals that have caused tremendous damage to small and medium-sized mammal populations across Australia. Domestic cats gone feral, sheep, cattle, camels, pigs, goats and an endless list of exotics all helped seal the mammal fate.

The above are hypotheses and cannot now be proven, but, in deadly combination, they clearly played a role in the drastic decline of Australian wildlife. To this list of extinct mammals can be added two species of rodent, Maclear's Rat and the Burrowing Rat, which once lived in the Australian Territory of Christmas Island in the Indian Ocean. This brings the total mammal extinction count to 20 species.

MARSUPIALS AND RODENTS AT RISK

Large numbers of other marsupials and rodents remain at risk, including some of Australia's most beautiful kangaroos and wallabies. The highly endangered Bridled Nailtail Wallaby has only one population remaining on Tauntan National Park in Central Queensland. The Yellow-

DISTRIBUTION
BRIDLED NAILTAIL WALLABY

Former range

Current range

Range of the Bridled Nailtail Wallaby (Onychogalea fraenata). Formerly abundant, it has been reduced to a small population in east Queensland.

Right The Southern Hairy-nosed Wombat (Lasiorhinus latifrons) *is similar in appearance to the Common Wombat but has finer and softer fur and a hairy nose. It occurs in southern Australia where it is locally abundant but populations are fragmented and suffer from competition with rabbits. It has also recently been discovered in New South Wales.*

Below The Numbat or Banded Anteater (Myrmecobius fasciatus) *is, unusually for a marsupial, active by day. Its numbers have declined dramatically and it is now extinct in New South Wales, Victoria, Northern Territory and South Australia.*

footed Rock-Wallaby in western New South Wales, the Black-footed Rock-Wallaby and Tammar Wallaby in western Australia, and the Rufous Hare-Wallaby in the Northern Territory are all presenting wildlife managers with extremely tough problems. The Rufous Hare-Wallaby (or Mala), considered the most endangered of all marsupials, now remains only in captive colonies. It is a classic example of the serious decline among desert mammal populations, for this species once inhabited more than 25 per cent of the continent.

The list of other famous marsupials in need of conservation help is extensive, but the following examples highlight the diversity in this marvellous animal group. The Northern Hairy-nosed Wombat remains in one isolated population (perhaps 65 animals) in Epping Forest National Park in central coastal Queensland. The Bilby, one of the most fragile and unusual looking of all the bandicoot family, has declined in numbers by approximately 70 per cent and now only remains with small threatened populations in three states. The Long-footed Potoroo, southeastern Australia's most endangered species, is being pushed to the brink by logging activities in Victoria and New South Wales. The Golden Bandicoot from north Western Australia and the Numbat from the southwest Western Australia are two striking examples of species that have been lost from more than 90 per cent of their former ranges in recent times. There is a successful conservation program for the Numbat involving captive breeding, reintroductions and relocations to parts of its former range, and it has come to symbolize the conservation fight in Western Australia.

Among the possums, three of the most endangered are Leadbeater's Possum, the Mountain Pygmy-possum and the Western Ringtail Possum. The first two are threatened by logging activities and ski resort development respectively. The ringtail possums in the east of Australia are often thought of as "pests," living happily in urban gardens, and most Australians are surprised to learn of the difficulties facing the western cousin.

Also suffering heavily are the fascinating dasyurids, small insectivorous or carnivorous marsupials. The largest dasyurids left on the mainland are the native "cats" or quolls. Extremely beautiful, agile, and fierce, they remain secure only in Tasmania. The Western Quoll

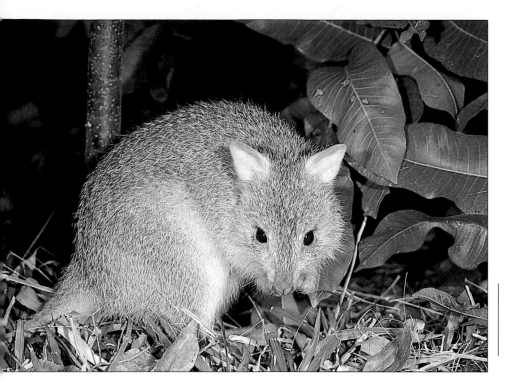

Left The Rufous Bettong (Aepyprymnus rufescens) is a small nest-building kangaroo that lives in open forests. Although it is still reasonably widespread, development pressures, grazing and perhaps forestry practice are having their effect.

or Chuditch is extremely endangered, surviving only in large jarrah forests in southwest Western Australia. Smaller dasyurids known to be at risk include the marsupial "mice," the Atherton Antechinus, the Cinnamon Antechinus, the Mulgara, the Dibbler, the Red-tailed Phascogale, and the Sandhill Dunnart.

The two endemic monotreme species, the Short-beaked Echidna, and the Platypus, are still common and maintain viable populations. But some scientists are concerned that the Platypus is a potentially vulnerable animal. It is extinct in South Australia, and is coming under increasing pressures from human use and pollution of its freshwater habitats in eastern Australia.

Although less appealing to many people than the marsupials, the rodents are a valuable component of the Australian fauna with a high degree of endemicity. A significant proportion of species, 8 out of 65, are extinct, and at least 25 species are thought to be under some degree of threat, ranging from highly endangered to potentially vulnerable.

The Greater Sticknest Rat is probably the best known of the rodents in trouble. Once found across the entire southern half of Australia, the species has not been seen on the mainland since 1933. It is famed for building above ground large sticknests, which can reach 1 meter (3 1/4 feet) high and 1.5 meters (5 feet) across. Less than 1,000 individuals remain, only on the Franklin island off the coast of South Australia. A new conservation program aims to reintroduce the rat to a part of its previous range in coastal and central Western Australia. One of this rat's close cousins, the Lesser Sticknest Rat, has also not been seen since 1933, and is now listed as extinct. Reported sightings still occur in the desert regions of South Australia, leading to some hopes that it may one day be "rediscovered." The threatened rodent list also includes the False Water Rat, the Thornton Peak Melomys, and a significant number of indigenous mice. Among these are the Smoky Mouse, now extinct in New South Wales and occurring only in Victoria; the Shark Bay Mouse from the Shark Bay region of Western Australia; and the Northern Hopping Mouse found only on Groote Eylandt in the top end of Northern Territory.

Northern Hopping Mouse (Notomys aquilo)

Shark Bay Mouse (Pseudomys praeconis)

False Water Rat (Xeromys myoides)

Right *The Australian Sealion* (Neophoca cinerea) *is the only seal endemic to Australia. Although they are no longer hunted, the populations do not appear to be increasing in number, but have been removed from the endangered list.*

DISTRIBUTION
SWAMP TURTLE

■ *Current range*

Western Swamp Turtle (Pseudomydura umbrina). *One of Australia's (and perhaps the world's) most endangered reptiles, there are probably fewer than 100 animals left in the wild. Although wildlife authorities have had some success with captive breeding, its future remains in peril.*

ENDEMIC BATS

Increasing numbers of endemic bats are worrying wildlife biologists. The Ghost Bat has recently been removed from the endangered list by Australian bat specialists, though is still regarded as "near threatened." It is the only carnivorous bat in Australia, and eats large insects, reptiles, frogs, birds, small mammals, and even other bat species. Occurring in the northern half of the continent, its habit of roosting in caves has contributed to its decline. In Queensland, for instance, a limestone mining company, with the full permission of the then Queensland government, blew up one of the species' main roosting caves at Mount Etna, near Rockhampton, causing international outrage. The spectacular, endemic Orange Horseshoe-Bat, also from northern Australia, has been badly affected by human interference, with entire colonies abandoning their roosts.

THE SEALION AND THE DUGONG

Two marine mammal species causing concern are the Australian Sealion and the Dugong. Hunted heavily in the last century, the sealion has still not fully recovered, though it has now been removed from the endangered list. Although the current population of approximately 80,000 animals makes the Australian Dugong population one of the healthiest in the world, it still remains vulnerable in its northern tropical coastal home, and is considered "critically endangered" in the southern half of the Great Barrier Reef Marine Park. Gill-netting fishing practices appear to be the primary cause of serious decline.

THE BIRDS

Australian birds have so far proved no more resilient than mammals to the depredations of human society. Twenty-three species and subspecies have been lost from Australia, though most are unique subspecies from island territories. These include the King Island Emu, the Grey Fantail from Norfolk Island, and the Tasman Starling from Lord Howe Island.

Australia is renowned for its broad array of parrot species, and an alarmingly high proportion of these are threatened to some degree. Those of particular concern include the Golden-shouldered, the Hooded, the Orange-bellied, and the Scarlet-chested Parrots. Habitat destruction has been mainly responsible for the decline of these species. Many are further threatened by the activities of wildlife smugglers, such as the Golden-shouldered Parrot and the potentially vulnerable Palm Cockatoo, both found in restricted habitats at the top end of the Cape York peninsula in Queensland.

Other well-known Australian birds continue to struggle against very stiff odds. The extremely beautiful Mallee Fowl builds a very large nesting mound – measuring 2–5 meters (6½–16½ feet) in diameter and one meter (3¼ feet) high – by filling an excavation with sand, dry leaves, twigs, and bark. The male carefully controls the temperature of the eggs inside this incubating mound by adding or removing sand as necessary. The Mallee Fowl is now vulnerable to extinction through loss of its essential mallee (dwarf eucalyptus), dry scrub habitat, and predation of eggs and chicks by introduced foxes.

Another attentive parent, the male Cassowary, has been observed sitting on the eggs for 48 days without getting up, feeding or drinking. This remarkable flightless bird, standing up to 1.8 meters (6 feet) tall, is also vulnerable to extinction, with possibly fewer than 4,000 birds left. Destruction of its rainforest home in north Queensland, illegal hunting, disease, and road kills have all taken their toll.

Far left *The cheeks of the spectacular Palm Cockatoo* (Probosciger aterrimus) *turn bright red when the bird is excited. It is much sought after by illegal traffickers and collectors.*

Left *The Diamond Python* (Morelia spilota spilota) *is restricted to the eucalyptus and rainforests of New South Wales. It is a distinct subspecies of the more widespread Carpet Python and, because of its attractive markings, has been widely collected for the pet trade.*

The Gouldian Finch and the Rufous Scrub Bird are other examples of highly endangered mainland Australian birds. But it is among the birds of Australia's island territories that the bulk of avian extinctions have been experienced to date. The Lesser Noddy, the Norfolk Island Parrot, the Norfolk Island Boobook Owl, and Abbott's Booby are a few of the many species threatened in these island habitats. The Norfolk Island Boobook Owl is unfortunately down to one remaining specimen – a solitary female. She has four hybrid offspring, with evidently insufficient viable genes to keep the species in existence.

REPTILES

Of Australia's 50 or so endangered and vulnerable reptiles, the Western Swamp Turtle is easily one of the most endangered. There are fewer than 100 remaining in the wild, isolated in two small ephemeral swamps near Perth in Western Australia, and the turtle's future depends upon intensive captive breeding programs. Although there have been a number of successful

DISTRIBUTION
PALM COCKATOO

■ *Current range*

In Australia, the Palm Cockatoo (Probosciger aterrimus) *occurs only at the extreme north of the Cape York peninsula, Queensland. It does also have an extensive range in New Guinea, but has been wiped out in most areas close to villages.*

batches of young to date, its long-term survival is still far from assured. Three snakes, the Diamond Python, the Broad-headed Snake, and the Western Black-striped Snake, all suffer from the dual threats of habitat destruction and the wildlife trade.

The reptile with perhaps the worst public image in Australia is the Saltwater Crocodile. The subject of much controversy, it was hunted to near-extinction after the Second World War. The Western Australian population is now extremely small and isolated. In Queensland, the population is under threat from habitat destruction, illegal trade and shooting, and removal from eastern coastal habitats by wildlife authorities for use in "farms." The Northern Territory's population is protected primarily so that it can be utilized in endorsed "ranching" operations, though permission has recently been given for the killing of wild animals for commercial export purposes. Many conservation organizations believe that the present export program is not in the best interests of the species' long-term survival.

On Australian islands, the reptile fauna has been as vulnerable as the mammals and birds, and includes three threatened skinks. The Pedra Branca Skink, while seemingly secure, is precariously linked to the well-being of Pedra Branca Island seabird colonies on which it feeds. Increasing commercial fishing near this Tasmanian island may have catastrophic results. The island home of the vulnerable Lord Howe Island Skink is located some 800 kilometers (500 miles) off the New South Wales coast. The endangered Lancelin Island Skink occurs off the southwest coast of Western Australia. Both skinks have been affected by introduced animals.

AMPHIBIANS AND FISH

The alarming declines among the amphibians of continental Australia have caused warning bells to ring around the country. In the last fifteen years or so, as many as a dozen frog species have disappeared from their rainforest haunts down the east coast of Australia. Nobody knows why, but one hypothesis is that the disappearances are linked to subtle effects of climatic change. Australia has the only frog that incubates its young in its stomach, the Platypus Frog, and one of the only two species in the world that uses sign language to communicate, the Eungella Torrent Frog. The former is highly endangered, having not been seen for a number of years, while the latter has also moved into this dubious category. The thirty or so other amphibians considered potentially vulnerable to extinction include the Baw Baw Frog from Victoria, and the Mount Glorious Torrent Frog from southern Queensland.

There is a relatively low number (about 200) of freshwater fish species in Australia, but

Right The Great White Shark (Carcharodon carcharias) *is still widespread in most of the warmer waters of the world but has suffered in recent years from a bad press, particularly after the release of the film* Jaws, *and is threatened in Australia. Very little is known of its life cycle or status.*

this is made up for by their diversity and the high proportion of endemics. Australian biologists have lately realized that a greater number of freshwater fish species are under threat than was previously thought. Competition from introduced game fish, pollution, and the damming of rivers have all produced large declines in numbers and range. Many of Tasmania's well-known, minnow-like galaxids are causing concern, including the Swan Galaxias and the Lake Pedder Galaxias. On the mainland, the Blind Cave Eel, which lacks eyes, body pigmentation and fins, has been collected less than a dozen times and is found only in subterranean waters in Western Australia. The Australian Grayling from southeastern Australia, and the Trout Cod from northeastern Victoria and southern New South Wales, both have very restricted distributions and are threatened with extinction.

So too, do increasing numbers of sharks. Sport hunting, commercial fishing, by-catch, beach netting and outright prejudice are finally having an impact on the Great White Shark, the Grey Nurse Shark and many others, including the "fish & chip" species, the School and Gummy sharks. Three other marine species of concern to Australian experts are the Eastern

DISTRIBUTION
TUATARA

■ *Current range*

The Tuatara (Sphenodon punctatus) *is found only on islands off the North Island and in the Cook Strait. Its two main strongholds are Stephens and North Brother.*

Left *The Tuatara* (Sphenodon punctatus) *is a reptile virtually indistinguishable from its ancestors that lived 135 million years ago in the Jurassic. Once widespread in New Zealand, its range has contracted within historical times and it is now confined to offshore islands.*

Gemfish, Orange Roughy and the Southern Bluefin Tuna. The Bluefin has been heavily over-exploited by national and international fishing fleets, and is listed by the World Conservation Union as "critically endangered."

NEW ZEALAND – LAND OF THE OLD NIGHT BIRD

New Zealand evolved in isolation for some 80 million years after splitting from Gondwanaland. It is both the largest and most diverse of land forms to have developed in the absence of terrestrial mammals. The amazing results of this isolated gestation period were birds such as the flightless kiwis and the giant ostrich-like moas, the very ancient reptile, the Tuatara, and many other animals that have come to symbolize New Zealand's wildlife heritage.

Evolution did not provide New Zealand with the sheer numbers of species found on islands such as New Guinea, but this is more than compensated for by the biological wonders among its endemic fauna. The endemic species comprised 3 mammals (excluding whales and dolphins), 150 birds, 40 reptiles, 3 amphibians, 25 fish, and 91 molluscs and arthropods. A further 137 birds and 3 freshwater fish were indigenous. Of these species, at least 16 vertebrates and 3 invertebrates are now extinct, while over 60 vertebrates and at least 40 invertebrates are threatened.

New Zealand was a land of forests and superlative mountain ranges. It was only 1,000 years ago, with the arrival of the Polynesians, that New Zealand first felt the impact of human interference. By the time the Europeans had firmly established their colonies, almost 25 per cent of New Zealand's forests had disappeared, and with them a large percentage of the birds, including the giant moas. Due to vastly increased forest destruction by Europeans, approximately 66 per cent of the lowland forest (80 per cent of the North Island, 55 per cent in the South) has been lost to farms, towns, cities, and exotic pine plantations. These and other developments represent prime threats to New Zealand's native wildlife.

INTRODUCED SPECIES

Introduced and now feral species wrought terrible damage on native animals and plants. The list of destroyers is almost endless and includes rats, mice, ferrets, stoats, cats, dogs, possums, wallabies, cattle, sheep, goats, rabbits, and many introduced plants. These exotic

Right Until about 100 years ago Hooker's Sealions (Neophoca hookeri) *bred on North Island, New Zealand, but they are now restricted to sub-Antarctic islands. During the nineteenth century they were exterminated on Macquarie Island, and the main population is now on Auckland Island.*

predators, browsers and colonizers killed and ate to extinction a large number of endemic vertebrates, and continue to seriously threaten many of the remaining species.

The only non-marine mammals indigenous to the country are three endemic bat species, called *pekapeka* by the Maori. The Greater Short-tailed Bat is already extinct, perhaps as recently as 1965. Some biologists hope that a few of these bats may still survive on one of the small rat-free islands near Big South Cape Island. The other two species are the vulnerable Lesser Short-tailed Bat and the Long-tailed Bat. What a catastrophe it would be if these remaining ambassadors of the mammals in New Zealand were also to be lost.

MARINE MAMMALS

Among marine mammals giving cause for concern are the White-headed or Hector's Dolphin, an animal found nowhere else in the world, and Hooker's Sealion, a species that inhabits Auckland and Campbell Islands just south of New Zealand. Hooker's Sealion is one of the world's most threatened sealions, with an estimated population of between 11,000 and 15,000

Left *The Kea* (Nestor notabilis) *is found at high altitudes on South Island, New Zealand. In the past it was persecuted because it was thought to kill sheep, but it is now protected.*

Kakapo (Strigops harbroptilus)

animals. The species is threatened by the activities of Japanese, Korean, and Soviet trawlers hunting for squid. The sealion also hunts squid, and it is known that hundreds of them become entangled in the trawling nets each trawling season.

THE BIRDS

The largest component of the vertebrate fauna, the birds, have borne the brunt of the unnatural extinction in New Zealand. Thirteen birds have already been lost, and at least 44 species are currently threatened. The plight of the endemic parrots – some believe the most spectacular and fascinating of all the world's parrot species – epitomizes the dramatic effects of human invasion upon New Zealand's wildlife.

All the endemic parrots are subject to illegal capture for sale, normally in overseas markets, and other threats. The Kaka is suffering from the felling of indigenous forests and competition with exotic browsers, to the extent that it no longer exists on the mainland. The Kea is the only alpine parrot in the world, and is regionally threatened by illegal shooting and poisoning, but it is the Kakapo that became most prominent in the battle to conserve endangered species in New Zealand. This parrot is the largest and most endangered parrot on Earth. Also known as the Old Night Bird or Owl Parrot, it is the most extraordinary parrot and the one nearest extinction, with only 50 remaining. This flightless creature of the night is the largest parrot in the world, weighing up to 3.5 kilograms (7³/₄ pounds). It may live to be 60 years old or more – but even with such longevity, it may not see out the century unless drastic action is taken. The bird evolved in the absence of large predators, except for a non-extinct giant eagle. So it has no defences, other than its natural camouflage of mottled green and yellow feathers and the instinct to freeze when threatened. The Kakapo exists now on only a few small islands, including Little Barrier Island which protects 16 of the remaining birds.

The endemic and highly endangered Takahe, a beautiful and endangered flightless rail, was once widespread in the alpine grasslands and upper beech montane forests of Fiordland. Thought extinct until 1948, when 200 were discovered near Lake Te Anau, the Takahe can now be seen at the Te Anau Wildlife Reserve where a captive breeding program is in place. Its decline in population has been caused by predation and competition for food with introduced species, in an already restricted range. The kiwis, familiar throughout the world as symbols of New Zealand, are also in some trouble. Like all of New Zealand's flightless birds, they are finding difficulty in maintaining range and numbers under continuing human pressures. The North Island Brown Kiwi is threatened by land clearance and accidental killing during pig and possum hunting. The South Island's Great Spotted Kiwi is facing imminent extinction unless urgent conservation action is taken soon. Conservation department officials say that the Kiwi's populations in Arthur's Pass and the Hurunui district, Canterbury are "slowly disappearing." Hunting pressure from introduced predators such as stoats and ferrets, and the overgrazing effects of introduced possums, is sending the species to the brink.

In contrast, the endangered Black (Chatham Island) Robin provides a good-news story. Over a decade ago the species was on the brink of extinction, with the last five Black Robins clinging on to survival on one of the islands. Although the species was always restricted to the Chatham Islands, some 800 kilometers (500 miles) east of mainland New Zealand, it was once widespread throughout the island group. Gross habitat disruption, destruction and predation reduced the population to a mere handful of birds in a tiny remnant patch of forest. But thanks to the intervention of the New Zealand Wildlife Service, and the unusual longevity and breeding capacity of one of the two surviving females, the population of Black Robins today stands in excess of 170 birds – a spectacular and welcome recovery.

REPTILES, AMPHIBIANS AND FISH

The endemic reptiles and amphibians of New Zealand have not been immune from the pressures of modern society. Indeed, New Zealand has one of the longest lists of threatened reptiles in the world. That well-known reptilian curiosity, the Tuatara, has a very restricted distribution and is further threatened by the illegal reptile trade and predation by rats. The Brother's Island Tuatara is vulnerable, while the Cook Island Strait Tuatara is of less conservation concern. New Zealand's only endangered reptile, other than the Brother's Island

Below The Takahe (Notornis mantelli) was confined to the Murchison mountains of South Island, New Zealand. There competition for food from introduced deer and predation by introduced mammals have caused a decline, and a population has been established on Maud Island.

Below right The Black Robin (Petroica traversi) was confined to Little Mangere Island in the Chatham islands of New Zealand, but in the 1970s the entire population was transferred to Mangere Island and there are now populations on Rangatira as well.

Tuatara, is the Chevron Skink. At least 16 other reptile species are thought to be vulnerable to extinction, including the Stephen's Island Gecko, the Grand Skink, and Whitaker's Skink.

New Zealand's three endemic amphibians are all frogs. Hamilton's Frog, with only two main populations surviving, is the only species listed as vulnerable. But as soon as the Maud Island Frog (currently one of the two populations of Hamilton's Frog) is formally described as a new species, the latter will be left with a population as small as 200–300 individuals. The other two endemic and rare frog species of New Zealand, Archey's Frog and Hochstetter's Frog, are regionally threatened by habitat destruction.

Many of New Zealand's galaxid fish are listed as threatened. The only species known to have become extinct is the New Zealand Grayling.

Above The New Zealand Hamilton's Frog (Leiopelma hamiltoni) *lives well away from standing water, in mists and clouds. It was discovered in 1915 on Stephen's Island in the Cook Strait, but by 1942 was believed extinct. It has since been found again there and, although it is still very rare, another colony was discovered in 1958 on Maud Island, where this one was photographed. Because of the scientific interest in the species, it was given protection in 1921, together with all other New Zealand frogs.*

THE FUTURE

This review has barely touched on the marine vertebrates and the land and marine invertebrates at risk. No one even really knows how many invertebrate species there are in the Australasian region as a whole. Guesses range from half a million to one million, and are probably serious underestimates. This indicates the amount we have still to learn about the region's biological diversity. Yet we must learn quickly, for the scale of environmental, and consequent species' degradation is already great.

The Indonesian, Papua New Guinean, Australian and New Zealand governments all have well-developed conservation programs, though the frenzied pursuit of economic development in the 1990s has taken its toll on environment budgets and priorities. There needs to be new regional focus and cooperation on the urgent issue of maintaining Australasia's biological diversity, before the millennium brings news of greater losses to come.

Antarctica

Mark Carwardine is a zoologist, writer, photographer, and broadcaster. He worked for several conservation organizations (WWF, in England; UNEP, in Kenya; and IUCN, in Switzerland) before going freelance in 1986. He has written more than 30 books – including the best-selling *Last Chance to See* (with Douglas Adams), *Whales, Dolphins and Porpoises*, and *The Guinness Book of Animal Records* – and writes regularly for magazines and newspapers such as *BBC Wildlife* and *The Mail on Sunday*. He is also an advisory editor of *The Good Book Guide* and a consultant to the Whale and Dolphin Conservation Society. Mark is a naturalist on cruise ships in the Antarctic every southern summer.

Right *The Antarctic peninsula near Argentine Island. The last nearly pristine wilderness in the world, Antarctica is now critically threatened by a wide range of developments, including mineral exploitation and other human activities.*

Below *Antarctica covers 10 per cent of the world's land surface and doubles again in size when the seas freeze in the winter. A great sheet of ice containing 99 per cent of the world's ice covers 98 per cent of the continent.*

AUSTRALIA

ANTARCTICA

Cold and windy, isolated and inhospitable, Antarctica is the last virtually unspoiled wilderness on Earth. Separated from all other continents by a permanently frozen sea and the stormy waters of the Southern Ocean, it is almost entirely hidden under a thick sheet of ice.

There are no native people in Antarctica. In fact, no human had set eyes on the continent itself until the Russian explorer Thaddeus von Bellingshausen sighted it in January 1820, and the first permanent research stations were not erected until as recently as the late 1940s.

But while Antarctica has so far escaped many of the destructive human activities that have become so familiar in other parts of the world, there is growing concern for its future. As scarce resources elsewhere in the world become even scarcer, some governments and businesses are looking south for new supplies of food and mineral wealth.

Yet many experts believe that the continent will be more valuable in the long term if it is left untouched. It is a critical component of the world's weather system, which is driven largely by the great temperature difference between the tropics and the poles; it provides a pristine open-air laboratory for monitoring global pollution and for other scientific research; and it is the largest wildlife sanctuary on Earth. Also, for a growing number of people, Antarctica has become a symbol of conservation, as the world's last remaining wilderness.

KRILL – A RICH FEEDING GROUND

The continent itself has relatively few permanent wildlife inhabitants. The plant life consists of only two native flowering species (a pearlwort and a hairgrass) and a few hundred representatives of groups such as mosses, lichens, algae, and liverworts. The animal life is also rather limited, consisting predominantly of microbes and small invertebrates, the largest of which is a midge less than 13 millimeters ($\frac{1}{2}$ inch) long.

But the surrounding sea, which covers more than twice the area of the land, is a thick soup of shrimp-like creatures called Krill. These tiny crustaceans are only about 5–6 centimeters (¼ inch) long, but they are full of protein and live in dense swarms throughout the Southern Ocean. They form the backbone of a rich food chain that supports a significant number of the world's great whales, and millions of seals, penguins, and other animals.

There were claims, in the mid-1980s, that Krill could solve the world's food crisis. At the time, more than half a million tonnes of the animals were being taken, mainly by the former USSR, and there were plans to catch considerably more. But this optimism was short-lived. With the collapse of the Soviet Union, there were fewer Krill ships plying the Southern Ocean. There was also a technological difficulty – which has yet to be overcome – because Krill is unsuitable for human consumption unless it can be processed immediately. Today, the catch levels are relatively modest. But, despite serious concerns that even a relatively small Krill fishery could have a serious impact on the struggling populations of whales and other animals, there are still plans to increase the harvest.

Krill (Euphausia superba)

WHALING AND SEALING

The first commercial activity in Antarctica was sealing, which began in 1820, and much of the stimulus for early Antarctic exploration came from the search for new sealing grounds. The sealers were interested mainly in Fur Seals, for the high commercial value of their fur, and Elephant Seals, for their high yield of fat. Both species were hunted almost to extinction. These days, sealing is regulated by the Convention for the Conservation of Antarctic Seals (CCAS), which bans the hunting of Fur, Elephant and Ross Seals and establishes regional and seasonal limitations as well as catch limits for Crabeater, Weddell and Leopard Seals.

Whalers first turned their attentions to Antarctic waters at the turn of the century, when they had wiped out most whale populations elsewhere in the world. Initially, the most sought-after species was the Blue Whale, and in the short 1930–31 season, an incredible 28,325 were

Below left An American Sheathbill (Chionis alba) scavenging behind a Gentoo Penguin (Pygoscelis papua) among Chinstrap Penguins (Pygoscelis antarctica). Chinstraps may have increased since the slaughter of whales, with which they competed for Krill.

Below Numbers of Crabeater Seal (Lobodon carcinophagus) have increased dramatically since the 1930s and it is believed this is directly linked to the decline in whales. Like the great whales, these seals feed on Krill, sucking them in as they swim through a shoal open-mouthed, and then sieving them through their cheek teeth.

killed in the region. As the Blue Whale catch declined, the whalers concentrated on other species and, one by one, the Antarctic's great whales were hunted to commercial extinction. Two million whales were killed in the Southern Ocean in less than a century.

Yet whaling continues to this day. The Japanese are still hunting the Southern Ocean for Minke Whales, stubbornly ignoring strong world opinion against them and despite an official ban on commercial whaling. In 1994, the Southern Ocean Whale Sanctuary was approved, covering an area of some 50,000 square kilometers (19,300 square miles) around Antarctica – but even this is being ignored.

MINING

One of the greatest potential threats to Antarctica is mining, which could cause irreversible damage on a massive scale. Research by several nations suggests that the continent might contain large quantities of oil and substantial deposits of other minerals, such as copper, platinum, and coal. If these reserves are ever exploited, oil spills would be inevitable and the continent would be besieged with ever larger numbers of people, increased shipping operations, huge quantities of equipment, and a variety of new buildings and exploration facilities. However, thanks to millions of signatures from concerned people all over the world, and several tanker disasters which finally convinced decision-makers that accidents are both inevitable and devastating, mining has been banned in Antarctica for an indefinite period.

RESEARCH AND TOURISM

There are more than 60 permanent scientific bases on the Antarctic continent and surrounding islands, populated by up to 1,000 people in the winter and more than 3,000 during the brief southern summer. The largest is the US government's McMurdo, on the shore

Below *The pollution on this beach on the British island of South Georgia is typical of an increasing problem throughout the Antarctic. Abandoned whaling and sealing stations, and modern scientific research facilities, all contribute litter to what was until very recently a totally unspoiled region.*

Below right *The* Explorer *is one of an increasing number of tourist ships visiting the Antarctic. If properly controlled, tourism can be a relatively benign form of development.*

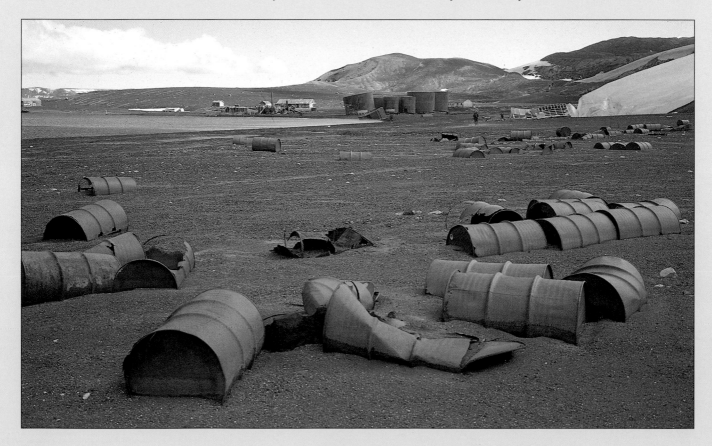

of Ross Island, which is like a small town. Dubbed Science City, it has two airfields built on the ice, its own sewerage system, a church, three bars, and even a bowling alley. The breadth of science on the continent includes everything from weather forecasting and the effects of the sun on the atmosphere to microbiology and the psychology of small groups of people living together during the harsh winter.

The first pioneer tourist trips to Antarctica were undertaken in the 1950s, and in the years since, tourism has become a serious commercial activity in the region. Nowadays, the number of tourists each season greatly exceeds the number of scientists and support personnel on the continent. Although tourism is currently limited to a relatively small number of cruise ships, there is concern that it may be approaching a rapid phase of expansion – with more disturbance to wildlife and a greater risk of introducing non-native organisms such as cockroaches and house plants. But efforts are being made to limit the growth and to control any potential harm, through the Antarctic Treaty and the International Association of Antarctic Tour Operators (IAATO). Meanwhile, any suggestion of land-based tourism, including the building of hotels and permanent airstrips, is strongly opposed by conservation groups.

ANTARCTIC TREATY

Restricting human activities – and environmental damage – in Antarctica is particularly difficult because the continent belongs to the world as a whole rather than to just one country. There were formal territorial claims to various sections as early as 1908 but, thanks largely to a remarkable international pact called the Antarctic Treaty, these have all been frozen. The treaty came into force in 1961 and provides a legal framework for all activities and decision-making in the region. Basically, it gives all countries the right to explore Antarctica's scientific mysteries but none the right to exploit its resources.

Above Krill (Euphausia superba), *a shrimp-like crustacean, occurs in such huge numbers that it dominates the Antarctic food chain. A wide range of animals feed directly on Krill, including fish, seabirds, penguins, Crabeater Seals, and the great whales, and many of these are, in turn, devoured by others. People's depletion of the great whales has irrevocably altered the balance of wildlife dependent on Krill.*

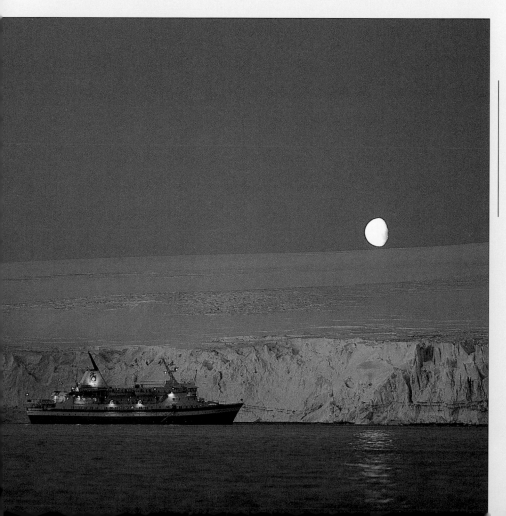

World Park

Ultimately, the long-term aim of some governments and many of the world's largest conservation organizations is to establish Antarctica as a World Park. This would be the first park of its kind and would give the last virtually unspoiled continent on our planet the level of protection it really deserves.

Oceania & Marine

Oceania can be broadly defined as all those islands, scattered across the world, which rise directly from the seabed and have never been part of a continental land mass. Alternatively, it can be defined as the majority of the Pacific Ocean islands. Oceanic islands support a higher number of endemic animal and plant species than any other region.

JAPAN

Midway Is.

Marianas

P A C I F I C

Marshall Islands

Caroline Islands

Micronesia

Gilbert Islands

Phoenix Island

BORNEO

New Ireland

NEW GUINEA

Solomon Islands

Vanuatu

New Hebrides

Samoan Islands

Fiji

New Caledonia

Tong

AUSTRALIA

NEW ZEALAND

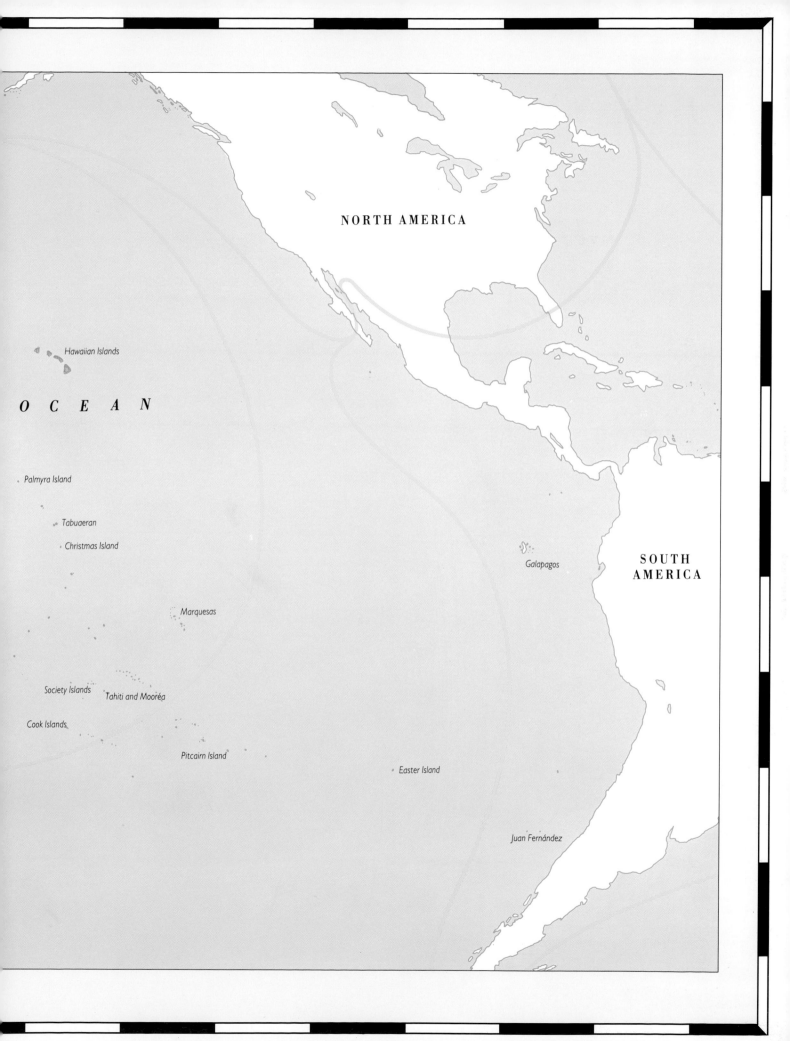

NORTH AMERICA

SOUTH
AMERICA

O C E A N

Hawaiian Islands

Palmyra Island

Tabuaeran

Christmas Island

Marquesas

Society Islands   *Tahiti and Mooréa*

Cook Islands

Pitcairn Island

Easter Island

Galapagos

Juan Fernández

Oceania & Marine

Teresa Farino is an environmental journalist and wildlife photographer with a special interest in the adaptations of animals and plants to the world's biogeographic zones. She is author of six books, has contributed to many other publications, and is Spanish correspondent for *BBC Wildlife Magazine*. Since 1986, she has been living in the Picos de Europa in northern Spain, and is currently compiling a field guide to the flora of these mountains.

Cindy Engel is an associate lecturer in Life Sciences with the Open University, and a freelance science writer. She spent a year studying the endangered Jaguar population of southern Mexico, and many years working on the social and pheromonal control of the wild rabbit in England. She is a consultant researcher and science adviser for an independent television company.

Oceania can be broadly defined as all those islands, scattered across the world's oceans, which rise directly from the seabed and have never been part of a continental land mass. Oceanic islands are usually volcanic in origin, formed of lava pushed up through points of weakness in the Earth's crust. In tropical regions, coral reefs soon form around new volcanoes. Over the course of millennia, the cone gradually sinks under its own weight and vanishes beneath the waves, leaving a coral atoll as the only evidence of its past existence.

All volcanic islands rise pristine from the seabed and are totally devoid of life at their formation. Natural colonization by animals and plants is a slow process. Creatures which can swim or fly – seals, marine turtles, and seabirds – may arrive under their own steam, sometimes carrying the seeds of plants in their fur or feathers, or even in their stomachs. Microscopic seeds and small invertebrates may arrive in the air streams of the upper atmosphere, while cyclones and hurricanes can cause rafts of fallen trees and other debris to be hurled far out to sea. Very occasionally such a raft may come ashore, depositing its living cargo.

Only a tiny fraction of the vast wealth of continental animals and plants will ever reach an oceanic island and, even then, survival is dependent upon finding a suitable habitat or a compatible mate. But those creatures that become successfully established on an oceanic island thrive in the absence of mainland predators, and have a multitude of new niches to exploit. Such isolated island populations start to change, both physically and behaviourally. Thus, oceanic islands support a higher number of endemic animal and plant species than any other biogeographic region.

The Hawaiian archipelago, which lies almost 4,000 kilometers (2,500 miles) from the nearest major land mass and 1,600 kilometers (1,000 miles) from the closest islands, is the

Right The coast of Napali on the island of Kauai in the Hawaiian Islands. Although superficially unspoiled, the impact of people can be discerned. Since their discovery by Captain Cook, the islands have been steadily depleted of their rich and varied fauna and flora through deforestation, hunting, and the introduction of exotic species.

most isolated island group in the world. Although most of the animals and plants that live there are related to families on other Pacific islands, over 90 per cent of the native flowering plants and almost all of the land birds and invertebrates – including some 8,000 insects - are found nowhere else in the world. But of the 69 endemic land birds known to be present on the Hawaiian Islands when Captain Cook arrived in 1798, 25 have since become extinct and most of the remainder are endangered, particularly forest species such as the honeycreepers. In particular, the island of Hawaii has lost 9 of its 16 endemic bird species in historic times. However, it is not only land birds that have been lost: the Hawaiian Islands have already lost 600 of their 1,061 endemic snail species, and it is estimated that between 200 and 400 of the remainder are endangered. Of the diverse endemic Hawaiian flora, about 300 species have disappeared for ever, and a further 800 are at risk.

Such horrifying statistics are unfortunately not confined to the Hawaiian archipelago. Generally speaking, oceanic islands have a greater number of endangered species than any other region of equivalent land area in the world. Only 20 per cent of all the bird species in the world are found on islands, but of the 104 species of bird known to have become extinct since 1600, 97 were island endemics. Similarly, about one-third of the 25,000 flowering plants that are considered to be threatened with extinction in the world today are found only on islands. On the Juan Fernández archipelago off the Chilean coast, the majority of the 116 endemic plant species are endangered, as are two-thirds of the 229 endemic plants of the Galápagos archipelago. Over a quarter of the 600 plants which are endemic to the Canary Islands are also at risk, while of the 280 plants native to Mauritius, 7 per cent are extinct and 79 per cent are in danger of vanishing for ever.

Just why are so many island species threatened with extinction? One of the main reasons is that small islands are only able to support small populations of any species, no matter how successful that species may be. In addition, in the absence of large herbivores, many plants have stopped expending energy on the production of grazing deterrents such as thorns and toxic chemicals. Similarly, the paucity of predators means that island birds do not have to take to the air to escape, nor do they need to nest in high, inaccessible places. So, during the course of evolution, many birds have lost the power of flight.

Such isolated communities of animals and plants are relatively stable as long as they remain undisturbed, but humans and their introduced herbivores and predators have wreaked havoc on the unprotected flora and fauna. In addition, the world's oceanic islands are no more able to withstand large-scale forest clearance, burning, soil erosion, and other human disruptions than any other terrestrial ecosystems.

EXPLOITING ISLAND LIFE

Hungry sailors rapidly annihilated the Dodo of Mauritius, which had previously never encountered large predators. The Hawaiian Goose, or Néné, a species with limited powers of flight, was hunted almost to extinction by the early twentieth century. Although reintroductions of captive-bred birds have saved this species from the grave, predation by mongooses, rats, and feral dogs and cats are preventing the population from expanding.

Top The Silver Sword (Argyroxphium sandvicense) *is one of the rarest flowering plants in the world, confined to the Haleakala Crater National Park, on the island of Maui, Hawaii. The spectacular flower grows 2 meters (6½ feet) high, takes 15 years to grow, and when it has bloomed the plant dies.*

Above *The Hawaiian Goose or Néné* (Branta sandvicensis) *was saved from extinction both by the introduction of strict protective measures in the Hawaiian Islands and also by a captive breeding program started by Sir Peter Scott in England, and the US Fish and Wildlife Service.*

Hunting has also depleted populations of Pacific-island pigeons, and those now endangered include the Tooth-billed Pigeon, reminiscent of the Dodo in appearance and endemic to the volcanic islands of Western Samoa; the Marquesas Pigeon found only on the island of Nuku Hiva in the Marquesas group; and the Society Islands Pigeon, which is restricted to Tahiti and nearby Makatea in the Tuamotu archipelago. In many areas hunting continues today, despite being illegal.

Birds are not the only island creatures to have suffered from overexploitation. In the equatorial Pacific, the Galápagos Islands were originally home to 14 distinct subspecies of Giant Tortoise *(Geochelone elephantopus)*, the largest measuring up to 122 centimeters (48 inches) in length and weighing some 270 kilograms (600 pounds). It is estimated that more than 200,000 Giant Tortoises were taken from the Galápagos Islands by passing ships between the seventeenth and nineteenth centuries, to provide sailors with fresh meat.

Right *The Galápagos Giant Tortoise* (Geochelone elephantopus) *once occurred on all the larger islands in the Galápagos, but is now extinct on Floreana and Fernandina and much reduced on most other islands.*

Of an original population of 250,000, only about 15,000 of these Giant Tortoises remain today. Two subspecies have vanished forever, and many of the remainder may not survive for much longer. The Pinta Island Giant Tortoise, for example, is as good as extinct, with only a single male surviving.

Most of the 55 species of flying fox are restricted to single islands or small island groups in the Pacific and Indian Oceans. They are the largest bats in the world, with a wingspan of up to 1.7 meters (5½ feet). Flying foxes are long-lived creatures that have a very low reproductive rate compared with other mammals of similar size. They also have complex social structures, specific food requirements, and a narrow range of potential roost sites. As a consequence, flying foxes are vulnerable to a wide variety of threats associated with human interference, particularly forest destruction and hunting.

Archeological evidence suggests that the Chamorro people of the Marianas Islands have been eating flying foxes for over 1,000 years. Although traditional hunting practices are thought to have had little impact on the populations of flying foxes in the North Pacific, the introduction of firearms and a cash economy has proved disastrous for many species. Today, all trade in flying foxes serves a single consumer market – the island of Guam in the Marianas

Above The Coconut or Robber Crab (Birgus latro) *is widely distributed in the Indian and Pacific Oceans. Considered a delicacy, it is hunted extensively for food, and is declining throughout most of its range.*

Islands. In the 1970s, having all but exterminated the Guam Flying Fox (now possibly extinct) and the Marianas Flying Fox, the hunters moved further afield. No fewer than 30,000 frozen flying fox carcasses were imported into Guam between 1981 and 1987, mainly from Micronesia and Samoa. Both the Cusp-toothed Flying Fox, endemic to the Solomon Islands, and the Rodrigues Flying Fox, endemic to Mauritius, are critically endangered.

Another animal unfortunate enough to be considered a delicacy – and reputed to have aphrodisiac properties – is the Coconut or Robber Crab. Living almost exclusively on small islands in the western Pacific and eastern Indian Oceans, it is probably the largest terrestrial invertebrate in the world. A mature male Coconut Crab can measure a meter (3¼ feet) from leg tip to leg tip and weigh up to 3 kilograms (6½ pounds), females being somewhat smaller. Hunted intensively by island peoples, it is also used as fishing bait, and whole crabs are dried and sold to tourists. As a result this species is now extinct on a number of islands.

The dark red resin of the Macronesian Dragon Tree was once believed to be the blood of dragons and is reputed to have magical and medicinal properties. This small tree has thus been "harvested" from all but the most inaccessible sites and is now extinct on four of the Canary Islands and on Porto Santo in the Madeiran archipelago.

FOREST CLEARANCE

Although direct exploitation has been responsible for the near-extinction of some island species, it is the wholesale destruction of the island habitat which has caused the most widespread damage.

When Mauritius, Réunion and Rodrigues (the Mascarenes), lying in the Indian Ocean due east of Madagascar, were colonized in the mid-1600s, they were almost entirely forested. Between 1638 and 1710, almost all the lowland ebony was removed for lumber, while in succeeding centuries widespread clearance of the lowland forests made way for cash crops such as sugar, tea and pine plantations. Today, sugar cane covers more than 95 per cent of the lowlands of Mauritius, and only a few square kilometers of dwarf upland forest remain.

The effect on the wildlife of these islands has been catastrophic. Among the endemic vertebrate species, Mauritius has lost 20 species of endemic birds, two of its three fruit bats, and 8 of its 12 reptiles, including *Leiolopisma mauritiana*, formerly the world's largest skink. Nearby Réunion has fared even worse, losing 16 of its 23 birds, both its fruit bats, and four of its six reptiles. On Rodrigues, all the native reptiles have been eliminated, including the world's largest gecko *Phelsuma gigas*, as well as one of the two fruit bats, and 10 of the 12 land birds endemic to the Mascarenes.

Similarly, people have wreaked havoc on natural ecosystems in the Seychelles, especially the once extensive forests of these granitic oceanic islands. Commercial logging and clearance for agriculture not only physically destroyed a large part of the native forests, but also led to the increased incidence of drought, accidental fires, and soil erosion. Not surprisingly, almost all of the 72 endemic vascular plants of the Seychelles (not including Aldabra) are in danger of extinction.

The clearance of upland forests on the main island of Mahé, along with the increased incidence of fire on the denuded island, has reduced the population of the forest-dwelling Seychelles Scops Owl to only 80 pairs. The Seychelles Brush Warbler is found only on Cousin Island today, having disappeared from Marianne during the major forest clearances of the nineteenth century. A similar fate has befallen the Rarotonga Flycatcher, known only from the greatly reduced upland forests of the Cook Islands and not seen since 1976.

INTRODUCED ANIMALS AND PLANTS

The native plants of oceanic islands are often unable to compete with the vigorous weeds which may become dominant following habitat degradation, while the indigenous animals are ill-adapted to feed on introduced vegetation. In the Mascarenes the invasion of exotic plant species is believed to have brought about the virtual extinction of the monotypic tree *Tetrataxis salicifolia*, now known only from seven individuals on the island of Mauritius, while only three individuals of the small tree *Badula crassa* survive today on the island of Réunion.

Perhaps the most insidious destruction has resulted from introduced domestic herbivores, especially the goat. Goats defoliate all vegetation within reach and can even climb trees to browse. They are also extremely prolific, the goat population on Pinta Island in the Galápagos increasing from just three individuals to around 20,000 in 12 years! In the sixteenth and seventeenth centuries, goats were automatically introduced to islands as soon as they were discovered to provide a ready supply of fresh meat for passing sailors.

One of the most tragic examples of environmental breakdown is that of St. Helena, a solitary island in the South Atlantic, which, when discovered in 1502, was densely covered with forests. In 1513, a small herd of goats was introduced and by 1588, the original herd had proliferated into thousands. Their voracious appetites not only stripped the island of much of its herbaceous vegetation but also prevented forest regeneration. This goat-manufactured ruin was aided and abetted by human felling of mature trees to fuel the lime-kilns that were needed to supply mortar for fortifications during the Napoleonic wars. By 1810, the original

Juan Fernandez archipelago

Sheep, cattle, horses, goats, and rabbits are threatening:

■ Crusoe's mayu-monte *(Sophora fernandeziana)*.

■ Selkirk's mayu-monte *(Sophora masafuerana)* – endemic to Isla Alejandro Selkirk.

■ *Lactoris ferndandeziana* – one of the archipelago's 98 endemic flowering plants.

■ *Ranunculus capparum* – only known from a single locality on Isla Alejandro Selkirk.

Overexploitation is severely endangering:

■ The Chonta Palm *(Juania australis)* – used for walking sticks, cabinet work, and its "edible heart" leaves.

Extinct in the wild since 1908:

■ The semi-parasitic tree *(Santalum fernandezianum)* – felled for its sweet-scented reddish wood, used in the production of prayerbeads and boxes for saintly relics for export to Peru.

forest was confined to a few fragments on the central ridges and precipices of the island, the remainder being overrun with some 260 species of European, American, and Australian weeds. Before human intervention, St. Helena had supported in the region of 100 endemic plant species. Today less than 40 endemics remain, about half of which are endangered.

Ship-borne rats have probably had the most devastating impact on island reptiles and birds of any unintentionally introduced animal. The Black Rat is originally native to Asia, but was spread by ship around the world during the great era of trade and exploration in the fifteenth and sixteenth centuries. It climbs well, raiding birds' nests for eggs and young, and takes a wide variety of terrestrial prey, including lizards and large invertebrates.

In the Galápagos archipelago, Black Rats have caused a severe decline in the endemic Galápagos Dark-rumped Petrel. Similarly, rat predation on the nests of the Aldabra Brush Warbler is the main reason why this bird is believed to be extinct. Apparently confined to a 10-hectare (25-acre) strip of coastal vegetation on Aldabra, only five individuals have ever been seen. In 1977 only two females were found, while a search in 1986 failed to locate any.

Below left *The natural forest cover of the island of Mauritius has largely been destroyed and a significant proportion of the land is now under cultivation for sugar cane.*

Below *The Coco de Mer* (Lodoicea maldivica) *has the largest seeds in the plant kingdom. Their size, together with their distinctive shape, made the seeds much-prized symbols of virility. The plant is confined to the Seychelles. Although extinct in many areas, it has been protected in the Valle de Mai since 1966.*

The stick insect *Dryococelus australis*, a 12-centimeter (4³/₄-inch) heavy-bodied, wingless species, is endemic to Lord Howe Island off the east coast of Australia. It was formerly abundant on the main island but was quickly exterminated by rats when they were introduced in 1918. It is possible that a small colony will survives on tiny Ball's Pyramid, a virtually unvegetated but presently rat-free offshore islet. Some 40 per cent of Lord Howe Island's indigenous species of forest bird had also become extinct within five years of the rats' arrival.

In a misguided attempt to control rats, the Indian Mongoose was introduced to a number of Pacific islands. This voracious predator hunts primarily by day, and so has relatively little effect on the nocturnal rats. After wreaking havoc on the native avifauna of Hawaii, the mongoose was imported to Fiji in 1873. Eight species of indigenous bird subsequently became extinct, while the endemic Long-legged Warbler has virtually disappeared, with only a handful of survivors confined to the montane forests of Viti Levu and Vanua Levu.

In the late nineteenth century, cats were released on Mangere Island in the Chatham group to control introduced rabbits. This example of biological control did indeed achieve its stated objective, but in the process no less than 12 indigenous bird species were also

Right *The Flightless Cormorant (Nannopterum harrisi) from the Galápagos Islands. Many species of birds occurring on oceanic islands are flightless, and it is thought that this reduces their chances of being blown away from their island home. Another theory is that with few land predators and easily available food, they had no need to fly.*

Round Island

Only 152 hectares (375 acres) in size, Round Island is home to seven reptilian species known only from the Mascarenes.

■ Endangered:
Günthers Gecko *(Phelsuma guentheri)*.
■ Keel-scaled Boa *(Casarea dussumieri)*, approximately 75 individuals left.
■ Vulnerable:
Round Island Skink *(Leiolopisma telfairii)*.
■ Recently extinct:
Round Island Boa *(Bolyeria multocarinata)*.

eliminated, three of which were endemic and have therefore disappeared from this world forever. In the Seychelles, predation by feral cats is thought to have been the main reason for the virtual extinction of the Seychelles Magpie-robin, known only from Frigate Island. The population of the Galápagos Hawk, a confiding species which was once abundant throughout the archipelago, has also been severely affected by cat predation. Only 130–150 pairs were recorded in a 1974 census, and these were found only in remote localities, far from human settlements. Other introduced mammals, such as pigs and feral dogs, are threatening the Giant Tortoises of the Galapagos by taking their vulnerable eggs and young. Attempts have been made on Chatham Island to control the feral dogs, but rats continue to be a problem.

In the 1970s, almost all of the 18 native birds on Guam in the Marianas Islands became extinct because of the Australian Brown Tree Snake, a venomous bird and egg predator introduced to the island after the Second World War. This snake, which locates its prey by smell and is capable of engulfing a chicken, has become so successful on Guam that its population is numbered in millions. One of its most spectacular victims was the endemic and flightless Guam Rail whose population on the island plummeted from over 80,000 individuals in 1968 to zero in 1988. Fortunately the bird is breeding prolifically in captivity, and an experimental population is to be introduced to the nearby, currently snake-free, island of Rota.

The world's largest terrestrial snail, *Achatina fulica*, native to Africa and Madagascar, was deliberately introduced to Réunion in the early nineteenth century, supposedly to make soup for the governor's mistress. From there it has spread as far afield as the Society Islands and Hawaii, reaching plague proportions among crops on many Pacific islands. In 1977, in the Society Islands, the large carnivorous snail *Euglandina rosea* of Florida, was introduced in an attempt to control this pest. Rather than tackle the African giant, however, *Euglandina rosea* preferred a diet of viviparous tree snails, two genera of which *(Partula* and *Samoana)* are found only on the island of Moorea. By 1980, no viviparous tree snails were found in that part of Moorea occupied by the carnivore, and it is feared that the majority of the 11 endemic species have become extinct in the wild.

Introduced animals also bring exotic diseases with them, such that native birds of Pacific islands have been seriously affected by bird pox, spread by mites and direct contact between birds, and avian malaria, spread by mosquitoes. The southern *Culex* mosquito, accidentally introduced to Hawaii in the mid-1800s, has carried avian malaria throughout the lowlands of the archipelago, killing off a great part of the native bird life.

Even in more recent times, with our better understanding of island ecology, accidental introductions can still be disastrous. In the 1980s, for example, a sap-sucking insect was accidentally introduced onto St. Helena, probably on plant material. This insect, *Orthezia insignis*, had no natural enemies on the island and threatened to take the endemic gumwood – the national tree – to extinction. A carefully chosen predatory beetle was therefore released onto the island in 1993 and 1994. This has dramatically reduced the population of insects and the gumwoods are slowly recovering. Conservation of these vulnerable island ecosystems is, therefore, a matter of constant vigilance.

MARINE

The oceans and seas cover more than 70 per cent of the face of the Earth and have an average depth of almost 4 kilometers (2½ miles). All are interconnected, forming one huge, three-dimensional habitat, which has been estimated to comprise about 99 per cent of all the

Below left The small Indian Mongoose (Herpestes auropunctatus) has been introduced into many islands including Mafia (Tanzania), Mauritius, Fiji, and several islands in the Caribbean and Hawaii. They have done considerable damage to populations of ground-nesting birds.

Below The Brown Tree Snake (Boiga irregularis) occurs in coastal northern and eastern Australia, north to New Guinea and Indonesia. This very aggressive snake has been introduced from Australia into Guam, where it has wiped out many of the native birds.

life-supporting space available on this planet. And indeed, life exists at all levels – from the shallow waters of the continental shelves to the vast expanses of the open ocean, and from the sunlit waters at the surface to the abyssal trenches reaching depths over 11,000 meters (36,000 feet). Some marine organisms have a cosmopolitan distribution in the world's oceans, while others are limited to areas of particular temperature, depth, and salinity.

Over the centuries the oceans have been regarded as a limitless resource: until recently, unregulated beyond national boundaries. People have vastly overexploited most commercial fish species, hounded seals and Sea Otters unceasingly for their skins, driven the great whales to the brink of extinction, and treated the oceans as a huge trashcan.

Pollution of the oceans is on all scales: from small plastic refuse to oil spills and world-wide contamination with toxic chemicals. Plastics are particularly dangerous as they break down very slowly. Over two million seabirds and 100,000 endangered marine mammals and sea turtles are known to die each year from accidental entrapment in, or ingestion of

Snails at risk

Of the 42 *Achatinella* tree snails endemic to Oahu, Hawaii, 16 are extinct and 24 are critically endangered by the introduced *Euglandina rosea*, predation by rats and fire ants, shell-collectors, and forest clearance.

■ More than 30 of 66 *Bulimulus* snails endemic to the Galapagos are seriously endangered by fire ants.

■ All but two of the 13 endemic endodontid snails of Rarotonga in the Cook Islands have been eliminated by the African ant.

discarded plastics. Other forms of pollution also take a heavy toll. For example, in one of the worst single oil spills in history, the tanker *Exxon Valdez* ran aground on 24 March 1989 in Prince William Sound, Alaska. Millions of gallons of crude oil were spilt, contaminating almost 4,000 square kilometers (1,500 square miles) of sea and claiming the lives of 950 Sea Otters, 9 whales, millions of fish, and 300,000 birds. But accidents are not the only way oil reaches the oceans: it is estimated that every year, humans pump 2–5 million tonnes into the oceans as waste. Other waste chemicals cause problems, too. The biological amplification of persistent chemicals such as DDT and PCBs, which are known to impair health and reproduction, threatens all marine filter-feeders. In addition, nutrient inputs from sewage sludge and agricultural fertilizers have been cited as causes of toxic algal blooms causing widespread destruction of marine life.

Incidental catches have a detrimental effect on marine organisms, with one of the most wasteful examples of exploitation being that carried out by tuna-fishing fleets in the eastern tropical Pacific. Tuna in these waters are frequently associated with surface schools of dolphins and porpoises; a fact which enables fishermen to locate their prey with ease. The massive purse-seine nets used to trap the tuna also accidentally drown over 120,000 small cetaceans each year. Not surprisingly, the East Pacific Spinner Dolphin has been reduced by about 80 per cent. Incidental deaths of dolphins has been so high that a voluntary agreement on Dolphin Mortality Limits (DMLs) has been agreed by members of the IWC. This helped reduce incidental deaths from 100,000 a year in 1989 to 3,000 a year in 1997. However, in 1993, 8,000 Harbor porpoises were killed in fishing entanglements, and the most endangered cetacean, the Vaquita Dolphin, is on the brink of extinction as a direct result of gillnet fishing.

In the Pacific Ocean, an estimated 48,000 kilometers (30,000 miles) of driftnets are set each night by the pelagic fisheries of Japan, Korea, and Taiwan. Each net is a plastic death trap which ensnares and drowns small cetaceans, seals, marine turtles, sharks and other non-target species. But the real threat is posed by the so-called ghost nets – nets which have come adrift and are swept along by the ocean currents, engulfing all creatures in their path. Japan, for example, is estimated to lose 16 kilometers (10 miles) of driftnets each night. When

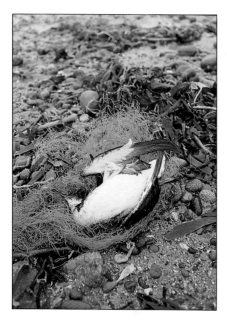

Above *Discarded fishing nets are a major cause of mortality in seabirds; millions drown every year. This Manx Shearwater was found on a beach in west Wales, close to its breeding site. As a result, its young may have starved to death.*

Right *Huge quantities of garbage end up in the seas. In addition, several thousand tons of hazardous waste are dumped at sea each year.*

the weight of carcases becomes too great, the ghost nets sink to the bottom, only to rise again to wreak yet more havoc when their cargo of corpses has rotted.

Shark barriers cause similar problems. These are weighted gillnets, set parallel to the shore to protect bathing beaches around the coasts of Australia and South Africa. Statistics from the Queensland nets alone make depressing reading, with 465 Dugongs, 317 porpoises, 2,654 marine turtles and 10,889 rays being trapped over a period of 16 years, as well as over 20,000 sharks, most of which belonged to species not remotely dangerous to people.

But it is probably overexploitation that has had the greatest impact on marine life, as these examples from some animal groups show.

FISH

Modern commercial fishing methods have caused a dramatic rise in catch numbers, from 18.5 million tons in 1952 to 82.5 million tons in 1992, and consequently many fish stocks have completely collapsed. In 1982 the UN Convention on the Law of the Sea provided a new regime for the management and exploitation of the oceans; the impact of which remains to be seen. In 1998 it was estimated that nearly 70 per cent of commercial fish species were fished beyond ecologically safe limits. When collapse comes, it is swift and can take both fishermen and scientists by surprise, as with the Great Bank Cod stocks off Newfoundland, Canada, in 1990. Both the Atlantic and Indian Ocean tuna fisheries have collapsed, and the Southern Bluefish Tuna looks likely to be next.

WHALES AND DOLPHINS

One of the most tragic examples of overexploitation of marine organisms is that of the great whales, hunted for over 1,000 years for their flesh and for the valuable fats and oils contained in the thick layer of blubber which insulates their bodies. In the early days of whaling the harvest was small, but when steel motor vessels appeared on the scene, armed with cannon and accompanied by factory ships able to process a large number of carcasses at sea, whaling began to have a serious impact on its target species. This century alone, over 1.25 million whales have been slaughtered.

The largest living animal, the Blue Whale, was originally found in all the world's oceans and seas, with an estimated total of around 200,000 individuals in the southern oceans alone. Recent surveys suggest that the oceans of the southern hemisphere today support a maximum of 2,000 Blue Whales, despite the species having been protected since 1965. Similar horror stories can be told for other great whales. The Fin Whale, or Common Rorqual, had an estimated pre-exploitation population of over 500,000 individuals, yet only 4,000 are thought to be present in the southern hemisphere today. While about 115,000 Humpback Whales formerly inhabited the oceans, a census in the 1980s revealed the presence of approximately 12,000 individuals world-wide.

The Bowhead, or Greenland Right Whale, which was once common in almost all arctic waters, has been virtually exterminated. Commercial whaling commenced in the sixteenth century, the prize being the Bowhead's enormously thick layer of blubber and long baleen plates. Bowheads swim close to the surface at low speeds while feeding, and conveniently float when dead, making them the "right" whales for people to exploit. By 1981 the North Pacific Bowhead population was estimated at about 2,200 individuals, with a few sporadic sightings in the North Atlantic. Its close relatives, the Northern Right Whale and the Southern Right Whale, once abundant along the coasts of major land masses, have also been brought

Above *An increasing amount of debris and waste litters beaches around the world. In many places, raw sewage is still pumped into the sea. Boatloads of household and industrial waste are dumped at sea, and most ocean-going vessels dump their garbage overboard. Plastics, in particular, can take many decades to decompose and may harm or kill birds and marine wildlife.*

almost to the point of extinction. Today, there are less than 600 Northern Right Whales and 4,000 Southern Right Whales.

Other baleen whales that have suffered huge losses through overexploitation include the Sei Whale, Bryde's Whale, and the Gray Whale. Among the toothed whales, the Northern Bottle-nosed Whale is today believed to be heavily depleted, while only 2,000 to 4,000 Sperm Whales are thought to survive, of an original southern hemisphere population of well over a million. Other toothed whales whose populations have declined dramatically include the Narwhal and the Beluga.

Although 1986 brought an international moratorium on whaling, over 19,000 whales were killed, mainly through legal loopholes, by Japan and Norway during the next ten years. As populations slowly recover, there is continuing pressure from these countries to resume commercial whaling.

The commercial slaughter of the great whales may have stopped for now, but they are still threatened by pollution and reduction of their food supply, and their smaller relatives – the dolphins and porpoises – continue to be threatened by hunting. Current estimates suggest that half a million small cetaceans are killed every year, particularly by Japan, Peru,

Below Sturgeon, like salmon, return to rivers in order to breed. The Atlantic Sturgeon (Acipenser sturio) *was once extremely abundant but was fished to the point of extinction in most rivers and pollution has often prevented recolonization.*

Below right The tail fluke of a diving Blue Whale (Balaenoptera musculus) *in the Indian Ocean. The Indian Ocean has been created a whale sanctuary, but some scientists believe that Blue Whale populations have fallen so low they may never recover.*

and Sri Lanka. In Sri Lanka, dolphin meat represents a vital source of protein, and the kill is in the order of 40,000 small cetaceans each year. The Japanese claim that eating whale meat is an essential part of their culture and religion. In 1988, Japanese kills accounted for nearly 50,000 small cetaceans, including such endangered species as Dall's Porpoise, found only in the North Pacific. The harvest of 17,000 Dall's Porpoise per year is currently the largest direct kill of cetaceans in the world.

SHARKS

The oceans are being purged of sharks as the demand for meat, skin, fins, and cartilage is high. Hong Kong's shark-fin imports were estimated at 10 million sharks in 1991. In addition, shark by-catch in high seas fisheries could be as high as 50 per cent of the commercial shark fisheries. Between 1989 and 1991, for example, 12 million elasmobranchs were discarded by the fishing industries.

An inoffensive beast hunted for centuries, especially in the North Atlantic, is the Basking Shark. It is the second-largest fish in the world, growing to lengths well in excess of 11 meters

(36 feet). It feeds on plankton and occurs more or less all around the world, often frequenting shallow coastal waters. The surface-feeding habit and gregarious nature of this fish make it easy prey, while its huge liver yields up to 900 liters (240 gallons) of oil, used as lamp-fuel, lubricants, and in the preparation of cosmetics. In a classic case of overexploitation, the Achill Island fishery managed to virtually eliminate the Basking Shark population along the western coast of Ireland, a kill of over 1,700 in 1950 dropping to an average of less than 50 sharks a year in the early 1970s. Although the Basking Shark is not considered to be endangered, numbers have declined dramatically in almost all fisheries, and it is feared that the remaining individuals may be too widely dispersed to reproduce efficiently.

In contrast, the Great White Shark is a fierce predator and it is this that has led to its relentless persecution around the world. Large predators always exist in far smaller numbers than the animals on which they feed, and the Great White is no exception: on average, only 27 have been caught for every 100,000 sharks of other species. Because Great Whites occasionally take a curious bite out of an unfortunate swimmer, the sensationalist press and the horror film industry have provoked an almost obsessive hatred of them. In addition, some sports fishermen regard the single-handed capture of a Great White as the ultimate "macho" status symbol, while its teeth fetch up to $200 on the open market and a full set of jaws around $5,000. Some researchers believe the Great White Shark is close to extinction, with only an estimated 35 to 40 remaining in southern Australian waters (once a stronghold of this species), most of which are virginal males.

SEALS AND OTTERS

Hunting for skins has severely affected many seal populations, especially those with a limited geographical distribution. The Juan Fernández Fur Seal, for example, is confined to five tiny islands off the Chilean coast, where it numbered over 3.5 million in pre-exploitation times. From the seventeenth century onwards, hunting was so intense that by the 1960s this seal was believed to be extinct. Fortunately a few small colonies were discovered in 1965, and following legal protection the Juan Fernández Fur Seal now numbers more than 2,500 individuals.

Many seals are viewed as competitors for the fish harvest by fishermen, who respond by killing large numbers. In some cases a "cull" is associated with a barely concealed demand for seal products. For example, the massacre of Harp Seals and Hooded Seals in Canada in the 1980s took place ostensibly because these species were depleting local fisheries, but had the lucrative spin-off of valuable pelts.

Among the most victimized of the fishermen's supposed competitors are the Monk Seals, already greatly depleted by sealing expeditions in the eighteenth and nineteenth centuries. The Caribbean Monk Seal is probably extinct, with no definite sighting since 1952, the last known colony of this species in Yucatan, Mexico, having been exterminated by fishermen in 1911. Although the Hawaiian Monk Seal was formerly widespread in the Hawaiian Islands, it is thought that the current population numbers no more than 1,500 individuals.

Similarly the Mediterranean Monk Seal occurs only sporadically in the eastern Mediterranean today, although its former range extended from Madeira and the Canaries throughout the Mediterranean to the Black Sea. Apart from persecution as a fish-eater, this seal is also suffering disturbance along its coastal habitats due to increased tourism, especially urbanization, pleasure boats and diving. Only about 500 Mediterranean Monk Seals remain, and there is a real possibility that this species will become extinct in the near future. The North Pacific Fur Seal, already hunted for fur, is competing with fishermen, and has

Basking Shark (Cetorhinus maximus)

Great White Shark (Carcharodon carcharias)

Dugong
(Dugong dugong)

American Manatee
(Triechechus manatus)

African Manatee
(Trichechus senegalensis)

Amazon Manatee
(Trichechus inunguis)

dramatically reduced in numbers since the growth of the Alaska Pollack industry which has taken its main food source.

The Sea Otter, measuring up to 2 meters (6½ feet) from head to tail, possesses a thick pelt which is regarded as being among the most valuable of all mammal skins. Originally present all around the rim of the North Pacific, from Japan to the shores of central California, its population was estimated at over 200,000 at the beginning of the eighteenth century. By 1911, when hunting finally ceased, it was estimated that only 1,000 to 2,000 Sea Otters remained. Following legal protection the otters have repopulated much of their range, but are still apparently absent from the Pacific coast of North America south of Alaska, apart from an isolated Californian population.

Sea Otters are also severely affected by oil spills. They may ingest the toxic oil while swimming through oil-contaminated waters, eating contaminated food or preening. Alternatively they may die from hypothermia, as, unlike most marine mammals, Sea Otters possess no blubber beneath the skin, relying on their fur for insulation, and it has been suggested that in the cold waters of the Northern Pacific only 10 per cent contamination of the coat can kill.

SIRENIANS

Possibly the only marine creature as yet annihilated by people is Steller's Sea Cow, a peaceable, slow-moving beast which measured 6–9 meters (20–30 feet) and weighed around 6,400 kilograms (14,100 pounds). This giant herbivore of the Pacific Arctic was discovered in 1741, but within 30 years it had been hunted to extinction for its oil, thick skin, and delicious meat.

West Indian Manatees were formerly widespread and abundant around the coasts of the southern USA, the Caribbean and northern South America, but the main viable populations today are confined to Florida, Belize, Guyana, and Surinam. Of over 10,000 manatees in Floridian waters in the 1940s, less than 1,200 remain today. The West African Manatee has suffered less from human depredations and still occupies a large part of its former range from Senegal to Angola. The Dugong is now extinct in the Mediterranean and severely depleted in the northern Indian Ocean. The largest known populations today occur in northern Australia, with a world maximum of around 50,000 in the entire Indo-Pacific.

Sirenians are long-lived creatures with a low reproductive rate. Female Dugongs live for about 50 years but have their first calf between the ages of nine and fifteen years, and subsequent offspring at intervals of three to seven years. A stable population of Dugongs can thus increase at a maximum of about 5 per cent per year; similar rates of increase apply to manatees. But many populations of Sirenians regularly sustain losses far in excess of this.

Despite legal protection in many countries, all living Sirenians are still hunted for their meat, oil, and hides. In addition, they become entangled and drown in the nets of commercial fishermen, while Dugongs are frequently counted among the unintentional victims of shark nets in Australian waters. Of the total population of around 1,200 Florida manatees, no less than 160 died in 1989, about a third as a result of collisions with powered pleasure boats.

Undersea meadows provide the main source of food for manatees and Dugongs, each animal needing to eat at least 5 per cent of its bodyweight in sea-grasses per day to sustain its bulk. But onshore forest destruction and soil erosion are increasing the turbidity of the water, thus killing off these meadows and starving the resident Sirenians to death. In Florida's Boca Ciega Bay, about a fifth of the sea-grass beds have been destroyed by trawling and

Left A West Indian Manatee (Trichechus manatus) *in the Crystal River, southern Florida. Elsewhere in the world they are hunted for their flesh. In Florida, they are strictly protected against hunters but face the new threat of damage from the propellers of speedboats.*

Green Turtle (Chelonia myas)

Kemp's Ridley (Lepidochelys kempii)

dredging activities, while herds of Dugong which feed on the sea-grass beds of the Arabian Gulf are threatened by reclamation schemes off Bahrain and regular oil spills which occur in the area. Oil released during the 1991 Gulf War threatened the last large herd of Dugong.

SEA TURTLES

Perhaps the most endangered group in the world's oceans today is the marine turtle, six of the seven living species having been severely depleted by overexploitation and incidental capture, pollution and coastal development.

The Green Turtle is a 1-meter (3¼-foot) long, herbivorous, circumtropical species. The females do not mature until 15–50 years of age, when they return to their ancestral beaches to lay their eggs. Many traditional nest sites support depleted numbers of females today, while others have been lost altogether. For example the largest Green Turtle rookery the world has ever known, on the Cayman Islands, had been completely exterminated by 1900. The Hawksbill Turtle is another circumtropical species which feeds mainly on invertebrates of the seabed associated with coral reefs. Unlike the Green Turtle, Hawksbill females emerge to lay their eggs singly or in small numbers. Although many nesting localities survive, their breeding populations are severely depleted. They are hunted for the highly valued decorative "tortoiseshell" and are declining in 38 of their 65 areas.

The Loggerhead Sea Turtle is a circumglobal, carnivorous species about the same length as the Green Turtle. Breeding densities have declined dramatically, the main nesting sites today being found on Masirah Island off Oman and in Florida. The largest sea turtle, the Leatherback, reaches some 1.8 meters (6 feet) in length and lacks a well-developed bony carapace. It is another circumglobal special, but today nesting occurs mainly in Pacific Mexico, French Guiana and western Malaysia.

Kemp's Ridley is the most precariously placed of the sea turtles whose females choose to lay their eggs only on a 20-kilometer (12-mile) stretch of beach near Rancho Nuevo, Tamaulipas in Mexico. This species is noted for its *arribadas*, in which thousands of female turtles emerge onto the beach simultaneously. In 1947 some 40,000 females emerged at Rancho Nuevo in a single day, but by 1992 only 1,200 mature females were seen. However, conservation measures may be helping as the number of nests made per season has risen from a low of 200 in 1985 to 580 in 1994. The related Olive Ridley is a more widespread species, known from the tropical Atlantic, Indian, and Pacific Oceans. While *arribadas* of more than 250,000 females per year were recorded on the Orissa coast of India between 1976 and 1996, none came in 1997 and 1998. At the same time, 10,000 were entangled and killed in shrimp-trawling operations off the Orissa coast.

One of the most severe threats to marine turtles is the collection of eggs for food, since whole generations of turtles are liable to be eliminated in one fell swoop. Loggerhead eggs are exploited on a large scale in Mexico, Cuba, Mozambique, and the Macronesian islands, while almost all the Green Turtle eggs laid in Sarawak over the past few decades have been collected by local people, mainly because they are regarded as an aphrodisiac.

Triton's Trumpet (Charonia gigas)

Queen Conch (Strombus gigas)

Right *The Hawksbill Turtle* (Eretmochelys imbricata) *is widespread in warmer waters and is the species most valued for "tortoiseshell." It is now protected in most parts of the world and the trade in its shell is controlled.*

All marine turtles are also hunted for food, mainly for local consumption, although the flesh of the Green Turtle is considered a great delicacy in the Western world. Green Turtles have also been exploited commercially as a source of oil and leather. Commercial harvesting of Olive Ridleys for the leather industry is still widespread, with more than two million adults being taken in Mexico between 1964 and 1969. Only the skin from the neck, shoulders and limbs is removed, the rest of the carcass being discarded. Stuffed juveniles of several species are sold to tourists as curios, particularly Hawksbills. In addition, the strikingly patterned shell of this species has been highly valued since the time of the Pharoahs.

Since most adult marine turtles are bottom-feeding creatures, accidental capture in shrimp trawls causes high mortality. Some 4,000 Loggerheads a year, for example, are drowned or battered to death in this manner in the south-eastern USA alone. Large numbers of Kemp's Ridleys are trapped in shark nets in Australian waters, while drift nets, long lines and ships' propellers cause problems for surface-feeding species such as the Leatherback.

Marine pollution is accounting for large numbers of juvenile turtles, especially Greens and Loggerheads, which are indiscriminate feeders and have been found choked to death on tar balls, styrofoam plastics, and plastic bags. Riverborne pollution in the Mississippi Delta is adversely affecting adult Kemp's Ridley Turtles.

In addition, uncontrolled coastal development is devastating marine turtle populations in many parts of the world. Even where such activities do not completely destroy breeding habitat, sand compaction by vehicles prevents the emergence of the hatchlings and deters further nesting, while speedboats kill and mutilate females waiting to come ashore. Also, the bright lights of coastal resorts cause disorientation both of nesting females and emergent hatchlings. Instead of making their way down to the sea, the turtles head inland.

INVERTEBRATES

Neither have invertebrates escaped overexploitation, and endangered species include a number of large marine molluscs. Large-scale exploitation for food and ornament is chiefly responsible for their decline. Research is underway to explore the food potential of the Giant Clam in commercial aquaculture. How this will affect the wild population remains to be seen.

Epidemics

In addition to pollution, interaction with the fishing and tourist industries, and over-exploitation, conservationists are alarmed by epidemics sweeping through already vulnerable marine populations. By far the most important threat to all marine turtles in the late 1990s, for example, is the epidemic of fibropapilloma tumors which took hold of the Green Turtle population in the 1980s and is spreading to other species of sea turtle. Another example is the world's rarest sea lion – Hooker's Sea Lion, off the southwest coast of New Zealand, which although currently protected, is still declining due to a mysterious disease which killed 60 per cent of pups and 20 per cent of adults in 1998.

Left A Giant Clam (Tridacna gigas) *among branching corals in the Galápagos Islands. Many of the larger and more spectacular molluscs have suffered from overcollection both for food and as souvenirs.*

Conservation
IN ACTION

National Parks

John Burton began his career in the British Museum in the Natural History Department. He moved into freelance writing and journalism and, from 1970 onward, became increasingly involved with wildlife conservation. John has written over 20 books and contributed to many others. In 1989 he was one of the founders of the World Land Trust, which he now directs, and is involved with land conservation in Belize, Costa Rica, Brazil, the Philippines and other parts of the world. He has been involved with numerous other conservation projects and is currently the UK Representative for the Programme for Belize.

Peter Earland-Bennett is a natural history researcher with an honors degree in Geology and a special interest in lichens and fungi.

The scale of destruction of the world's wild places is escalating rapidly. In the developing world, the demand for natural resources is often one of the prime reasons for this. In the developed world, other factors such as the increase in leisure pursuits can add to the degradation and destruction of habitats. Whatever the reasons, the need for the protection of natural habitats becomes ever more urgent.

Although parks and areas of forest and other habitats were set aside for hunting by monarchs in medieval times and even earlier, the establishment of nature reserves, national parks, and similar protected areas is much more recent. By the end of the eighteenth century the vast expansions in human populations associated with the Agricultural Revolution and then the Industrial Revolution, were taking an increasing toll on nature. Among the earliest naturalists to realize this was the Englishman Squire Charles Waterton, who in 1824 expressed his horror at the way Americans were commercializing Niagara. By 1826 he had enclosed his estate with a high brick wall, protecting all the wildlife within it and creating a sanctuary very much in the modern style. However, the origin of protected areas is not normally traced to the eccentric behavior of an English squire, but to an American cemetery.

In 1831 a rural cemetery known as Mount Auburn was created in the outskirts of Boston. As well as providing a place for burying the dead, within a few years of its creation, its

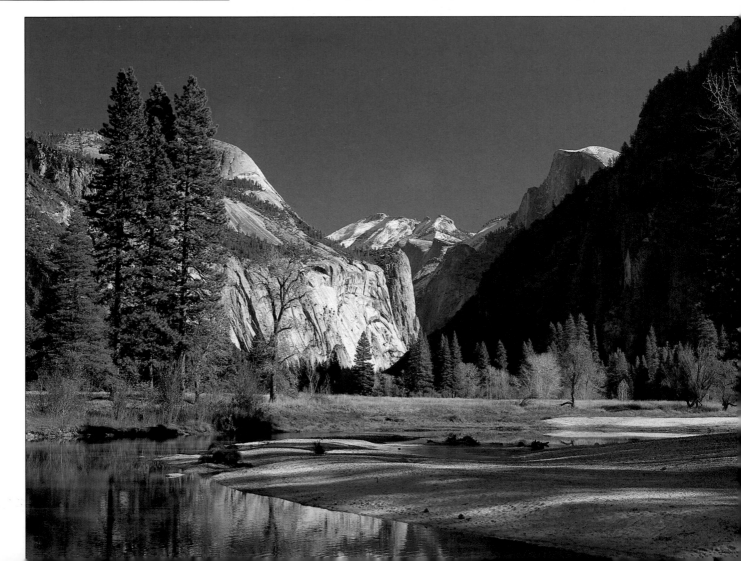

attractively planted landscape had made it a popular place of recreation for Bostonians. Today it is a mature arboretum and, during the migration season, an important locale for viewing myriad warblers and other songbirds on passage.

A year after the creation of Mount Auburn, the famed artist of native Americans George Catlin proposed that a "nation's park" be created in the west of the emerging USA. Another American, Frederick Law Olmsted, inspired by London's Victoria Park, was one of the designers of New York's Central Park in the 1850s. Although such city parks are far removed from modern concepts of a nature reserve, the seeds of the idea had been sown. They soon germinated, and between 1879 and 1885, Frederick Law Olmsted got the state of New York to restore the cataracts of Niagara and its environs to their natural state. Ontario followed suit and made the Canadian side a provincial park in 1888. In the 1880s and 1890s a start was made on protecting the 13.5 million hectare/6 million acre Adirondack Park of up-state New York.

It was in 1864, when Yosemite valley was set aside by Congress for protection as a state park, that the modern national park movement can be said to have been truly born. A national park surrounding the Yosemite valley was established by Congress in 1890, but by then Yellowstone (1872) had been a national park for nearly two decades. Like the majority of the early parks in America, both Yosemite and Yellowstone were preserved for their monumental scenery and recreational value rather than for their wildlife. It was not until the Everglades of Florida became a national park in 1947 that an area can be said to have been put aside in the USA purely for the wildlife it contained.

While the Americans undoubtedly created the concept of national parks, there were significant developments in other parts of the world. The Gran Paradiso National Park in Italy has a strong claim to be one of the oldest parks, and colonial powers subsequently set aside for protection large areas in Africa and Asia.

Above China's nature reserves. The ones shown on this map were all established to protect endangered species of animals. In addition, there are reserves established to protect important ecosystems, and others to protect endangered vegetation types. (Based on China's Nature Reserves by Li Wenhua and Zhao Xianying.)

Far left Yosemite National Park, California, like most other parks in North America, was created primarily for its scenic value rather than as a wildlife refuge. However it does contain a wide range of animals and plants, including many rarities.

Left The alpine meadows of Gran Paradiso National Park provide a refuge for some of Europe's rarest fauna and flora. It was there that the Ibex (Capra ibex) was saved from extinction. Situated close to the border with France, it adjoins the Vanoise National Park.

As the twentieth century nears its end, the heightened awareness of the plight of wildlife is leading to the establishment of a rapidly growing network of national parks and other protected areas. The following examples illustrate some of the better known, more accessible and larger ones, arranged on a geographical basis. Those selected are intended to give an idea of the diversity of wildlife to be found within a region's parks. The 1997 UN list of parks and protected areas lists a grand total of over 6 million square kilometers/2,300,000 square miles (89 per cent) of the world's land mass.

AFRICA

Ethiopia has created spectacular parks, including the Awash National Park (75,000 hectares/ 185,325 acres). This contains mainly a grassy plain in the Ethiopian highlands, crossed by the Awash river. Here the rare Swayne's hartebeest can still be seen, together with Beisa Oryx, Anubis Baboon, Ostrich, and other wildlife.

The national parks of Kenya are among the best known in the world. Despite its small size and proximity to the city, Nairobi National Park with its backdrop of downtown skyscrapers is still a haven for big game. Lake Nakuru National Park (18,800 hectares/46,455 acres) was established in 1967 around the large shallow Lake Nakuru and swamps. Greater and Lesser Flamingo congregate there in flocks reaching over a million strong at times, as well as

Right Tsavo West National Park in Kenya was the center of a controversy over elephant culling in the 1970s. Some people thought that the numbers of African Elephant (Loxodonta africana) were so high they would totally destroy the natural habitat. Culling did not occur and now the populations are threatened by poaching.

Spoonbill, pelican, cormorant and Night Heron. Tsavo, Amboseli, Samburu, the Aberdares, and Malindi Watamu Marine national parks are just a few of the other areas that make Kenya justly popular with tourists. However, the wildlife in them is considerably reduced compared with half a century ago.

Tanzania's protected areas included the Ngorongoro Conservation Area (828,000 hectares/2 million acres). This provides an extraordinary variety of important habitats for wildlife in a huge volcanic bowl, and also encompasses the Olduvai gorge, rich in fossils of early humans. There are large populations of ungulates, such as wildebeest, Zebra, Eland, and both Thomson's and Grant's Gazelles, alongside Elephant, Lion, Rhinoceros, Leopard, African Buffalo, and Flamingo, Stork and Ostrich. Close by, the Serengeti National Park (1.47 million hectares/3.6 million acres) is perhaps the most spectacular of all the African parks. The undulating plains are filled with the greatest remaining concentration of plains game in Africa, particularly during the annual migration in May to June when huge herds trek in search of water. Wildebeest, Zebra, Thomson's Gazelle, Lion, Leopard, Cheetah, African Hunting Dog, Spotted Hyena, Elephant, Black Rhinoceros, Hippopotamus, Giraffe, Oryx, and African Buffalo are among the many animals still abundant there.

In Uganda, Kabalega (Murchison) Falls National Park (384,000 hectares/950,000 acres) contains these magnificent falls on the River Nile. Most of the park is rolling grassland and savanna, with isolated forest patches, swamp and river. It once held some of Africa's largest concentrations of Crocodiles, Buffalo, Giraffe, Lion, and Black and White Rhinoceros, as well as Elephant and Hippopotamus. Unfortunately the White Rhino is extinct there and the security of several other species is in doubt. In the 1990s two new large national parks were created in the Rwindi Impenetrable Forest (32,000 hectares/79,000 acres) and Rwenzori Mountains (100,000 hectares/247,000 acres).

In West Africa, Senegal's Niokolo-Koba National Park (913,000 hectares/2.26 million acres) was established in 1954. It has impressive savannas, flooded grassland, marsh, and dry forest. The mammals include Lion, Leopard, Elephant, and Giant Eland. All three African crocodiles, the Abyssinian Ground Hornbill, and Martial Eagle are also found there.

The "W" National Park (1 million hectares/2.5 million acres), also established in 1954,

Below *Mount Kilimanjaro in Tanzania seen from Amboseli National Park, Kenya, with a Giraffe* (Giraffa camelopardalis) *in the foreground.*

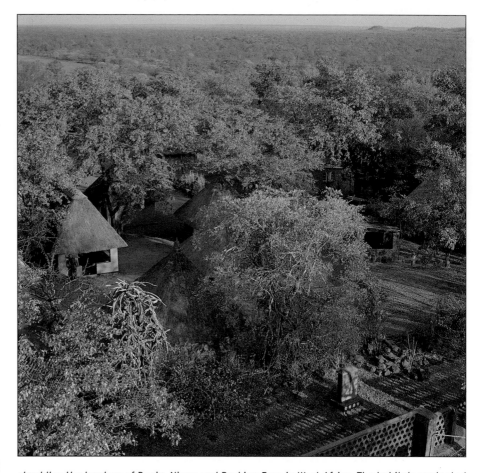

Right Robin's Camp, Hwange National Park, Zimbabwe. Essential components of most national parks are facilities for visitors, since tourists provide vital revenue. The facilities should be as unobtrusive as possible, as in this example.

White Rhinoceros

The story of the survival of the White Rhino is one of markedly fluctuating fortunes. By the early part of the present century it had been wiped out from most of the southern parts of its range, surviving only in the Umfolozi and Hluhluwe Game Reserves in South Africa. However, it was still widespread in the northern parts of its range, with as many as 1,000 in Zaire in the 1960s, and substantial populations in the Sudan, Uganda and elsewhere. By the late 1980s less than 20 of the northern population survived, in the Garamba National Park in former Zaire. But the southern population had increased to such an extent that they were being reintroduced elsewhere, sent to zoos, and even culled.

straddles the borders of Benin, Niger, and Burkino Faso in West Africa. The habitats protected include forest, savanna, and semi-desert, with populations of Elephant, Lion, Cheetah, Leopard, Hippopotamus, Buffalo, Reedbuck, Hyena, Crocodile and African Fish Eagle.

In the Cameroon the Bouba Ndjida National Park (220,000 hectares/540,000 acres) encompasses closed-canopy woodland and light forest with populations of Black Rhinoceros, Giant Eland, Elephant, Cheetah, Lion, Hippopotamus, Giraffe, Kob (waterbuck), and Buffalo. More recently, with help from the World Wide Fund for Nature, a large area of forest has been protected in Korup.

The Democratic Republic of the Congo (former Zaire) contains some of the largest tropical forests in the world, and the Virunga National Park (780,000 hectares/1.9 million acres) was among the first areas there to be protected as a national park in 1925. Congo has a total of over 14 million hectares (35 million acres) of parks and reserves. The Virunga National Park, contiguous with Ruwenzori National Park in Uganda and Volcanoes National Park in Rwanda, contains lakes, marshy deltas, peat bogs, savanna, lava plains, equatorial forest, high altitude glaciers and snowfields. The animals found there include Elephant, Lion, Hippopotamus, Buffalo, Kob, Topi, Defassa Waterbuck, Okapi, the endangered Mountain Gorilla and the Chimpanzee. Zambia's Kafue National Park (2.24 million hectares/5.53 million acres) includes open grassy floodplains, forest and swampland. The animals found there include Giant Eland, Kudu, Little Duiker, the rare Red Lechwe, Elephant, Black Rhinoceros, Buffalo, Lion, and the Yellow and Chacma Baboons.

Zimbabwe's network of parks includes the famous Hwange (Wankie) National Park (1.46 million hectares/3.6 million acres) which was established in 1949. It has great teak forests, moist woodland, savanna and grassy plains with substantial populations of Elephant, Buffalo, Giraffe, Zebra, Wildebeest, Impala, Eland, Lion, Leopard, Cheetah, Bateleur Eagle, and Vultures.

South Africa has lost much of its wildlife, but does have some impressive protected areas totalling over 6.6 million hectares/16.3 million acres. The Kalahari Gemsbok National Park (959,103 hectares/2.36 million acres) established in 1931, crosses the border of South Africa and Botswana, and joins an area of over 2.7 million hectares (6.7 million acres) in Botswana. A huge, open expanse of sand dunes with scattered grass and trees, it is home to substantial populations of Gemsbok, Springbok, Wildebeest, Eland, Cape Pangolin, Cheetah, Lion, Jackal, Bat-eared Fox, Secretary Bird, Giant Eagle Owl, and Ostrich.

The Kruger National Park (2 million hectares/5 million acres), established in 1926, was one of the first parks and is among the best-known wildlife reserves in the world. Despite limited rainfall, it supports about a million large mammals, including Elephant, Buffalo, Impala, Zebra, introduced Black and White Rhinoceros, Hippopotamus, Giraffe, Lion and Cheetah.

In Namibia's Etosha National Park (2.2 million hectares/5.5 million acres) the arid savannas are scattered with some trees and shrub acacia, but it is largely open arid country. The animals present include Elephant, Lion, Leopard, Cheetah, Zebra, Black Rhinoceros, Giraffe, Eland, Black-faced Impala, Ostrich, and Red-crested Korhaan.

ASIA

Although not as widely known as many of the African and North American parks, there are many impressive reserves throughout Asia. Since these lack the extensive savannas and open grasslands that dominate many of the African parks, the wildlife is generally less obvious, but nonetheless exciting.

India's Gir National Park (25,800 hectares/63,750 acres) is the last home of the Asian population of Lion, which earlier this century ranged from Arabia across the Middle East to India. It comprises most arid, overgrazed scrub forest of stunted acacia and teak trees.

The habitats of Kanha National Park (94,000 hectares/232,300 acres) include grassland, forests and dense bamboo thickets. It is home to some of the largest populations of several endangered mammals, including Tiger, Barasingha (Swamp Deer), Leopard, Sloth Bear, Dhole (a wild dog), Striped Hyena, and Asiatic Jackal.

Below *Giraffe* (Giraffa camelopardalis), *Thomson's Gazelle* (Gazella thomsoni), *Ostrich* (Struthio camelus) *and Gemsbok* (Oryx gazella) *at a waterhole in the Etosha pan, Namibia.*

Below left *The Gemsbok Kalahari National Park on the borders of Namibia and Botswana is one of the largest areas of wilderness in the world. It has spectacular sand deserts as well as large herds of Gemsbok* (Oryx gazella) *and other antelopes.*

Kaziranga Wildlife Sanctuary (43,000 hectares/106,240 acres) is an amply watered area, with swampy plains, open grassland and reedbeds. It is one of the remaining strongholds of the Great Indian (One-horned) Rhinoceros (the largest rhino species).

Keoladeo Ghana Wildlife Sanctuary covers a relatively small area (2,850 hectares/7,000 acres) consisting of a sparsely wooded, shallow basin. After monsoon rains this becomes a vast expanse of lake and marsh, and attracts huge flocks of water-loving birds. In total, India's national parks and sanctuaries comprise over 14 million hectares/35 million acres.

Nepal's Royal Chitwan National Park (93,200 hectares/230,300 acres) ranges from low grassy plains to the icy heights of Mount Everest, and is home to Tiger, Leopard, Himalayan Black Bear, Sloth Bear, the endangered Gaur (a wild ox), and sightless Ganges Dolphin.

With over 13 per cent of its territory protected as parks and reserves, Sri Lanka is way up in the world leaders, at least in designating protection. Sri Lanka's Wilpattu National Park (Yala Park) (131,000 hectares/324,500 acres) covers a wide coastal strip and shorelines along Portugal and Dutch Bays. It is noteworthy for its great concentrations of Leopard, which on this island are normally diurnal, and for being the last refuge in the area of the Dugong.

Above right *A grassy plain in the Royal Chitwan National Park, Nepal, with the permanent snows of the Himalayas in the background.*

Right *A solitary Asiatic Elephant* (Elephas maximus) *in the Yala National Park in Sri Lanka. The park is also renowned for its spectacular rock formations.*

The hundreds of islands that comprise Indonesia are home to a wide diversity of wildlife. They are also home to some of the most rapidly expanding human populations in the world, and a network of protected areas is essential if the wildlife is to survive. So far, over 34 million hectares/84 million acres have been designated as national parks or offered some sort of conservation status. The Ujung Kulon Nature Reserve (123,000 hectares/304,000 acres) in the lowlands of Java with many streams and swamps is mostly covered by dense tropical vegetation. It was established primarily to provide a refuge for the last survivors of the nearly extinct Javan Rhinoceros, and also harbors Banteng, Muntjac, Giant Squirrel, Javan Macaque, and Monitor Lizard.

Malaysia's Kinabalu National Park on the island of Borneo contains forested mountains and tropical lowlands. Among the species found there are the rare Sumatran (Asiatic Two-horned) Rhinoceros, Orang Utan, Gibbon, Tarsier, Flying Lemur, Giant Ground Squirrel and Pangolin; it covers an area of 75,000 hectares/185,000 acres.

Thailand's Khao Yai National Park (216,000 hectares/534,000 acres) was created in 1962, and is mostly lush tropical rainforest, with palms, bamboos, evergreens, and deciduous trees. There are healthy populations of Asian Elephant, Sun Bear, Tiger, Leopard, Gibbons, and great numbers of Hornbills.

Japan has many parks, the majority chosen for their scenic beauty, but an increasing awareness of wildlife has led to more areas being given protection to preserve threatened species. The Akan National Park (90,481 hectares/223,580 acres) comprises mountains, forests and lakes, including Kutcharo, the largest crater lake in the world, and Mashu. The scenery is spectacular, especially in the fall when maple and birch turn crimson and yellow, and in spring with the rhododendrons and azaleas. It also provides a refuge for Eurasian Brown Bear, Raccoon Dog, Sika Deer, and other wildlife.

Turkey's tiny Lake Manyas National Park (50 hectares/125 acres) contains a shallow lake fringed with willows and reedbeds, and nearby woods and low-lying, often flooded areas. Although tiny, it is a veritable bird paradise, harboring White Stork, Glossy Ibis, Squacco Heron, White-winged Black Tern, huge flocks of migratory pelicans, and many other birds.

The states of the former USSR have an impressive network of protected areas covering habitats that range from arctic tundra to tropical forest. In 1995 after the break-up of the USSR, Russia had 90 reserves, totalling 29,671,500 hectares/73,318,300 acres, or 1.46 per cent of the total area of the country. At the point of disintegration of the USSR there had been 173 State Nature Reserves. The Barguzin State Nature Reserve in Siberia (260,000 hectares/ 643,000 acres), established in 1916, is a refuge for the varied and fascinating fauna and flora of the Lake Baikal taiga. Over 600 species of flowering plant have been recorded there, while the freshwater lake, the deepest in the world, is home to the endemic Baikal Seal and many other unique animals.

The Kavkazky (Caucasus) Biosphere Nature Reserve (263,000 hectares/650,000 acres) was created in 1924. A mountain reserve, it has over 1,500 plant species, including many endemic forms, plus 157 birds and 59 mammal species, including Wolves, Bears and over 600 Bison (reintroduced).

"Kedrovaya Pad" Nature Reserve (17,900 hectares/44,000 acres) protects 17 species of plant listed by Russia as endangered, including Genseng *(Panax ginseng)* and *Rhododendron schlippenbachii*. It also harbors Leopard and endemics such as Maack's Swallowtail Butterfly.

In Turkmenistan, the Repetek Biosphere Nature Reserve (34,700 hectares/85,700 acres) is a remarkable area in the Kara-Kum sandy desert, close to the Iranian border. Around 200

Above *The peaks of Mount Kinabalu from Panar Laban, Sabah Malaysia. Mount Kinabalu towers to a height of 4,090 meters (13,455 feet) and is the highest peak between the Himalayas and New Guinea. The park embraces all the ground over 610 meters (2,000 feet) and pitcher plants are especially abundant.*

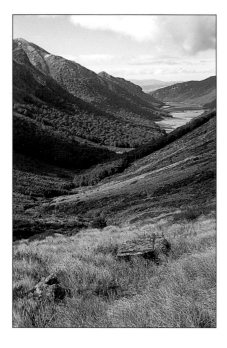

species of bird, including Rufous Bush Chat and Pander's Ground Jay, have been recorded, as well as a wide range of reptiles.

Wrangel Island Reserve (796,000 hectares/1.96 million acres) in the Chukchi sea off northeast Siberia is a sanctuary for breeding Snow Goose, Sandpiper and other shorebirds, and Polar Bear and Walrus.

AUSTRALIA AND NEW ZEALAND

Australia includes some huge areas of largely unexplored natural habitats ranging from arid deserts to the 2,000 kilometer (1,250 mile) long Great Barrier Reef. Green Island, off Queensland (7 hectares/17 acres plus 3,000 hectares/7,500 acres of surrounding waters) is a small coral bay giving access to the Great Barrier Reef. There, much of the undersea wildlife typical of the reef can be seen, including staghorn, golden leaf, brain and many other living corals, together with a wide variety of brilliantly colored fish.

Lamington National Park, Queensland (20,600 hectares/50,900 acres), designated as long ago as 1915, is a rugged volcanic plateau, deeply cut by winding river gorges providing hundreds of waterfalls. The plentiful rainfall supports varied plant life, including rainforest. More than 20 species of orchid, King Parrot, Crimson Rosella, Red-necked Wallaby, Bandicoot, Brush-tailed Possum, Sugar Glider, and many others have been recorded.

The fantastic sandstone formations of Ayres Rock – Mount Olga National Park, Northern Territory, are among the better-known natural features of Australia. In contrast, Phillip Island in Victoria (530 hectares/1,300 acres), once a farming community, is now several small reserves, providing refuge for such typically Australian animals as Fairy Penguin and Koala. There are also large breeding colonies of Short-tailed Shearwaters.

Sherbrooke Forest Park in Victoria (800 hectares/2,000 acres) is richly vegetated with luxuriant tree ferns and towering Mountain Ash (Giant Gum Tree). Among the special attractions is the lyrebird.

Tidbinbilla Nature Reserve in New South Wales is a treasury of plant and animal life, and striking geological formations. Gray and Red Kangaroo, Emu, Red-necked and Swamp Wallaby, Wombat, Honeyeaters, and Peregrine Falcon are among the animals that can be seen.

Left *The horses of the Camargue, though not wild, typify the region. Much of the Camargue has been heavily modified by people but it remains important for breeding birds such as flamingoes and herons and rare mammals such as Wild Boar (Sus scrofa) and beaver (Castor fiber).*

The Stirling Ranges National Park, Western Australia, is an area (115,000 hectares/284,000 acres) of rugged peaks with cloud forest remnants, dry eucalyptus forest and mallee heath. It contains many rare wildflowers, as well as Gray Kangaroo, Wallaby, Wombat, Emu, Purplecrowned Lorikeet, and several species of Honeyeater.

Western Australia has a considerable number of protected areas that have been gazetted and given numbers, but as yet, no name.

Mount Field National Park (16,265 hectares/40,175 acres), Tasmania, created in 1916, encompasses forested mountains, waterfalls and high bogs. Its wildlife inhabitants include Platypus, Tasmanian Devil, Tasmanian Echidna, Bandicoot, Wombat, Wallaby, Tasmanian native-hen, Yellow Wattlebird, and Green Rosella.

New Zealand's Egmont National Park (33,500 hectares/82,800 acres), North Island, is in forested mountains. Several of the birds unique to New Zealand still occur there, including Brown Kiwi, Kaka, Shining Cuckoo, North Island Tomtit, and North Island Wattled Crow. Urewara National Park (212,600 hectares/525,300 acres), also on North Island, covers an area of densely forested mountains, waterfalls, and lakes. Many of New Zealand's rare endemic birds are found there including Kiwi, Weka, Paradise and Blue Duck, Kaka, Shining Cuckoo, New Zealand Pigeon, and Morepork.

Fiordland National Park, South Island (1.2 million hectares/3 million acres) is one of the world's largest national parks and also one of the most unspoiled. Among the birds found there are two species of Kiwi, and Takahe, Kakapo (Old Night Bird), and South Island Wattled Crow. In addition there are Fur Seal and Sealion.

EUROPE

Almost everywhere in Europe shows signs of human activities, but there are still some remarkable parks and reserves. Although these may be modified or even managed, they are often spectacularly beautiful, particularly in spring, and home to the remnants of the large mammal fauna that was once widespread over the continent.

Austria's Marchauen-Marchegg Nature Reserve (1,120 hectares/2,770 acres) contains some of the most luxuriant of Europe's remaining riverine forests. Inhabitants include Red

Otter Trust

Over the majority of its European range, the otter is critically endangered, if not already extinct. The causes for its decline include pesticide poisoning, hunting, and probably road deaths. In areas where adequate protection can be given, reintroductions have taken place, and in England the Otter Trust has been breeding them very successfully in captivity. In cooperation with English Nature (formerly NCC), the Otter Trust has successfully reintroduced into the wild captive-bred otters. Subsequent monitoring of these animals has shown that they are now breeding and rearing cubs successfully.

Deer, Roe Deer, Wild Boar, Marten, European Lynx, seven species of Woodpecker, Black Kite, White-tailed Eagle, Honey Buzzard, and Heron. Neusiedler See and Seewinkel National Park (8,000 hectares/19,770 acres) on the Austro-Hungarian border encompasses a remarkable steppe lake and shallow marsh. These form a vast breeding ground that attracts more than 300 species of bird including Great White Egret, European Spoonbill, Baillon's Crake, and Red-necked Phalarope. In addition to the national park, Austria also has nearly 50,000-hectares/ 123,500-acres of nature reserve on the Neusiedler See.

The Hautes Fagnes Nature Park and State Nature Reserve (over 70,000 hectares/173,000 acres) is in Belgium, one of Europe's smallest and most densely populated countries. It protects a high plateau of peat moor ringed by woodland and is inhabited by Red Deer, Roe Deer, Wild Boar, and the rare European Wild Cat. The flora includes many rare species such as Marsh Gentian, Bog Asphodel, Bog Pimpernel, White Beak-sedge, and Common Sundew, although it was not until the 1950s that any large areas were designated in Belgium, several large areas had been protected in its African colonies much earlier in the century.

One of France's most spectacular protected areas is the Camargue Zoological and Botanical Reserve (13,000 hectares/32,000 acres) around the Rhône Delta on the Mediterranean coast. It is one of Europe's most important bird reserves and over 320 species of bird have been recorded. Flamingo, four species of Tern, Bee-eater, Roller, and Great Spotted Cuckoo are among the birds breeding there.

La Vanoise National Park (52,000 hectares/128,500 acres) adjoins the Gran Paradiso of Italy on the French side. It has magnificent alpine scenery containing coniferous forest, interspersed with heath, alpine meadowland, glaciers, and permanent snow. The mammals include Ibex, Chamois, and Alpine Marmot. Among the 115 species of bird found there are Water Pipit, Alpine Accentor, and Black Grouse.

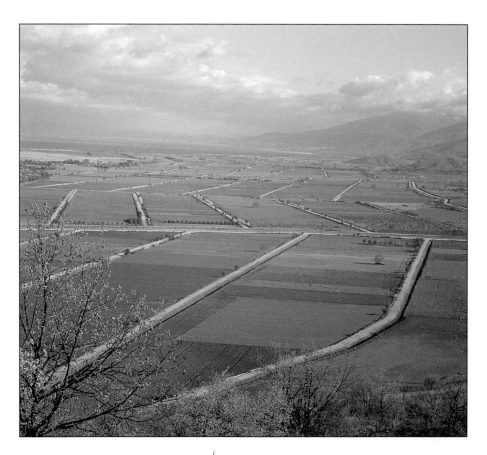

Right The shores of Lake Mikri, Greece harbor an extraordinary variety of birds. The lake, which is surrounded by farmland, was given protected status in 1971 and is known as the Lake Mikri Prespa National Park.

Above *The Badlands National Park, Texas is not only known for its dramatic scenery, but also as the home of one of the last remnants of the prairie grasslands.*

In Eire's Killarney National Park (10,000 hectares/24,700 acres), the oceanic climate encourages luxuriant growth of mosses and ferns within the fine natural Oak and Yew wood-land. Unusual species include Strawberry Tree, Irish Spurge, the large-flowered Butterwort and Kidney Saxifrage, and Red Deer and the introduced Sika Deer.

Much of Germany is forested, though mostly with second-growth forests or plantations. The Bavarian Forest (Bayerischer Wald) National Park (13,000 hectares/32,000 acres) was designated in 1970 and is inhabited by three species of grouse – the Capercaillie, Black Grouse and Hazel Hen – Tengmalm's Owl, Goshawk, Three-toed Woodpecker, and Ring Ouzel, as well as Roe and Red Deer, and Pine Marten. The Berchtesgaden National Park (21,000 hectares/50,400 acres) is a stunningly beautiful enclave of alpine scenery. It offers a wide range of habitats including deciduous woodland, spruce-beach-fir woodland, subalpine coniferous forest, mountain-pine scrub, and alpine grassland. Among the rarer inhabitants are Juniper, Arolla Pine, Dragonmouth, Apollo butterfly, Marmot, and Golden Eagle.

Great Britain's wildlife is among the most impoverished in Europe, but the Cairngorm National Nature Reserves, Scotland (93,000 hectares/230,000 acres) is a magnificent wilderness area containing vertical rocky cliffs, cauldron-like corries, steep-sided glens, and vast areas of high moorland. Among the birds to be encountered are Golden Eagle, Osprey, Peregrine Falcon, Merlin, Snow Bunting and Ptarmigan, while the flora includes Bell Heather, Mountain Crowberry, Creeping Azalea, Dwarf Cornel, and Alpine Lady's Mantle.

Lindisfarne National Nature Reserve and the Farne islands, England, comprise 28 small islands renowned for their wildfowl, seabird, and Gray Seal populations. In complete contrast is the New Forest, formerly a royal forest, created by the Norman kings in the eleventh century. Although without formal status overall, it includes extremely important conservation sites, being among the richest areas in the British Isles for both plants and animals. Uncommon species include Honey Buzzard, Hobby, Goshawk, Nightjar, Sand Lizard, Smooth Snake, Mole Cricket, and several of Britain's rarest butterflies.

Minsmere Bird Reserve, England (600 hectares/1,500 acres) is one of the most outstanding in Britain. Its reedy marshes and pools, woodland, heathland, and hedge are mainly human-made habitats, but they attract some 250 species of bird, mostly waterfowl and

Right The Farne Islands off the coast of Northumberland, England are a breeding ground for large colonies of seabirds such as these Puffins, Kittiwakes, and Guillemots.

shorebirds. These include Avocet, Bittern, Nightjar, Marsh and Hen Harrier, Garganey, Snow Bunting, and Black Tern.

Dartmoor National Park (95,400 hectares/235,700 acres), England, is a high plateau of ancient granitic rocks comprising moors and bogs, rocky outcrops and steep-sided, wooded valleys with fast-flowing streams. The rich and distinctive flora includes the rare Heath Lobelia, Sanicle, Royal Fern, and Opposite-leaved Golden Saxifrage.

Greece's Lake Mikri Prespa National Park, established in 1971, is one of the least known but certainly one of the most important of Europe's protected areas. The lake and its shores harbor an extraordinary variety of birds. They include nesting colonies of Dalmatian and White Pelicans, both of which are declining rapidly, Spoonbill, Pygmy Cormorant, Gray and Purple Herons, Squacco Heron, Night Heron, Little Bittern, Glossy Ibis, Great White and Little Egret.

Italy's Gran Paradiso National Park (70,200 hectares/173,500 acres), one of the world's oldest protected areas, is in a beautiful part of the Italian Alps. Created in the last century as a reserve for Ibex, it also harbors 1,500 species of alpine plants, Chamois, and Golden Eagle, Alpine Swift, Crag Martin, Alpine Chough, Snowfinch, Black Grouse and Ptarmigan. It was designated a national park in 1922.

The Texel and Terschelling Reserves (280,000 hectares/700,000 acres) of the Netherlands are very valuable bird reserves in the Waddensee, a huge expanse of tidal flats and shallows. They are home to breeding colonies of Spoonbill, Avocet, Eider, Curlew, Black-tailed Godwit, Ruff, Redshank, Shelduck, and Tern.

Norway has a small human population spread over a huge area and in its Rondane National Park, an area of 58,000 hectares/143,300 acres of largely unspoiled high mountain ranges, some of Europe's rarest mammals can be found, including wild Reindeer and Wolverine.

Poland has an extensive network of parks and reserves, the most famous of which is the Bialowieza National Park which was formally established only in 1932 but has a much longer history. Together with its neighboring Russian area, it preserves remnants of the primeval forest which once spread over the central European plain. For four centuries it has been the principal home of the once greatly endangered European Bison. It also contains Elk (Moose),

Left Dartmoor, Devon, England seen from Pew Tor. Like most of Britain's national parks, there is much evidence of human activity, with the landscape heavily modified by grazing and farming. The Dartmoor National Park contains many important archeological sites as well as herds of semi-primitive ponies.

European Lynx, Gray Wolf, Beaver, Bechstein's Bat, and most other species associated with the great forests.

The Danube Delta National Biosphere Reserve (580,000 hectares/1.4 million acres) in Romania is a maze of shifting channels, reedy swamps, sandbars, low islands, and floodplains rising barely above sea level; it was given Biosphere Reserve status in 1991. Although a large part has been destroyed or drastically modified in the past few decades, it is still among the most important wetlands in Europe. There are herds of Wild Boar, as well as small populations of Wolf, and European Wild Cat, Mink, and Otter. The birds include White and Dalmatian Pelicans, nesting Pygmy Cormorant, Glossy Ibis, and Night Heron.

Spain's Coto Doñana National Park (50,700 hectares/125,300 acres) is one of the most valuable wildlife areas of western Europe and, sadly, one of the most threatened. Amid the sand dunes and marshes of the Guadalquivir river delta lives one of the last of the Iberian

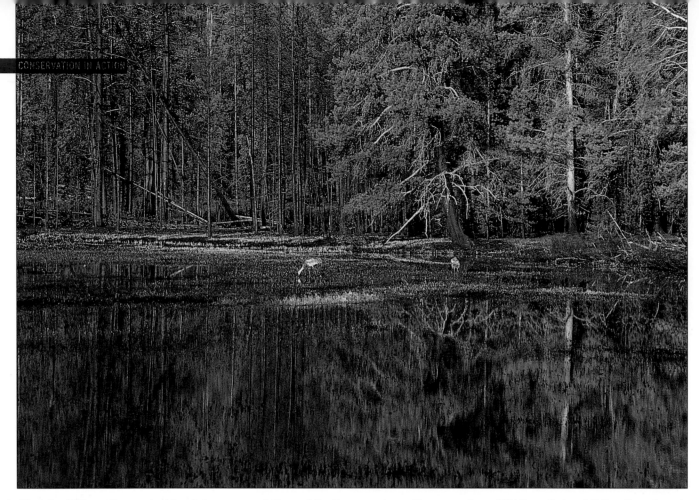

Above Sandhill Cranes (Grus canadensis) *against a backdrop of scorched trees in the Yellowstone National Park, Wyoming, USA. In the past, fires were normally controlled even within parks but in recent years the National Park Service has occasionally allowed them to take their natural course.*

populations of the European Lynx. Also present are Wild Boar, Red and Fallow Deer, Avocet, Black-winged Stilt, Slender-billed Gull, Crested Coot, Black-necked Grebe, Griffon, and Black Vultures. In 1998 it was seriously threatened by pollution.

Just south of the high peaks of the Pyrenees lie the spectacular crags and escarpments of the Ordesa y Monte Perdido National Park (15,600 hectares/38,500 acres). There are a number of rare species including Spanish Ibex, Chamois, Wild Boar, Wild Cat, European Brown Bear, Lynx, and, among the birds, Lammergeier, Alpine Swift, Alpine Chough and Rock Thrush.

Sweden's Stora Sjöfallet National Park (127,000 hectares/313,800 acres), when combined with adjacent protected areas, is by far the largest reserve in Europe. It is mostly primeval coniferous forest mixed with birch woods, dwarf birch and willow scrub, alpine heath and tundra, and also includes extensive areas of marsh and bog. It shelters some of the last populations of Europe's larger mammals including European Brown Bear and Lynx, Gray Wolf, Wolverine, Pine Marten, and Elk (Moose). Birds found there include Golden Eagle, Gyrfalcon, Merlin, and Rough-legged Buzzard.

The Swiss National Park (16,887 hectares/41,728 acres) was an early reserve, established in 1914. It contains long stretches of magnificent pine forest, remote untouched valleys, and impressive peaks of dolomitic limestone. The mammals found there include Ibex, Chamois, and Marmot, while among the birds are Alpine Swift, Snow Finch, Ptarmigan, Black Grouse, Alpine Chough, Capercaillie, Raven, and Nutcracker.

NORTH AMERICA

The vast, largely unexplored, northern tundras of Canada and Alaska include some of the world's largest protected areas. Canada alone has over 94 million hectares/232 million acres of protected areas. Wood Buffalo National Park, Alberta (4.5 million hectares/11 million acres) was established in 1922 to protect the last remaining herd of Wood Bison. Today's descendants, numbering 12,000, are mostly hybrids of Wood and Plains Bison, but a pure, isolated herd of about 200 Wood Bison was found in 1957 in the Nyarling river – Big Buffalo lake area of the park. The park also contains Moose (Elk), Woodland Caribou, Black Bear, and Timber (Gray) Wolf.

The United States park system got underway with the protection by Congress of the spectacular Yosemite valley and surrounding countryside – but this still did not save California's symbol, the Grizzly Bear, from extinction in the state. Yellowstone National Park, Wyoming (899,000 hectares/2.2 million acres) is the oldest (1872), and, together with the Grand Teton National Park (124,000 hectares/306,400 acres) and other contiguous protected areas, forms one of the largest wilderness areas in the United States. It is a high, rolling, volcanic plateau bounded by rugged mountains and containing the spectacular geothermal features, most famous of which is the geyser known as Old Faithful. There are huge numbers of Elk (Wapiti), as well as Black Bear, Grizzly Bear, Bison, Moose (Elk), Mule Deer, Pronghorn Antelope, Golden Eagle, and Trumpeter Swan.

The Badlands National Park, South Dakota, contains remnants of one of the world's great grasslands, on the edge of the prairies. Bison, Pronghorn Antelope, Prairiedog, Bighorn Sheep, and Mule Deer roam there, and it was one of the last natural habitats for the Black-footed Ferret.

Big Bend National Park, Texas (286,000 hectares/706,700 acres), encompasses wide expanses of arid flatland, sheer canyons, forested slopes and mountain meadows. Although it lies in the USA, much of its flora and fauna is more typical of Mexico and Central America. In the desert areas there are cacti, yucca, and agave as well as many species of desert rodent, Kit Fox, and Peccary. The wooded areas are home to Mountain Lion and Gray Fox, while 385 species of bird have been recorded there.

The Great Smoky Mountains National Park (209,000 hectares/516,400 acres) in Tennessee and North Carolina is connected to Shenandoah National Park (85,000 hectares/210,000 acres) in Virginia by a 755-kilometer (469-mile) scenic road known as the Blue Ridge Parkway. It was established to preserve remnants of the eastern hardwood forest.

Bald Eagle

The Bald Eagle was chosen by the United States of America as the nation's Great Seal, soon after Independence. It was a controversial decision, since not everyone liked the idea of a scavenger being used. However, there is no doubt that it is a majestic and impressive bird. Despite its status as the national bird, Bald Eagles were persecuted widely, and then in the 1950s and 1960s their populations declined catastrophically, almost entirely due to pesticide poisoning. The bird disappeared from many states, and became rare almost everywhere except Alaska. Fortunately, with the introduction of some controls on the use of pesticides, strict protection and imaginative reintroduction programs, the species is now re-established over most of its former range.

Left Great Egrets (Egretta alba) *in the Everglades National Park, Florida, USA. Public outrage at the hunting of breeding egrets for their plumes eventually led to the protection of the Everglades, making it one of the few parks in the USA established primarily to preserve wildlife.*

The Everglades National Park, Florida, comprises over 609,000 hectares (1.3 million acres) of subtropical swamps. It is home for a large number of North America's endangered animals: Florida Cougar, North American Manatee, Sea Turtles, American Crocodile and Alligator, Everglades Kite, and huge nesting colonies of Herons and Egrets. However, much of the water which used to flow into this area has been diverted, shrinking the marshes. Despite concerns, the Everglades are under constant pressure from surrounding drainage projects.

SOUTH AMERICA

Tikal National Park, Guatemala covers an area of 57,600 hectares (142,000 acres) around a restored Mayan temple city in dense tropical forest. Although the main attraction is the archeological site, the park is rich in mammals, such as Brocket Deer, Peccary, Agouti, Jaguar, Puma (Mountain Lion), Ocelot, and Coatimundi, and birds including Trogons, Tanagers, Motmots, and Hummingbirds.

The Rio Bravo Conservation and Management Area in Belize is owned by private groups which bought it with the intention of developing tourism as a long-term sustainable resource. The wildlife includes Jaguar, Ocelot, Margay, Tapir, Howler and Spider Monkeys.

Right A herd of Marine Iguanas (Amblyrynchus cristatus) *sunning themselves on the dark volcanic rocks of the Galapagos islands. They swim out to sea to graze on marine algae.*

Trinidad is important for migrant birds and has significant breeding populations. The Caroni Swamp Wildlife Sanctuary and Asa Wright Nature Center contain brackish shallow waters, mudflats and rainforest. Some 10,000 Scarlet Ibis breed there as well as Cattle Egret, Roseate Spoonbill, Limpkin, White, Little Blue and Louisiana Herons, Blue-gray, Palm, Silver-beaked, White-lined and Bay-headed Tanagers; and Hummingbirds.

Galápagos National Park, Ecuador, in the Pacific contains the 16 major islands, and many more smaller ones, spread over 520,000 hectares (1.28 million acres) of ocean. On the islands are some damp forests, but much of the habitat is arid with the remains of volcanic cinder cones and craters. The many endemic animals, several of which are endangered, include sea lion, Galápagos marine and land Iguana, Giant Tortoise, Galápagos Hawk, Flightless Cormorant, Galápagos Penguin, and 13 species of Darwin's Finch. There are also huge colonies of Magnificent Frigate Bird, Waved Albatross, and Masked, Red-footed, and Blue-footed Booby. However, the rapidly growing human population in the Galápagos is creating enormous pressure on the natural resources and wildlife.

The mighty falls of Iguazú, one of the world's most spectacular sights, are now protected in Iguazú National Park and Iguazú District Nature Reserve, Argentina and Iguaçu National Park, Brazil. Luxuriant tree ferns, bamboos, and palms border the falls, and bromeliads,

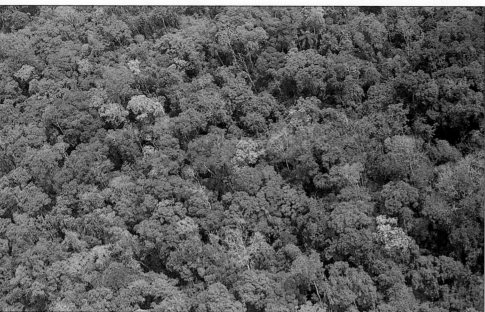

orchids and vines festoon the trees, where macaws and other parrots are still common.

Nahuel Huapi National Park, Argentina, contains over 770,000 hectares (1.9 million acres) of dense forest with Antarctic Beech, Myrtle and Larch. Above the treeline are perpetual snowfields and glaciers. The mammals include Pudu, Guemal, Vicuña, and Guanaco and among the birds there are Black-necked Swan, Ashy-headed Goose, Steamer Duck, Blue-eyed Cormorant, Chilean Flamingo, Austral Parakeet, and Austral Pygmy Owl.

High in the Andes of Peru is the 6,500-hectare/16,000-acre Pampa Galeras National Reserve, containing rolling, treeless grasslands, with broad valleys separated by flat-topped ridges. The reserve was established to preserve the Vicuña, which has steadily increased in numbers under strict protection. Peru's largest national park comprises the 1.5 million hectares/3.7 million acres of the Manu Park, which is exceeded by the 2 million hectares/4.9 million acres of the Pacaya Samiria National Reserve.

Itatiaia National Park in Brazil was one of the earliest to be established in South America, dating back to 1937. Its 30,000 hectares/74,000 acres contain mountainous tropical rain- and cloud forest, and among their large inhabitants are Maned Wolf, Jaguar, Ocelot, Tapir, Giant Anteater, Woolly Spider Monkey, Sloth, Harpy Eagle, Guan, and Toucan.

In finishing this brief summary of protected areas, it is perhaps also worth noting those areas lacking an adequate network. According to the 1997 UN List, the United Kingdom had not introduced any significant protected areas for several of its remaining colonies, namely Anguilla, British Indian Ocean Territory, Gibralter, Monserrat, and Pitcairn. A number of other countries were, according to the UN List, very poorly represented. They include: Vanuata, Andorra, Cape Verde, Comoros, Equatorial Guinea, Grenada, Guinea Bissau, Guyana, Iraq, Lesotho, Liberia, Maldives, Malta, the Marshall Islands, Micronesia, Myanmar (Burma), Aruha (Netherlands), Sao Tomé, the Solomon Islands, Syria and Yemen.

Protected areas

With the rapid expansion of the world's human population, natural areas are increasingly confined to national parks and reserves. Those shown here are a selection, chosen from those listed by World Heritage. It is notable that some of the largest protected areas occur in the poorer countries of the world, while the wealthier nations of the developed world often protect only a tiny fraction of their land, usually in areas too small to be of major significance. Antarctica is still the subject of dispute between those nations which recommend a World Park and those which refuse to give up mineral exploitation rights permanently.

Percentage of country's total land area (including marine areas) classified as protected in 1997

- 25.0 and over
- 17.0 - 24.9
- 12.5 - 16.9
- 6.0 - 12.4
- 1.0 - 5.9
- 0.0 - 0.9

World Heritage Sites

- Natural sites

- combined natural and cultural sites

Greenland
(to Denmark)

ICELAND

CANADA

UNITED STATES OF AMERICA

MEXICO

BAHAMAS

CUBA
JAMAICA
BELIZE
GUATEMALA
EL SALVADOR
HONDURAS
NICARAGUA
COSTA RICA
PANAMA

DOMINICAN REPUBLIC
Puerto Rico
HAITI
ANTIGUA AND BARBUDA
DOMINICA
ST LUCIA
ST VINCENT
BARBADOS
GRENADA
TRINIDAD AND TOBAGO

VENEZUELA
COLOMBIA
GUYANA
SURINAM
French Guiana

ECUADOR
Galapagos

PERU

BRAZIL

BOLIVIA

PARAGUAY

CHILE
ARGENTINA
URUGUAY

Falkland Islands
(to U.K.)

IRELAND
UNITE
KINGD
FR

PORTUGAL SPAIN

Canary Islands
(to Portugal)
MOROCCO
ALG
WESTERN
SAHARA
MAURITANIA
MAL
SENEGAL
GAMBIA
GUINEA BISSAU
GUINEA
SIERRA LEONE
LIBERIA
IVORY
COAST
GHANA
TOGO
BURKIN
EQUATORIAL GUINEA

International conventions

Greenland
(to Denmark)

ICELAND ▲

▲▲▲▲▲ NETHERLANDS
▲▲▲▲ BELGIUM

CANADA ▲▲▲

UNITED
KINGDO

▲▲▲ IRELAND
▲▲▲ CZECH
▲▲▲ AUSTRIA
▲▲▲ HUNGARY
▲▲▲▲ SWITZERLAND

UNITED STATES OF AMERICA ▲▲▲

▲▲▲▲ PORTUGAL SPAIN

Canary Islands
(to Portugal)

MEXICO ▲▲

MOROCCO

ALG

WESTERN
SAHARA

BAHAMAS ▲▲

CUBA

MAURITANIA

MAL

BELIZE JAMAICA
DOMINICAN REPUBLIC
Puerto Rico
ANTIGUA AND BARBUDA ▲

HAITI

▲▲▲ SENEGAL
▲▲ GAMBIA

▲▲ GUATEMALA
▲ EL SALVADOR

HONDURAS
NICARAGUA

DOMINICA
ST LUCIA
ST VINCENT

BARBADOS

GRENADA

GUINEA BISSAU

GUINEA

BURKINA

▲ SIERRA LEONE

▲▲ COSTA RICA
▲▲▲ PANAMA

TRINIDAD AND TOBAGO ▲▲▲

▲▲ LIBERIA

VENEZUELA GUYANA ▲▲
SURINAM ▲▲

COLOMBIA

French Guiana

▲▲▲▲ IVORY COAST
▲▲▲ GHANA
▲▲▲▲ TOGO
▲▲ BENIN

ECUADOR ▲▲▲
Galapagos

PERU ▲▲▲

BRAZIL ▲▲▲

▲ EQUATORIAL GUINEA
▲▲▲ GABON

BOLIVIA ▲▲

PARAGUAY

▲▲▲ CHILE

ARGENTINA ▲▲▲

URUGUAY ▲▲

Falkland Islands
(to U.K.)

International treaties and conventions
are a useful aid to conservation, and
are a general indication of a nation's
willingness to protect wildlife.
However, enforcement is often
expensive and can be beyond the
resources of the smaller developing
countries. Since the root cause of
most conservation problems is the
uncontrolled consumerism of the
developed world, many
conservationists argue that these
countries should provide greater
support for the conservation efforts of
the poorer countries.

Signatories to major conventions

▲ CITES (Convention on International
Trade in Endangered Species)

▲ RAMSAR (Convention on Wetlands
of International Importance
especially as Waterfowl habitat)

▲ BONN (Convention on the
Conservation of Migratory Species)

▲ ITTO (International Tropical Timber
Organization members)

Conclusion

It is difficult not to be pessimistic about the future of the world's wildlife when natural environments are threatened world-wide. However, no one can doubt the huge increase in public awareness of those threats over the past half century.

GATHERING INFORMATION

In the 1960s the first Red Data Books were published. These are compilations listing endangered species. Some are international, dealing with particular groups of species, such as birds or mammals, but the majority are national or more local. These deal with states, or even with units as small as counties, or their equivalent. The Red Data Books are the basic reference for the concerned conservationist. When arguing against undesirable developments such as major road works, aggregate extraction, or construction of polluting industries, a Red Data Book proves that species concerned may be threatened. Increasingly they are called upon as evidence, and they are also used as the basis for listing species that need legal protection.

The threatened species lists in each Red Data Book are based on information provided by numerous scientists and naturalists working in the field. However, our knowledge of the natural world no longer relies solely on traditional field research, but also on sophisticated new technology such as satellite imagery, Global Information Systems maps, underwater surveys, and remote-control photography.

Below A map of part of the Rio Bravo Conservation and Management Area in northern Belize. The map was generated from computer data using GIS, and enables scientists to work out which areas need the greatest protection, and also provides data for sustainable harvesting of lumber.

MODERN TECHNOLOGY

Within the past quarter of a century, both computing and communication systems have been developing rapidly, and Global Information Systems (GIS) are a remarkable means of providing detailed data that can be utilized for conservation. Using satellites, Global Positioning Systems (GPS) can pinpoint observations to within a few meters, making it possible to locate individual trees, points on a river bank, etc., together with an almost infinite amount of biological data recorded at that spot. This can be sorted in a data base and used to generate maps which are based on analyses of the data. The Programme for Belize, in a project funded by the European Union, has plotted huge areas of forest, including data on all trees above 10cm (4 in) in diameter. This data

Left *A satellite photograph of North America taken at night. The large conurbations, such as New York and Chicago are clearly visible. Light pollution from cities is now known to affect migratory birds, insects and other wildlife. Plants even alter their growth periods in towns.*

has been utilized to calculate the sustainable production of lumber and allow for a balanced management plan for the forest that includes wildlife such as jaguars, tapirs, and howler monkeys.

Satellite imagery has also enabled scientists to look at the world from a new perspective. Infra-red photography allows scientists to see where vegetation has been disturbed by slash-and-burn agriculture, and to monitor pollution and other assaults on the environment. Perhaps some of the most striking images are those taken at night, showing huge amounts of light pollution. Since many birds migrate at night and are known to use the stars for navigation, this form of pollution is thought to have an adverse effect. It is well known that birds are disorientated by powerful lights such as marine lighthouses, but they are also pushed off course by lights from skyscrapers, and even by street lights. Many

Above By using automatic cameras set along forest trails scientists can record the passage of wildlife such as tigers. Additionally, since the markings on the face of a tiger are as distinctive as human fingerprints, the activities of individual animals can be monitored.

conservationists are now campaigning for darker skies. You can help by switching off non-essential outside lights and using curtains to contain your household lights.

For years it has been known that humans can be identified by their fingerprints. Now it is also known that many animals have distinctive patterns that identify individuals. Years ago, the late Sir Peter Scott started identifying every Bewick's Swan that visited the lake in front of his studio at Slimbridge, UK. Now scientists use remote-controlled cameras to photograph tigers, ocelots, jaguars, and other wildlife. By setting the camera up on a trail and using automatic focus, flash, and other modern attachments, first-rate photos can be taken and the individual animal recognized by its markings.

ACTION PLANS

Since the first edition of this book was published in 1991, there has been an upsurge in the development of Action Plans to conserve threatened species. The first of the international action plans published by IUCN came out in 1988, and ten years later nearly 30 have been published. Numerous other regional and local plans have also been published, particularly in North America. The USA has led the world in the production of Recovery Plans, which lay down in greater detail the actions needed for individual species. Encouragingly, several of these have been crowned with success.

CAPTIVE BREEDING AND LAND PURCHASE

Captive breeding of endangered animals and the propagation of plants now plays a major role in zoos and botanic gardens throughout the world. Despite a tendency by some to exaggerate the benefits of captive populations, there is no doubt that captive breeding, together with the knowledge gleaned about the species in the course of captive breeding, has played an important role for the survival of some species. Captive breeding is most successfully carried out in specialist centers, such as the Jersey Wildlife Preservation Trust, UK (founded by the late Gerald Durrell).

Above Captive-bred Black and White Ruffed Lemurs at Jersey Wildlife Preservation Trust. Founded by the late Gerald Durrell, the JWPT specializes in breeding endangered animals and carries out extensive research into the requirements of threatened species in the wild so that it will be possible to reintroduce captive-bred populations.

Realistically, however, only a handful of the thousands of threatened species can be saved in captivity. And, inevitably, these will tend to be the more spectacular or appealing species, such as the Tiger, macaws, and the Giant Tortoise, rather than the less "cuddly" invertebrates. Nor is captive breeding cost-effective. The cost of maintaining a viable population of most endangered species is huge compared with the cost of maintaining that same sized population in the wild. There are plenty of areas in the tropics where several hundred thousand acres of rainforest could be purchased for around $10 million, and then, for less than $1 million a year, given full protection, including research. This amount of money would conserve viable populations of thousands of species, whereas it would only protect a handful of species in captive conditions.

However, the two policies are not mutually exclusive, they should work together. Some species, such as marmosets and tamarins, hover on the brink of extinction in the wild, but are now flourishing in captivity. Provided suitable protected habitat can be acquired, it will not be too difficult to re-establish them in the wild.

THE ROLE OF THE WORLD WIDE WEB

The technological leaps that have taken place in the last two decades mean that the Internet is now part of the everyday life of many of the people who will read this book Some of the information used to compile the maps, particularly for subjects like natural disasters and forest fires, was collected from the Internet. Much of IUCN's data, including Red Data lists, is available on their web site The interested reader can easily follow up on most of the information in this book by accessing the numerous well-designed web sites that have been developed by the majority of wildlife conservation organizations.

For example, I happen to run a relatively small international organization devoted to conserving threatened habitats, particularly tropical forests. Despite our small size, by using

Below Tourists watching an elephant in the Ngorongoro Conservation Area, Tanzania. For many less developed countries, tourism is a very important source of foreign exchange. If it is handled with sensitivity, it can have minimal impact, but major benefits for local communities.

dedicated volunteers, we have created a web site (Search for World+Land+Trust), and we know that our information is now freely available globally. From our web site, it is easy to connect to all our partner organizations, and from them to visit other sites. We plan to incorporate reports and research data, thus making freely available information that we hope will produce a new generation of well informed, and, consequently, concerned citizens.

THE ROLE OF ECO-TOURISM

National Parks play an increasingly important role in the preservation of habitat for endangered wildlife. However, over the past half century, the rapid development of international tourism has made most of these parks accessible to many more people. This creates a new set of problems since the pressure of too many visitors, the infrastructure that is required to support them, and the garbage they create can have a vast impact on what was once a pristine wilderness.

So-called eco-tourism is becoming increasingly fashionable. It is a new term for a form of tourism that has been going on for a long time - environmentally sensitive, with a strong educational element. It has much to recommend it, but if we bear in mind that a family going on an international vacation consumes about half their household energy budget on that one journey, we can appreciate that the real eco-tourist stays at home. Yet here is the dilemma. The developing countries need those tourists to visit their national parks to generate income – otherwise why preserve them in the face of other economic pressures. The gorillas of the Parc des Volcans in Rwanda are a classic example. Rwanda is a tiny country with vast human population problems, yet the Park has been preserved because it is a major source of foreign exchange – the overwhelming reason for tourists visiting the country is to view the gorillas.

WHAT CAN YOU DO?

On a practical level there is a lot that the individual can do. By joining one or more of the many environmental pressure groups and wildlife conservation societies individuals can increase their awareness of environmental issues and add weight to the pressure that such groups can bring to bear on government. The oft quoted adage "think globally, act locally" is particularly relevant today. Those of us living in North America or Europe cannot control what happens in the forests of the Congo or the Amazon. But we can clean up our own backyard, and we can make sure that our elected representatives are environmentally sensitive. And they, in turn, may be able to influence national and, ultimately, foreign policy. The Earth Summit at Rio in 1992 may turn out to have been little more than an enormous cloud of hot air. However, what little it did achieve was largely due to the fact that the politicians attending were well aware that the public who had voted for them were concerned and well informed about the issues being discussed.

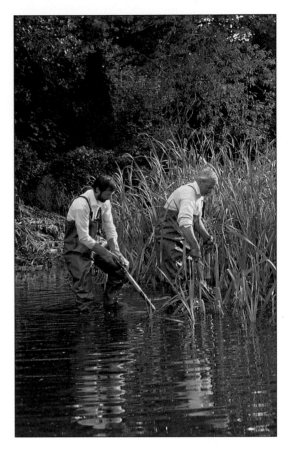

Above A group of British Trust for Conservation Volunteers at work clearing a pond. Volunteers working with such groups not only help with the management of wildlife sites, but receive training in traditional and modern skills.

By joining environmental and wildlife groups, such as Naturalists Trusts and Audubon Societies, it is possible to become involved in a wide range of practical, hands-on activities. Small-scale nature reserves, particularly those close to urban areas, often need considerable maintenance in order to keep them "natural." Visitor centers need guides, the shops need staff, and children need teaching. With increasing amounts of leisure more people are visiting nature reserves, and there is a greater need for volunteers prepared to put in a few hours on a regular basis. Enabling young people to acquire traditional rural skills is useful in itself, but it also leads to an increasing awareness of the importance of the natural environment. Volunteering can be hard work, but it is very satisfying to know that you are making a difference (however small) and, as an added bonus, it is also fun and a great way of getting to know like-minded people.

Even if you do not have time to be an active volunteer, there are two other ways in which the individual can have an impact. The first is with financial support. Most conservation organizations rely heavily on public donations to finance their activities – which may range from buying land to preserving a particular species. Second, if you cannot raise funds, you can influence politicians. Politicians generally take serious notice of letters from their constituents. Finally, in any country with a democratically elected government, it is the responsibility of each individual to ensure that in the 21st century we aim only to elect environmentally sensitive politicians.

Threatened species

Greenland
(to Denmark)

ICELAND

UN
KIN

F

SPAIN

PORTUGAL

Canary Islands
(to Portugal)

MOROCCO

AL

WESTERN
SAHARA

MAURITANIA

MAL

SENEGAL
GAMBIA

GUINEA BISSAU   GUINEA

BURKIN

SIERRA LEONE   IVORY
COAST   GHANA

LIBERIA   TOGO

EQUATORIAL GUINEA

3 10 2 3

CONGO

10 19 9 985

CANADA

50 35 52 4669

UNITED STATES OF AMERICA

MEXICO

Hawaii
(to U.S.)

BAHAMAS

CUBA   DOMINICAN REPUBLIC
JAMAICA   Puerto Rico
BELIZE   HAITI
HONDURAS

GUATEMALA
EL SALVADOR   NICARAGUA

COSTA RICA

PANAMA   VENEZUELA GUYANA
SURINAM
COLOMBIA   French
Guiana

ECUADOR
Galapagos

PERU

BOLIVIA   103 71 25 1358

B R A Z I L

PARAGUAY

CHILE   ARGENTINA   URUGUAY

Falkland Islands
(to U.K.)

Red Data lists of threatened species
have not been compiled for all
countries - and clearly they reflect the
intensity of scientific research, rather
than the real number of threatened
species. The reason birds figure so
prominently is that they are better
studied than other groups of animals.
However, even a superficial
examination reveals that the number
of threatened plants far outnumbers
all the animal species put together.

**Number of threatened species in
selected countries**

100

50

0

Birds

Mammals

Reptiles and amphibians

Plants

Svalbard
(to Norway)

NORWAY

4 4 6

SWEDEN

FINLAND

ESTONIA

LATVIA

J. LITHUANIA

ER. POLAND

BELARUS

CZECK SLOV.

USTRIA HUNGARY

ROMANIA

UKRAINE

MOLDAVIA

KAZAKHSTAN

MONGOLIA

RUSSIAN FEDERATION

38 31 5

214

B. YUG.

M. BULGARIA

GEORGIA

AZERBAIJAN

UZBEKISTAN

KYRGYZSTAN

ITALY

ALB.

GREECE

TURKEY

ARM.

TURKMENISTAN

TAJIKISTAN

CHINA

90 75 16

312

TUNISIA

CYPRUS LEBANON SYRIA

ISRAEL

IRAQ

IRAN

AFGHANISTAN

N. KOREA

S. KOREA

JORDAN

KUWAIT

PAKISTAN

J A P A N

LIBYA

EGYPT

QATAR U.A.E.

SAUDI
ARABIA

OMAN

INDIA

73 75 19

1236

BHUTAN

BANGLADESH

TAIWAN

GER

YEMEN

MYANMAR

LAOS

VIETNAM

PHILIPPINES

CHAD

SUDAN

ERITREA

DJIBOUTI

SRI
LANKA

THAILAND

CAMB.

C.A.R.

ETHIOPIA

SOMALIA

SEYCHELLES

34 42 14

490

MALAYSIA

CONGO

RWANDA

UGANDA

KENYA

BURUNDI

DEMOCRATIC
REP. OF
CONGO

TANZANIA

I N D O N E S I A

PAPUA
NEW GUINEA

SOLOMON
ISLANDS

ANGOLA

MALAWI

COMOROS

Mayotte (to France)

VANUATU

FIJI

ZAMBIA

MOZAMBIQUE

MADAGASCAR

ZIMBAB.

New
Caledonia
(to France)

NAMIBIA

BOTSWANA

AUSTRALIA

45 58 62

2245

SWAZILAND

SOUTH
AFRICA

LESOTHO

NEW ZEALAND

44 3 12

211

16 33 26

2215

Endangered Wildlife

Since the first edition of this book was published the list of endangered species has grown dramatically. This is not entirely because the threats to wildlife have increased, but also because our knowledge has improved. The internationally accepted lists of threatened species are published by IUCN (see p. 265), and in early 1998 the most comprehensive list of threatened plants ever compiled was published. Because the lists of endangered species are now so extensive, it would take a book considerably larger than this one simply to list them.

The lists published in this edition therefore are summaries, mostly by families. Anyone wishing to know more about individual species should consult either the National Red Data Book for the country concerned, or one of the IUCN lists. An increasing amount of information is also available on the internet – try starting with IUCN's site.

Below *Elephantidae – African elephant.*

MAMMALS

Family	examples	
Abrocomidae	*Chinchilla rat*	1
Balaenidae	*Northern right whale*	1
Balaenopteridae	*Whales*	4
Bovidae	*Barbary sheep, Wild yak*	53
Bradypodidae	*Maned sloth*	1
Burramyidae	*Mountain pygmy-possum*	1
Caenolestidae	*Chilean caenolestid*	1
Callitrichidae	*Marmoset and Tamarins*	13
Camelidae	*Camels*	1
Canidae	*Wolves and Wild dogs*	5
Capromyidae	*Hutia*	10
Cercopithecidae	*Black colobus*	36
Cervidae	*Deer*	11
Cheirogaleidae	*Mouse lemur*	3
Chinchillidae	*Chinchilla*	2
Chrysochloridae	*Golden moles*	11
Craseonycteridae	*Hog-nosed bat*	1
Ctenodactylidae	*Gundi*	1
Cynocephalidae	*Flying lemur*	1
Dasypodidae	*Giant armadillo*	6
Dasyproctidae	*Azara's agouti*	3
Dasyuridae	*Dibbler and Dunnarts*	15
Daubentoniidae	*Aye-aye*	1
Delphinidae	*Dolphins*	1
Didelphidae	*Opossum*	21
Dinomyidae	*Pacarana*	1
Dipodidae	*Jerboa*	8

| Above Equidae - Grevy's zebra

Myoxidae	Dormice	8
Myremecobiidae	Numbat	1
Myrmecopha	Giant anteater	1
Mystacinidae	Short-tailed bat	1
Myzopodidae	Sucker-footed bat	1
Natalidae	Natalus tumidifrons	1
Notoryctidae	Marsupial mole	2
Nycteridae	Ghost bat	3
Ochotonidae	Pikas	4
Octodontidae	Red vizcacha rat	2
Otariidae	Fur seal and Sea lion	6
Pedetidae	Springhare	1
Peramelidae	Bilby and Bandicoot	4
Petauridae	Troik and Gliders	5
Phalangerida	Cucus	4
Phocidae	Seals	3
Phocoenidae	Harbor porpoise, Vaquita	2
Phyllostomidae	Long-nosed bat	29
Physeteridae	Sperm whale	1

Dugongidae	Dugongs	1
Echimyidae	Porcupines	5
Elephantidae	Elephants	2
Emballonuridae	Sheath-tailed bats	13
Equidae	Zebras	4
Erethizontidae	Columbia tree porcupine	1
Erinacediae	Moonrat and Gymnure	5
Felidae	Cheetah, Lynx, Snow leopard	10
Furipteridae	Amorphochilus schnablii	1
Geomyidae	Gopher	6
Herpestidae	Mongoose	6
Heteromyidae	Kangaroo rat	7
Hippopotamidae	Hippopotomus	1
Hominidae	Gorilla and Chimpanzee	4
Hylobatidae	Gibbon	4
Hystricidae	Crested porcupine	1
Indridae	Sifaka	5
Lemuridae	Lemurs	8
Leporidae	Hares and Rabbits	12
Loridae	Loris	2
Macropodidae	Tree-kangaroos, Wallabies	16
Macroscelididae	Elephant shrew	7
Megadermatidae	Ghost bat	1
Megaladapidae	Lemurs	2
Microbiotheriidae	Dromiciops gliroides	1
Molossidae	Javan mastif bat	20
Monodontidae	White whale	1
Mormoopidae	Moustached bat	1
Moschidae	Musk deer	1
Muridae	Rats and Mice	237
Mustelidae	Wolverine and Otters	13

| Above Megaladapidae - Mongoose lemur.

| **Above** Trichechidae - West Indian manatee.

| **Above** Ursidae - Giant panda.

Platanistidae	Dolphins	4
Potoroidae	Potoroo	4
Procaviidae	Hyrax	3
Procyonidae	Coatis	7
Pseudocheridae	Ringtails	3
Pteropodidae	Fruit bats, Flying foxes	6
Rhinocerotidae	Rhinoceros	4
Rhinolophidae	Leaf-nosed bats	27
Rhinopomatidae	Horsehoe bat	2
Sciuridae	Flying squirrels	37
Solenodontidae	Solenodon	2
Soricidae	Shrews	114
Suidae	Warty pigs	4
Tachyglossidae	Long-beaked echidna	1
Talpidae	Desman and Moles	10
Tapiridae	Tapirs	3
Tayassuidae	Peccary	1
Tenrecidae	Shrew-tenrec	10
Thyropteridae	Disk-winged bat	1
Trichechidae	Manatees	3
Tupaiidae	Tree shrews	6
Ursidae	Giant panda	5
Vespertilionid	Gray bat	68
Viverridae	Civet and Genet	10
Vombatidae	Northern hairy-nosed wombat	1

BIRDS

Family	examples	
Accipitridae	*Sparrowhawk*	24
Aegothelidae	*Owlet nightjar*	1
Alaudidae	*Lark*	8
Alcedinidae	*Kingfisher*	11
Alcidae	*Murrelet*	1
Anatidae	*Teal and Duck*	25
Apodidae	*Swift*	8
Apterygidae	*Kiwi*	3
Ardeidae	*Heron*	7
Atrichornithidae	*Scrub-bird*	2
Bucerotidae	*Hornbill*	10
Callaeidae	*Kokako*	1
Campephagidae	*Cuckoo-shrike*	7
Capitonidae	*Barbet*	3
Caprimulgidae	*Nightjar*	6
Casuariidae	*Cassowary*	2
Cathartidae	*Condor*	1
Charadriidae	*Plover*	9
Ciconiidae	*Stork*	5

| **Above** Gruidae - Japanese cranes.

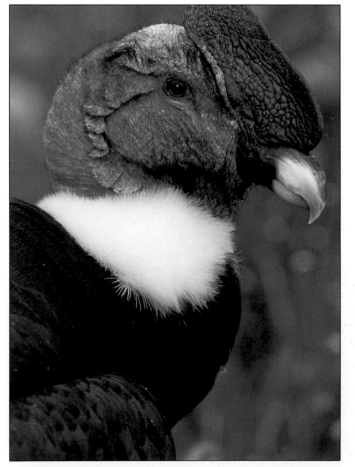

| **Above** Cathartidae - Condor.

Cinclidae	*Rufous-throated dipper*	1
Columbidae	*Pigeon*	55
Coraciidae	*Ground-roller*	4
Corvidae	*Crow*	13
Cotingidae	*Cotinga*	15
Cracidae	*Curoassow*	14
Cuculidae	*Cuckoo*	8
Dendrocolaptidae	*Woodcreeper*	1
Dicaeidae	*Flowerpecker*	5
Dicruidae	*Drongo*	2
Diomedeidae	*Albatross*	3
Drepanididae	*Akikiki*	16
Emberizidae	*Brush-finch*	51
Estrildidae	*Parrotfinch*	12
Eurylaimidae	*Broadbill*	2
Falconidae	*Falcon*	6
Formicariidae	*Antbird*	32
Fregatidae	*Frigatebird*	2
Fringillidae	*Linnet*	8
Furnariidae	*Canastero*	24
Galbulidae	*Jacamar*	2
Glareolidae	*Courser*	1
Gruidae	*Crane*	7
Haematopodidae	*Oystercatcher*	1
Heliornithida	*Masked finfoot*	1
Hirundinidae	*Swallow*	4
Hydrobatidae	*Storm petrel*	1
Icteridae	*American blackbird*	8
Indicatoridae	*Woodpecker*	9

Irenidae	*Leafbird*	1
Laniidae	*Bush-shrike*	11
Laridae	*Tern and Gull*	10
Megapodiidae	*Scrubfowl*	8
Melophagidae	*Honeyeater*	11
Mesitornithidae	*Mesite*	3
Mimidae	*Mockingbird*	3
Motacillidae	*Pipit*	3
Muscicapidae	*Warbler*	159
Musophagidae	*Turaco*	2
Nectariniidae	*Sunbird*	6
Oriolidae	*Oriole*	3
Otididae	*Bustard*	4
Paradisaeidae	*Bird of Paradise*	6
Parulidae	*Conebill*	12
Pedionomidae	*Plains wanderer*	1
Pelecanidae	*Pelican*	2
Pelecanodidae	*Diving petrel*	1
Phalacrocoracidae	*Shag*	8
Phasianidae	*Peafowl*	49
Philepittidae	*Asity*	1
Phoenicopteridae	*Flamingo*	2
Phytotomidae	*Plantcutter*	1
Pipridae	*Manakin*	2
Pittidae	*Pitta*	7
Ploceidae	*Weaver*	16
Podicipedidae	*Grebe*	4
Procellariidae	*Petrel*	27
Psittacidae	*Lovebird, Parakeet*	89
Ptilonorhychidae	*Bowerbird*	2

Pycnonotidae	*Bulbul*	12
Rallidae	*Rail*	32
Recurvirostridae	*Stilt*	1
Rhinocryptidae	*Bristlefoot*	3
Rhynchopidae	*Skimmer*	1
Rhynochetidae	*Kagu*	1
Scolopacidae	*Sand-piper*	10
Sittidae	*Nuthatch*	6
Spheniscidae	*Penguin*	5
Strigidae	*Owlet*	21
Sturnidae	*Starling*	7
Sulidae	*Abbots booby*	1
Threskiornithidae	*Ibis*	7
Tinamidae	*Tinamaou*	7
Trochilidae	*Woodstar, Hummingbird*	27
Troglodytidae	*Wren*	7
Trogonidae	*Quetzal*	2
Turnicidae	*Buttonquail*	5
Tyrannidae	*Tyrant*	22
Tytonidae	*Masked owl*	5
Vangidae	*Vanga*	3
Vireonidae	*Vireo*	4
Zosteropidae	*White-eye*	21

REPTILES AND AMPHIBIANS

Family	examples	
Agamidae	*Agama lizards*	3
Alligatoridae	*Alligators, Caiman*	2
Ambystomatidae	*Axolotl*	4
Anguidae	*Alligator lizard*	5

| ***Above*** *Gavialidae - Gharial.*

Above Iguanidae - Gálapagos iguana.

Boidae	Boa	6
Bufonidae	Toads	11
Carettochelyidae	Pig-nose turtle	1
Chamaeleonidae	Chameleon	6
Chelidae	Turtles	13
Cheloniidae	Loggerheads and Kemps	6
Chelydridae	Alligator snapping turtle	1
Colubridae	Racers and Giant garter	18
Cordylidae	Girdled lizards	5
Crocodylidae	Crocodiles	7
Cryptobranchidae	Japanese giant salamander	1
Dermatemydi	River turtle	1
Dermochelyidae	Leatherback	1
Elapidae	Pygmy copperhead	7
Emydidae	Terrapins and Wood turtles	29
Gavialidae	Gharial	1
Gekkonidae	Geckos	12
Heleophrynidae	Ghost frog	2
Helodermatidae	Beaded lizard	2
Hydrophiidae	Laticauda crokeri	1
Hylidae	Tree frogs	11
Hynobiidae	Salamanders	9
Hyperoliidae	Tree frog and Reed frog	3
Iguanidae	Iguanas	19

Kinosternidae	Mud turtle	4
Lacertidae	Giant lizard	7
Leiopelmatidae	Hamilton's frog	1
Leptodactylidae	Lake Junin frog	20
Microhylidae	Rain frog	4
Myobatrachidae	Torrent frogs	15
Pelomedusidae	River turtles	8
Pipidae	Xenopus gilli	1
Plethodontidae	Salamanders	16
Proteidae	Olm	1
Pygopididae	Delma	6
Ranidae	Frogs	14
Salamandridae	Vietnamese salamander	5
Scincidae	Skink	26
Sphenodontidae	Tuatara	1
Teiidae	St Lucia whiptail	2
Testudinidae	Tortoise	23
Trionychidae	Softshell turtles	9
Typhlopidae	Blind snakes	2
Varanidae	Komodo dragon	2
Viperidae	Adders	16
Xantusiidae	Island night lizard	1

Siluriformes	Catfish	37
Salmoniformes	Galaxias	36
Percopsiformes	Canefish	4
Gadiformes	Cod and Haddock	3
Ophidiiformes	Cusk-eel	7
Batrachoidiformes	Toadfish	5
Lophiiformes	Spotted handfish	1
Atheriniformes	Rainbow fish	42
Cyprinodontiformes	Pearlfish and Pupfish	63
Beloniformes	Buntingi	13
Gasterosteiformes	Ellinopygosteos	3
Syngnathiformes	Sea horses	37
Synbranchiformes	Anguila ciega	1
Scorpaeniformes	Peafish and Sculpin	9
Perciformes	Perch, Cod, Grouper, Darter	227
Pleuronectiformes	Halibut and Flounder	2
Tetradontiformes		3
Coelacanthiformes	Coelacanth	1

INVERTEBRATES

Family	examples	
Arachnida	Spiders	10
Chilopoda	Centipedes	1
Crustacea	Amphipods, Shrimps, Crayfish	407
Insecta	Beetles, Butterflies, Dragonflies	537

| **Above** Arachnida - Red-kneed tarantula.

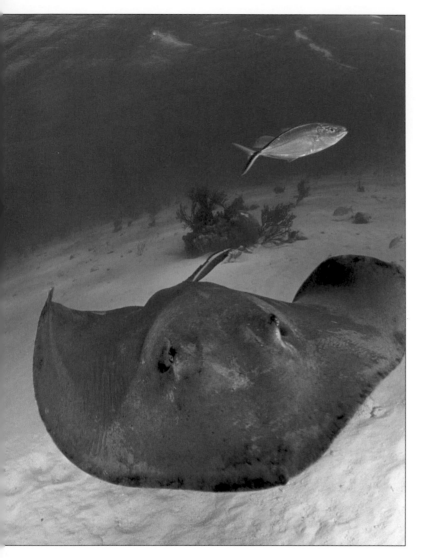

| **Above** Myliobatiformes - Stingray.

FISH

Family	examples	
Petromyzoniformes	Lamprey	3
Hexanchiformes	Bluenose sixgill shark	1
Orectolobiformes	Sand tiger shark	1
Lamniformes	White shark	4
Carchariniformes	Dusky shark	4
Squaliformes	Kitefish shark	1
Pristiformes	Sawfish	4
Myliobatiformes	Stingray	1
Acipenseriformes	Sturgeon	25
Osteoglossiformes	Bony tail fish	1
Clupeiformes	Venezuelan herring	4
Cypriniformes	Chub and Shiners	191
Charachiformes	Naked characin	1

| Above *Anthozoa - Sea anemone.*

Onychophora	Velvet worms	6
Oligochaeta	Washington giant earthworm	5
Polychaeta	Marine bristle worms	1
Bivalvia	Mussels and Clams	114
Gastropoda	Snails	806
Enopla	Nemertine worms	2
Anthozoa	Sea anemone	2

VASCULAR PLANTS

		Families with over 50% threatened	
Fern allies	87		
True Ferns	683	Laxsomataceae	2 (50%)
Gnetopsida	1		
Pinopsida	327	Araucariaceae	30 (78.9%)
		Taxaceae	15 (75%)
		Cephalotaxaceae	5 (71.4%)
		Taxodiaceae	10 (62.6%)
		Podocarpaceae	70 (56%)
		Pinaceae	133 (53.2%)
Ginko	1	Ginko	1 (100%)
Cycadopsida	149	Cycadaceae	20 (57.1%)
		Zamiaceae	128 (88.9%)
Dicotyledons	25,524	Brunelliaceae	57 (91.9%)
		Limnanthaceae	8 (72.7%)
		Penaeaceae	14 (70%)
		Trigoniaceae	17 (65.4%)
		Calycanthaceae	3 (60%)
		Meliosmaceae	16 (59.3%)
		Chrysobalnaceae	225 (50%)
		Hoplestigmataceae	1 (50%)
		Roridulaceae	1 (50%)
		Tovariaceae	1 (50%)
Monocotyledons	6,646	Ruscaceae	4 (50%)
TOTAL	**33,418**		

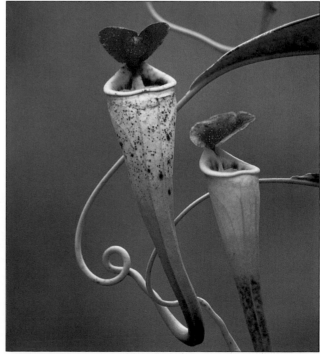

| Above *Sarraceniaceae - pitcher plants.*

Conservation Organizations

The best source of information on North American wildlife conservation organizations, of which there are literally hundreds is the Conservation Directory, published annually by the National Wildlife Federation. It is now in its 40th year or so and lists the organizations by state, as well as listing national and international bodies. They also have an excellent web site, that will lead you to many other points of contact. The NWF claims nearly 6 million members and affiliated organizations.

The other main organizations are:
The Nature Conservancy
1815 North Lynn St, Arlington, VA 22209, USA.

American Bird Conservancy
1250 24th St, NW, Suite 400, Washington DC 20037, USA.

National Audubon Society (and the independent state Audubon Societies)
700 Broadway, New York, NY 10003, USA.

International Union for Conservation of Nature – The World Conservation Union
The major international federation of Government Agencies and NGOs. HQ in Switzerland, but many National Committees and centers of operations worldwide.

IUCN – The World Conservation Union, Rue Mauverney 28, CH-1196 Gland, Switzerland.

IUCN Publications, 214 Huntingdon Rd, Cambridge CB3 0DL, UK.

World Wide Fund For Nature
The largest conservation body (with branches in many countries).

WWF – UK, Panda House, Weyside Park, Godalming, GU7 1XR, UK.

WWF – USA, 1250 24th St, NW, Washington DC 20037-1175, USA.

WWF – Australia, G.P.O. Box 528, Sydney, NSW 2001, Australia.

Wildfowl and Wetlands Trust
Founded by the late Sir Peter Scott it now manages many reserves, but its main collections of waterfowl and HQ are at Slimbridge.

Wildfowl and Wetland Trust, Slimbridge, Gloucestershire GL2 7BT, UK.

Fauna & Flora International
Founded as the Society for the Preservation of the Fauna of the Empire, in 1903, FFI publishes the quarterly journal, Oryx, which is a major reference on endangered species.

FFI, Great Eastern Rd, Tenison Rd, Cambridge CB1 2DT, UK.

Wildlife Trusts
The Federation of County Wildlife Trusts in the UK. Most counties have active trusts conserving wildlife by owning reserves at a local level.

Wildlife Trusts, The Green, Witham Park, Waterside South, Lincoln LN5 7JR, UK.

Jersey Wildlife Preservation Trust
Founded by the late Gerald Durrell. The foremost collection of captive animals being kept and bred for conservation. Many other zoos are active but Jersey is preeminent. It also publishes Dodo, a journal devoted to captive breeding and conservations.

JWPT, Les Augres Manor, Trinity, Jersey, JE3 5BP, Channel Islands.

Conservation Foundation
Largely working behind the scenes, the Conservation Foundation seeks to promote co-operation between industry and wildlife conservation. It also produces lists of addresses of UK-based conservation organizations.

Conservation Foundation, 1 Kensington Gore, London SW7 2BR, UK.

Linnean Society of London
The premier academic society concerned with natural history, with an extensive library. The Linnean Society also organizes many conferences and symposia on the scientific aspects of wildlife conservation.

Linnean Society, Burlington House, Piccadilly, London W1V 0LQ, UK.

Convention on International Trade on Endangered Species of Wild Fauna & Flora (CITES)
Secrétariat CITES, Case postale 456, 1219 Châtelaine/Genève, Switzerland.

TRAFFIC International
The TRAFFIC network (with 18 offices worldwide) monitors the legal and illegal trade in wildlife and its derivatives. It publishes bulletins and case studies.

TRAFFIC International, 214 Huntingdon Rd, Cambridge CB3 0DL, UK

TRAFFIC Oceania, G.P.O. 2528, Sydney, NSW 2001, Australia.

TRAFFIC North America, 1250 24th St, N.W. Washington DC 20037, USA.

TRAFFIC North America-Canada, c/o World Wildlife Fund Canada, 90 Eglinton Ave East, Suite 504, Toronto, Ontario M4P227

Bibliography

The purpose of this bibliography is to help the reader interested in following up the topics discussed in this book. The titles listed nearly all contain extensive bibliographies which will enable most topics to be researched in greater detail, if the reader wishes.

Simon, N., *The Guinness Guide to Nature in Danger*, Guinness, 1993

Baillie, J. & Groombridge, B., *The IUCN Red List of Threatened Animals*, IUCN, Cambridge, 1996

Walker, K. S. & Gillet, J. H., *The IUCN Red List of Threatened Plants*, IUCN, Cambridge, 1998

Red Data Books. A large number of Red Data Books have been published for most parts of the world, often in great detail at the local level. Most are listed in the bibliographies of the lists above, and can also be accessed through the IUCN Website: http://iucn-psu@wcmc.org.uk

Matthew, B. & Burton, John, A., *CITES Guide to Plants in Trade*, 1994

Harcourt, C. S. & Sayer, J. A.,*Conservation Atlas of Tropical Forests of the Americas*, Simon & Schuster, New York, 1996

Sayer, J. *et al, The Conservation Atlas of Tropical Forests: Africa*, Macmillan, London, 1992

Davis, S. D. *et al, Centres of Plant Diversity – A Guide and Strategy for their Conservation*, 3 vols. WWF/IUCN, Cambridge, 1994-1997

Matthews, J. R., *The Official WWF Guide to Endangered Species of North America*, Beacham Publishers, Washington DC, 1990-1997

Collar, N. J. *et al, Birds to Watch 2. The World List of Threatened Birds*, Birdlife International, Cambridge, 1994

IUCN publishes the widest range of specialist publications (including international Red Data Books) relating to threatened wildlife and habitats. Publications include Action Plans for most of the better known groups of mammals and birds, as well as some plants, and other animals. Specialized newsletters on endangered species, including *Species*, and topical reviews are also published. An up-to-date list of publications is available from IUCN Publications, on their Web site, or from IUCN Publications, 214 Huntingdon Rd, Cambridge CB3 0DL, United Kingdom.

Index

Acknowledgments

The publishers would like to thank the following for providing photographs and for permission to reproduce copyright material:

British Trust for Conservation Volunteers 15; Dr. Barbara huy][plStudies/University of Newcastle) 174; Cindy Buxton, Survival Anglia Ltd 133r; Phillip Cribb 155; Michael Cullen 236; Stephen Davis 179, 180; Ian Edwards 123l, 123r, 124, 128r; Paul Glendell 216t; David George 172br; David Given 185; Image Bank 256, 258t, 259 bl, 260, 261, 262r; Nick Hanna 175b; Jersey Wildlife Preservation Trust/William Wood 251; Paul Kay 216b, 217; Sabina Knees 59b, 94t, 94b 129; Programme for Belize/World Land Trust 248; Royal Botanic Garden, Edinburgh 122; Philip Steele/ICCE 182; Ruth Taylor 152, 153.

All other photographs supplied by Bruce Coleman Ltd.